FROM WARSAW TO ROME

FROM WARSAW TO ROME

*General Anders' Exiled
Polish Army in the Second World War*

MARTIN WILLIAMS

Pen & Sword
MILITARY

First published in Great Britain in 2017 by
PEN & SWORD MILITARY
an imprint of
Pen & Sword Books Ltd
47 Church Street
Barnsley
South Yorkshire
S70 2AS

Copyright © Martin Williams, 2017

ISBN 978 1 47389 488 4

The right of Martin Williams to be identified as
Author of this work has been asserted by him in accordance
with the Copyright, Designs and Patents Act 1988.

A CIP catalogue record for this book is
available from the British Library.

All rights reserved. No part of this book may be reproduced or transmitted
in any form or by any means, electronic or mechanical including
photocopying, recording or by any information storage and retrieval
system, without permission from the Publisher in writing.

Printed and bound in Malta
by Gutenberg Press Ltd.

Pen & Sword Books Ltd incorporates the Imprints of
Pen & Sword Aviation, Pen & Sword Family History, Pen & Sword Maritime,
Pen & Sword Military, Pen & Sword Discovery, Pen & Sword Politics,
Pen & Sword Atlas, Pen & Sword Archaeology, Wharncliffe Local History,
Wharncliffe True Crime, Wharncliffe Transport, Pen & Sword Select,
Pen & Sword Military Classics, Leo Cooper, The Praetorian Press, Claymore
Press, Remember When, Seaforth Publishing and Frontline Publishing.

For a complete list of Pen & Sword titles please contact
PEN & SWORD BOOKS LIMITED
47 Church Street, Barnsley, South Yorkshire, S70 2AS, England
E-mail: enquiries@pen-and-sword.co.uk
Website: www.pen-and-sword.co.uk

Contents

Introduction viii
1. The First Blitzkrieg 1
2. A Polish Army in the USSR 11
3. Exodus to the Middle East 49
4. Along British Lines 67
5. A Year of Challenge 85
6. Ready to Fight 101
7. The Move to Italy 123
8. Mountain Warfare and the Defence of the Sangro River 135
9. The Monastic Fortress 155
10. Preparations for Battle 167
11. Assault on the Gustav Line 183
12. A Brief Respite 193
13. Victory at Monte Cassino 201
14. Breaking the Adolf Hitler Line 209
15. The Aftermath 227
Notes 235
Appendices
1. Orders of Battle for Polish II Corps May 1944 241
2. Personnel Statistics and Equipment Holdings of II Corps 253
Bibliography 257
Index 263

List of Maps

1. Polish II Corps, from Warsaw to Rome — ix
2. Poland 1939 — 3
3. The Soviet–German Front 1941 — 15
4. The Soviet–German Front winter 1941/42 — 29
5. Evacuation of the Polish Army from the USSR, April and August 1942 — 52
6. The Polish Army in the Middle East, September 1942–June 1943 — 77
7. Polish II Corps in Palestine and Lebanon, June–December 1943 — 106
8. Polish II Corps arrive in Italy, January–April 1944 — 126
9. Polish II Corps Sangro River defence, January–April 1944 — 145
10. Victory at Monte Cassino, 12–18 May 1944 — 203
11. Initial Assaults on Hitler Line, 19–21 May 1944 — 213
12. Capture of Piedimonte, 22–25 May 1944 — 223

List of Tables

1. Polish Independent Carpathian Rifle Brigade 1939–1942 — 10
2. Development of Principle Formations of the Polish Army in the USSR, August 1941–August 1942 — 43
3. Development of the Polish 2 Armoured Brigade — 80
4. Development of Principle Formations of the Polish Army in the East into the Polish II Corps 1942–1943 — 87
5. Polish order of Battle in the Mediterranean following General Sosnkowski's Organizational Plan, November 1943 — 115
6. II Corps Organization for the Battle of Monte Cassino — 165
7. Line of Evacuation for Battlefield Casualties — 180

Introduction

The march from Warsaw to Rome was not a manoeuvre the Polish Army or any other nation had envisaged. Following the defeat of Poland in September 1939 the tens of thousands of soldiers incarcerated in Soviet prisoner-of-war camps were essentially written off as a lost cause. Hitler's invasion of the USSR in June 1941 changed this; these men now represented a vital, potentially decisive addition to the Allied fight against Germany. The struggle to get these Polish soldiers back into action depended on close cooperation between the diplomatic and military missions of Britain, Poland and the USSR. It was to prove a most challenging endeavour.

These three countries, compelled to cooperate through the necessity of war were Allies, not friends. They had nothing in common, no shared ideology or post-war outlook; the relationship was characterized by antipathy, mistrust and open aggression. The only common ground was the objective of defeating Germany. The feat of getting these countries to work together was never realized, even the pacts between them were made individually and not as a tripartite agreement – together the three could agree on nothing.

In military circles things were different. The unprecedented effectiveness of Hitler's war machine was obliterating all before it and no nation was able to even slow the onslaught. Something drastic had to be done. The result of the panicked process was a wildly ambitious and risky plan; to release Polish soldiers held in Soviet prisoner-of-war camps, recruit them into a brand new Polish Army to be raised in the Soviet Union, equip them from Britain and then send them to war on the Soviet or Mediterranean front! Amazingly, the scheme did work, not perfectly, but well enough to get tens of thousands of Polish soldiers back in the war and fighting the Germans. That any measure of success was achieved at all was purely down to the dogged determination of the Poles in the Soviet Union to strike back at Hitler, with their dying breath if need be, to wreak vengeance for the plight of their nation. And this they did in good measure.

The creation of the Polish Army in the East and subsequently the II Corps represents the largest non-UK or Dominion fighting force ever raised by Britain; it was a mammoth undertaking without parallel before or since. To grasp the scale

Introduction ix

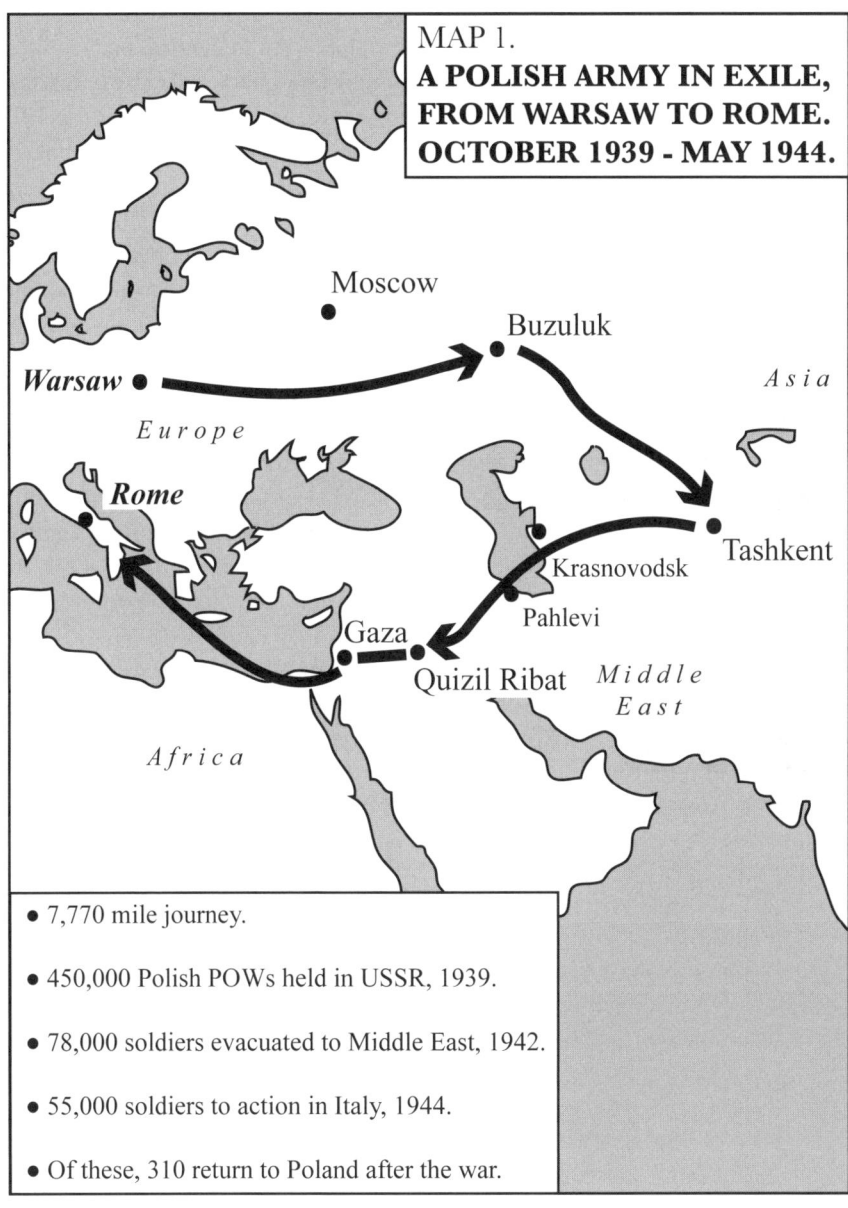

MAP 1.
A POLISH ARMY IN EXILE, FROM WARSAW TO ROME. OCTOBER 1939 - MAY 1944.

- 7,770 mile journey.
- 450,000 Polish POWs held in USSR, 1939.
- 78,000 soldiers evacuated to Middle East, 1942.
- 55,000 soldiers to action in Italy, 1944.
- Of these, 310 return to Poland after the war.

of this feat it is helpful to make a brief comparison of troop numbers: the Polish II Corps on 30 April 1945 totalled 83,023[1] personnel, on 1 January 2016 the British Army totalled 84,960.[2] Their first parent British formation, Persia and Iraq Command, summed up the achievement and is clear about where the real credit is due: 'The triumph belongs first of all to the greatness of the Poles themselves, and the glory of their subsequent fighting on the Italian front to them alone.'[3]

The exiled Polish soldier's lot was a tough one characterized by disease, fatigue, hard choices, isolation and great emotional and political pressure. This cauldron could boil over and led to some scalding arguments and bitter rebukes, notably from Churchill who was perennially frustrated with political infighting amongst the Polish commanders. There was always hope in the story though, characterized by one constant of the Polish Army – they were an incredibly tough and ferocious bunch whose spirit to carry on fighting proved to be one of the most outstanding displays of human endurance ever seen. You would not want them as your enemy; as a fighting ally, there could be no better choice.

The following quote from the introduction to Stefan Kleczkowski's 1942 information publication *Poland's First 100,000* sets a poignant opening for this book: 'So it is right that British minds should be stirred and their ignorance dispelled by such an account as this of what has been and is being done to regain freedom for Poland . . . [and that for Poland's ongoing fight against Hitler] we and the United Nations owe a historic debt of gratitude. Fully to repay it may be beyond our power. At least we can and should recognize and endeavour to understand it.'[4]

This book is an attempt to answer the call from 1942; the debt of gratitude was never repaid, the least we can do now is to appreciate the struggle of our wartime Ally and the role we played in their tragedy, one sadly characterized by ignorance and fear of the Stalinist USSR.

A fitting wartime phrase frequently used by the Poles when describing their struggle was: For our freedom, and yours. Here then, is their story, and ours.

1

The First Blitzkrieg

The summer of 1939 found the pivotal character of this saga, Lieutenant General Władysław Anders, in northeast Poland commanding the Nowogrodek Cavalry Brigade, whilst only a few miles away the German Army was massing across the border in East Prussia. Poland's military commanders were exasperated by the weeks of political vacillation which had left the nation's borders in a flimsy state of readiness – only in August had they been permitted to dig in and erect barbed-wire entanglements. The great flat plains of Poland lay open from the German border to the capital of Warsaw. The general mobilization order calling up all reservists was issued on 28 August, but was soon cancelled. This cautious approach was taken at the behest of the British, French and American ambassadors, who were all too aware that in every previous conflict involving Poland the defensive strategy adopted by Polish generals was that of pre-emptive attack. It was hoped that by not antagonizing the Germans unduly, war could be averted even at this late stage.

Their efforts were to no avail and on 1 September 1939 the Second World War broke out with the German invasion of Poland. General Carlton de Wiart headed the British Military Mission to Poland, his instructions from London making clear that his mission was to provide no more than moral support: 'In view of the difficulties of rendering direct military support by British Armed Forces to the Poles, the question of inspiring confidence is of great importance.'[1] In response to Nazi aggression Britain launched a leaflet-dropping campaign over Germany: the Poles were dismayed. Carton de Wiart advocated the Polish Army pulling back to firm defensive lines behind the River Vistula which were not actioned, while the Polish commander Marshal Edward Rydz-Śmigły steadfastly insisted on fighting for every inch of Polish soil; however the bulk of the Polish Navy was evacuated at the beginning of hostilities at the behest of the British Admiralty.

For Carton de Wiart and his staff the campaign was a revelation as the German all-arms Blitzkrieg rapidly overwhelmed the Polish Army and openly attacked civilians. Despite a valiant defence, the Polish troops were forced to fall back to defensive positions in the south-east of the country along the rugged Tatra Mountains bordering neutral Romania, holding out for the assistance of Britain and France, neither of whom the Poles realistically expected to do anything. Indeed the French Army announced it would take two years to prepare for an offensive. Such a response convinced the Polish General Staff that Britain and France were intending to allow Germany to seize Poland, whereafter the Entente would sue for some kind of peace settlement. The Polish defence was finally put paid to on 17 September due to the unforeseen invasion by the USSR and with the defence of the Tatra pocket no longer feasible the Polish Government ordered the evacuation of its army into allied Romania. Axis forces overcame the last elements of the army on 6 October. The country was subsequently divided between the two victor nations, although no formal surrender was ever issued by the Polish Government. Among the tens of thousands of captured soldiers was Lieutenant General Anders, who had been captured in the southern Polish village of Jesionka Stawiowa (now known as Yasenka Stets'ova) following a night of hand-to-hand fighting in which he sustained multiple wounds.

On 1 October 1939, Winston Churchill broadcast a radio message to the British people: 'Poland has been again overrun by two of the great powers which held her in bondage for 150 years, but were unable to conquer the spirit of the Polish nation. The heroic defence of Warsaw shows that the soul of Poland is indestructible, and that she will rise again like a rock, which may for a spell be submerged by a tidal wave, but which remains a rock.'[2]

The eastern region of Poland was appropriated by the Soviets and garrisoned by large numbers of troops detailed to stop the Polish Army from evacuating and being reconstituted abroad, a point one of General Anders' detaining officers made clear to him shortly after his capture: 'We are now good friends with the Germans, together we will fight international capitalism. Poland was the tool of England, and she had to perish for that. There will never be a Poland again.'[3] Along with the plunder extracted by the Soviets was the estate of General Carton de Wiart, who resided in Poland – the authorities removed his possessions and placed them in the Minsk city museum.

Commensurate with the Sovietization of eastern Poland, the captured Polish soldiers in this zone, along with countless civilians were deported by the NKVD (a forerunner of the KGB) deep into the Soviet Union to Turkmenistan, Kazakhstan, Siberia and other remote regions. All persons deemed to be actually or potentially hostile to the Soviet regime, a broad swathe of society encompassing all military personnel above the rank of private, all police officers, teachers, doctors, landowners and so on, were interned in camps and put to hard labour. This included the extraction of tree sap in arctic Siberia for the chemical industry, mining for asbestos and heavy metals, labouring on civil engineering projects and toiling on collective farms. The work took a heavy toll in lives for these deportees, the vast majority of whom had no experience of such hardships. The exact number of casualties has never been certain, but all those who survived the experience had clear recollections of the deaths of many of their compatriots.

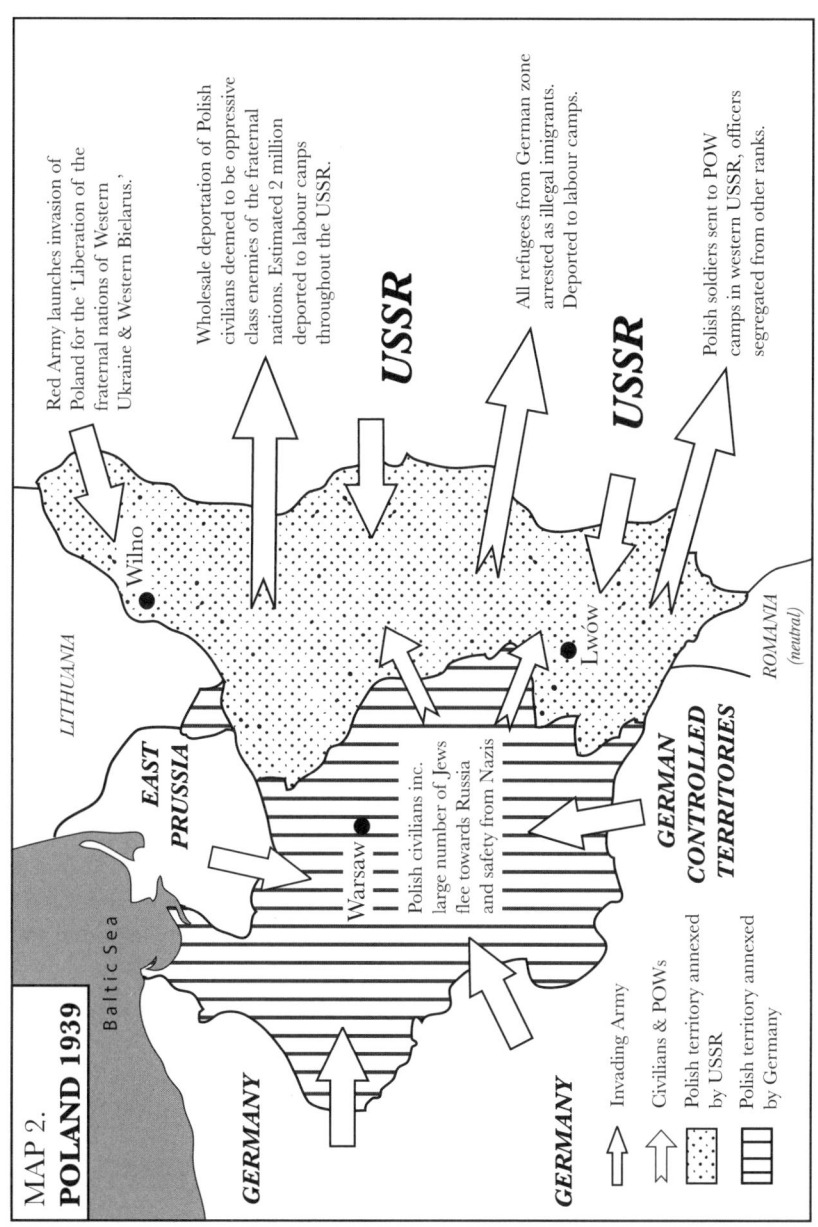

Meanwhile, having conveyed much useful information about German warfare, General Carton de Wiart travelled from Paris to meet General Ironside, the Commander-in-Chief of the Imperial General Staff. He recounts that the opening remarks went as follows: '"Well! Your Poles haven't done much!" I felt the remark was premature, and replied: "Let us see what others will do, Sir."'[4] Carton de Wiart was justifiably enraged by the dismissive attitude of the General Staff and when Prime Minister Neville Chamberlain enquired with all sincerity as to the effectiveness of the Royal Air Force's leaflet campaign the General's reply was far from complimentary. The full impact of Germany's Blitzkrieg had yet to register with the western powers, and many senior military and political figures could not adapt to the requirements of this completely new form of warfare. In the coming weeks both Ironside and Chamberlain were replaced, the latter of course by Churchill, a military innovator who far outpaced his contemporaries in his grasp of the impact of technology on warfare.

The Polish Government and General Staff had escaped to Romania along with the foreign military missions. A significant proportion of government figures including the prime minister and many soldiers were subsequently interned, as Romania was not at war with Germany and sought to appease German ambitions. Those who fled to Hungary faced a similar situation; both countries were neutral and had no desire to antagonize the Germans by playing host to the exiled Poles.

Of the Polish soldiers who evaded capture and escaped through Hungary and Romania, the majority headed for France and the centre of General Władysław Sikorski's exile Polish Army based at Coetquidon in Brittany. Sikorski was appointed both prime minister and Commander-in-Chief of the Polish Army, at the urging of the French government. Sikorski was politically distanced from the leadership that had led his country to defeat, so his reputation was in far better shape than that of most senior officers in the eyes of the Polish soldiery and the international community. He also possessed a good reputation with the French, having spent much of the previous thirteen years in Paris and was most familiar with the leading French politicians and military figures. And the British Army held him in good stead, particularly General Ironside, who on his first inspection of the Polish Army observed that during Sikorski's tenure as Minister of War, 'The progress made by the Polish Army during the last years is remarkable.'[5] General Sosnkowski was appointed Minister of Home Affairs and set to his business of organizing resistance warfare in occupied Poland, a role he had performed before against the Russians at the turn of the century. He was also appointed as the President's successor.

The French were however distraught that war had broken out with Germany. They believed it to be totally avoidable and blamed the British for what they saw as an ill-conceived pact with Poland. Far from brimming with fighting spirit, they nonetheless were obliged to play host to the exiled Polish Army. Sikorski was adamant that only joint military participation in the war effort would guarantee the Allies' commitment to Poland, and the creation of an army became a means of gaining international commitment to the Polish cause. Some 80,000 soldiers escaped capture and assembled in France before pressure from the Germans resulted in the route through Hungary and Romania being closed altogether, so that later evacuees had to make for the French Levant (Syria and Lebanon), where they joined the French colonial forces. From the winter of 1939 these men were billeted in Foreign Legion barracks in Homs, Syria and were organized as part of the French Army of the Levant, with their training and equipping well underway by January 1940. The formation was transferred to Polish command on 2 April 1940, becoming the Polish Carpathian Brigade, its staff and commander, Colonel Stanisław Kopański, arriving from Marseilles two weeks later.

The military campaign in France was a disaster for the Allies. An overwhelming German onslaught swept aside the armies of all opposing nations, leading to the capitulation of France and the need to evacuate all other Allied contingents to Britain. The Poles were acutely aware of this terrible situation and on 16 June prepared their first evacuation scheme, based on the principle that the struggle must be continued at the side of Britain. A consequence of the Franco-Polish alliance was that Polish units engaged at the front could not pull back and must fight to the end, an obligation Sikorski ordered his men to fulfil. However with the French signing their armistice with the Germans on 17 June, the obligation to send any more Polish troops into battle ceased. Sikorski met with Marshal Pétain that day and came to the conclusion that any help in the task of evacuation could only come from Britain. With this very much in mind, Churchill ordered an RAF bomber to fly to Bordeaux to collect the General and fly him direct to London for immediate talks with the British high command. Sikorski agreed to attend on the proviso that he be flown back to France straight after the talks to coordinate his army. Arriving on British soil Sikorski sent an appeal to Churchill on 18 June, which, while recalling the terms of the Anglo-Polish pact, contained a request for the provision of British warships and transports for the evacuation to Britain of the Polish units in France. 'I desire to renew the assurance, that Poland stands resolutely at the side of H.M. Government in the camp fighting against Germany and I place my soldierly trust in you, Mr. Prime Minister, confident that at this hour of trial you will issue the necessary orders for the rescue of the Polish troops...which desire to continue the struggle at the side of the armies of His Majesty.'[6]

Sikorski was invited to meet Churchill that very morning at 10 Downing Street, where he told the prime minister that the Polish Army was determined not to surrender. His army was in fact threatened with total annihilation, the Germans having received orders to take no Polish prisoners; every Pole, officer or enlisted man, was to be executed. They had fought desperately, remembering the fate of their martyred countrymen at home. The close of the meeting was captured by the *Sunday Express* journalist George Slocombe (14 July 1940): ' "Tomorrow, I return to France...and I have to face my Army. What am I to tell them?" "Tell them," replied Mr. Churchill, "that we are their comrades in life and death. We shall conquer together or we shall die together."...The two Prime Ministers then shook hands.' 'That handshake,' General Sikorski told Mr Slocombe afterwards, 'meant more to [me] than any treaty of alliance, or any pledged word.'[7] Immediate plans for evacuation were prepared and executed, some 23,000 soldiers and 8,000 airmen being transported to Britain over the following days.

Lieutenant General Sir Alan Brooke, commander of the United Kingdom Home Forces, called upon Sikorski on 31 July to arrange the employment of Polish troops, Brooke being responsible for coordinating Britain's anti-invasion preparations. The discussions led to the signing of the Anglo-Polish Military Agreement on 5 August 1940, formalizing Sikorski's earlier pledge. The British Government recognized the autonomy of the Army of the Sovereign Polish Republic under the Supreme Command of the Polish Commander-in-Chief, though in practice the British high command would direct operational strategy and control joint operations. Lieutenant General Sir Alan Brooke made this point plain in his diary with the phrase '[the] Polish Troops being now under my orders.'[8] The Polish Army was to be formed under Polish operational command and military laws, unlike the much smaller Polish Air Force and Navy that became integral parts of the British Armed Forces – this was largely because the British establishment recognized that the Polish Army was now the only surviving Polish institution of any size and the sole remaining symbol of their sovereignty. Polish soldiers were nevertheless subject to British criminal and civil law, which was seen as necessary to curb the practice of duelling amongst the officers.

The collapse of France shattered all hopes that the war might be over quickly and Poland's necessary dependence on military cooperation with Britain meant that the war had now to be seen from the British perspective, as a global conflict, along with the realization that Polish troops would have to fight on battlefields away from Europe. The only immediate military option open to Sikorski was to form an expeditionary force from the

Poles in the French Levant, whose ranks had swelled to some 3,000. This growing force was however in a difficult situation, being based in Vichy French territory, and the French commander of the Levant Army, General Huntziger, ordered the arrest of Colonel Kopański when the latter refused to disarm and instead insisted on leaving Syria with full military equipment. Kopański's firmness won through, he openly refused to yield to threats and the Brigade marched out of Syria and into Palestine with colours flying. Thanks to secret assistance from the French General de Larminat, the Poles were able to acquire arms and munitions, and thus equipped they joined the British Army in Palestine. The British commanding officer in Palestine, General Sir Henry Maitland Wilson, noted that the evacuated soldiers contained a high proportion of officers, in fact larger numbers than could be absorbed. A special unit of ex-officers had therefore to be created, christened the Polish Officers' Legion.

The first real test of this Anglo-Polish pact came with the Italian declaration of war on 10 June 1940, bringing the possibility of military conflict between the Allied troops in the Suez region and Italian troops from Ethiopia and Eritrea. In response, the British proposed using the Polish Independent Carpathian Rifle Brigade for the defence of Egypt in October 1940. The Polish troops in the Middle East now numbered 5,500 men and the British, although welcoming them, were somewhat perplexed as to how they should be employed. Poland was not at war with Italy, indeed the two countries had long enjoyed close relations, while the long-standing relationship with France meant that Polish troops could not be used against Vichy French forces in Syria. This situation infuriated the British commanders, who refused to rearm the Poles with British weaponry, leaving the Brigade in a state of inactivity. The force was utilized as a garrison in Jerusalem until late September, when it transferred to Alexandria to perform further garrison duties, along with preparing the city's fortification against possible attack from the Axis. The Officers' Legion remained in Jerusalem to train new recruits as they arrived from the Balkans.

This period of inaction came to an end on 13 November, when Sikorski severed diplomatic relations with Italy, affirming that Britain's enemies were Poland's enemies and that the Poles were willing to fight alongside the British. The Polish Independent Carpathian Rifle Brigade was subsequently fully re-equipped during December 1940 and trained in mountain warfare. The nature of the Anglo-Polish alliance was clearly set out: Poland was the junior partner. This was not to belittle the contribution of the Polish contingent, as demonstrated at the close of October when Anthony Eden visited the Middle East and inspected the British and Allied contingents. 'Most dramatic of all was a parade of the Polish Brigade. These men, so far from their own land, so isolated by language, climate and ways of life, were yet compactly sufficient to themselves and unmistakably military material of the finest quality.'[9]

The contribution of the Polish forces was welcomed by the British authorities in the Middle East, a region that was both politically turbulent and also the only theatre of war in which the British and Commonwealth forces were still engaged in land combat with Germany and its Axis partners. Fighting in the desert was initially a British–Italian conflict, but as Italy's fortunes ebbed Mussolini called upon Hitler for assistance. The Germans responded by sending the outstanding General Erwin Rommel and the specially created Afrika Korps, who proved to be extremely effective desert soldiers. Indeed, at this stage of the war the Germans were very much in the ascendancy; it was Germany making territorial gains and German commanders dictating the nature of the fighting. The British and Commonwealth forces reacted to German initiatives, in both strategy and tactics. Each new threat or thrust from the Germans entailed much reorganization of the limited and widely spread Allied forces, whose near constant reorganization and redeployment reflected this, as did the high turnover of generals and commanders-in-chief in the region. The need to win battles and to safeguard oil supplies was vital both strategically and for morale. Military forces in the region were administered by Middle East Command, based in Cairo under the command of General Auchinleck, a man popular amongst his troops and of resolute good character, later described by General Anders as a 'splendid soldier'.[10] The command's forces were spread over a huge area with the main combat force, the Western Desert Force, focused on the task of defeating Rommel's Afrika Korps.

The advance of the Afrika Korps across northern Africa was causing much internal unrest and tension in the countries of the Middle East. In 1941, a coup d'état in Iraq installed Rashid Ali's pro-Axis government that went on to besiege the British Royal Air Force training base at Habbaniya. Alarmingly, the new regime was readily acknowledged by the USSR. Hostilities commenced on 2 May, with the airfield defence troops eventually able to overcome the Iraqis and, with the arrival of British troops deployed from Palestine, pushing on to capture Falluja. These elements combined to form Habforce, which took Baghdad after a brief artillery exchange, bringing the rebellion to an end. The soldiers stationed in Iraq became known, unimaginatively, as British Troops in Iraq and were supplied and maintained from India, while under the operational remit of Middle East Headquarters. The formation was under the command of Lieutenant General Edward Quinan, a strikingly individual officer who possessed an intense dislike for the trimmings of office along with a thorough disregard for his own comfort. The small, weather-beaten, grey-haired gentleman was extremely popular with the men of his command.

Despite the presence of British Troops in Iraq the territory was still considered to be under Axis threat from the French Levant. This territory comprised the French colonies of Syria and Lebanon that were now administered by the puppet Vichy French government in league with the Germans. Vichy France had allowed its airfields to be used as staging posts for German aeroplanes supporting Rashid Ali's revolt, and the further development of enemy air bases in the French Levant would afford the Axis the ability to launch air raids against Iraqi oil installations, with Baghdad lying within two hours' flying time. The decision was therefore taken to launch Operation Exporter, the invasion of the French Levant. The taskforce was formed from the British, Australian, Indian, Free Czechoslovakian and Free French Armies, who overcame the stubborn defence of the Vichy French forces between June and July 1941 and subsequently occupied the territories. The Polish Independent Brigade had been earmarked for service in Syria though Sikorski fervently refused to allow Polish soldiers to fight Frenchmen.

The Polish Brigade had yet to see action, coming closest on 9 April 1941 when ordered to embark for Greece and the Balkan Front. However, pressure from Rommel in Libya changed matters, so that the Polish Brigade and two British infantry divisions were obliged to remain for the defence of Egypt. The Polish Independent Carpathian Rifle Brigade was deployed to a fortified camp at Mersa Matruh, near Alexandria, to protect the approaches to the Nile delta and to provide guards for twelve prisoner-of-war camps housing 65,000 Italians captured in Libya. There the Poles remained for continued training until finally, on 15 August, Colonel Kopański was informed his Brigade was being sent to relieve the besieged garrison at Tobruk, where the Polish troops fought with distinction.

Aside from these conventional military activities the Polish Intelligence Corps in the Middle East and North Africa achieved notable success, with a network of spies established in Vichy territories handled by Polish officers under Major Mieczysław Zygfryd Słowikowski, codenamed Rygor. The information gathered in Tunisia proved most useful in the planning of Operation Torch, the Allied amphibious invasion of Tunisia in November 1942 that enabled the final rout of the Axis in Africa. The spying role diminished as the war progressed and the Intelligence Corps became focused on intercepting enemy transmissions and the interrogation of prisoners, along with establishing counter-intelligence procedures to deny the Germans knowledge of Allied plans.

Table 1
Polish Independent Carpathian Rifle Brigade 1939–1942

1939	
October	Polish soldiers escaping Poland arrive in Syria to enlist in the French Army of the Levant.
1940	
April	**Polish Carpathian Brigade** formed in Homs, Syria and transfered to Polish command.
August	Brigade evacuated to Palestine following surrender of France and signing of British-Polish Military Agreement. Renamed **Polish Independent Carpathian Rifle Brigade**. Deployed on garrison duties in Palestine as Poland not at war with any beligerents in Middle East.
November	Poland breaks diplomatic relations with Italy, Brigade considered for use in North Africa.
December	Retrained and re-equiped for modern warfare.
1941	
April	Designated for action in Greece.
June	Greek operation aborted, Brigade employed guarding Italian POWs around Alexandria.
August	Brigade sent to relieve Australian garrison at Tobruk.
December	Battle of Gazala.
1942	
February	Brigade transferred to Palestine pending expansion into **Carpathian Rifle Division**.

2

A Polish Army in the USSR

The fate of the interned Poles in the USSR appeared far from hopeful. Lieutenant General Anders found himself moved around various detention centres and hospitals on a circuitous journey that led him down an inexorably deteriorating standard of captivity until, frostbitten from being held in a $-30°C$ cell, he was in March transferred to Moscow and the Lubianka headquarters of the NKVD. The Lubianka was an oddity of the Soviet penal system, originally a luxury hotel it had been used as a prison since the Bolshevik revolution of 1918, being reserved for persons of special interest to the Central Office of the NKVD. An eerie silence prevailed inside the establishment, as inmates and guards alike were permitted to speak only in whispers and the corridors were thickly carpeted to absorb all normal sounds. The inmates' conditions were luxurious for the Soviet system – baths and showers were taken, beds and bedlinen provided, as well as clothing, regular meals and haircuts; the prisoners were expected to be presentable for interrogation by high-level officials.

Anders' repeated interrogations took the form of attempts to pressure him into joining the ranks of the Red Army and of disclosing the location of Polish resistance units. When he refused to accede to these demands Anders' faith in the British-Polish Military Pact was attacked, with the interrogators telling him, 'Don't think that we are the genuine friends of Germany: We hate only the English more.'[1] Soviet propaganda played strongly upon Britain and France's lack of immediate action to assist Poland during the German invasion, the Soviets aiming to capitalize on any resentment in the Poles to bring them round to their own view: that Germany and Britain were equal enemies. Anders' refusal to yield to his interrogators led to a transfer to solitary confinement at Butyrki prison, where for the several months of his captivity powerful lights were kept permanently trained on his eyes, night and day, until they became inflamed, and so filled with pus he could no longer see. In September, Anders was returned to the Lubianka and left on the back burner, allowing him time to recover and absorb the permitted literature on the glory of

Soviet achievement and also some news about the German conquest of Europe. This respite allowed the General, always a man of intellectual as well as physical rigor, to inform himself about current affairs and thus armed with up-to-date information he began to make plans.

The General's pace of life accelerated rapidly when, from July 1941, the sound of bombs exploding could be heard outside in the streets of Moscow. Anders surmised that Germany had turned on the USSR and thought the Soviets must have been fighting the Germans for some time. The other prisoners were not so convinced as Anders recalled, 'They began to argue whether the aircraft were German or British. That they should have considered that the aircraft might have been British was not strange, for the Russians never disguised their detestation of the British, and reviled them at every opportunity. The Germans they dreaded, but at the same time regarded with a peculiar respect.'[2] This anti-British sentiment featured prominently in the minds of the senior Soviet leaders, who strongly resented Britain's intervention in the Russian civil war of 1918–19 and Britain's failed attempt to destroy the Bolsheviks by force of arms.

Anders' long period of captivity began drawing to a close in early August 1941, when he was brought before the head of the Lubianka, Colonel Kondratik. After telling Anders all Polish generals were cowards, Kondratik smiled and asked after the General's health and well-being and if Anders was aware of current events. Anders asked if there was a war between the USSR and Germany, Kondratik replied the explosions were only exercises. Anders then asked if there was a treaty of alliance between Britain and the USSR, the curt answer coming that there was; and whether conversations were taking place with General Sikorski's government – they were. The following day Anders was shaved and sprinkled with eau-de-Cologne in readiness for his meeting with the head of the NKVD, Laurenti Beria. In a luxuriously furnished study Anders came face to face with Beria and his deputy Merkulov, and after exchanging brief pleasantries Anders asked immediately if he was still a prisoner or a free man. The reply came from Beria, simply, 'You are free.'[3] There followed a friendly and lengthy conversation on the need for Poland and the Soviet Union to fight together to defeat the Germans and about the fact that a Polish Army in the USSR was to be created with Anders as commander, a selection the Soviets were especially pleased with and Stalin himself took a great personal interest in. On 4 August Anders walked out of the Lubianka, still in his prison fatigues, whereupon a chauffeur-driven limousine collected him at the gate and drove him to his new luxury apartment in Moscow, where his cook had prepared a banquet for him including caviar and vintage French champagne. Colonel Kondratik was placed at Anders' disposal and tried most awkwardly to explain his previous behaviour towards the General. From now on Anders was afforded the courtesy and respect due to a high-level foreign military dignitary.

Events had indeed developed rapidly when, on 22 June 1941, Hitler launched the German invasion of the Soviet Union codenamed Operation Barbarossa. The desperate situation Stalin now faced forced him to release many Soviet generals who had been imprisoned for spurious counter-revolutionary crimes during the Great Terror of the 1930s. Amongst them was General Meretskov, who had been so badly beaten with rubber truncheons that he was almost completely crippled, so he was the only person in the USSR permitted to remain seated in Stalin's presence. General Rokossovsky was also freed; in his case the suffering had consisted of having all his fingernails ripped out. Disturbingly, they like Anders were made to work with their torturers upon release. No one was exempt from the tentacles of Stalin's terror; the Poles, to their horror, had been no exception.

Stalin was now forced by fate to join the Allied camp. During these first weeks after the German invasion the immediate aim of the British Secretary of State, Anthony Eden, was to restore relations between the Polish Government in Exile and the Soviet Government – it was felt that the USSR had an obligation to create a new friendship with the ally on whose behalf Britain had gone to war with Germany. Britain saw its role as a facilitator between the two in their negotiations, but a tripartite agreement between Britain, Poland and the USSR was not pursued, both western governments wishing to retain freedom of manoeuvre, to pursue their own agenda with the Soviets.

The British desired to form an Anglo-Soviet military pact as soon as possible and to facilitate this it would be beneficial for Polish-Soviet relations to improve. Sikorski understood the situation and transmitted a radio broadcast to Poland on 23 June, the transcript of his message reviewed beforehand by Anthony Eden, who insisted that it should not contain any language that might inflame the Soviets. Sikorski stated that an understanding could be reached between the two countries provided the Soviets recognized the terms of the 1921 Treaty of Riga and agreed to the release of all Polish deportees and prisoners of war to fight the common enemy. General Sosnkowski wrote to Sikorski within days, urging a policy of cooperation with the USSR.

On 4 July, the Soviet government issued their response to Sikorski's broadcast to Anthony Eden via the Soviet ambassador in London, Ivan Maisky. It was clear the Soviets intended to release the Polish prisoners of war but that these men would be subject to the control of a Polish National Committee to be set up in the USSR. Allusions were also made to the independence of the Polish state and the possibility of a treaty against the Germans. The Foreign Office found the message particularly vague and non-committal, but Sikorski interpreted it as a significant development of Soviet policy and was quick to propose that the Polish government should send a representative to Moscow, there being no desire for a National Committee that would inevitably be created as a puppet of the Soviet regime. Sikorski considered it unnecessary to discuss Polish frontiers at this early stage, all that the Polish government in exile required was for the Soviet Union to nullify the treaties made with Germany in 1939. Anthony Eden found this position very reasonable and passed these comments on to Mr Maisky, indeed Sikorski's attitude was seen as most pragmatic and a constructive presence in Allied-Soviet relations. On 6 July, the Soviet Ambassador met Sikorski in Sir Alexander Cadogan's room at the Foreign Office, whereupon Maisky undertook to submit to his government five points that summed up the Polish position:

1. Discussion of the frontiers to be left aside for the moment, provided the Russians denounced the treaties with Germany of August and September 1939;
2. Normal relations to be resumed between the two governments and a Polish ambassador appointed to Moscow;
3. Poland would be prepared to collaborate in the common fight against Germany;
4. A Polish army to be formed on Soviet territory, to be transported elsewhere if desired;
5. Polish military and political prisoners to be released.[4]

The establishment of a Polish Army in the USSR initially appeared to offer little of benefit to the British war effort until General Claude Auchinleck, Commander-in-Chief Middle East Command, wrote to the War Office on 3 July (at the height of Rommel's advance) passing on General Kopański's suggestion that Polish soldiers could be moved from the USSR to the Middle East to replenish the Independent Carpathian Rifle Brigade. The motion was proposed to the Chiefs of Staff that 15,000 Polish soldiers could be evacuated to the Middle East for the purpose. The Chiefs of Staff immediately saw the advantages of deploying the large numbers of Polish soldiers in the Caucasus region, with a view to their eventual transfer to British control.[5]

British-Soviet relations were also being cultivated with haste during this period, with the Anglo-Soviet Agreement being negotiated by the British Special Envoy to Moscow, Sir Stafford Cripps. Cripps met Stalin on 8 July and found that all the Soviets wanted by way of an agreement at that time was

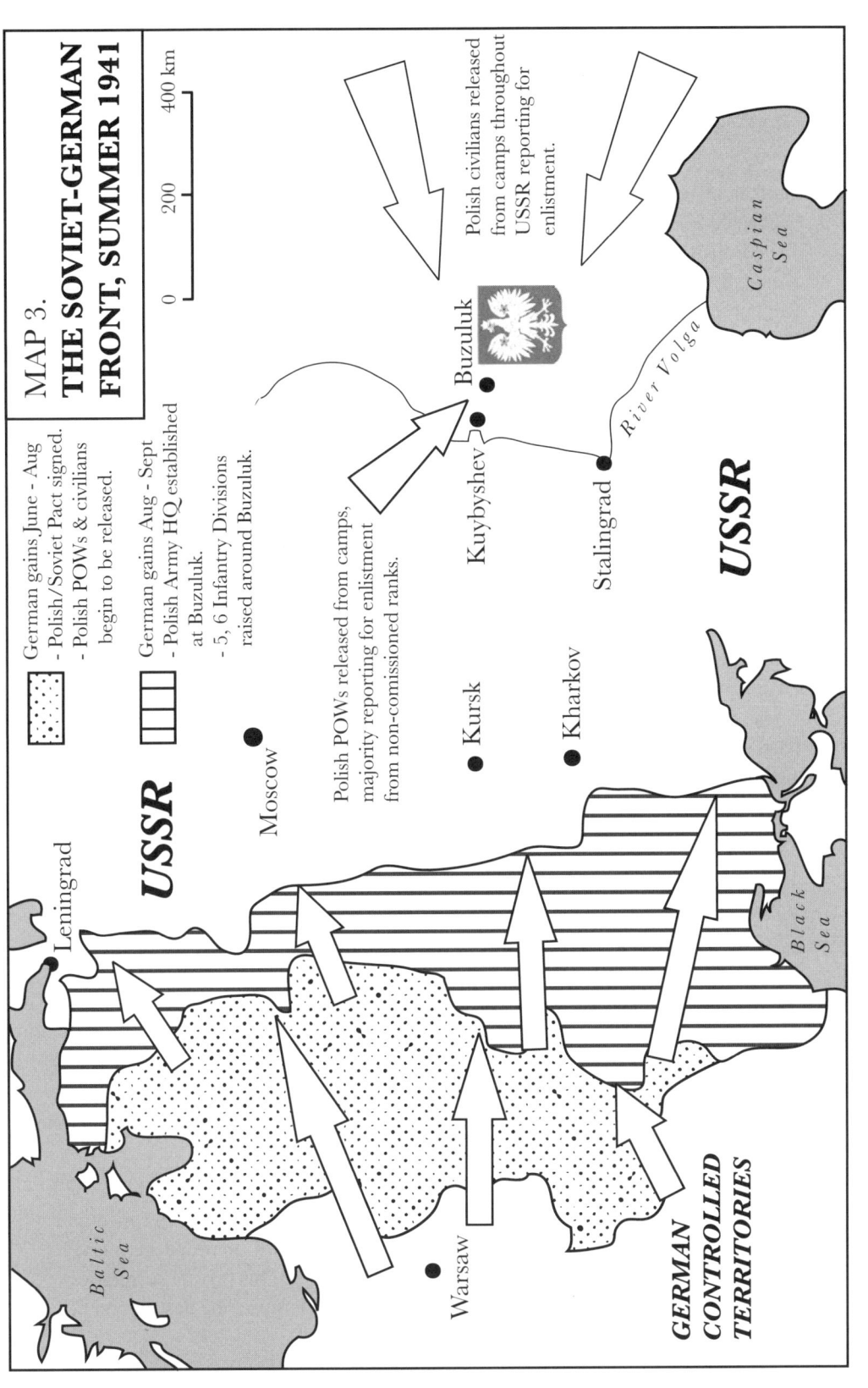

a pledge of mutual help without precise statements about quantity or quality, and an undertaking on both sides not to conclude a separate peace. The British accepted Stalin's position and the agreement was signed in Moscow on 12 July. The Polish-Soviet negotiations were more heated and only after many difficult meetings between General Sikorski and Mr Maisky was Sikorski able to reach an agreement with the Soviet government on 30 July. The process was greatly aided by Anthony Eden and, crucially Sir Stafford Cripps, who obtained a universal amnesty for all Poles in the USSR. The decision was not an easy one for Sikorski, the Soviets having invaded his country and enslaved its people, but with Britain forging ahead with a rapprochement policy towards the USSR it was evident to Sikorski that he would have to do a deal with the Soviets in order to remain an active and influential member of the Allied camp.

To reassure any sceptics, Sikorski broadcast a speech on 31 July expressing his opinion about the act: 'The present agreement only provisionally regulates disputes which have mutually divided us for centuries. But it does not permit even of the suggestion that the 1939 frontiers of the Polish State could ever be in question. It does not allow of any idea Poland has renounced anything... the condition of our brotherhood in arms must be respect for our sovereignty.'[6] Anthony Eden acknowledged Sikorski's statesmanship as deserving credit for creating the Polish-Soviet Agreement and said that the British part 'was only patient diplomacy tinged with anxiety for what the future must hold for the Poles as the weaker partner.'[7] Such anxiety weighed heavily on the Poles and many were horrified that Sikorski had not demanded firm reassurances on Poland's frontiers from the Soviets, while at the same time failing to obtain a formal security guarantee from the British. In light of what to many in the exile community were vital omissions, Deputy Prime Minister General Sosnokowski and Ministers August Zaleski and Marian Seyda resigned from the government. These ministers also objected to the wording of the agreement, in particular the use of the word amnesty in relation to Polish citizens in the Soviet Union; it suggested that the Poles, who were deported by the Soviet Union during the military occupation of the eastern provinces of Poland, were guilty of a crime. Zaleski, Sosnokowski and Seyda believed that this vagueness in the wording of the treaty would hamper the fight for an independent Poland at the end of the war.

Both the agreements signed with the USSR by Britain and Poland were in all practicality a display of solidarity and common cause rather than firm alliances; few of those involved realistically expected the Soviets to hold out for long against the Germans and both Britain and Poland harboured deep concerns about becoming allied to the communist state. Churchill confided his grave doubts about any alliance with the Soviet Union to one of his private secretaries on the eve of the German invasion, 'I have only one purpose, the destruction of

Hitler. If he were to invade Hell, I would make at least a favourable reference to the devil in the House of Commons.'[8]

General Sikorski and the London Poles now busied themselves forming a Polish Military Mission to the USSR whose task was to obtain information on the situation in the Soviet Union and to secure as much assistance from the Soviets as was possible to facilitate the creation of a Polish Army on Soviet soil. The mission was purely militaristic in its purpose; political and strategic responsibility remained the business of the Polish Embassy in Moscow. The Polish Military Mission was headed by Major General Zygmunt Bohusz-Szyszko, with Major Leon Bartnowski as his deputy. Major General Bohusz-Szyszko met with Anders four days after his release from the Lubianka prison. Anders was notably thinner, slightly dragged one foot and leant on a stick, but his gaze and voice were still energetic and he held himself with a noble stance. Major General Bohusz-Szyszko provided him with a new Polish uniform and a watch and Anders loudly voiced his joy at being not only a free man but also a Polish soldier once again. Soon after, Lieutenant General Anders called on Major General Sir Noel Mason-MacFarlane, chief of the newly arrived British 30 Military Mission Moscow. Before departing London for this posting MacFarlane had visited the Hotel Rubens in Buckingham Palace Road, effectively the seat of the Polish Government in Exile, where he met and befriended General Sikorski. Sikorski entrusted him with delivering a letter to Anders with his instructions for the creation of the Polish Army in the USSR. He made it clear that if the future of Poland's eastern border could not be agreed then the Poles were to be evacuated from the USSR, and that in the interim the Poles should be concentrated in areas that would facilitate their evacuation; Sikorski favouring the Arctic port of Archangel, with the Caucasus region of the southern USSR as an alternative. Anders was in agreement with Sikorski that even during these formative days of the Polish Army in the USSR, consideration should be given to its possible evacuation.

The creation of the army commenced from 6 August, following negotiations with the Red Army's Chief of Staff, Marshal Boris Shaposhnikov, focusing initially on the outline organization and rules for recruitment. There followed further meetings joined by Lieutenant General Anders and from the Soviet side by Generals Alexei Panfilov, Alexander Vasilevski and NKVD General Georgi Zhukov (not to be confused with the illustrious Red Army General of the same name). On 8 August, Major General Bohusz-Szyszko presented Sikorski's organizational plans to Stalin for approval and he, after making several amendments, consented to the Polish-Soviet Military Agreement that was subsequently signed by Major General Bohusz-Szyszko and General Vasilevski on 14 August 1941. It was agreed that the Polish Army was to be raised as the national army of the sovereign Polish Republic, under Polish command but falling under Soviet Supreme Command for operations on the Soviet western front. The army was to be ready for action in the shortest possible time and was to consist of land forces only, for which the availability of manpower, supplies, and equipment would determine the size of the army. Recruits had to be of Polish nationality and those who had previously served in the air force or navy would be transferred to Polish units in Britain. Responsibility for the supplying and equipping of the new army was to be shared between the USSR and Britain. The energetic and outspoken campaigning by General MacFarlane greatly accelerated the signing of the agreement, and the process was also greatly facilitated by the fact that the Soviets were still reeling from the shock of being caught off guard by the German invasion. Anders was particularly struck by Major General MacFarlane's habit of wearing shorts, an eccentricity that endeared him to Anders and also indicated to him how different the experience of working with the British would be.

In London, the British Chiefs of Staff commenced their deliberations over the Polish forces in the Soviet Union from 11 August, following a series of telegrams from Major General MacFarlane who sought a policy direction on the armament and equipping of the Poles. The Chiefs of Staff delegated the investigation into the requirements and usefulness of the Poles to the Allied Forces (Official) Committee, who made the following recommendations at their meeting on 15 August:

(a) That it would be desirable to bring to this country from Northern Russian ports in accordance with the order of priority laid down by the Chiefs of Staff:-
   (i) Any trained or partially trained air crew personnel or ground personnel of skilled trades.
   (ii) Any officers and ratings formerly belonging to the Polish Navy.
   (iii) If any further shipping space were available, any technical military personnel such as artificers, tank crews, and other AFV personnel.
(b) That this would only be possible if the troop ship on its way to Russia could be made available for the transport of these men. There was regular accommodation for about 800 men, though more could probably be carried if necessary.
(c) That the Foreign Office should suggest to the Polish Government that the latter should endeavour to make the necessary arrangements for the detachment and transport of these men to the North Russian ports, with the military authorities in Moscow through the Polish Military Mission. Technical details could be left for discussion between the Polish authorities in London and the Service Departments.

(d) That General Mason MacFarlane should be informed of the action being taken and instructed to lend what assistance he could to the Polish Military Mission in their negotiations with the Soviet Military Authorities.
(e) That the Foreign Office should suggest to the Polish authorities that His Majesty's Government would see some advantage in part of the Polish military forces being assembled in the Caucasus region with a view to their eventual transfer to the Middle East or for other purposes, and that it was hoped that this object might be secured in their negotiations with the Soviet authorities.

[...] The Allied Force (Official) Committee has invited the Foreign Office, in conjunction with the War Office, to examine the problem of transporting Polish Military personnel from the Soviet Union to the Middle East.[9]

Only the Air Ministry made direct requests for Polish personnel, receiving 60 officers and 200 airmen between October 1941 and mid-March 1942.

Meanwhile, the Poles were busy raising an army. The appointment to the position of commander of the Polish Army in the USSR was of great importance. The Polish Exile Government in London had initially nominated General Stanisław Haller, formerly Chief of the Polish General Staff to be the commander of the Army – Sikorski considered him the most suitable candidate for the task of organizing and commanding the Polish armed forces in the USSR. However, when he could not be found Sikorski entrusted the task to General Anders. General Haller was not the only missing soldier; several thousand Polish officers taken prisoner were unaccounted for. Crucially for Sikorski, Anders was politically distant from the pre-war regime and this made him a more attractive candidate than the more experienced Major Generals Boruta-Spiechowicz and Karaszewicz-Tokarzewski. Anders had served in the Russian cavalry before the revolution, distinguishing himself in the struggle for Polish independence and also possessing good references from his captors, the latter proving decisive for Soviet approval of his appointment. The leader of the Polish Military Mission in the USSR, Major General Zygmunt Bohusz-Szyszko noted, 'From the outset, Anders commanded the respect, trust and affection of his men, and even the most insurmountable obstacle seemed within his reach. Not only was his record battle proven, but he also took upon himself the role of friend and guardian, for he had shared their privations. They would now follow wherever he led.'[10] Anders was the right man, in the right place at the right time.

Generals Anders and Zhukov debated the shape of the Polish Army from 16 August, through a week of negotiations. The Soviet military mission was headed by General Panfilov, although real authority rested with the NKVD representative General Zhukov, assisted by Colonel Volkovyski as his liaison officer. The British were represented by General Mason-MacFarlane with Colonel Leslie Hulls appointed as British military assistant to Anders. Anders became close friends with Hulls, who was one of the few western officers to comprehend the Soviet mindset and consistently proved himself a great help to the Polish cause. Amongst the first matters discussed were crucial questions about how many Polish soldiers were held by the Soviets and could be released, and about the provision of uniforms, arms and equipment. General Panfilov informed Anders that approximately 20,000 men were available, in light of which Anders proposed the creation of two infantry divisions plus a reserve. Furthermore, it was agreed that Poles already serving in the Red Army could be transferred to the Polish Army. Anders requested that the Soviets provide the money, instructors, food and arms for these men. The request was accepted on 19 August and went along with the formation of the Army Training Centre and a 365 million rouble loan from the Soviets. General Panfilov also conveyed the instruction that the force should aim to be ready for combat deployment on 1 October – an impossible time-frame of just over one month to recruit, equip, train and deploy two infantry divisions.

The location the Soviets chose to raise the Polish Army lay between the River Volga and the Ural Mountains, where they were concentrating their reserves. The region was known for its harsh winter climate. The town of Buzuluk near the city of Orenburg became the headquarters of the new army, with the 5th Division based at Tatishchev on the banks of the River Volga whilst the 6th Division and Army Training Centre were situated at the town of Totskoye. The formations were established on the standard Red Army pattern of three regiments of three battalions, along with numerous supporting regiments of artillery and cavalry and battalions of engineers, signals and medical staff.

The men arriving at the 6th Infantry Division's Totskoye camp were greeted by the sight of a great number of tents surrounded by thick broad-leaved forests; it looked like, and indeed was a summer training camp for the Red Army. As the year advanced the camp's unsuitability for winter rapidly became evident. There were very few permanent huts but numerous double-roofed tents. These were dug in, so that anyone entering had to step down to floor level – in effect, they were holes in the ground and as rain fell they grew waterlogged and with the winter winds and snows became freezing and miserable. The men endeavoured to erect low walls for shelter and utilized discarded metal barrels as stoves. Much time was devoted to gathering firewood and to basic survival. A cause for alarm was that the number of officers arriving to volunteer was far below the 15,000 envisaged and concern was growing as to the welfare of the rest. Captain Czapski was tasked with investigating the non-appearance of these Polish officers who had been detained by the NKVD. An Information Office was established at the Totskoye camp, where Czapski interviewed all new arrivals for information on the missing men, as well as pressing the issue with the Soviet authorities. He never received any satisfactory answers as to their fate and the Poles' suspicions about Soviet intentions towards them grew.

The Anglo-Soviet Pact was soon put to the test when on 25 August 1941, Operation Countenance, the Anglo-Soviet invasion of Persia was launched. Persia was vital to the Allied war effort in two ways: firstly, the British-owned Anglo-Iranian Oil Company operated a vast refinery at Abadan which supplied the bulk of Britain's oil; secondly, the only means of delivering military supplies into the USSR via an ice-free port was through Persia. The ruling Shah Pahlavi was amenable towards the Axis having accepted captured Czechoslovakian arms from the Germans earlier that year. A sizeable fifth column of Nazis posing as businessmen had begun fomenting tribal unrest from 1940 and German spies operated overtly throughout the territory. The Shah was requested by Britain and the USSR to give practical evidence of his neutrality by removing from Persia those Germans engaged in political activity hostile to the Allies. He failed to do so, and the Allies felt obliged to safeguard their interests by sending troops into the country. Lieutenant General Quinan attacked from the west with Iraq Force (formed from elements of British Troops in Iraq), whilst General Kozlov invaded from the north with three armies of the Transcaucasian Front. Quinan's forces seized their objectives and raced on to occupy Hamadan before the Soviets could reach it. The invasion was completed within three days and, following the expulsion of Germans from the territory, cordial relations with the Persians were resumed with only a minimal British military presence maintained in the west of Persia.

The Soviets by contrast garrisoned their zone heavily, displaying all the hallmarks of an occupier aiming for the long haul. The Soviets occupied and administered the northern fringes of Persia, from Lake Urmia near the Turkish border eastwards, including the entire Caspian Sea coast. Western Persia and Iraq's northern front were to be secured by Lieutenant General Quinan's Tenth Army; the new designation for British Troops in Iraq following the full transfer of responsibility of that force to Middle East Command in January. Sharing a joint administration of Persia with the USSR was not an ideal situation for the British, and Churchill in particular expressed concern as to the long-term intentions of the Soviet garrison. To safeguard Persia's future it would be altogether more desirable to remove the Soviet troops at the first opportunity.

The Anglo-Soviet invasion of Persia was launched only two weeks after the signing of the military agreement and demonstrated that the British and Red Armies could be deployed together on the same front. Stalin was most keen to capitalize on this success by pushing for a second front to be opened in Western Europe or for

British forces to fight directly on the Soviet Front. Both notions had grabbed the attention of the British public, where popular opinion was shouting for a second front to help the Russians. Churchill dismissed any notion of a cross-Channel landing but in early September he did telegram Stalin, stating, 'We are ready to make joint plans with you now.... We are hoping to raise our armies in the Middle East to a strength of three quarters of a million by the summer of 1942. Once the German-Italian forces in Libya have been destroyed all these forces will be available to come into line on your Southern flank.'[10] To which Stalin replied, 'It seems to me that Great Britain could without risk land in Archangel twenty-five–thirty infantry divisions, or transport them across land to the Southern region of the USSR. In this way there could be established military collaboration between the Soviet and British troops on the territory of the USSR.'[11]

These optimistic visions of cooperation between Britain and the USSR were still in view when on 1 September, General Panfilov decreed that the quantity of supplies the Soviets possessed would be sufficient to maintain 25,000 men with food provisions and weapons, whilst he insisted the British were to provide uniforms and other equipment. The Soviets were soon able to promise more supplies and on 6 September announced they could maintain a force of 44,000 men and that with the anticipated influx of men to the Army Training Centre a new formation would be created – the 7th Infantry Division. Alongside the men of the Polish Army, reporting for duty was also a sizeable contingent of women volunteers, who performed duties ranging from health care to administration, education and guard duties under the title of the Polish Women's Service.

Positive as these developments were, they were soon to be undone by the misfortunes of war. The formation of the Polish Army came at a time when the Red Army was heavily engaged in fighting the Germans, who had by the autumn captured the breadbasket of the USSR – the Ukraine and Belarus. This led inevitably to the harvest being lost and resulted in severe food shortages as production fell by over half. Accordingly the Soviet government announced on 10 September that food supplies could only be guaranteed for one Polish formation, the 5th Infantry Division that was already in receipt of light arms and some allocation of animals for transport and as such was envisaged as ready to join battle in October. Sikorski had repeatedly stressed to Churchill that his formations in the USSR should be entirely dependent on supplies from Britain and America; this would not only better the conditions of his men but would also put the responsibility for the Polish Army in the USSR with the Allied planners from its creation.

In light of these developments Sikorski drafted a note to Churchill on 17 September 1941:

Note relative to the formation of Polish Forces in Russia

Recent reports from Russia led to a general estimate of our military possibilities on the Eastern Front. There are about 1.5 million Poles who have been deported into Russia. Over 100,000, nearly 60% of whom are trained soldiers could be called up to the Polish Forces.

Lt. General Anders, GO Commanding Polish Forces in Russia, hopes to be able to organize 4 to 6 divisions including special units and services at the disposal of the Army and Army Corps Commands. Unfortunately, the shortage of equipment in Russia does not make it possible to organize immediately a greater number of divisions. The Soviet military authorities have declared their ability to arm only one infantry division. This armament however will not be complete, particularly in regard to artillery and anti-tank equipment.

The formation of a Polish Army in Russia is therefore entirely dependent upon the supply of armaments and equipment from Great Britain or the USA.

Two alternatives may be considered with regard to the organization of a Polish Army in Russia. This will depend on the available equipment.

Either   (i) – 1 armoured division,
*   3 infantry divisions (as fully mechanized as possible).*
Or   (ii) – 4 infantry divisions
*   2 tank brigades co-operating with infantry.*

Both alternatives should include –

*   2 regiments of heavy artillery*
*   (of 3 troops of 3 batteries of 4 guns)*
*   2 engineer battalions*
*   2 signals battalions*
*   2 groups of AA artillery*
*   2 reconnaissance groups*
*   services according to British organization for each division and Army Corps*
*   2 mobile hospitals of 600 beds.*

Moreover, full kit and personal equipment will also be required for 50,000 men as well as 5,000 outfits for the Women's Auxiliary Services.

Prevailing conditions in Russia demand the organization of independent supply of provisions. It would be therefore necessary to provide one million iron rations.

> *The difficulties connected with equipping and supplying of such an army will no doubt be considerable. It is only by overcoming these difficulties, however, that a Polish Army can be formed.*
>
> *It is most important to consider without delay the possibilities of organizing, arming and maintaining the Polish Forces in Russia and to carry out the determined scheme.*
>
> *I also wish to strengthen the Polish land forces in Britain and Africa by evacuating 8,000 men from Russia to Great Britain and 2,000 to complete the Polish Brigade Middle East. All the airmen and seamen will be evacuated to Britain. The first transport of 200 airmen was due to leave Archangel on 16th September.*
>
> *I am convinced that a full support from His Majesty's Government in this direction would greatly facilitate my endeavours.*
>
> *I am as much concerned with the matter of evacuation to Britain and Africa as with the organization of Polish force in Russia. The establishments of our Army in Great Britain are not complete and our Brigade in Egypt is already suffering losses and will require complements.*
>
> *Sikorski.*[12]

To address this and other material concerns with the Soviets, an Anglo-American Supply Mission, headed by Lord Beaverbrook and his deputy Averill Harriman, President Roosevelt's delegate, prepared to embark for Archangel to conduct negotiations. Prior to their departure from England, Sikorski's note was forwarded to both Beaverbrook and Harriman on Churchill's instruction, since the note highlighted the recurring problem facing the western Allies of reaching the Poles in the heart of the USSR. Supplies had begun arriving at the Soviet Union's northern ports in early September, but distribution was proving an insurmountable problem.

The mission landed in Archangel on 22 September to a bleak and unfriendly welcome, and the main meeting took place a week later in Moscow. The conference was concluded within four days and Stalin was pleased at the resulting promised quantities of supplies and the speed with which the arrangements had been made. Not that this was the result of any fervent desire to supply the Soviets with the equipment so badly needed by the British Army, especially as there was a total lack of information from the Soviets concerning the strategic situation and details of how the supplies would be used. No Soviet military information was shared; indeed even the order of battle of Red Army divisions remained unknown. It was clear to the negotiators that the Soviets would not reveal any detailed information for some considerable time to come, if ever, and that any agreement would have to be on the basis of good faith, as noted by Lieutenant General Ismay in summing up the conference:

> *The Russian General Staff tell them [the British Military Mission] precisely nothing. This may be accounted for partly by the intense centralization which obtains in Russia, and partly by the feeling of mutual distrust and dislike between the Russians and ourselves, which has prevailed for over 20 years. But whatever the reason, anything in the nature of joint planning, whether in London or Moscow, would in present circumstances be valueless. It is hoped that a new atmosphere and a new set of conditions will be created by the punctual fulfillment of our promises of help.*[13]

The western military authorities were not pleased that the military situation in the USSR remained a mystery and that in-depth discussions had not been pressed harder. The best source of information the British had on the Soviet war effort remained the Polish authorities.

The agreement reached on 1 October secured supplies for the USSR and raw material exports to Britain from October until June 1942. The agreed nature of the aid meant supplying the Soviet front as a whole, not by individual formation; it therefore remained for the Soviets to organize the distribution of supplies to the Poles.

The USSR's northern ports were poor places of entry for vast amounts of military material, partly due to the perilous sea passage involved and their ice-bound nature in winter, and partly to the poor rail and road facilities for the distribution of supplies. The British and Americans therefore agreed it was best to bypass these ports as far as was practicable and instead to develop the 'Trans-Persian routes...to the maximum extent and with the greatest possible speed.'[14] The Soviets expressed confidence in their ability to deal with any traffic likely to cross the Caspian Sea and stated that they were improving the port facilities at Bandar Caspian. What did capture the attention of the Anglo-American delegation was that the Soviets were surprised, even startled, at the proposals to increase Trans-Persian supply routes:

> *We had a definite impression that they were keen on keeping us as far away as possible from the Caspian Ports. They insisted, for example, that they must be responsible for the road traffic from Kavzin to Pahlevi, even of traffic which arrived by road at Kavzin (which is also the railway terminal for Pahlevi traffic) even though this procedure is obviously uneconomical in both time and transport.*[15]

The Anglo-American Supply Mission ran out of time to discuss Polish issues, having been so overwhelmed with the scale of Soviet demands. Ambassador Kot arranged for discussion of the re-equipment of Polish Forces in the USSR in a specific meeting to be held in Moscow on 2 October, the day after the conclusion of the main talks. At the American Embassy in Moscow, Beaverbrook and Harriman met with the Polish Ambassador, Lieutenant General Anders and General Bofors. Also present were the British and American Ambassadors, Lieutenant General Ismay and Major General Mason-MacFarlane, General Burns and Major General MacReady. Sikorski sought to take full advantage of this meeting to further the interests of and protect the Polish Army in the USSR. Not only had the troops to be spared from destruction on the faltering Soviet front, but also from the ravages of the Russian winter. With this in mind General Sikorski had written to Major General Szyszko-Bohusz on 27 September 1941; prior to the Beaverbrook mission's scheduled discussion on the Polish Army in the USSR:

> *Please put the following before General Sir Hastings Ismay.*
>
> *In view of latest developments on the Eastern front and particularly the rapid German drive in the Southern sector towards the Donetz Basin and the Caucasus the latter has become eminently important to the final issue. The protection of the Caucasian Oilfields is now vitally urgent. I desire the Polish Divisions to take part in the defence. We are not responsible for the delay in their organization or equipment. I do not wish to put forward to the Soviet Government the suggestion of moving the Polish forces to the Caucasus being most anxious to avoid occasioning any suspicion. I would be grateful if you will*
>
> *(1) give your kind assistance in the speeding up of equipment-transport from Archangel to the Polish forces.*
>
> *(2) Induce the British representative to put forward the proposal to move the Polish troops without delay or regard for their stage of organization to the Caucasus and to equip and arm these troops to the extent which will make it possible for them under the prevailing geographical conditions to render vital service to both Soviet Russia and the Allies.*
>
> *Sikorski.*[16]

The sending of this letter so far in advance of the meetings revealed that the Poles had great reservations over Lord Beaverbrook's commitment to the Polish cause. In an article in the *Sunday Express*, 31 March 1940, he wrote, 'The British were not interested in raising Poland and Czechoslovakia out of the gutter, dusting them down, and putting them on pedestals with arms in their hands, only for them to be overthrown again.'[17] With such a man tasked with promoting Polish interests they were not optimistic and focused their attentions on convincing the British military representatives of the merit of their schemes, hoping that the Generals could out-flank Beaverbrook.

The Polish representatives stated that they had enough men for four divisions, already amounting to about 44,000 and that they eventually expected to raise a force of 100,000. The Soviets had only armed one division, and had said that they could do no more; indeed Molotov had advised Anders to try to obtain arms on his own account. Following his discussions with the Soviets, Beaverbrook remarked that the Polish Army numbered only 40,000. From this Anders rightly deduced that the Kremlin would like to stop at that number for the present, to avoid being forced to agree to too great a concession in regard to the allocation of armaments for the Poles, and that this explained the unexpected hold-up of transports for the Polish Army in the past few days and also the procrastination over releasing further Polish detainees for service in the army. Lieutenant General Anders advocated the expansion of the army and this was supported and elaborated on by Major General MacFarlane, but Beaverbrook would not even entertain discussion on the issue, nothing could be done over and above the existing obligations to the USSR. Beaverbrook was enraged to hear from MacFarlane that 50,000 complete sets of equipment were on their way to the Polish Army, at which a greatly annoyed Major General MacReady turned to the Polish Ambassador and whispered, 'Our command surely has the right to send anything at its disposal, and we shall go on doing so.'[18]

Beaverbrook and Harriman were in agreement that it was the Soviets' responsibility to equip the Poles, however if they were unable to do so the British and Americans would try to assist them in the matter, so far as transport would allow. Harriman made a timid intervention, saying that the Americans wanted to supply the Poles with armaments over and above the Soviet programme. Later that evening during a meeting with Molotov, the latter reiterated to Beaverbrook and Harriman his earlier point to General Anders, 'that the Russians could do nothing beyond the equipping of a single division. The Russian Government would not, however, object to the United States and Great Britain taking decisions in the direction of arming the Poles.'[19]

Back in London and following the Beaverbrook mission, the British Chiefs of Staff turned their full attention to the events unfurling in the USSR and the course the Polish forces should take at their meeting on 2 October 1941:

> *Sir John Dill said that from the point of view of increasing resistance to the Germans in the oil fields area it was most desirable that Polish Forces should be concentrated in Caucasia. Moreover, these Polish Divisions might be of inestimable value to us as a means of reinforcing our army in the Middle East without the cost of shipping.*
>
> *The Russians could arm only one of the six Polish Divisions. It was doubtful whether under winter conditions, quite apart from German operations, it would be possible for us to send arms to the Poles via Archangel. It might be easier to send them equipment via Persia. If things were to go badly wrong in Russia, it would be desirable that the Poles*

> should be able to get out and this they could do more easily from the Caucasus.
> Sir John Dill mentioned that the supplies so far sent to the Poles amounted to equipment, clothing and necessaries for 50,000 men, and that similar supplies for another 55,000 men were to be sent.
> In discussion it was agreed to suggest to the Foreign Office that our Ambassador in Moscow should be instructed to support General Sikorski's proposal, and to press it.[20]

Following this discussion, Anthony Eden was asked by the British War Cabinet to inform the Soviet Government that the British Government preferred the Polish forces to be placed as near as possible to the Persian border to facilitate their supply. To enable this to be achieved the Polish Army had to be taken out of the Soviet order of battle for the defence of Moscow and to this effect Sikorski issued Anders precise orders on 2 October, forbidding him to release any Polish units for the front, at a time when the Soviets were asking for reinforcements. Anders was made personally responsible for ensuring that Polish troops should not be wasted by formations being sent prematurely to the front where their presence would have little impact militarily or politically. These decisions began the process of disengagement with the Soviets and the transferring of the Polish Army in the USSR to the British sphere of operations.

There was good reason for the timing, The Germans had launched Operation Typhoon, the capture of Moscow on 30 September, and it was proceeding to plan. Many of the battles that followed displayed a curious phenomenon: the Germans and Soviets were fighting each other with Polish rifles and grenades plundered during their individual occupation of Poland. The Soviet way of fighting was far from appealing either to the Polish command or the soldiers. Stalin ruthlessly forced thousands of his troops into battle without guns, due to the total lack of preparation for war with Germany. Countless thousands of Red Army soldiers lost their lives because the only way they could survive was to scavenge weapons from the dead and dying. This was the type of action the Poles feared for themselves, given their lack of armaments.

The German onslaught was overwhelming; the Red Army was soon in full retreat just like every other army that stood against Hitler. However, the Soviets were different in that they had vast resources of war materials, reserves of personnel, a huge territory within which to maneouvre and a winter that could bring any invader to a halt. What the leadership required was time to coordinate these elements together with a stabilized front from which to counter-attack. In an attempt to stop the retreat of the Red Army drastic measures were introduced and the infamous Blocking Units were sent in. These companies took up position behind Soviet troops going into

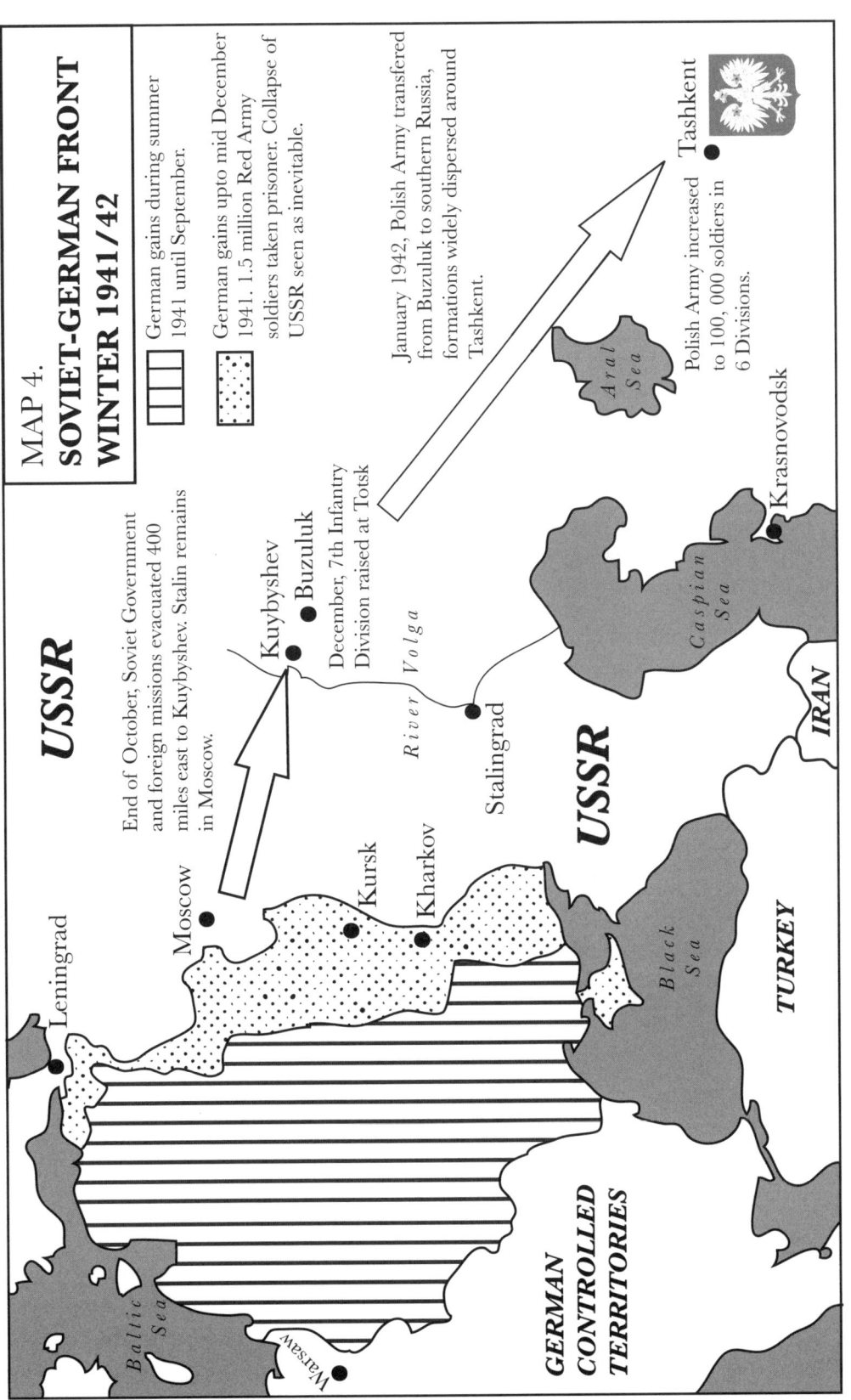

battle and their job was to mow down any men who tried to retreat. Hence the terrifying scenes of Soviet soldiers finding themselves driven back by the Germans only to be cut down by machine-gunners from behind. Such draconian measures proved only a limited success as huge gaps in the front began opening up as Operation Typhoon powered forwards. Nevertheless, in several sectors Soviet resistance was beginning to stiffen and near suicidal Red Army counter-attacks began to slow the German advance. Such desperate fighting by the Soviet troops bought time, both to improve Moscow's defences and to call upon available reserves.

On 5 October, Anders refused to let the partially armed 5th Infantry Division be sent into action. The decision resulted in an immediate change for the worse in Polish-Soviet relations, since the Soviets detested anyone who refused to fight. The situation was indeed grave and when, on 6 October, the renowned Red Army commander General Zhukov arrived at the Western Front HQ, he remarked that 'there was no longer a continuous front in the west, and the gaps could not be closed because the command had run out of reserves.'[21] On 13 October, Stalin issued orders to evacuate the upper echelons of government and the military to Kuibyshev, the city that was to serve as the temporary capital if Moscow fell.

Stalin was still insistent that his western Allies should fight on the Soviet front and if the Poles would not join battle then he was convinced the presence of even a few British troops would make a great difference to Soviet morale. Thus Anthony Eden made an offer on 16 October to send a brigade group to the Caucasus, providing a token British presence. The offer was immediately refused by Molotov, the Soviets now favouring British intervention at Rostov, the principle port city on the north-eastern coast of the Black Sea.

The threat of a German invasion of the Middle East through the Caucasus was perceived as very real to the British Chiefs of Staff. In addition to requesting the Poles be used to defend the Caucasus region on Soviet territory, a major reorganization of British forces in the region was instigated to counter possible German offensives from both the north and west. The commander of the region, General Auchinleck, reorganized the forces of Middle East Command during November 1941, and the northern front was held by amalgamating British and Commonwealth troops in Syria and Lebanon into the Ninth Army under General Sir Henry Maitland-Wilson. In the west the Eighth Army was formed under General Sir Edward Cunningham. The existing garrisons in Palestine, Trans-Jordan and Egypt formed a supporting Base and Line of Communication Area. British Troops in Iraq were tasked with creating the infrastructure for 10 divisions and 30 squadrons of aircraft, and for developing to the greatest extent possible a supply route to the Soviet Union through Persia.

The proposal to relocate the Polish Army southwards was supported by the British, Polish and also the Americans. On 7 November, the Chiefs of Staff met to discuss a draft telegram the American President intended to send to Stalin and that Roosevelt wished Churchill to approve beforehand. It included the following words:

> *[That] the Polish troops now in the Lower Volga area for whom the Russians could not provide arms and equipment, should be withdrawn to a designated area in Persia and there rearmed and equipped for return to the Russian Front in due course.* [22]

The committee instructed the Secretary to inform the Prime Minister that the Chiefs of Staff were in general agreement with the terms of the proposed telegram and the message was sent to Stalin later that day, endorsed by Churchill and Avril Harriman. Further meetings of the Chiefs of Staff in early November included discussions on draft proposals for the evacuation of 'Polish Forces, now in Russia, to India or the Middle East in order to enable them to be equipped and reorganized.'[23]

Churchill was now onboard with the idea of relocating the Poles and encouraged Sikorski to press for the transfer of Polish troops southwards, ideally to Persia where they could release the Soviet garrison to fight on the front. This would have suited Churchill's objective of getting Red Army soldiers out of Persia, however the Soviets would have had no desire to lessen their presence in this way, and the transferring of several Polish divisions totalling 100,000 men, to a rest and refit depot in a foreign country at the behest of foreign governments formed no part of their strategy. Thus reasoning, the Chiefs of Staff concluded the project would most likely fail and that the transfer of the Poles to India would be a less contentious alternative to maintaining the Polish Army. But Churchill's mind had been made up and he stuck with his idea and now pressed Sikorski to travel to Moscow and suggest the plan in person to Stalin – prompted largely by the fact that the British found it near impossible to form relationships with senior Soviet figures who possessed a deep mistrust of all westerners, a situation that frustrated even the excellent negotiator Lieutenant General Ismay. Churchill also felt that it would increase Sikorski's standing with Stalin if he presented the idea himself, reinforcing the portrayal of the Polish Exile Government as a sovereign body pursuing a Polish agenda.

General Sikorski visited the USSR at the close of 1941 and on his arrival in Kuibyshev he was reunited with Anders for the first time since before the war. Sikorski now witnessed at first hand the severe winter cold, as low as –52°C, with relentless icy winds that swept the snow into deep drifts, and many of the men in the camps froze to death inside their lightweight tents. British supplies of uniforms and equipment had begun arriving at the Polish Army camps from the second half of November, but there was a continuing lack of heavy weaponry from the Soviets that was causing Lieutenant General Anders much concern. It should be noted that it was standard procedure in the Red Army at this time not to issue weapons and ammunition to soldiers until they arrived on the battlefield itself, so the Poles were not singled out in this respect.

Major General Bohusz-Szyszko met with Major General MacFarlane in Kuibyshev on 21 November to discuss the relocation of Polish forces to Persia or India. They both agreed with the Chiefs of Staff's analysis that the Soviets would dismiss out of hand the notion of exchanging Red Army for Polish troops in Persia, but MacFarlane also felt that a relocation to India would prove just as disagreeable to them, and made the following points:

1. The Soviets might find themselves compromised by the shifting of the whole Polish Army from the USSR to a foreign country.
2. They would not agree to the release of two Polish Divisions already organized and armed.
3. They might require that the Polish Army, after the formation and arming in India, be returned to Soviet soil to fight on the Soviet-German front.[24]

With this less than promising briefing concluded, Generals Anders and Sikorski together with other Polish officials met with Stalin on 3 December, for a very demanding conference on Polish-Soviet affairs. The minutes of the meeting are reproduced in Ambassador Kot's post-war memoirs and the military discussions are included here. They provide a fascinating insight into the issues and personalities of those involved.

SIKORSKI: We Poles see the war not as a symbolic, but a genuine struggle.

(Stalin gestures his agreement.)

ANDERS: We want to fight for the independence of Poland here, on the continent.

SIKORSKI: In Poland we possess a strong military organization to which I have forbidden all publicity, since the Germans shoot for every [hostile] word. (Stalin assents. General Sikorski gives a number of instances of the methods the Polish nation is using to fight the Germans.) Our troops are fighting everywhere. In Great Britain we have a corps which requires reinforcements. We have a navy, which is functioning perfectly. We have in operation seventeen air divisions, which are being given the very latest British machines and are fighting magnificently. Polish pilots have accounted for twenty per cent of the losses of German aircraft over England.

STALIN: I know the Poles are brave.

SIKORSKI: When they are well led. Thanks to providence and to you, Mr. President, we have here General Anders, my best soldier, whose eight stars for wounds testify to his valour. You shut him in prison because he wanted to link up with me. He is a loyal commander, not a politician, and he will not allow his subordinates either to engage in politics.

STALIN: The finest politics is to fight well. (Turning to Anders) How long were you in prison?

ANDERS: Twenty months.

STALIN: And what sort of treatment did you receive?

ANDERS: In Lwów exceptionally bad. In Moscow rather better. But you can realize for yourself what 'better' means in prison, when you've been there for twenty months.

STALIN: Well, it couldn't be helped; such were the conditions.

SIKORSKI: I have one brigade, in Tobruk, which is to be transferred to Syria and reorganized into a motorized division with two tank battalions. If the need arose, I could transfer it here to the East. We have several naval vessels. When I decorated the sailors of our submarine stationed in Malta, which sank an Italian cruiser and one transport ship, the crew were so enthusiastic that the vessel sailed into a Greek port and despite a damaged periscope sank yet another cruiser and one Greek transport. It returned without loss. That's how the Polish soldier will fight when he is well led.

Our country is under occupation, and the only reserve of youth we have is here. I want you to send some 25,000 to Scotland and Egypt to make up complements; with those left it would be desirable to form some seven divisions. That is extremely important for Poland, which has its eyes fixed on the Polish Army as a symbol of its resistance and its independence. We want to fight, and so the troops in Scotland will be used as an advanced guard for the formation of a second front, or transferred here, to the East. In that case I would take over the command personally.

The present difficulties in regard to commissariat, equipment and training are causing me some anxiety, lest the formations organized in such conditions should be completely useless. Instead of devoting their health and life to the common cause the men are vegetating or are perishing pointlessly. The war will be a long one. Great Britain and the United States have disarmed themselves overmuch, and their war industry, especially that of America, will require a long time to achieve full production capacity. In time an avalanche of war materiel will be poured in. But I already have Roosevelt's and Churchill's assurance that they will arm our divisions parallel with yours, without affecting your supplies, but on the condition that our army will be formed in areas which supplies can reach without great difficulty. The present state of equipment of our divisions is completely inadequate. Divisions in such conditions are unfit for battle....General Anders will explain this to you in detail. (Anders explains the state of the equipment received, stressing the insurmountable difficulties which arise every day.)

STALIN: (enquires about certain details concerning artillery.) Russia entered the war with divisions consisting of some 15,000 men, but in practice they proved too heavy, so we have gone over to a lighter division of about 11,000 men.

SIKORSKI: The conditions in which the Polish Army is now being formed are quite unsatisfactory. The soldiers are freezing in summer tents, they feel the lack of food and are simply condemned to slow death. For this reason I propose to transfer all the troops and all the human material fit for military service to Persia, for example, where the climate and the guaranteed British and American aid would enable us in a short time to restore their health and form a strong army, which would return to your front, to occupy its own sector there. This is agreed with Churchill. For my part I am ready to make a declaration that these troops will return to the Russian front and that they might even be reinforced by several British divisions.

ANDERS: (Continues with his exposé of the situation of the troops already in formation, and declares that in these conditions of food, housing, sanitation and medical care and in the hard climate it is quite impossible to organize units capable of waging war.) This is only a state of wretched vegetation, in which all efforts are put into maintaining existence, and that very badly. But we want the Polish Army to be ready for battle as quickly as possible and to fight for Poland together with her allies; in these conditions this is quite impossible. So it is necessary to transfer the troops to climatic, food and supplies conditions which will enable us to go ahead on these lines. In view of the difficulties with which Russia is faced we must take the facilities for Anglo-American supplies into account. All the actual serving soldiers and all the men fit for military service should be sent there. When we take part in battles our army's blow should not be merely symbolic, but should serve the end for which we are fighting all over the world, the fight for Poland.

SIKORSKI: I would like the Soviet Government to have confidence in my proposal. I am a man, who, when he says 'yes' means 'yes', and when he says 'no means 'no', and when I say nothing, I either cannot or don't wish to tell the truth.

STALIN: (in an irritated tone and obviously dissatisfied) I am an old and experienced man. I know that when you go to Persia you will not return here. I see that England has much work and needs the Polish soldiers.

SIKORSKI: We are linked with Great Britain by an alliance which she is observing loyally. Also in Great Britain we have genuine sovereignty. I can even bring a corps here from Scotland, and they certainly won't make difficulties for me in England in consequence. Similarly, I can add the forces in Tobruk to our troops here.

KOT: The Pole fights particularly well if he is close to his homeland.

STALIN: Iran isn't all that far, but the English can force you to fight the Germans in Turkey, or tomorrow Japan may enter the war.

ANDERS: We want to fight for Poland. We believe that even the strongest airforces and navies will not finish the war. It will be ended by battles on the continent. We all without exception love our fatherland, and we want to be the first to enter it, we want to be ready to fight as quickly as possible, but in the conditions we have now it is impossible to prepare for it.

SIKORSKI: England today and formerly are as different as heaven and earth. At present the English have enough troops to defend their islands, so they have no reason to stop our corps from going.

(Molotov proposes to call General Panfilov into the conference and gives instructions to his secretary, who goes out.)

ANDERS: (Explains the difficulties of army formation and the living conditions in Koltubiansk, Tatishev, and Totskoe, the [Soviet] failure to observe the dates fixed for supplies of food, fodder, equipment, instruments, etc.) Such a life is only a wretched vegetation and the months are wasted. In these conditions it is quite impossible to form an army.

STALIN: (irritably) If the Poles don't want to fight let them go. We cannot detain them. If they want to go, let them go.

SIKORSKI: If we could have created our formations we should have been fighting already, but how much time has been wasted here through no fault of our own! In the present areas of location we have no prospects of any conditions for training soldiers. (A moment of silence.) In that case I ask for another solution.

STALIN: If the Poles don't want to fight here, let them say so straight out, yes or no. I am sixty-two and I know that where an army is formed, there it remains.

SIKORSKI: (in a sharper tone) Then please suggest some other solution to me, for conditions for organizing our army don't exist here, and I don't want the people to perish uselessly. I'm not presenting any ultimatum, but when there is a severe winter, wind, and frosts, from which people are dying, I cannot look on and say nothing.

ANDERS: The frosts have already reached [minus] 33 degrees [Centigrade] in our area. The men are living in single tents, the majority of them without stoves, which are being supplied to us in inadequate quantities. They wake up in the morning with frostbitten noses and ears. That's not forming military forces, that's wretched vegetation.

SIKORSKI: We cannot fling an untrained soldier against the Germans. We most not expose ourselves to the risk of being compromised. The Polish Army must be well armed and must fight as a whole.

ANDERS: As it is I'm amazed at our soldiers, who despite their great sufferings during the past two years and the horrible conditions in which they are now living – they received an issue of boots only a few weeks ago, and before that 60 per cent had been going barefoot – yet they made no complaint though they've never received all the food due to them, and for a long time not even their pay.

SIKORSKI: (resolutely) You have annoyed me, Mr. President, by saying that our soldiers don't want to fight.

STALIN: I am blunt, and I want to know clearly whether you want to fight or not.

SIKORSKI: (resolutely) That we do is shown not by words but by the facts.

ANDERS: That's what we are forming an army for, in order to fight here, and we realize that our struggle must be waged on the continent. According to my calculations I can have 150,000 soldiers, in other words, the equivalent of eight divisions. Meanwhile we have only two divisions and those not up to full strength. We are not getting the requisite food, and none of the promises to settle this question are kept.

STALIN: (to General Sikorski) It's as you wish.

SIKORSKI: I don't want the issue to be put like that. I'm still waiting for a new formula, and I'm ready to accept any equitable solution.

STALIN: (with a touch of sarcasm) I see the English need good soldiers.

SIKORSKI: That is not a correct appreciation [of the situation]. The English value us, but don't exploit us. Also I know Churchill well; I know he wants to do everything to help Russia.

ANDERS: Sixty per cent of my men are reservists, but after two hard years these men must be put on their feet and retrained. The volunteers also are arriving in a very bad state and must be given requisite training, for which time and suitable conditions are necessary.

STALIN: (irritated) That means we're savages, we cannot put anything right now. It seems to imply that the Russian can only strangle a Pole, but is not capable of doing anything for him. But we shall manage without you. We can hand over the lot. We'll shift for ourselves. We shall conquer Poland and then we'll give it to you. But what will people say to this? The world will sneer that we here cannot do anything.

SIKORSKI: I have not received any answer to the question where I am to create an army so that it can take part in the war and not perish in terrible climatic conditions. I ask for a definite counter-proposal. I assert once more categorically that we want to fight for Poland and at your side.

STALIN: If you go to Iran you may have to fight in Turkey against the Germans; if Japan enters the war tomorrow then against Japan. Just as the English order. Maybe in Singapore.

ANDERS: We want to fight on the continent against the Germans and for Poland. Our people have not seen their country for a long time, and no one loves his fatherland like the Pole. The nearest route for us is from here.

SIKORSKI: The patriotism of the Poles does not need attestation. I maintain that I still have no definite counter-proposal.

STALIN: If you must have it, then one corps, two or three divisions can go. But if you wish, I shall assign a place and resources for the formation of seven divisions. But all the same I see the English need Polish soldiers. For I have received a demand from Harriman and Churchill to evacuate the Polish Army.

SIKORSKI: Things aren't going so badly for the English that the Polish Army formed here will decide their fate. They are slow, but today they already constitute a considerable force. It was myself who demanded that Churchill should take action on the question of evacuating our troops. But I demonstrate my good will and am ready to leave the Army in Russia if you indicate a favourable concentration area and assure us of supplies and accommodation creating conditions in which training is possible.

MOLOTOV: Panfilov is ready. Do you object to his coming in? (They all agree; a moment later General Panfilov, Deputy Chief of Staff of the Red Army, enters.

A conversation ensues between Stalin, General Anders, and General Panfilov on the conditions necessary to the creation of a Polish force, in which the two sides cite contradictory details.)

ANDERS: I categorically state that I am not receiving adequate food, or fodder for the horses. The divisions have not received all the requisite food, nor even such necessary articles of equipment as heating stoves for the tents. Several months have passed since the promise was made to send tractors, but they still have not arrived. All our requests have no effect and the promises made by the Soviet military authorities are not fulfilled. I have typhus in the divisions, and I cannot get agreement to my request for a hospital train. The soldiers have not received any soap, building materials, boards, or nails, for several months. A large number of food products are not included in the diet at all. The means of transport are quite inadequate and are in very bad shape. A few weeks ago the number of rations was suddenly reduced from 44,000 to 30,000, and despite the promise you yourself gave, Mr. President, to our Ambassador that the rations would be restored to 44,000, this has not yet been done. On 1 December the entire camp at Totskoe got no food at all. (He goes on to specify a number of other shortages of food and supplies.) It is not correct that we have not mentioned these things. I have appealed again and again to the liaison officer, Colonel Volkovyski, and have myself sent telegrams and letters. I have travelled personally to get these matters put right many times.

STALIN: (very sharply to Panfilov) Who is to blame for all this?

PANFILOV: The requisite orders have been issued, General Khrulov issued the instructions.

STALIN: When did I give the instruction to increase the number of food rations?

PANFILOV: Two and a half weeks ago.

STALIN: Then why hasn't the instruction been acted on yet? Have they got to eat our instructions?

(All this part of the conversation is carried out by Stalin in a very sharp tone. Panfilov stands to attention, going red and white.)

SIKORSKI: Only the excessively great difficulties which we are meeting with here, and the bad conditions, have forced me to raise this issue.

STALIN: We can give the Polish Army the same conditions we give the Red Army.

SIKORSKI: In present conditions not even a corps will result.

STALIN: I realize they're bad. Our own forces are being organized in better conditions. I say this honestly, that if they can give you better conditions in Iran, so far as we're concerned we can only give you the same as our Army gets. But our food nourishment is better than what the Germans get.

ANDERS: If I get full nourishment such as is due to soldiers I regard it as sufficient, but it should be supplied without the continual shortages we suffer from. I must have the possibility of running my own commissariat, creating our own reserves, and not living from day to day, with the result that if transport breaks down the men frequently go hungry.

SIKORSKI: I declare yet again that we want to fight together with you against the Germans as our common enemy.

STALIN: But I have got the impression that the English need your soldiers.

SIKORSKI: No, it was I who, seeing the difficulties we are up against here, asked the English and Americans to feed our soldiers in better conditions.

ANDERS: (Hands over a detailed statement of the numbers of Polish soldiers in the southern areas of Russia, mentioning the respective localities. A discussion follows as to the places in which further forces are to be formed. The names Uzbekistan, Turkestan, Trans-Caucasia, are mentioned.) I reckon on 150,000 men, i.e., eight divisions, together with auxiliary services. There may be even more of our people, but this includes a strong Jewish element which does not want to serve in the army.

STALIN: The Jews are rotten soldiers.

ANDERS: Many of the Jews who have applied to join are speculators or people who have been punished for smuggling; they will never make good soldiers. The Polish Army doesn't need these. Two hundred and fifty Jews deserted from Buzuluk on the false report that Kuibishev had been bombed. Over sixty deserted from the fifth division on the eve of an anticipated distribution of arms to the soldiers.

STALIN: Yes, the Jews are poor soldiers.

(A discussion follows, Stalin, Anders and Panfilov taking part, on the question of armaments and their shortages.)

SIKORSKI: When shall we be given the new area and learn other details concerning the [new] formations?

(Stalin confers aloud with Panfilov and gives the names Uzbekistan, Turkmenistan and Trans-Caucasia as indications.)

SIKORSKI: After formation and training it will be necessary to concentrate the units in a single whole for striking as an army, for that alone will have the necessary impact on the imagination of the Polish nation.

STALIN: That will take a long time.

ANDERS: Not if everything is carried out properly; after arms have been received the formation will not take long.

(Stalin raises the issue of forming an army not based on the corps as a unit.)

SIKORSKI: Perhaps that would be better. We'll agree to that, only then the divisions must be equipped and armed more powerfully.

STALIN: Organization without a corps base is better, for where you have the existence of corps the army commander throws all that responsibility on to the corps commanders, and in the end no one is responsible for anyone. It would be better for your army simply to have divisions, the same as we have.

SIKORSKI: I shall watch to ensure that equipment arrives for you from abroad in a greater flow. Given good will it will be possible to do this.

STALIN: We supply a part. The English should send the rest. But sea transports don't always reach us in time. They can be delayed, and that has to be taken into account.

SIKORSKI: Twenty-five thousand men must be evacuated from here, because I need them for the air force, the navy, and armoured detachments. Apart from these we can form seven divisions. After all, our sole human reserve is here. Have you enough aeroplanes?

STALIN: There are never enough aeroplanes. Quantitatively we are no worse off than the Germans. Qualitatively we even have predominance. But the situation regards tanks is much worse.

SIKORSKI: Part of the German air force has already been destroyed in Libya.

STALIN: We have not been conscious of German air superiority for two months. They have very inexperienced young pilots now. Their planes are relatively slow. But how many planes do you have in a division?

SIKORSKI: Twenty-seven; eighteen in the first and nine in the second line.

STALIN: That is equal to our air regiment.

SIKORSKI: We shall be able to send several air divisions from England for our army. Our people there are burning to come.

(Stalin praises the British airmen now in Russia.)

SIKORSKI: Our airmen have perfect sight and swift orientation.

STALIN: The Slavs are the finest and bravest of airmen. They react very quickly, for they are a young race which hasn't yet been worn out.

SIKORSKI: The present war is rejuvenating the Anglo-Saxons. The British are not the French, who have ended their role in the war.

STALIN: I don't agree with that opinion.

SIKORSKI: The lower strata are good, but the majority of the top stratum are of no great value. (A long conversation on the subject of Pétain and other generals.)

STALIN: The Germans are strong, but the Slavs will defeat them.

SIKORSKI: Now I would like to go and review the Army and visit the centres of the civilian population, and then return to Moscow to see you once more.

STALIN: By all means; I am at your service.

(There follows discussion about Sikorski's radio broadcast to all countries under German occupation, to which Stalin is amenable.)

SIKORSKI: And now I regard the military issue as agreed and settled. In the Mixed Commission, which should meet as soon as possible in order to give these questions finality, General Anders will take my place. Perhaps you would like to nominate your men of trust for the visit to the camps.

STALIN: I agree. (He names Vyshinsky and Panfilov, asking whether they meet with Sikorski's approval. Sikorski answers affirmatively and takes his leave, with the Ambassador and General Anders. Stalin detains Anders. Stalin questions Anders concerning cooperation with Panfilov; Anders declared that it had gone amicably, but General P. could not do much.)

ANDERS: Now you have promised to eliminate the difficulties, I'm sure the development of our Army will be handled properly.

STALIN: I greatly regret I haven't seen you before.

ANDERS: It is not my fault that I have not been summoned by you, Mr. President.

STALIN: I shall be very pleased to see you again at any time.

ANDERS: Mr. President, I am at your disposition at any time.

(The main conversation lasted two hours. That between Stalin and Anders several minutes.)'[25]

The following day saw more detailed negotiations during which General Anders submitted his proposals for an army of seven divisions containing 110,000 soldiers. The Soviet delegation agreed to a force of six divisions totalling 96,000, with an additional 27,000 being sent to Britain and the Middle East. The soldiers for the enlarged army were to be recruited solely from Polish deportees in the three southern provinces of Uzbekistan, Turkistan and Trans-Caucasia, where the army was to be based. Poles residing in other regions of the USSR were not included in the levy. Following a browbeating by Stalin, General Panfilov was ordered to supply the 5th and 6th Infantry Divisions that were to remain on Soviet establishments, whilst the 7th, 8th, 9th and 10th Infantry Divisions were to be developed according to British practice and supplied by the British.

The conclusion of these talks was the signing by Stalin and Sikorski of the Declaration of Friendship and Mutual Assistance, whereby Stalin attempted to push Sikorski into settling the question of Poland's post-war borders there and then, stressing that if Poland did not fight on the Soviet front such borders would come into question later in the war. Sikorski chose to refuse the invitation as he was in no way convinced that the Soviet Union would be able to achieve anything militarily other than its own survival and felt it would be the Western Allies that would secure Poland's frontiers. This stance exposed him to immediate criticism from his opponents, who viewed it as a weakness in his dealings with the Soviets. The talks were concluded with a dinner punctuated by many toasts and speeches, amongst which Stalin gave a pro-Polish speech saying, 'You have twice in history taken Moscow. The Russians have several times been in Warsaw. It is time to stop the strife between the Poles and Russians.'[26] Sikorski was unable to attend his second audience with Stalin as he fell ill with a kind of gastric flu no doubt due to the changes of climate (in four days by seventy degrees), so Lieutenant General Anders and Ambassador Kot were authorized to represent him in these final discussions. Sikorski flew back to London via Tehran after concluding his inspection of the camps, to recuperate before travelling to Washington.

Following these talks Sikorski aired his concerns at the autonomous nature of Anders' position in the USSR and sought an affirmation from Anders that he would follow the lead of the Polish Government in Exile and General Staff

Table 2
Development of Principle Formations of the Polish Army in the USSR, August 1941–August 1942.

1941							
June	Polish-Soviet pact signed by Sikorski and Molotov.						
August	**5th Infantry Division** Formed at Tatishev. 13, 14, 15 Regiments 5th Light Artillery Regiment			**6th Infantry Division** Formed at Totsk. 16, 17, 18 Regiments 6th Light Artillery Regiment			
December	**5th Infantry Division** Cont. training		**6th Infantry Division** Cont. training		**7th Infantry Division** Cadres raised at Totsk. 19, 20, 21 Regiments		
1942 January	All formations in USSR transfered to Southern Russia, widely dispersed around Tashkent.						
February	**Soviet Organization**		**British Organization** (as far as practicable)				
	5 Inf Div	6 Inf Div	7 Inf Div	8 Inf Div	9 Inf Div	10 Inf Div	Army Organization Centre
	13, 14, 15 Regiments 5th Light Artillery Regiment	16, 17, 18 Regiments 6th Light Artillery Regiment	22, 23 Regiments 7th Light, 7th Heavy Artillery Regiments	20, 24 Regiments 8th Light, 8th Heavy Artillery Regiments	25, 26 Regiments 9th Light, 9th Heavy Artillery Regiments	27, 28 Regiments 10th Light, 10th Heavy Artillery Regiments	19, 21 Regiments No artillery
April	Training continued in USSR.		Above units evacuated from USSR to Palestine.				
August	Evacuated from USSR to Iraq.		Reorganization and training in Palestine.				

in London and not act as an independent agent. Anders gave his word that he and his men were Poland's men. What had come to concern Sikorski was how Anders viewed the nature of the Polish relationship with the Soviets. Sikorski wished to pursue the Polish-Soviet-British military effort for as long as possible, with the withdrawal of the Polish Army from the USSR as a last resort. Sikorski envisaged the army in the Soviet Union becoming a recruiting and dispatch base for men being moved to the British zone of military operation, thus retaining a presence in the Soviet Union whilst committing the bulk of his forces to military cooperation with the Western Allies who he felt would be more politically significant in deciding Poland's post-war settlement. Anders however had experienced the reality of the Soviet regime first hand and possessed a very different perspective on the Soviets. Anders saw it as inevitable that at some stage the Soviets would withdraw their support for Poland and assimilate any Poles remaining in the Soviet Union; it was therefore paramount to move the army south where they could cross the border to British-occupied territories, by foot if necessary. To prevent too great a number of Poles being abandoned in the USSR in such an eventuality it would be necessary to recruit as many men and women into the army as possible, not solely to increase the fighting capability but effectively so that civilians could be smuggled out in military uniform. By raising the largest possible army and evacuating it from the USSR altogether, Anders could end the need for any reliance upon the Soviets – who were losing the war badly – and achieve the freedom of the Poles all in one move.

The issue of sending British troops to the USSR raised its head again in December, as Anthony Eden prepared for his trip to Moscow, and he was most keen to know what offers he could make to Stalin with regards to troops for the southern USSR. Unfortunately, owing to the Libyan offensive going badly there were none available. That was until 3 December, when General Ismay produced a memo from Churchill at a Chiefs of Staff meeting to the effect that the 18th and 50th Divisions were to be offered to the Soviets for their southern front. Lieutenant General Sir Alan Brooke was aghast at the notion, since it would have led to the closing down of the North African campaign. The idea was universally unpopular and Lord Beaverbrook suggested that 500 tanks be sent instead. Anthony Eden was growing increasingly distraught; he had no wish to appear before Stalin without bearing gifts of troops, but ultimately Churchill resolved to send the Soviets nothing and to continue fighting in the desert, after which ten Royal Air Force squadrons would be made immediately available to the Soviet southern front. Unfortunately, by the time Eden arrived for his talks with Stalin the squadrons were no longer destined for the Soviets, the situation had moved on and they would have to be sent to Singapore to face the Japanese onslaught.

These failures to deliver men and equipment for the Soviet front did not actually threaten the continuation of the Anglo-Soviet Agreement. What was to prove the ultimate stumbling block for further Anglo-Soviet cooperation was the question of the Polish-Soviet post-war frontier: the Soviets resolutely insisted upon retaining their 1941 border, a demand both Poland and Britain refused to accept. Molotov summed up the Soviet position, stating that, 'In the absence of a settlement of the frontier question, no sound basis would be created for relations between Great Britain and the Soviet Union.'[27] No solution to this problem was forthcoming, the decision on these frontiers was not settled until much later in the war, and for the near future all sides agreed to leave the matter unresolved so as to permit a working relationship.

The New Year opened with the Soviets undertaking the southward relocation of the Polish Army that was completed by February 1942. The Polish Army was now gathered in the southern USSR, along the Afghan and Chinese borders in a marginally more hospitable environment. Each encampment consisted of thousands of pitched tents sprawling across the muddy treeless plains, set amongst the vast expanses of cotton fields and above which towered the majestic Pamir Mountains, capped in snow. The majority of troops and civilians arrived by donkey and camel from the railheads. Polish recruitment teams had proved extremely successful and a great number of men made their own way to the recruitment centres from all corners of the Soviet Union. The large army now numbered approximately 96,000 men in six divisions and a further 30,000 in army level formations. The 5th and 6th Divisions remained on Red Army establishments, whereas the new divisions were established along the lines of a British two-brigade infantry division. The Army headquarters was based at Yangiyul near Tashkent, with the formations dispersed over a vast area.

The Army now faced a considerable challenge from the thousands of civilians who naturally began to flock to them, seeking help, sustenance, and ultimately the possibility of evacuation from the USSR. Consular delegates were despatched to the various Polish encampments in the southern USSR with the purpose of collecting information, rendering financial help where needed and preparing a list of names to be considered for evacuation by the Soviets. The delegates were typically junior officers, each furnished with a horse-drawn wagon and a considerable amount of roubles to dish out. They visited every *kolkhoz* (collective farm) within a 30-mile radius. The soldiers were appalled by what they witnessed: these people were eking out a primitive subsistence existence the like of which had not been seen on such a scale in Europe for over a century. Poverty, despair and fatalism had sapped their vigour while disease and malnutrition exhausted their bodies. All were mere shadows of their former selves and many faded out altogether on the steppes of the southern USSR. The people were however united in one common goal, to get out of the USSR as fast as possible.

To achieve this the men seeking to join the army and their dependants had to register with the Soviet levy commission. Upon their arrival at a collective farm the levy commission and delegates were swamped by crowds of bedraggled men, women and children, all begging to be registered. There was a strong belief that by registering their name on the list they would receive the patronage of the Army, its protection and a place on an evacuation out of the Soviet Union. Ambassador Kot described some of the difficulties encountered during recruitment in a letter to the Polish Consulate in Jerusalem: 'The levy commissions were exclusively Soviet in the field with a Polish delegate present, and on the spot rejected Jews... . A second [Soviet] examination took place in our army... and even those Jews who had been passed in the field were rejected. ... the Soviets simultaneously spread through their agents among the Jews the story that they were doing this on the demand of the Polish authorities.'[28]

When the waiting crowds were informed that only Polish citizens who were both ethnically Polish and Christian could be registered for evacuation or army service, near riots erupted. It was beyond their comprehension that religious distinction should be a factor at all, especially coming from the fervently atheist communists. All strongly proclaimed themselves to be Polish citizens; some even falsified their religious affiliation in order to register their names on the list. The stipulations reflected the Soviets' insistence in their initial agreement to establish a Polish Army in the USSR, that only Polish citizens could be recruited and they must meet strict Soviet requirements. The Soviet Government considered all Jews, Ukrainians and Byelorussians from the areas of eastern Poland that the Soviet Union had seized in 1939 to be Soviet citizens, and the Polish authorities were expressly forbidden from recruiting Soviet citizens. Many tried desperately to bribe their way onto the list and the young delegates compiling the names felt huge pressure at having to deny such people the chance of leaving the USSR. The Soviets wasted no time in drafting those individuals who could not be registered into the Red Army and associated war industries – indeed many of the fittest men were diverted into Soviet service.

The lot of the Polish soldiers in their various camps did not improve by any noticeable measure. The only sources of drinking water available to the encampments were the local rivers, which resulted in widespread dysentery followed by malaria, typhoid and other diseases. The initial evacuees to this region were greeted by freezing cold, but the change of season brought an intense heat that persisted both day and night, sapping yet more strength from the Poles. All were malnourished from having to split the available army rations with the civilian population and all existed in absolute poverty. The doctors and medical staff worked with great sacrifice, labouring under appalling conditions and completely without medicines, hospital accommodation, linen or adequate food. The inadequate weaponry supplied by the Soviets, combined with the incredibly hard living conditions, made it increasingly clear to all that the face of the USSR was firmly set against them.

In these difficult circumstances the Poles continued to train with enthusiasm, while maintaining a stubborn silence about their exasperation with the Soviet system. But their patience grew steadily shorter and frustration with the Red Army's lack of enthusiasm eventually began to boil over into open condemnation of the Soviet regime; Colonel Gielgud, Chief of Staff of the 7th Infantry Division sent a particularly harsh letter to the District Executive Committee in Kermin on 14 February 1942, demanding the local Soviet make immediate improvements to the road network and adding, 'Failure to carry out this present instruction will involve you in material and criminal responsibility for any possible accidents and from damage to motors during the war to the detriment of the Seventh Polish Motorized Infantry Division.'[29] The Colonel's letter caused outrage to the very top of the Soviet system and serves well to illustrate how antagonistic relations between the Poles and Soviets had become.

Further stress was placed upon relations when, on 2 February, General Zhukov requested that the 5th Division be sent into action on the front in April, as a symbol of goodwill and cooperation between the two countries. With that division lacking much of its heavy weaponry Anders did not favour the notion, but if ordered he would deploy the division and lead it himself. Anders immediately contacted Sikorski for his decision, of which he was not certain as Sikorski had previously offered to Churchill that he would send two divisions to defend the Caucasus oilfields even if they were as yet unarmed. However, Sikorski's reply was forthright: the 5th Division would not be sent to the front as an individual formation, the Army would fight only as a whole as had been stated in the initial negotiations. Sikorski insisted to Anders that the Army must serve Polish interests and that this would best be achieved by the force remaining large and intact. The issue did not go away, as the Soviet General Panfilov renewed pressure on Major General Wolikowski of the Polish Military Mission to despatch the division to the front on 19 February. Wolikowsi informed Anders that due to the hard fighting expected in the coming months, pressure from the Soviets to see the Poles in battle on the Eastern Front would only grow.

With the Poles not committing their forces to battle, the Soviet Union now lost altogether its enthusiasm for supporting the creation of a Polish Army on its territory. The greatly displeased General Khrulov, who was responsible for rationing, informed Anders on 6 March that the food provisions available to the Poles were to be reduced to 26,000. Anders now appealed directly to Stalin, with whom he had become personally acquainted, and at his request attended a meeting in Moscow on 18 March. Stalin announced the shortages were due partly to the desperate struggle against the Germans in the Battle for Moscow into which the Soviets were throwing every available resource, and partly to reduced shipments of US grain that the Polish rations were to be taken from, as a result of Japanese naval activity. General Anders drove home his argument concerning supplies, by saying that the only way to maintain his army was to evacuate it to the Middle East where the British had offered full support. Stalin said he would feed 44,000 soldiers and agreed to the withdrawal of the remainder of the Polish Army from the USSR, sketching out the evacuation route there and then on a scrap of paper. Within a week General Zhukov commenced the transportation of half the army, some 40,000 soldiers and their dependent civilians to the Soviet-Persian border. Anders took this momentous decision himself, without consulting Sikorski or the Polish Government in Exile, on whom the realization now dawned that Anders was a powerful figure who could and would deal with the Allies directly and without government sanction. The British military authorities welcomed the evacuation, as was well summed up at the Chiefs of Staff meeting on 19 March:

> *Sir Alan Brooke read out a telegram (MIL 3715, cipher 19/3) from No. 30 Military Mission asking that we should accept in Persia at once 40,000 Poles and further contingents as they were recruited to prevent them from early starvation since the Russians had now said that they could only feed 44,000. The Poles, when properly armed and trained, would form a useful addition to our forces in the Middle East.*
>
> *It was pointed out that our main difficulties were with personnel reinforcements and it would be easier to send equipment for the Poles than to send out formations.*
>
> *The Committee:*
>
> *Invited the War Office to do everything possible to facilitate the evacuation of the Poles from Russia.*[30]

3
Exodus to the Middle East

The next stage in the development of the Polish Army in exile took place under British patronage as part of the broader Allied front in the Middle East. Persia provided a perfectly sited interface between Britain and the USSR where the handover of the Polish troops could be effected both quickly and cheaply – no expensive shipping or aircraft would be required. More amiable relations with the Persians were cemented by the January 1942 Treaty of Alliance between Britain, USSR and Persia, which secured Persian support for the development of supply lines to the USSR, whilst the Allies agreed to defend Persia from German assault. To safeguard the overland supply route more troops were needed in the Middle East to bolster the already massively over-stretched British Troops in Iraq whose commander, Lieutenant General Quinan, was asking for urgent reinforcements. He was offered a surprising solution – the Polish Army in the USSR would provide his manpower.

On 23 March, the Chiefs of Staff Committee discussed a telegram from the Commander-in-Chief, Middle East, General Claude Auchinleck, who recommended that 'all Poles evacuated from Russia should be retained in the Middle East, with the exception of navy and air force personnel and that a Polish Division, to include the present Polish Brigade Group, should be formed in the Middle East.'[1] In response to Auchinleck's proposal the Chief of the Imperial General Staff, Sir Alan Brooke, drafted a communiqué for Churchill to dispatch to General Sikorski recommending that the majority of the Polish forces evacuated from the Soviet Union should be retained and re-equipped in the Middle East.

Practical planning could now commence for the Poles' reception and onward passage to the extensive training facilities established in Palestine. The Polish evacuees were to be shipped from Krasnovodsk, on the eastern coast of the Caspian Sea, to Bandar Pahlevi, a rudimentary seaside resort with a shallow harbour on the Persian shore that had been utilized by the Soviets during the invasion of Persia. It was arranged that the reception and accommodation of the evacuees should be managed largely by a Polish staff headed by Colonel Okulicki and the Chief Medical Officer, Lieutenant General Szarecki, under the direction of a small British staff and with other British Army assistance. The evacuees were scheduled to arrive at the rate of 2,500 a week, and small parties were sent to Pahlevi to reconnoitre on that basis, including an advanced party of Polish officers from the USSR accompanied by Colonel Hulls. There was however an unfortunate hold-up in communication between the Soviet authorities in Tehran and Moscow. It was not until 24 March that the former were able to tell the British that the first transport of Poles would be arriving in three days' time, with the additional information that the rate of arrival, instead of being 2,500 a week, would be 6,000 a day.

The port of Krasnovodsk worked around the clock loading the military and civilian evacuees on to all available cargo vessels. The Soviet authorities made careful checks of everyone's paperwork to ensure that only Polish nationals boarded the vessels, but the embarkation itself was chaotic. With the Poles desperate to board the ships they had for so long dreamed of, in the bustle to mount the gangways several people were knocked overboard into the oily dock. Once aboard, the vast majority made the voyage across the Caspian Sea on the open decks of coal merchants and oil tankers with no protection from the elements, so tightly packed they could barely move and with no sanitary provision. The effects of bad weather and dysentery in such conditions must have been miserable and indeed many died during the two-day voyage, their bodies being cast into the sea. Though they were aware in advance of the dangers, the lure of freedom from the Soviet Union was so great that everyone who could possibly make the port crowded to gain passage. The loaded passengers, keen to bring their countrymen with them, sacrificed all comforts to enable as many as possible to make the crossing to Pahlevi. Upon arrival the ships anchored off the harbour, the limited depth of which curtailed the berthing of the convoys. Instead a host of tenders and lighters proceeded out to the ships to carry the disembarked Poles to the shore.

The commander of the British Base Evacuation Staff, Lieutenant Colonel A. Ross of the Highland Light Infantry, arrived on 25 March to find Pahlevi thickly carpeted with snow and the first transport, carrying 1,387 evacuees already lying off the harbour. The first meeting of the British and Poles took place when 'A grinning Polish major with a close-clipped beard, wearing a British battle-dress buttoned tightly around him, stepped ashore from a Russian lighter at Pahlevi, on the Caspian Sea, and saluted a high British officer waiting on shore. "Polish officer from Russia reporting, sir" he said in perfect English, "and waiting further orders."'[2] The landing of this soldier was accompanied by an almighty cheer, as thousands of Polish troops aboard the Soviet ship filled the decks to witness these first steps to freedom.

In the first eight days over 29,000 evacuees arrived. The ships came without notice at all hours of the night and day, one carrying as many as 5,000. The soldiers, though underfed, were properly clothed in British battledress and equipped with British kit. The civilians, however, had received no new items of clothing and many wore old and tattered garments; almost half were infected with lice. Some of the women were heavily pregnant, and among the children were seventy orphans aged between three and twelve years. The reactions of this variegated multitude who had survived so much in the USSR and now at last gained freedom in the Middle East were predominantly shock and disbelief. Once disembarked on to the wharf they spilled over on to the beach, standing in huddled groups or in the roadway; many sat down in the soiled snow, where curious Persian children gathered round them. Many were silent, others voluble. Some, excited by freedom and feverish with typhus, wandered off into the town. A few lay down and died. It was impossible in the first days to make a proper register of these people, impossible even to number them, for they strayed and eddied from the first moment of stepping ashore.

The reception staff could aim at two things only: to supply their immediate needs and to keep under some control the disease that they brought with them. The Polish and British reception staffs soon organized a great camp to house the newcomers, and although it was after dark and they had arrived days before they were expected, beds and food were soon ready for the most vulnerable. These were the first beds and hot meals they had had for many a long day, and they showed high appreciation. Pahlevi's only cinema and other suitable buildings were organized to house them, while others for whom accommodation could not be found and who were in a better physical state were given three heavy blankets and caddies filled with hot tea, then placed under tarpaulins among the sand dunes of the beach overnight. Next morning the local bathhouses were taken over as medical inspection centres and the troops began passing through at the rate of 4,000 a day. The Polish soldiers had spent their first night bedding down, and on their second attended a great concert at which Polish battle songs were sung by a choir of many thousands. Morale amongst the soldiers was high and at the top of their agenda was establishing their issue of equipment and entry into battle against the Germans.

A scouring of the town yielded provisions, notably 2,000lb of Government flour, and also the bakers to turn it into loaves. Disinfection centres were improvised. Tents arrived sufficient to shelter 8,000, and three companies of Polish sappers got to work on camp construction. There was a 'dirty' camp for new arrivals at one side of the town and a 'clean' camp at the other. These were operational by 28 March, three days after Ross's arrival. Medical facilities were provided by the 34 British Commonwealth General Hospital (BCGH) and the staff were Indians, together with a dozen senior medical personnel from Queen Alexandra's Royal Army Nursing Service. The nurses were appalled by the state of the incoming Poles – the majority were emaciated and skeletal in appearance, malaria, typhus and dysentery were epidemic and all were encrusted in mud, blood and excrement; the stench was unbearable. What these

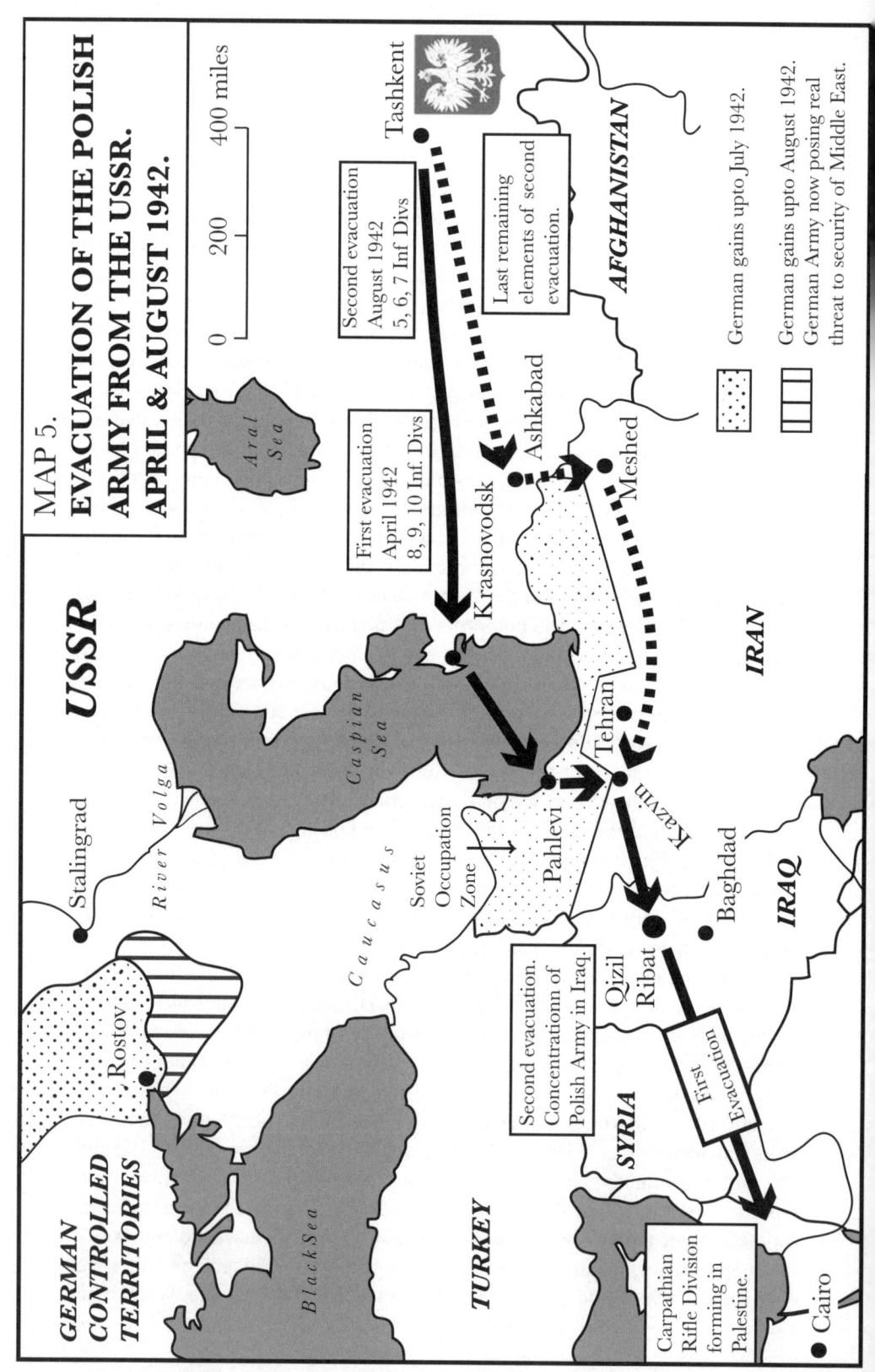

people must have been through was unimaginable. The evacuees, soldiers and civilians alike, were dying around them at an alarming rate, the local carpentry firm was producing fifty coffins a day and could not keep up with demand, guards had to be posted at the mass grave that was hastily dug, as wild animals were beginning to devour the corpses.

The processing of the Polish evacuees was conducted at high tempo, the numbers arriving at Pahlevi being so great that any delay would have led to disaster for these soldiers and civilians, already exhausted and demoralized by their long ordeal and most of whom required medical care. It was essential to bring order to the proceedings and maintain a professional military approach to both the evacuation and reception. With the arrival of Lieutenant General Józef Zając on 31 March, the very able Colonel Bolesławicz was appointed to take charge of the Polish staff, having previously commanded the Polish 9th Infantry Division in the USSR.

By 6 April, 19,000 Poles had already been moved on from Pahlevi, and Lieutenant General Zając paid a second visit, emphasizing to all concerned that things would only go smoothly if the arrangements made by the British were faithfully followed. Improvements were accelerated. More than 5,000 a day were now being put through the disinfection centres, and the hospital was coping successfully with a population that had risen to above 200. The final convoy departed Pahlevi on 25 April, scooping up a few stragglers who emerged at the last moment from unknown retreats in the town, many suffering the effects of arak, the local moonshine. Altogether, nearly 44,000 had gone through the evacuation centres. Although the majority of personnel were ethnic Poles, there were also some other nationalities who had managed to join the units of the Polish Army, most notably Belarusians and Ukrainians. Evacuation convoys had been organized to take the soldiers towards Iraq, whilst the civilians travelled to Tehran. The very poor physical condition of these men had not been anticipated by the British and the Polish soldiers would not be fit enough to serve in the defence of the region for the foreseeable future. Instead of gaining deployable military formations, the British were confronted with the prospect of providing lengthy convalescence for a great many ill soldiers.

With the ranks of the Polish Army under the command of the exile government in London now swelling rapidly, General Sikorski called a meeting of the senior Polish military leaders, including Anders, in London to discuss the future structure and disposition of the Polish Armed Forces. On his journey to London Anders stopped off in Cairo, where he met General Auchinleck and the resident British Minister, Richard Casey. Anders made full use of his stopover to lobby for the evacuation of all remaining Polish Army formations from the USSR to the Middle East. Anders convinced the General that the remaining troops were in far better condition than those currently arriving in Persia and would be ready for military action. Anders undoubtedly made a good impression upon Middle East Command and Auchinleck recommended Anders' proposals strongly to the War Office on 4 April, doubtless keen to receive as many additional infantry divisions as could be mustered.

Anders arrived in London on 21 April and met with Sikorski and Churchill before briefing Lieutenant General Sir Alan Brooke, Chief of the Imperial General Staff, on the Polish experiences with Germany and the USSR. The following day the Defence Committee and the Chiefs of Staff agreed to support the proposal to evacuate all Polish troops from the USSR to the Middle East. The specification of the area of deployment was influenced by Auchinleck's memo stating that 'Stalin favoured concentration of the Poles in the Middle East and if he heard they were going elsewhere he might close doors on further evacuation.'[3] A notion that was doubtless conveyed to him most strongly by Anders.

Two days later on 23 April, Sikorski held an afternoon reception at the Dorchester Hotel for 300 Allied representatives including Sir Alan Brooke, in honour of General Anders who was invested with the Order of Militari Virtuti, Fourth Class for his actions during the defensive campaign of 1939. There followed the planned Anglo-Polish meeting on the future of the Polish Armed Forces. The most important senior officers in attendance were Lieutenant General Anders (General Officer Commanding Polish Troops in the USSR), Lieutenant General Józef Zając (General Officer Commanding Polish Troops in the Middle East), Lieutenant General Marian Kukiel (General Officer Commanding the 1st Polish Army Corps in Scotland), Major General Tadeusz Klimecki (Chief of Staff), Major General Stanisław Ujecki (Inspector General of the Polish Air Force) and Admiral Jerzy Swinski (Commander of the Polish Navy). A number of other senior generals also attended including Major General Stanisław Kopański (General Officer Commanding the Polish Carpathian Rifle Brigade which was being moved from Libya to Palestine before being fleshed out to division size by increments from the USSR).

The agenda at this meeting was the future growth and distribution of the Polish Armed Forces. Sikorski presented his organizational plan that focused on the need for Polish troops to be as widely dispersed as possible to exploit any opportunity to strike towards Poland. With Polish forces now in the USSR, Middle East and Britain, the troops would be able to advance into Poland through the Ukraine, Balkans and France respectively. The Army was to comprise three principle formations: I Corps in Scotland, II Corps in the Middle East and III Corps in the Soviet Union. Manpower for this organization would be provided by the soldiers evacuated from the USSR in April, 14,000 were to be transferred to Britain to create I Corps, and the remaining soldiers from the evacuation would be used to bolster Middle East forces to form II Corps.

Generals Klimecki and Kukiel favoured the concentration of all Polish troops in the United Kingdom, arguing that this was essential as the future liberation of Europe would, in their opinion, be most likely launched from England. Major General Ujecki urged the need for replacements for his squadrons and concurred with the view that Britain offered the best location for retraining and re-equipping the army. Anders, supported by Zając, argued that all Polish troops should be concentrated in the Middle East, including the Air Force, since it was the Balkans that provided the most direct route to the Polish homeland. Anders also suggested that deployment in the Middle East would enable the Poles to fight on the Soviet front if ever required, at the same time highlighting that the Soviets would be certain to suspend recruitment if evacuated Poles left the Middle East for Britain en masse.

The two opposing camps were now clearly evident to the British; Sir Alan Brooke noted in his diary that from this meeting he was 'in favour of the latter. Any forces in the Middle East this summer will be a Godsend to us.'[4] Alan Brooke's favourable opinion of Anders was reinforced by a personal meeting between himself and Anders the following day, where he 'found Anders most interesting. Luckily he is a strong supporter of leaving as many Poles as possible in the Middle East.'[5] Following these discussions in London, Anders took the opportunity to review the Polish troops based in Scotland for a week. These forces were undergoing reorganization and training along British lines; Anders was most impressed by the soldiers, in particular the parachute brigade, and was delighted to be reacquainted with many familiar faces.

Sikorski collected the various elements of the discussion together and on 24 April wrote a letter to Churchill outlining his proposal for the use of Polish manpower evacuated from the USSR. The decisions were not easy, Sikorski had to take into account the various wishes of his commanders, the plans of General Auchinleck and Britain's strategic planning and available transport resources. The latter were gearing towards the major cross-Channel invasion of Europe which made the British reluctant to dispatch much-needed extra manpower to the Middle East – it was felt the deployment of the evacuated Poles in that region would answer that problem as previously highlighted by General Auchinleck. Sikorski had to abandon his plans for the large-scale expansion of his forces in Scotland, instead having to adopt the British focus on the Middle East. Sikorski's letter read:

> *After having given prolonged and deep consideration to the problem of the Middle East and the future of the Polish Forces in all theatres of war I have come to the following conclusion:*

> *Although it is against the opinion of some of my collaborators I have decided that in the interests of the Allied cause – as seen as a whole – and in that of Poland herself, the main Polish Forces which have been and I hope will continue to be evacuated from Russia should remain in the Middle East.*
>
> *In accordance with the wishes of General Auchinleck these troops will form the nucleus of the Polish Corps and, I hope, an Army in the future. I must ask, however, that arrangements should be made to bring over the following reinforcements which are urgently needed for the Polish Air Force and the Polish Navy which are fighting in England;*
> > *1,200 men for the Navy,*
> > *1,500 men for the Air Force,*
>
> *who may be partly selected from the younger men of about 16 years of age, who are now in civilian organisations of semi-military nature. In fact I would like all of them (about 1,500) to be transferred to Great Britain where they could be taken care of.*
>
> *In addition I am most anxious that the armoured division now being formed in Scotland should be reinforced by a minimum of 5,500 soldiers. I should mention that in order to help with the reorganization I have decided, if absolutely necessary, to disband the 1st Polish Brigade and incorporate its soldiers with the armoured division.*
>
> *These decisions have not been easy for me to take – and they may be subject to considerable criticism on the part of some of my countrymen.*
>
> *I have taken my decision in this matter and wish to inform you of it at once.*[6]

Sikorski forwarded his organizational plan to the Polish Government. The Polish forces of all services in Britain would be bolstered by the arrival of over 8,000 men taken from those evacuated from the Soviet Union. In the USSR, III Corps would comprise the existing 5th, 6th and 7th Infantry Divisions of 44,000 men under the command of Lieutenant General Anders, assembled along Soviet organizational plans. The Middle Eastern force would be assembled by amalgamating the 35,000 evacuated soldiers along with the Polish Independent Carpathian Brigade to form the 3rd Carpathian Rifle Division and the 4th Rifle Division, thus creating II Polish Rifle Corps under the command of Lieutenant General Zając. The Corps was to fight in the Middle East under British command and organization, comprising two infantry divisions each of two brigades and a tank brigade of two tank battalions, corps artillery and other corps level formations. Sikorski highlighted that this army distribution was essential so that Polish manpower remained dispersed, to exploit success on as many fronts as possible. At the same time Anders stressed to Sikorski most strongly that he felt every effort should be made to secure the evacuation of the remaining Polish soldiers in the USSR, an event Anders saw as inevitable given the Soviets' proven inability to supply the arms and equipment necessary to bring the remaining divisions to a combat-ready state.

Sikorski was growing ever more annoyed with Anders' contrary stance and made the shrewd move of offering him the choice of a position in London or command of the troops in the Middle East. However, Anders accepted neither, instead insisting on returning to the USSR to complete his work evacuating the remainder of the Polish Army. Acceptance of either position would have effectively led to the termination of Anders' command in the Soviet Union, allowing Sikorski to appoint a general of his choice to implement his organizational plans. Command of the Polish troops assembling in Persia and Iraq was thus to remain with Zając, for as long as Anders remained in the USSR, whilst Anders was awarded the largely ceremonial title of Inspector of the Troops in the Middle East.

Concern was expressed by some Polish commanders at the conference (notably by Major General Gustaw Paszkiewicz commanding 1 Infantry Brigade in Scotland), that if Polish units were brought up to full operational strength they would inevitably be deployed by the British, who would do so for their own ends and manpower would be rapidly depleted. Whereas if formations were maintained at cadre strength the units would not be readily deployable, preserving Polish manpower for concentration and deployment as and when the Polish Government deemed advantageous. Sikorski disagreed, aware that it was vital to Poland's position in the Alliance to be an active, fighting participant in the war, and therefore decided to bring all Polish formations in Britain up to full strength through the transfer of personnel from the Soviet Union via the Middle East. Major General Paszkiewicz took up command of the 4th Rifle Division in Palestine during May.

The London conference decided the fate of the troops from the first evacuation, but those remaining in the USSR were still to be fought over between Anders and Sikorski, who continued firm in their convictions – Anders in his drive to evacuate the whole army to the Middle East and Sikorski wishing the recruitment of Polish soldiers to continue in the USSR and insisting that any new formations raised should remain in the Soviet Union. On 1 May, Sikorski wrote to Anders articulating overall Polish military goals and strategies. In his instructions to the General, Sikorski demanded he follow the decisions of the Polish Government, and Anders was categorically forbidden to plan for a possible single command for Polish troops in the Middle East and the USSR: the two corps were not to be brought together unless in the event of the collapse of the Soviet Union. This distribution of manpower would, Sikorski proposed, prevent Polish troops being concentrated in one theatre alone which could lead to their severe depletion in combat. It was therefore necessary for Anders and his men to hang tough in the USSR. The only issue the two agreed upon was that recruitment into the Polish Army be resumed immediately. Anders' early reservations about the ability of the Soviets to supply the Poles appeared to be confirmed by the Soviets when Molotov wrote to the Polish ambassador on 14 May stating that, as the limit of 44,000 troops had been reached no further recruiting would be permitted and that no further evacuation out of the USSR would be possible due to transport difficulties.[7]

While Sikorski was formulating broad strategic goals for the future, the British were hard at work trying to secure the movement of the Poles out of the USSR to bolster their forces in the Middle East, a plan that appealed greatly to the Polish troops themselves. Anders' willingness to fight alongside the British Army made him the obvious focal point for Churchill, a position that was tacitly acknowledged by the Foreign Office as Colonel Leslie Hulls had begun introducing General Anders to British officials in the Middle East for discussions on future plans for the Polish Army. These developments led to growing resentment amongst the Polish leadership in London, as the British would only accept Polish propositions if they coincided with their own. If there was a divergence Poland had to follow Britain's preferences, and if the Polish Government's agenda did not fit operational demands then other Polish figures would be favoured instead. Thus Lieutenant General Anders' standing with British commanders and politicians steadily grew whilst their government's position weakened.

On his return journey to the Soviet Union, Anders travelled via Cairo, meeting General Auchinleck on 20 May for a lengthy conference on how the organization of the Polish forces in the Middle East would be affected by the arrival of more units from the USSR. Anders conducted these talks without the prior knowledge of or consent from Sikorski or the government and obtained from Auchinleck what he interpreted as British approval and support for a full evacuation from the USSR. In Cairo Anders also met Major General Mason-MacFarlane whose tour in the Soviet Union had drawn to a close and who was heading for his next assignment, commanding the garrison at Gibraltar. Mason-MacFarlane had come from the USSR via Tehran, where he received a hero's welcome from the Poles he encountered. Mason-MacFarlane considered his contribution in securing the release of the Poles as one of his most important and satisfying contributions to the Allied cause.

Towards the end of May Anders returned to Soviet soil, where the lot of the Poles had not improved by any measure; arms and equipment were not forthcoming. Anders convened a meeting of Polish unit commanders to appraise the situation and their findings were dire: the army was starving. Frustrated that Sikorski's partial evacuation had not improved the lot of the Polish formations, just as he had foreseen, Anders pursued with renewed vigour the possibility of evacuating the entire army, even if that meant going against Sikorski's instructions. Pursuant with this agenda Anders sought an audience with Stalin in June to discuss the possibility of moving the whole army to the Middle East, though the talks proceeded no further than his preliminary discussion with NKVD Colonel Tishkov. As well as gaining Soviet consent, Anders also had to convince Sikorski that the only possible option remaining to the Polish Army in the USSR was to evacuate and he wrote to the latter on 7 June stating that he considered the wholesale evacuation of the Polish Army was inevitable in the near future. Sikorski refuted Anders' claims in a letter dated 11 June and ordered Anders to follow government policy. But Anders understood that the Poles' time in the USSR was drawing to a close; it was clear the Soviets held them in no great esteem and he proceeded to press for the evacuation without further reference to London, confident he would enjoy full support from the British and the eventual agreement of the Soviets.

Anders would not have to wait long; Molotov met with Churchill and British officials in London from 20 May to 9 June, during which talks Churchill commented that if there were any surplus Polish troops in the USSR, the British would gladly take them over. Stalin made the final decision on evacuation without reference to the Polish Government. Sikorski's plans for a Polish Army to be left in the Soviet Union were thwarted by the utter determination of the Poles there to get out, the British requirement for manpower and the willing cooperation of Stalin, who wanted rid of the Poles in a manner which would not upset the major Allies. Stalin officially proclaimed his solution on 30 June to Sir Archibald Clark-Kerr, the British Ambassador to the USSR. Stalin instructed Molotov to issue the statement referred to below by the British War Cabinet:

> *The Soviet government had been watching with concern the developments of the military situation in Egypt leading up to the fall of Mersa Matruh. He had recalled that the Prime Minister had told him in London that if there were in Russia any Polish soldiers over and above the needs of the Soviet Government, His Majesty's Government would be glad to take them over and equip them for use in the Middle East. There were in Russia three Polish divisions, well trained but not fully armed. While the Soviet Government were loathe to weaken their own front, and while the transfer of these Polish troops therefore presented some difficulty, they were ready to place them at the disposal of His Majesty's Government in order to fill the gaps caused by recent severe fighting.*[8]

Churchill responded to Stalin, writing: 'I am sure it would be in our common interest, premier Stalin, to have the three divisions of Poles you so kindly offered join their compatriots in Palestine, where we can arm them fully...if we do not get the Poles, we should have to fill their places by drawing on the preparations going forward on a vast scale for the Anglo-American invasion of the continent.'[9] In the same letter Churchill also grudgingly acknowledged that Britain would accept Polish civilian refugees along with the soldiers and that Britain would somehow endeavour to support them, but that the success of the evacuation of the Polish Army depended on keeping the numbers of civilians to an absolute minimum.

The news was a complete surprise to the Polish Government who were informed of the decision on 2 July. Sikorski responded with a letter to the British Government the following day giving his conditional support to the scheme, and stipulating the need to gain consent from the Kremlin for the continued evacuation of Polish civilians capable of bearing arms, along with the families of service personnel. The British Ambassador in Kuibyshev, Sir Alan Clark-Kerr, on 7 July informed Anders of the news that the Soviets had proposed the evacuation of the remaining three Polish infantry divisions. During the briefing Anders was delighted when the meeting was interrupted by the arrival of a telegram for the Ambassador, requesting he gain permission from the Soviets for the evacuation of families and children alongside the soldiers. Three weeks of negotiations ensued whereby the Poles attempted to secure the further recruitment of new soldiers in the USSR and evacuation of as many civilians as possible. To facilitate this they proposed creating a dedicated recruitment and reserve centre to remain in the USSR following the Army's departure to be headed by Major General Bohusz-Szyszko. No progress was achieved on these issues.

The Soviets officially informed Anders of the evacuation through a telegram issued by Zhukov on 26 July: 'The Government of the USSR agrees to satisfy the efforts of the commander of the Polish Army in the USSR, General Anders, for the evacuation of Polish forces from the USSR to the Middle East and has no intention of placing any obstacles in realizing their immediate evacuation.'[10] The Soviets carefully worded the announcement to state that they were granting the Polish commander's request to evacuate from the USSR and in so doing they transformed Anders from a General into a legend, a position which afforded him considerable clout in the Polish émigré community. Conversely, Anders and the Polish Government could be held responsible by the Soviets for the evacuation and ensuing political ramifications, which in due course they were.

Stalin now embarked on the creation of a new, communist Polish Army to fight as part of the Red Army that was to be raised from former prisoners of war who accepted communism and service in the Soviet forces. The Soviets thus had no further requirement for dealings with the Polish Government or for their recruiting of soldiers. To this end Zhukov informed Anders during a discussion on 31 July, 'The Soviet Government cannot agree to the further formation of Polish units in the USSR…because the Polish Government, contrary to the agreement between the USSR and Poland, does not consider it possible to use such forces recruited in the USSR on the Soviet-German front.'[11] Further difficulties continued as regards the evacuation of Polish Jews, with Anders holding a conference with Jewish leaders on 3 August to allay their concerns that the Polish authorities were cooperating with the Soviets to leave them behind in the Soviet Union. A deep mistrust of the Polish authorities' intentions persisted amongst the Jewish community, who felt deeply betrayed.

That a Polish Army was formed in the USSR at all was due solely to the dire situation the Soviets found themselves in following the German invasion. The perennial difficulties of any Polish-Soviet cooperation stemmed from the Soviets' requirement for the rapid deployment of combat forces on the Eastern Front while paying little attention to the fact the Poles had been taken prisoner by them, had lost their families and had no desire to embrace the harsh authoritarianism of wartime Soviet communism. These factors led repeatedly to obstacles and conditions being attached by both sides to almost every suggestion; there was a total absence of trust. Had the evacuation of the Army not been agreed many thought it likely that the Soviets would have eliminated the Poles, in the same way that other anti-communist elements were purged from Soviet society – as highlighted by Anders in his memoirs they lacked only the means to immediately 'destroy and annihilate these army groups themselves.'[12] General Mason-MacFarlane drew similar conclusions from his experiences: '[The] Russians have an oriental contempt for the value of human life which is almost beyond the understanding of westerners and to them the killing of a few thousand Poles, quite apart from the fact the victims were "class enemies" who had contemptuously rejected all attempts at Marxist indoctrination, was a matter of little moment.'[13]

The situation was more civilly summarized by the Foreign Office: 'These preoccupations, coupled with traditional antipathies, naturally made it difficult for the two sides to co-operate whole heartedly… The truth of the matter was perhaps that General Sikorski's agreements of 1941 with Premier Stalin attempted too much. Events showed that it was not possible for enemies to become fully co-operating allies overnight, especially at time of such serious strain and stringency as obtained in Soviet Russia in 1942.'[14]

The British Chiefs of Staff were not so surprised by the announcement of the full evacuation – they had envisaged such an event earlier and the British authorities in Iraq had already heard news of a possible second evacuation from the USSR later in 1942, but permission was only given for skeleton staffs, British and Polish, to remain behind at Pahlevi. Confirmation of this second evacuation came on 10 July and the first transport actually arrived on 10 August, affording the staffs exactly one month to make their preparations. Five reception camps were constructed along the eastern beach, stretching – with a special children's camp added later – over a distance of four and a half miles and having a total capacity of 44,000. Separate camps were built for the staffs. By the time the first transport arrived there was shelter ready for 12,000, with cookhouses for 20,000. An additional 2,000 beds were provided by 18 Indian General Hospital, which was also assigned to bolster 34 BCGH. A special jetty had been allotted for disembarkation, repaired by the Soviet port authority and equipped with floodlighting and a first-aid post.

Once again thousands of Polish evacuees travelled from their encampments in Uzbekistan and Kyrgyzstan to the port of Krasnovodsk. The summer heat was intense and the rail transports taking two days were stifling hot. Arrival at Krasnovodsk brought no relief; there was no cool sea breeze, only baking hot, stifling air filled with the odour of oil from the Baku oilfields; it was impossible to reach the shoreline and sea as both were covered in thick crude oil. The fleet of cargo ships was supplemented by many fishing vessels and livestock carriers and the crammed conditions prevailed again, this time exacerbated by the relentless sun making the sea passage even more uncomfortable. This, combined with a lack of drinking water led to yet further weakening of the evacuees.

The reception of the second evacuation was quite different from the first, being properly organized well in advance. The British team was much the same, with Lieutenant Colonel Ross again in command. The Polish staff had profited greatly from experience; the actual disembarkation was now controlled by Polish officers with admirable efficiency and without any assistance at all. The Persian officials were extremely kind and helpful. There were troubles of course, the greatest being the effects of torrid heat and little food on men who were already far from well. The sickness rate was about five times that of the first evacuation, the most prevalent complaints being dysentery, malaria, typhoid and deficiency diseases. Thanks to the warm weather there was no typhus. The need for a great quantity of medical supplies had been foreseen, the hospitals were clean and aseptic, suitable food for cases of malnutrition was also procured. Again, the pace of processing the evacuees was conducted as fast as possible for, as well as there being a great number to help, the German Army was advancing so quickly into the Caucasus Mountains that the sound of their artillery fire could be heard clearly in Pahlevi. The threat of German invasion was imminent, all British and Commonwealth forces were pulling out and heading south, away from the Soviet occupation zone of northern Persia.

Several days after the last convoy of evacuees had arrived, a lone ship was spotted heading for Pahlevi. The worst was immediately suspected, that the German invasion fleet was on its way across the Caspian Sea. However, on its arrival, it was a dilapidated Soviet livestock carrier that anchored off the harbour, and the stench of excrement and decaying bodies could be smelt from the shore – it was no invasion but the last straggling transport of Poles and it was to prove the most harrowing for the evacuation base staff. The cattle pens were crammed with 1,000 orphaned children and babies. No food or water had been provided for them and no one was assigned to their care, 200 babies had died on the crossing and in the heat their bodies were fast decomposing; the conditions were beyond dreadful. The surviving children were in such a state of terror they could not even cry, and none could speak for several days. A special children's camp was established for them and Polish women with previous healthcare experience volunteered to help in any way possible. Thankfully the vast majority of the children were nursed back to physical health, though the emotional and psychological damage they suffered could never be undone. The evacuated soldiers and civilians also showed a power of physical recuperation that amazed the doctors; their recovery of spirit was not less astounding. Some seemed to pass straight from the deepest depression into gaiety; the most emaciated, after a few days of decent feeding, recovered their individuality. They were human beings once more. The base evacuation staff could only wonder in horror as to what the Poles had been subjected to in the USSR.

Although the military evacuation had turned into a humanitarian relief effort, the business of fighting the war remained preeminent, with Churchill travelling to the Middle East in August 1942, determined that Allied strategy should become more aggressive in its efforts to route Rommel's Afrika Korps. Churchill wrote, 'The Levant-Caspian front is almost bare. If General Auchinleck wins the Battle of Egypt we could no doubt build up a force of perhaps eight divisions which with the four Polish divisions when trained, would play a strong part in delaying a German southward advance.'[15] Churchill's questioning of Auchinleck's ability to win the day was telling – he and the Imperial General Staff had decided that changes of command were required to instil new vigour into the Army. General Alexander replaced General Auchinleck and Montgomery now became head of the Eighth Army. Alexander was not a man of intellectual pretensions but was adept at grasping problems and working out a solution intuitively. His charm and common-sense approach won him many advocates. On 18 August, Churchill announced the creation of Persia and Iraq Command to cover the region's northern flank and take some of the pressure off Middle East Command. The territories of Iraq and Persia were initially administered by the Tenth Army, but the combined task of operational planning and overseeing the vast lines of communications proved too great for the Tenth alone. Middle East Command assigned an Inspector-General of Communications, while an area command known as PI-Base was formed in Basra to deal with internal security and local administration in the base and lines of communication areas. These elements were combined into Persia and Iraq Command from 21 August, with General Sir Henry Maitland-Wilson at the helm, his headquarters based in Baghdad opening on 15 September 1942. The Tenth Army with its headquarters at Arāk, Persia, was now able to concentrate on the tasks of securing the oil fields, supply lines and defending the northern flank of the Middle East region from possible German assault.

This change of command personnel brought with it two men who were to accompany the Poles for the remainder of their wartime exploits; Generals Alexander and Wilson. Alexander had served in Eastern Europe following the First World War, where his experience of commanding the multi-national Baltic Landeswehr stood him in good stead for the challenges of command in the Middle East and Italy. Alexander was utterly committed to his lifelong calling of soldiery; his personality lacked any trace of self-doubt or inner conflict. He possessed a character abounding in good humour and was renowned for his tolerance and common sense, which gave him the qualities of compromise and compassion and through which he attributed great worth to an individual's character, the element that he saw as the measure of the man. He could not help but be impressed by Anders. Alexander's appreciation of the arts and his personal friendships with many painters led him to having his friend the landscape painter Edward Seago appointed to his headquarters as camouflage officer. The prominent Polish art critic and then head of II Corps public relations department, Major Józef Czapski must have been a welcome visitor to his headquarters, as the General always enjoyed the company of painters and those who appreciated art. Anders' appointment of Czapski to this role demonstrates his thorough grasp of politics.

The arrival of General Wilson greatly improved things for the Poles, his energy and enthusiasm accelerated the reorganization and re-equipping of the Polish Army. Wilson was a jaunty, individual fellow with an amiable sense of humour, combined with a formidable intellect, capable of tackling complex and varied problems with decisiveness. Very much the soldiers' soldier, he had amassed a great deal of military knowledge and experience by the outbreak of war, whereupon proving himself an exceptional staff and training officer. General Wilson provided Persia and Iraq Command with a stalwart commander of whom it was said in the command's official history, 'it was beyond imagination that the Nazis could seriously interfere with a man like this'.[16] A fascinating insight into the command's operation can be gained from the diary of Wilson's secretary, the Countess of Ranfurly, who described Anders as possessing 'a fine, handsome but rather sad face and great charm.'[17] Lieutenant General Carton de Wiart made a similar observation of the Poles in general, they were 'vivacious and gay, especially the women, but they all seem possessed by a racial sadness that knows little joy or even contentment.'[18] Their recent ordeals would have done nothing to lift that mood.

Following the meeting in Cairo Anders departed to oversee the second evacuation at Pahlevi, General Wilson requesting his presence afterwards at his headquarters in Baghdad. Anders returned to Tehran via Qizil Ribat in Iraq, inspecting the area earmarked to become the centre of the Polish Army. Upon his arrival at Pahlevi on 28 August, Anders visited the evacuation station. He inspected the camps and addressed both soldiers and civilians, and 15,000 Polish soldiers and women of the auxiliary service marched past the general, many still weak, but all erect and proud. The convoys ran until late August when German planes had begun bombing the ships, so the remaining evacuees were directed overland, to the Persian railheads of Bandar Shah and Sharud and thence by train to Teheran. A number of civilians crossed over the border on foot, arriving at Meshed and onwards finally to Tehran.

The evacuation camp at Pahlevi separated those likely to become fit enough for military service from the unfit, old men, women and children. General Wilson noted that in selecting the Polish families and individuals for removal from Poland the better educated had been chosen, which meant that many of the civilian men had previously served in the Polish Army as officers in the interwar period. These men were sent to Iraq along with the Army and, although their numbers were too great to be readily absorbed at that time a special Officers Reserve unit was created.

The departure of civilians from Pahlevi was very different and led to a worldwide dispersal. At Kavzin the military and civilian convoys had parted, and women who had lost country, homes and possessions had also to say farewell to their men. Their destination was Tehran, where the Polish Ministry of Labour and Social Welfare had from 1 April been readying a special 'concentration camp' as the British authorities referred to it. General Wilson visited the non-combatants' encampments around Tehran and was most impressed by the way in which the Poles had organized themselves and were relying on their own efforts to provide clothing and amenities, as well as education, without relying on the staff of the camps to do everything. As the numbers increased the overflow was moved to Ahwaz and when they regained a reasonable level of medical fitness a great number sailed on to areas of the British Commonwealth which had offered to receive them, in India and East Africa. Some settled in Palestine and others remained in Tehran and other towns in Persia and Iraq. These Polish civilians became receptionists in officers' clubs, assistants in canteens, hospital nurses, clerks in offices – a lucky few women were reunited with their men after the war, having moved to Britain along with the demobilized combat forces.

The emigration of Poles out of the USSR finally ceased on 1 September, the Soviets having closed the border between the USSR and Persia, ending any further attempts to evacuate those Poles who remained behind. The Soviet Union declared that all Poles resident on Russian soil after 1939 were now Soviet citizens effective from January 1943, citing Anders' withdrawal of the Polish forces to Persia as a breach of the military agreement of 14 August 1941. This had the effect of hindering the development of the Polish Army, as the source of further recruits and reinforcements was now cut off. In all over 100,000 Poles were evacuated from the USSR into Persia, including a great many civilians, and such a movement of people was only permitted by the Soviets thanks to intense personal negotiations by Lieutenant General Anders at the highest level of Soviet authority.

4

Along British Lines

The next stage in the evolution of the Polish Army began with the restructuring of the troops evacuated during April 1942 to British organization, thus making them an integral Allied force in the Middle East. Lieutenant General Zając presided over the Polish forces in the region, who were gathered under the provisional title of the Polish Rifle Corps. The available manpower precluded the immediate formation of Sikorski's envisaged two infantry divisions of two brigades each, so instead it was decided to form one infantry division of three brigades and an embryonic armoured brigade of two tank battalion cadres along with the necessary supporting corps level units.

General Sikorski issued orders on 28 April for the creation of the Carpathian Rifle Division by disbanding the existing Polish forces in the Middle East, principally the Independent Carpathian Rifle Brigade, and amalgamating them with the incoming soldiers evacuated from the USSR. The 4th Rifle Division never grew beyond its cadre staff.

Given the manpower availability the reorganization was to be undertaken in two stages; the first raising the nucleus of two infantry brigades from the former Carpathian Rifle Brigade, the second stage taking the evacuated troops from the USSR to establish 3 Carpathian Rifle Brigade, then bringing all brigades and supporting divisional formations up to full strength. The division began formation around the Palestinian settlements of Quastina, Isdud and Beit Jura under the auspices of Colonel Łakinski, as Major General Kopański had been recalled to London. The Polish formations in the Middle East commenced their restructuring in Palestine during the summer of 1942, aided by high morale after the news of the German defeat in Libya.

From early May the fittest of the evacuated soldiers travelled onwards from Iraq towards Quastina in Palestine – these troops were mainly from the 25th, 26th and 27th Battalions of the former 9th and 10th Infantry Divisions. Their morale was good but their state of health poor after their ordeals in the USSR. Only about 40 per cent of the men in these formations were former soldiers, the remainder had received a rudimentary military training in the USSR. In recognition of the long awaited reunion of the Polish forces a ceremony was held on 3 May, Polish Constitution Day, attended by Lieutenant General Zając and Brigadier Erlington, with Major General McConnel, GOC Palestine and Trans-Jordan, reviewing the formation a week later. By the end of June the Carpathian Rifle Division was at full strength with 1 Brigade based at Isdud, 2 Brigade at Beit Jura and 3 Brigade at Quastina. These tented and barracked facilities totalled some 50 square miles and reflected the fact that the Polish Army was the largest Allied military force in Palestine. The division was bolstered further by the transfer of a number of officers from the Polish Army in Scotland. Other Polish institutions established in Palestine included four hospitals, each providing 500 beds, with nurses drawn from women volunteers. The 1 and 3 Military Hospitals were based at Reshovot, 4 at Gedera and number 2 was transferred to Mosul, Iraq in June. Other facilities included the Polish Embassy and Soldiers' Home in Jerusalem, and in Tel-Aviv the Polish Consulate and the welfare facilities of the Polish Red Cross.

The Carpathian Rifle Division was busy from June with extensive training carried out at the Central Army School at Beit Jura. The training was largely conducted by Polish staff from the former Army Training Centre evacuated from the USSR, with men drawn from 19 and 21 Infantry Regiments. These training cadres had to rapidly acquire new skills, methodology and language, and were hard pressed. Here the Polish soldiers were introduced to modern mechanized infantry techniques, with courses on driving a variety of vehicles and motorcycles. Despite the heat, marches were conducted in the desert; attacking and defensive tactics were practised, also reconnaissance. The instructors were particularly active in familiarizing the men with the full range of British weaponry, all of which from rifles to heavy artillery were new to them. The evacuees quickly regained their traditional dash and buoyancy and were regarded by British military experts as tough, war-hardened fighters. The former Warsaw correspondent of the *Daily Mail*, Stefan Kleczkowski, noted the comments of one of the British military advisors: 'They are as hard as nails', as one of them puts it, 'and their discipline is noticeably good.'[1]

The division was dispersed throughout Palestine with the principal officer and non-commissioned officer schools based at Julius in the north. Other Polish units being formed included the tank battalions and corps level formations of engineers, artillery, signals, transport, electro-mechanical engineers and medical services. The principle camps and training facilities used by the Poles were at Bar Bara, Beit Jura, El Hanut, El Bureir, Naid, Julius and Quastina. Amongst the first of these Polish units to be deployed with the Allied forces was the construction company of the 1st Railway Engineers Battalion, who from 18 July constructed 28 kilometres of track on the Beirut–Haifa railway, assisted by New Zealand engineers and Arab labour.

The Polish tank formations leaving the USSR in the first evacuation also made their way to Palestine. The Armour Training Centre landed at Pahlevi on 26 March 1942, and following subsequent moves between quarters in Pahlevi, Tehran and Ahwaz sailed for Palestine from the port of Abadan near Basra on 27 April. The centre became established in the vicinity of Gedera Hill 69 in mid-May, becoming the 1st Tank Battalion before adopting the title of 4th Tank Battalion on 4 August, at which time Major Gliński, newly arrived from London took command. The 1 Krechowiecki Lancers Regiment also left the USSR in the first evacuation, travelling onwards to Palestine and the small town of Bashit near Gedera. The regiment was initially designated as the 2nd Tank Battalion but soon became the 5th Tank Battalion, unofficially maintaining its Krechowiecki title. The battalion was bolstered by the arrival of 250 men from the Carpathian Lancers who had already seen action at Tobruk and Gazala as part of the Independent Carpathian Rifle Brigade. In June 1942, the 4th and 5th Tank Battalions both attended training courses in Egypt at the British Royal Armoured Corps' Cowley Training Camp at Abbassia. Here the troops trained in Mk VIB light tanks for several weeks, the 4th Battalion being reinforced by additional troops from the former Carpathian Lancers. Following the training period the battalions returned to Palestine.

Of invaluable service to the Polish Army were the large numbers of women volunteers. The Polish Women's Auxiliary Service Corps abbreviated to PWSK and referred to affectionately as the *Pestki* was raised in Palestine by merging the many pre-war women's institutions, namely the Women's Defence Corps, the Sisters of the Military Health Service and the women nurses of the Polish Red Cross who were serving with the Army. These women were evacuated out of the Soviet Union alongside other military personnel, forming the Polish equivalent of the British Army's Women's Auxiliary Territorial Service under the oversight of Chief Inspector Colonel Bronisława Wysłoucha. From August these women were officially defined as soldiers on active service and became subject to Army discipline. The PWSK were employed in various branches including the medical facilities, as drivers, teachers and training centre staff.

The arrival of the second evacuation was anticipated by General Auchinleck, who decided to relocate the Carpathian Rifle Division from Palestine to northern Iraq in late 1942. This would both bolster the defences of the Middle East's northern flank and facilitate the reorganization of the Polish Army with the arrival of more Polish soldiers from the USSR. During August 1942, the Polish troops in the Middle East were joined by thousands more who departed Pahlevi in long convoys travelling out of Persia through rugged mountains, a journey not without danger. Two trucks carrying men of the 6th Division plunged into a ravine as the drivers failed to make a hairpin bend, all aboard were lost. At Hamadan the Poles passed through the final Soviet checkpoint; orders were given for the men to hold their temper and their tongues as they departed the Soviet system for good. The convoys took on extra water at the Kermanshah staging camp for the final leg across the desert to their destination of Qizil Ribat, 500 miles away in Iraq. The 5th, 6th and 7th Infantry Divisions from this second evacuation retained for now their organization as it had been in the USSR and along with other Polish formations were consolidated in the eastern area of Iraq, stretching from Khanaqin in the south to Mosul in the north, and forming the Polish Army Corps. This influx of soldiers would enable the creation of the second infantry division as envisaged, but there were also an additional number of soldiers who had to be put to employment, which necessitated a review of the existing plans.

Exactly how this array of Polish formations were to enter battle was a point of considerable debate between the British Imperial and the Polish General Staffs, and also in the Polish command itself, principally as to how to structure an army that could sustain combat casualties and keep sufficient reserves to replenish the formations. General Sikorski wrote to Churchill concerning the disposal of Polish forces in the Middle East on 3 August; he stressed that the Polish Government attached primary importance to the principle of assembling the Polish forces in the Middle East into one indivisible operational entity, which would not be disrupted when ready for action to carry out different military operations. He added that this point of view corresponded with the feelings of the Polish nation, which eagerly followed the activities of the Polish forces abroad, wishing for their concentration and not for their further dissipation. Sikorski proposed the creation of an army of two corps, each of two infantry divisions and a tank brigade. His plans were based on the premise that recruitment of Poles in the USSR would resume, affording him a vast pool of recruits to fulfil his plans and that this army, once operationally ready, would ideally return to the USSR to fight on the Soviet-German front as per the Polish-Soviet Pact of 30 July 1941.

That such a large force was envisaged reflects the political aspirations of the Polish leadership more than the actual operational requirements of the Middle East. As with the formation of the Polish Army in the USSR, Sikorski was not willing to have Polish formations comprise only a minor constituent of the British command – a role that he felt would not allow them to realize their longer-term ambitions of creating a national army for post-war Poland. For Sikorski the principal function of the Polish Army remained the safeguarding of Poland's post-war interests and as such he strove continuously to preserve and enlarge its structure. As in his earlier discussions with Anders, where Sikorski had expressed his preference for retaining as many troops in the USSR as possible for political leverage, Sikorski now planned to do likewise with the British by creating a large army in the Middle East. The British, were however keenly focused on the practical and immediate fighting of the war in the Middle East and as such aimed to raise a tactical fighting formation for deployment as soon as possible, rather than embarking on the long-term growth of an army-sized formation.

Two days after General Sikorski's submission to the War Office an Anglo-Polish conference was held in London, at which the British opposed creating a Polish Army as favoured by Sikorski. Although the numbers of Polish soldiers made the plan feasible on paper, the poor general health of the men combined with the epidemic disease problems of malaria and typhus meant that the available pool was in fact far smaller. The British cited these points in particular for their rejection of Sikorski's plan, coupled with the Poles' near total lack of equipment. The Foreign Office also expressed its displeasure at the fact that Sikorski's plan would create such a sizeable force that it would hold effective control of whatever territory it was based in. Instead the War Office proposed that the army should be used as a reinforcement pool, primarily to bolster the Polish Air Force in Britain, with a standing force in the Middle East consisting of two infantry divisions each of two rifle brigades, a tank brigade, an independent infantry brigade and associated corps units. Denied the opportunity to raise his desired force in the Middle East, Sikorski willingly agreed to the transfer of many of the evacuated troops to Britain, greatly augmenting the 20,000 Polish service personnel already stationed there. The force currently assembling in the Middle East was five times the size of this, and could potentially have become the focus of British-Polish relations – by transferring troops out of the Middle East, Sikorski aimed to redress the imbalance and retain the primacy of the London Poles. The draft of this new organization was to be delivered to the commanders in the Middle East by the Chief of the Polish General Staff, Major General Tadeusz Klimecki.

Following the rejection of Sikorski's plans for the Polish Army, the British now turned their full attention to the opinion of General Anders, who met with John Miles, the British military attaché to the USSR, to discuss the organization of the evacuated Polish units. Following this meeting Anders was summoned to Moscow to see Churchill and Generals Wavel and Sir Alan Brooke, who were in conference with Stalin. General Sir Alan Brooke had taken the opportunity to survey the Red Army's Caucasus defences by flying low over the Caspian Sea coast on his way to Moscow in mid-August. Flying at under 200 feet to evade German fighter aircraft he gained an excellent view of the terrain, a ten to twenty-mile wide strip of flat land lying between the Caspian shore and the Caucasus mountains. He was most disappointed to observe that the defences amounted to only 'a half completed anti-tank ditch, badly revetted and without any covering defences! ... in fact the back door seemed to be wide open to the Germans to walk through for an attack on the Russian Southern supply route, and more important still, the vital Middle East oil supplies of Persia and Iraq.'[2] He therefore advocated preparing on the largest possible scale for the defence of Syria and Persia, and accordingly the War Office instructed General Wilson to prepare for the German invasion of Persia and Iraq they envisaged being launched in October 1942.

Unfortunately, time ran out before Anders could talk with Churchill, the meeting being rescheduled to take place in Cairo on 22 August by Colonel Leslie Hulls, who assisted greatly in introducing Anders to the British commanders in the Middle East. The trip to Moscow was far from wasted, however – Anders' meeting with General Alan Brooke was to prove a revelation to the latter. The meeting took place at Alan Brook's hotel suite and Anders' behaviour baffled the British General: 'When he came into my hotel sitting room he beckoned to me to come and sit at a small table with him. He then pulled out his cigarette case and started tapping the table and speaking in a low voice. He said, "As long as I keep tapping this table and talk like this we cannot be overheard by all the microphones in this room!"'[3] Anders proceeded to recount to Alan Brooke yet more revelations about the Soviet system and the treatment of the Poles in the USSR. As things became clear to the General, he developed a negative opinion of the Soviet regime, in particular their utter disregard for anyone not of the USSR, whom they saw no use for other than getting everything they could out of them.

Anders bade farewell to General Zhukov on 19 August, grateful for his expedition in arranging the evacuation of the Poles, and left the USSR for the final time, flying to Tehran. Awaiting him was a telegram from Sikorski, who was most taken aback that Anders should be conducting negotiations on army organization directly with the British and without consulting the Polish Government. Accordingly, Sikorski forbade him to travel on to Cairo, instead dispatching Major General Klimecki from London to conduct the negotiations. Sikorski was most concerned that Anders would be prepared to make unacceptable concessions to the British in order to join battle at the first opportunity. He also strongly suspected that Anders had already made such suggestions and that this accounted for the rejection of his own plans – his hunch would turn out to be correct. Anders ignored the order and travelled to Cairo on 22 August to meet with Churchill and General Sir Henry Maitland-Wilson at the British Embassy. Churchill opened the meeting, announcing that he had studied Anders' plans for the organization of the Polish Army and that these had been passed on to the Imperial General Staff and General Wilson. There was a general consensus between all parties on the shape of the Polish force: two infantry divisions, an independent infantry brigade and a tank brigade that were to be established under the direct control of General Headquarters, Persia and Iraq Command. Anders expressed his eagerness to form part of General Wilson's army, and Churchill promised to send equipment to the Poles at the first opportunity. Following the meeting Anders returned to Tehran to oversee the second evacuation. Klimecki arrived in Cairo on 24 August and after an introductory briefing with Brigadier Erlington began to suspect that Sikorski's concerns about Anders' involvement were correct.

Numerous changes to the existing basic organization were proposed during a more detailed Anglo-Polish conference held in Cairo on 28 August where Major General Klimecki attempted to represent Sikorski's interests. He was too late; he was informed that Brooke and Churchill had taken Anders' plans back with them to London and that pressure would be applied to Sikorski to accept them. The conference proceeded to elaborate on the joint Anders-British plan and announced that the Carpathian Rifle and 5th Divisions were to be the principle infantry formations and were to be expanded to include three field artillery regiments, a reconnaissance regiment and a heavy machine-gun battalion, as per British practice. General Wilson had further reviewed the plans and advocated the reduction of the Corps' allocation of heavy anti-aircraft artillery to a single regiment, and to redistribute this and all other manpower to bolster the new formations. Tanks were to be made immediately available for training. The nascent 4th Rifle Division was to be disbanded and the 8th Infantry Division would be liquidated and transferred to Great Britain to reinforce the Polish Army and Air Force there. Klimecki, taken aback by the rapid course of events conditionally approved this organization before flying to Tehran to confront Anders and inform him of the British revision of his plans.

Anders recalls the meeting in his memoir as being a difficult conversation with several points of disagreement. Undoubtedly there was a ferocious clash of authorities as the worlds of London and the Middle East collided. Anders stood firm and won out, he was confident of full British backing for his plans and this was more important than the approval of the Polish Government. Klimecki forwarded General Wilson's amendments to the plan, to which Anders proposed further amendments to enable the Polish forces to continue at an army level of organization and retain the more prestigious title of Army, by including a third front-line division. To achieve this he proposed the reorganization of the evacuated 6th Infantry Division, renaming the division's infantry brigade 6 Independent Rifle Brigade and including 2 Tank Brigade in its order of battle. The highly effective German panzer grenadier divisions had inspired this mixture of infantry and armour. Anders accepted maintaining only one tank brigade and suggested the renaming of the 7th Reserve Division as the 7th Infantry Division; he made no objections or amendments to the Carpathian Rifle and 5th Infantry Divisions proceeding along the British template.

Anders then proposed that these changes, which in effect amounted to nothing more than changes of name, would provide a continuity with the units raised in the Soviet Union that would greatly improve morale in the Polish forces evacuated from the USSR. His own amendments also made no change to the types of formation the British wanted, thus enabling the Polish Army to be readily deployed in the British order of battle. His insistence on having the force named an Army was likely to be agreed by the British, as improving the prestige of Allied forces in the region, particularly in the eyes of the Soviets. This minimal tweaking of the British plans demonstrated the successful pragmatic approach of Anders: 'Devoid of romanticism, Anders was blessed with a sober clear-sightedness and approached matters, be they of a personal or more general nature, in a decisive and business-like manner. In communicating with the Allies these traits were of not inconsiderable help.'[4]

Following his meetings with Generals Wilson and Anders, Klimecki reported back to Sikorski on 5 September, suggesting the rejection of Anders' plans in full; the short-term fighting agenda was at odds with the Government's plans for continued development and post-war goals and risked squandering Polish forces for a British agenda. There followed many telegrams between Sikorski and Anders that culminated three days later with Sikorski abandoning his own organizational plans, informing Anders that he accepted his measures. The pressure on him was too great, and with Anders' plans now being the only available route forward he reluctantly informed the War Office on 12 September that he agreed to the proposed Polish organization. To refuse or to argue further would alienate him from the Allied table; to preserve any future influence and authority amongst the Allies he would have to accept that Anders had outmanoeuvred him. On 16 October, Sikorski received confirmation from the British that the plan had been accepted.

The result was a defeat for Sikorski; Anders and the British got their way. The British gained another corps for deployment in the Middle East and Anders achieved the title of Army with three frontline divisions to deploy, while Sikorski received the consolation prize of a few thousand extra personnel for his forces in the UK. Anders emerged from the process with greatly elevated prestige amongst his troops and having fashioned himself into the figure the British would choose to deal with in future with regard to the Poles in the Middle East. Major General Bohusz-Szyszko then commander of the 5th Infantry Division, observed that 'Anders had no difficulty in establishing relations with the British and rapidly winning their trust and support for his organizational plans.'[5]

In light of the agreed organization and as recognition of the status of the Polish forces in the Middle East, General Sikorski officially bestowed upon them the title of Polish Army in the East on 12 September 1942, just as Anders had recommended. Lieutenant General Anders was named Supreme Commander, with the Army's headquarters based at Qizil Ribat in Iraq and the majority of military units based around Khanaqin. Here a large and well-organized encampment was established on the banks of the River Gilan, providing all the facilities needed to be self-sufficient as well as an officers' casino, clubs and shops. Polish soldiers had begun arriving from temporary encampments in Persia since 28 August. The heat of the Iraqi desert, combined with contaminated drinking water supplies, led to many cases of disease amongst the soldiers already weakened from their experiences in the USSR. A unique spectacle was provided at the Qizil Ribat camp by 333 Field Butchery – the large quantities of carcases disposed of each day attracted a huge number of nocturnal scavengers. The nights were filled with the sound of squabbling hyenas, foxes and bears, the desert darkness punctuated with hundreds of pairs of glowing eyes.

The British staff of Persia and Iraq Command were both amazed by the scale of the plan for the Army and appalled by the condition of the evacuated Polish soldiers: 'On the face of it, this project seemed to be wildly ambitious. The majority of the men who were to compose this army had suffered extreme privation and it would have appeared no easy task to make them fit for the ordinary life of civilians; few, when they left Pahlevi, looked as if they would get through any army medical board for many months.'[6] Here in the Iraqi desert, life began to move at a fast pace, perhaps too fast for some. The climate, hot in the daytime, cool at night, was somewhat easier to bear than what they endured in Uzbekistan. However it was not the new climate that benefited the Poles so much as the knowledge that they were now an integral army in the Western Allied forces. They were looked after by people who cared about and understood their situation and their need for good food, appropriate for the climate and their weakened physical condition. Medical care was immediately available, with modern equipment and medication in abundant supply. In the Iraqi desert, despite the efforts of the medical staff, malaria unfortunately not only persisted but spread far and wide at an alarming rate. It caught up with men deployed on training courses as far afield as the British base at Basra. Despite the medics' copious provision of Mepacrine tablets no real headway was made against the disease. The military hospitals were filled with men who, after their discharge, were directed to the special convalescence companies of 7 Infantry Brigade for their recovery and from there, back to the units, only to find themselves back in hospital, felled by renewed attacks of malaria. It was a vicious cycle, but training had to go on, and it did so at all costs, paid for by a steady toll in lives and a constant reduction in the strength of the Polish formations.

Beneficial as the climate was, it was not ideal for the malaria-ridden evacuees. What was really required was a far more temperate region, but before such a relocation the Polish Army would have to reorganize itself to the British pattern and become fully trained in modern warfare. With British assistance the Poles were fully exerting themselves in their training to become a modern fighting force capable of defeating their German adversaries, and despite the raging malaria, the troops' hopes and morale were very high, as noted by Persia and Iraq Command: 'In exiles the flame of patriotism burns very fiercely, and these soldiers had accounts to settle with the Germans. If they needed inspiration they had it in full measure from Sikorski, and their own commander, General Anders. No exertion or hardship was beyond these men.'[7] Indeed, Anders issued orders to his troops in September emphasizing that the Poles were entering a new stage in their struggle: 'We had to become a modern army... We must try to merge the forces arriving from the Soviet Union and the units stationed in the Middle East into a single unit for the liberation of a strong and happy Poland.'[8]

Pursuant with this agenda Persia and Iraq Command were working intensively to introduce and equip the Poles according to British methodology. Persia and Iraq Command also provided all their supplies – a huge amount of time, effort and resources were dedicated to the Polish Army in the East. The task was on a truly industrial scale, deploying vast numbers of men on a myriad of tasks and using a variety of equipment all focused on making the Poles a decisive military force. Principal among these changes was the mechanization of the Polish Army that required the training of 20,000 drivers. The large 26 British Military Mission was attached to the Poles to keep their staff running on British lines and to assist in their specialist training. Led by Brigadier Way the unit comprised British liaison officers assigned to each headquarters and branch of the Polish combat arms and supporting services. Colonel Leslie Hulls became Anders' personal liaison officer.

Supplies for the Polish formations in Iraq were not as forthcoming as had been hoped, hampered by the rail supply route having to be routed through neutral Turkey, with accompanying false paperwork and markings. Suspicious of such activity and aware of the Germans having knowledge of the affair, the Turks detained a train of covered wagons destined for Iraq in June. The Turkish government notified the British authorities in Iraq that the train would be returned to Syria unless the sealed wagons were opened for inspection. The British refused to open the wagons and the train was sent back, along with its cargo of uniforms and equipment destined for the Polish Army.

The reorganization of the Polish divisions from Soviet to British orders of battle commenced in earnest after General Wilson's headquarters was up and running in Baghdad, commencing with the 5th Division on 22 October and continuing with the other formations through December. The formations evacuated in August were bolstered by the transfer of Polish forces from Palestine to Iraq during November and December of 1942, with the largest formation, the Carpathian Rifle Division sailing from Suez via Aden and arriving at Basra in November. This transfer suited both the Poles and the British – the former attained Sikorski's wish to have all the Polish forces pooled together and the

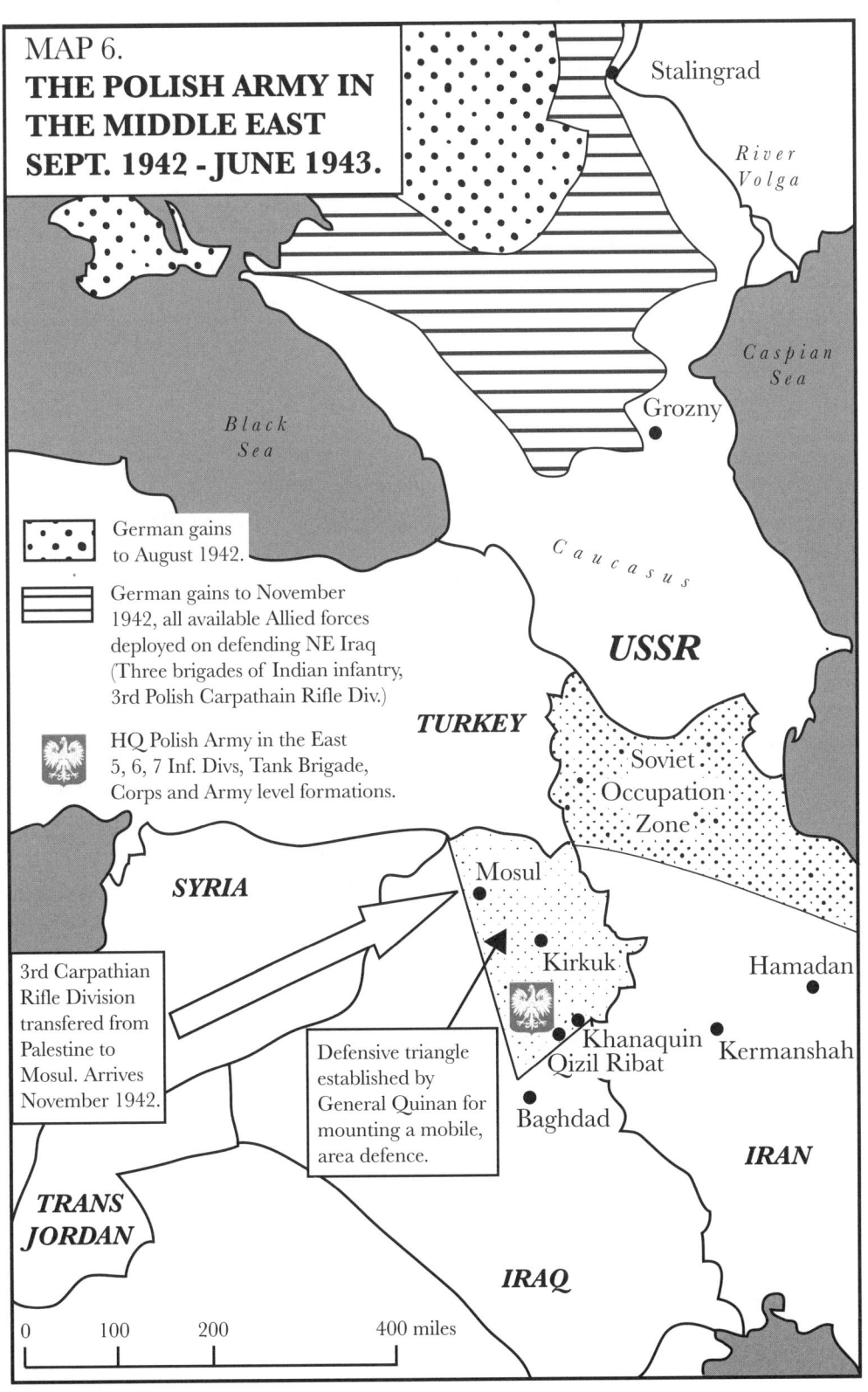

latter gaining an extra division for the defence of the Middle East's northern front. The Polish Army in the East became established on the template of a British expeditionary corps, being conceived of as a large, self-contained operational unit. Principal changes comprised the reduction of the Carpathian Rifle Division to a two-brigade structure from 9 November and being renamed the 3rd Carpathian Rifle Division on 11 November. The disbanded 3 Brigade and all other surplus infantry went into bolstering the ranks of the army level units and the 5th Division. This formation also underwent a reorganization whereupon the existing battalions were split in two, creating two new infantry brigades, 3 and 4, whilst the 6th Division absorbed 2 Tank Brigade as per Anders' plan. In support of the main army establishment there was also a Base, which comprised the grouping of the reserve and replenishment units: 7th Reserve Infantry Division, training facilities, hospitals, supporting services and administration. Further rear echelon and base duties were also undertaken by the cadre strength 8 Infantry Brigade. The Carpathian Lancers Regiment arrived in Iraq during November, having transferred from Egypt. The regiment's commander, Major Władysław Bobiński and his officers had become highly experienced in the modern armoured cavalry role from their battles in North Africa, and with their assistance training was accelerated for the two remaining divisional armoured reconnaissance regiments, the 12th Podolski Lancers and 15th Poznan Lancers.

The non-divisional arms and services formations at corps level were however of a larger organization than that of a British corps, including a number of organic units normally provided at army level in the British organization. Such front line units included the Artillery Group Polish Army, anti-aircraft artillery, engineers, signals and a number of service units. Such organization was desirable to the British command because there were national and language differences that promoted the case for the Poles possessing a more autonomous structure; also for the Polish side it provided the opportunity to expand the army in the future. This incorporation of higher army level formations into the Polish Army in the East did much to elevate its prestige amongst the British and Polish authorities – though numerically small, it was in effect a complete army in miniature.

Differences between the British and Polish structures were evident at almost the highest level, with Poles creating the post of Deputy Corps Commander held by Lieutenant General Zając. The appointment was necessary to keep the corps running whilst Anders was engaged at inter-Allied conferences and with army level responsibilities. In the Polish organization the part played by the Corps Chief of Staff, Colonel Kazimierz Wiśniowski, was considerably larger than in a similar British formation; in addition to strictly military matters he dealt with recommendations received from the central

Polish authorities. Further, in accordance with traditional Polish practice, his duties embraced not only the supervision of operations but also the issue of instructions to the administrative staff and ensuring cooperation between the commanders and the two respective services directorates. Other differences to the standard template included the provision of 20 interpreters, while the total staff of the Corps Headquarters amounted to 300 officers and nearly 800 other ranks.

The artillery and tank regiments of the Polish Army now underwent a massive expansion. Artillery cover for the infantry divisions trebled in size and new corps and army level formations were raised. Similarly, the small number of evacuated armoured troops was swelled by the conversion of cavalry and reconnaissance regiments into tank battalions.

For the intense bombardment of enemy positions two heavy artillery regiments were created at army level. The 10th Heavy Artillery Regiment was formed in May 1942 at Barbara Camp in Palestine, from soldiers evacuated from the USSR in the first wave of transports in March and April of that year. The regiment was initially outfitted with sixteen 155mm howitzers, before transferring to the Mullah Azis camp near Khanaqin on the banks of the Alwand River in Iraq. Here the regiment was outfitted on the same pattern as a British heavy artillery regiment and was equipped with modern 5.5in. guns. On 19 October 1942, this regiment was joined by 11 Heavy Artillery Regiment, formerly 7 Medium Artillery Regiment that had supported the 7th Infantry Division since its creation in the USSR and was now equipped with sixteen 4.5in. guns. The two regiments formed a unit titled Heavy Artillery, whose guns were the largest calibre artillery pieces used by the Polish Army at this stage of the war.

The Polish Army in the East included the integral 2 Tank Brigade, which comprised a brigade headquarters and 4th, 5th and 6th Tank Battalions tasked with providing close infantry support. The Polish tanks were transferred from Palestine to Qizil Ribat in Iraq during September, where they were joined by a further unit, the 6th Reconnaissance Battalion that had left the USSR as part of the second evacuation, arriving in Iran on 22 August 1942 along with the last remaining training and administrative elements of the Armoured Corps. This Battalion was installed at Qizil Ribat two weeks later and was redesignated the 6th Tank Battalion on 8 October, thus establishing the third battalion of the Brigade. The new armoured brigade was now strengthened with the arrival of officers and men from England. In October 1942 the 6th Infantry Division was created from 2 Tank Brigade and 6 Independent Rifle Brigade. During this period more in depth training was provided in Egypt for the senior 4th Battalion in tactics, engineering and other specializations. On returning to Qizil Ribat these men aided the establishment of a modern Armoured Corps Training Centre and began the training of soldiers and NCOs from the other battalions, the officers travelling to Egypt for training.

Along with the fighting formations adopting British organization, the supporting services supplying and maintaining them had also to convert to British methodology. This reorganization caused more opposition from the staff officers than was the case in the fighting units – a number of Polish planners held the opinion that Britain was interfering enough in the affairs of the Polish Army

Table 3
Development of Polish 2 Armoured Brigade.

1941			
August	5th Tank Battalion 6th Tank Battalion	5th Cavalry Sqdn 6th Cavalry Sqdn	6 Reconn. Regt 6th Inf. Division
December		7th Cavalry Sqdn.	
1942			
January	Amalgamated into Armoured Training Centre	Amalgamated into 1 Krechowiecki Lancers Regt.	Training in USSR.
April	Evacuated from USSR to Palestine.		
	Tank Brigade		
	1st Tank Battalion	2nd Tank Battalion	
August	Training in Palestine and Egypt.		Evacuated to Iraq.
September	**2 Tank Brigade**		
	4th Tank Battalion	5th Tank Battalion	
November	2 Tank Brigade transfered to Iraq and incorporated into the 6th Lwów Division.		
	2 Tank Brigade		
	4th Tank Battalion	5th Tank Battalion	6th Tank Battalion
1943			
March	6th Lwów Division disbanded, 2 Tank Brigade becomes an independent formation.		
June	Tank battalions deployed on oil field defence duties in Iraq and continued training.		
August ↓ December	Brigade transfers to Palestine, issued with modern Sherman tanks.		
December	**2 Armoured Brigade**		
	4 Skorpion Armoured Regiment	1 Krechowiecki Lancers Regiment	6 Children of Lwów Armoured Regiment

and that the Poles could organize their own supporting services. However, the Polish Army in the East had of necessity to be closely integrated with the British supply system; if the Polish services were organized very differently then cooperation and collaboration between Polish and British units would be extremely difficult. The British services organization differed from the Polish by affording the service departments much greater executive autonomy and full recognition of their importance, whereas the supply and transport formations of the Polish Army had been very much secondary to the combat units. This difference was manifest in the British organization, with the Quartermaster's position being held of equal importance to that of Chief of Staff. This became ever more vital as military technology advanced at pace, as did the volumes of ordnance consumed in battle. The supporting services became more and more pivotal to the fighting efficiency of the troops on the front line. The British organization of the Polish arms and services were in practice adjusted to the Polish way of working and tradition. Churchill took the matter very seriously and wrote a memo to General Ismay on 21 December 1942, stating: 'I regard the equipment of the Poles as of first importance and urgency... . Let a scheme be prepared showing dates by which the various divisions can be equipped... It is not necessary to adhere exactly to British standards. These can be attained later. Let me have the earliest date when these fine troops will have the minimum equipment to acquire substantial fighting value.'[9]

The shortage of Polish manpower could not be overcome in all the supporting service branches, transport and signal companies being particularly short. The solution was to employ women. Two transport companies, 316 and 317, were formed exclusively from PWSK volunteers and by the close of 1942 women were being trained as radio telegraphers and telephone exchange operators. Women in the Polish Army were expected to work much closer to the front line than in other Western armies; as such they were the only women to carry firearms in regular service during the war. Even with the addition of female staff the signals branch grew to such a size that British soldiers had to be deployed in the Polish formations; the British Royal Signals Corps provided the Technical Maintenance Sections for the divisional signals battalions with some sixty men.

To aid familiarizing the Poles with British methodology, General Wilson devised specialist exercises for all commanding officers and headquarters' staff of the Polish Army; they were assisted in these tasks by the Chief of Staff PAIC, Major General J. Bailon and the Administrative Officer, Major General Selby. During this period Anders frequently discussed Polish-Soviet relations with General Wilson, stressing the need for Allied intervention on behalf of the Poles in the USSR. It was this sort of quasi-diplomatic role that suited Wilson well, his management of politico-military relations in the Middle East showcased his talents in this field of inter-Allied relations. The British Minister of State for the Middle East, Richard Casey inspected the Polish troops in Iraq during October, and was most impressed by both Anders and the Polish Army; the two men got along well and Anders took the opportunity of asking Casey to press the British and American governments to push for more Poles to be released from the USSR.

Persia and Iraq Command's plans for the Polish Army in the East were laid out during an Anglo-Polish conference at the command's headquarters in Baghdad. The Poles came under the direct control of General Headquarters Persia and Iraq Command and were tasked with supporting the defence of the oilfields and mountain passes of northeast Iraq. General Wilson decreed that following intensive training the Poles should achieve operational readiness by May 1943, with the 3rd Carpathian Rifle Division ready before then. The 3rd Division was the most fully armed and equipped Polish formation, though it still lacked much of its heavy weaponry and vehicles, new supplies of which were distributed to the other divisions engaged in intensive training during the winter months. The 3rd Division was detailed by General Wilson to relieve the Indian 8th Infantry Division in northeast Iraq. The division's headquarters and 2 Carpathian Rifle Brigade were deployed to the Mosul region, with 1 Brigade garrisoning the Qaiyara area. The division's objective was to defend the mountain passes linking Persia and Iraq from German attack through the Caucasus. Such an attack was now expected from April onwards, the winter and spring months being unfavourable for movements through the rugged and wild mountainous terrain.

Upon arrival at their new encampments the division was busied adapting the tented accommodation for the coming winter, which in this location is characterized by heavy rainfall and temperatures that drop to zero and below. New roads were constructed, kitchens built and the tents given extra lining. Nonetheless, the prevailing climatic hardships and the difficulty in supplying the formations through the poor local road network caused many frustrations. The mood was elevated on 15 December when the troops celebrated the first anniversary of their victory at the battle of Gazala, a ceremony was held and attended by Lieutenant Generals Anders and Zając and Bishop Gawlina. That month also saw the 5th Infantry Division awarded the name Wileńska. The 5th, 6th and 7th Infantry Divisions remained in the area Khanaqin-Qizil Ribat and continued their intensive training during the cooler winter months. During this period a number of Polish officers were selected to attend the British Army Staff College in Haifa, Palestine.

The Polish work in Iraq was not limited to purely matters of military organization; Major Czapski began writing in Baghdad for the Polish Army newspapers

White Eagle and *Polish Courier*. Other amenities included a Soldiers' Home provided by the Polish YMCA, a Polish Red Cross station and the offices of the Polish Consulate. The city of Mosul to the north housed No. 2 Polish Hospital, the Soldiers' Home, and the hugely popular Polish Parade Theatre established in the King Faisal Theatre, where performances were always sell outs to audiences of Polish soldiers, Iraqi civilians and RAF personnel. The royal box was often graced by the Regent of Iraq and his Prime Minister, with Generals Quinan and Wilson making attendances. One of the most popular pastimes to be enjoyed whenever the training schedule permitted was hunting the abundant game – in the vicinity of the camps were huge flocks of desert partridges, ducks and geese, as well as boar, antelope and leopards. Those who enjoyed such pursuits were thrilled by the opportunities, none more so then Lieutenant General Anders himself: 'I remember shooting on one day eight and a half brace of partridges, three duck, three hares and a boar, and then going out the same evening and bagging seven foxes and two wolves.'[10] The experience of the rank and file of the Polish Army was not so glamorous for they were the hunted, preyed upon by scorpions and poisonous spiders which insisted on sharing the soldiers' tents. The locale was far from hospitable.

The Corps' strong individual character was reinforced by the work of the Public Relations Section directed by Major Czapski to promote Polish identity and traditions. These were necessary morale measures to create and maintain esprit de corps and cohesion, factors that General Anders saw as crucial to maintaining the exiled Poles' distinct status as the national Army of Poland. The public relations staff worked closely with the Education and Welfare Section to provide libraries, and in the production of numerous pamphlets and leaflets for the troops, liaising with local communities and journalists from other Allied armies as well as providing embedded journalists such as the renowned Melchior Wańkowicz to various elements of the Army. As director of the Public Relations Section and Chief Liaison Officer, Major Czapski moulded the public image of the Army and coordinated all cultural activities within the Polish formations. Additionally, each formation had its own Public Relations Section, that performed a valuable role in raising awareness of the contribution of the Polish Army amongst the other Allied forces. The sections also instructed the Polish soldiers in local customs and foreign languages by means of phrase books.

One of the most popular recollections of the Polish Army in the East is that of Wojtek, the Syrian Brown Bear who became the mascot of 22 General Transport Company. The story goes that in 1942 a local boy found a bear-cub near Hamadan in Persia, that he sold to soldiers of the Polish Army stationed nearby for a couple of tins of canned meat. As the bear was less than a year old it initially had problems swallowing, and was fed with condensed milk from an empty vodka bottle and given a washing-up tub to sleep in by Lance Corporal Piotr Prendys. Wojtek took on many aspects of human behaviour including crying like a baby whenever his master left him. The bear proved quite an attraction for soldiers and civilians alike, and soon became an unofficial mascot for the units stationed nearby. The British authorities refused to allow any animals to travel with troop movements, so Wojtek was officially drafted into the Polish Army as a soldier, with accompanying paperwork, being listed among the soldiers of 22 Artillery Supply Company, thus allowing him to travel unhindered.

Wojtek was fed with fruits, marmalade, honey and syrup, and was often rewarded with beer, which became his favourite drink. He also enjoyed eating cigarettes, though only after they had been lit for him. As one of the officially enlisted 'soldiers' of the company, he lived with the other men in their tents or in a special wooden crate transported by truck. Wojtek favoured sleeping amongst the soldiers and could not relax unless cuddled up with them, frequently awakening them by licking their faces.

Wojtek was not unsurprisingly a soldier-bear who enjoyed a great many escapades. He ran into trouble with the Women's Signal Corps in 1942 at Qizil Ribat, where one afternoon he decided to plunder the women's washing line and proceeded to wrap their underwear around his head before uprooting the whole line and dragging it round the camp. Wojtek was disciplined, and aware he had done wrong, covered his eyes as his master bawled him out. The women took pity on him, however, feeding him sweets to cheer him up. At Christmas Wojtek received a great many carefully wrapped presents of food. Not being a patient bear he ate the wrapping paper as well, followed by a bottle of white wine and then beer. Later that night he broke into the store tent and gorged himself on fruit, jam and honey before passing out.

5

A Year of Challenge

The threat of a German invasion of the Middle East soon faded as the Soviets began to turn the tide of war from January 1943, the attendant risk to the Middle Eastern oilfields also decreasing. With this change in the strategic environment, General Sir Alan Brooke met with Lieutenant General Sir Arthur Grasett (Chief Liaison Officer, Allied Contingents) at the War Office to discuss the future of the Polish forces in the Middle East from 19 February; the decision was taken to transfer the Polish Army to another theatre of war. Persia and Iraq Command received a new commander on 6 January, Lieutenant General Sir Henry Pownall, who informed General Anders on 15 March that he should prepare his forces for future amphibious and mountain warfare in the Mediterranean. This decision coincided with the reduction of PAIFORCE (Persia and Iraq Command) to a garrison and line of communication basis that enabled the transfer of the fighting formations, stores and equipment to other theatres.

Following these discussions and the conclusion of the winter training period, Sikorski decided on 10 March to consolidate the Middle East forces into formations ready for deployment in the line. This he envisaged would concentrate the somewhat thinly spread manpower into two fully operational infantry divisions of two brigades and an independent tank brigade.[1] General Anders was in agreement with Sikorski's reorganization of the Army, adapting its structure to existing manpower. The 6th Infantry Division, the concept of which the British General Staff were not convinced about, was disbanded, with 6 Independent Rifle Brigade joining the 5th Infantry Division, whose existing 3 and 4 Infantry Brigades were amalgamated into 5 Infantry Brigade, a move made necessary by the high number of malaria cases in that formation. At the same time 2 Tank Brigade became an independent formation and the 7th Infantry Division was further reduced in strength and was primarily assigned with providing Base and administrative facilities. The 5th Wileńska Infantry Division adopted the name Kresowa on 27 March at a ceremony attended by General Wilson; the constituent brigades were also named as 5 Wileńska and 6 Lwów Infantry Brigades. The name Kresowa refers to the eastern borderlands of Poland, from where the majority of the division's personnel originated, the brigades being named after prominent cities in the region.

March saw the Heavy Artillery expanded further to include a headquarters, a signals unit and the 7 Horse and 9 Light Artillery Regiments to form 2 Army Group Polish Artillery, that from April moved to the Khanaqin region for further extensive training and practice firing. These two regiments were formed after the downsizing of the 7th Division and the disbandment of the 6th.

The life of 2 Tank Brigade was also in fast-forward at this time. The Brigade began to be issued with Valentine Mk III tanks during February, the first allocation went to the 4th Battalion, subsequent issues to the 6th and 5th. Training with the Valentine tanks continued in earnest and was reviewed by General Sikorski on 12 April. Other mechanized formations progressing rapidly were the four reconnaissance regiments of armoured cars and mounted infantry, one for each division and one at corps level. The growth of artillery and mechanized units was achieved through further downsizing of second line units.

During April 1943 the status quo of Polish-British relations was rocked by a huge political fracas between Poland and the Allies. It erupted following the publicizing by the Germans of their discovery of several mass graves containing some 4,500 Polish officers buried at Katyn near Smolensk. All had been shot in the back of the head, allegedly by the Soviet NKVD. By making the discovery public the Germans knew they could achieve a huge propaganda victory, driving a wedge between Poland and the USSR. The Soviet response was to completely deny the allegations, claiming it was the Germans who had killed the prisoners; the Western Allies chose to accept the Soviet version of events to hold the wartime alliance together. The Poles did not accept it, however, and held the Soviets fully accountable for the atrocity. Anders' response was swift. On 18 April in his orders for the day he called for a requiem mass to be observed for the dead, and criticized the events at Katyn and the Soviet government. The order was also published in the daily Polish language newspaper *Dziennik Polski*.

Anders' order drew a sharp response from the Soviet ambassador in Britain and more importantly for Anders, a rebuke from General Pownall, commander of Persia and Iraq Command. Pownall issued Anders with precise orders demanding the suppression of all criticism of the Soviet Union by members of the Polish Army in the East. Sikorski issued similar orders, writing to Anders that 'politics was not the business of military commanders' and in a private letter called on Anders to 'dismiss conspirators from his entourage and from the Army.'[2]

The Soviet Union responded by suspending all relations with the Polish Government in Exile on 25 April, stating that by accusing the Soviet Union of

Table 4
Development of Principle Formations of the Polish Army in the East into the Polish II Corps 1942–1943.

1942					
April	**Polish Independent Carpathian Rifle Brigade**, based in Palestine. **First Evacuation from USSR**, Polish soldiers arrive in Palestine.				
	Polish Independent Carpathian Rifle Brigade	**8th Infantry Division**	**9th Infantry Division**	**10th Infantry Division**	**Army Organization Centre**
	Liquidated.	Disbanded, personnel to UK.	Liquidated.	Liquidated.	Becomes Army Training Centre
May	Liquidated formations combined in Palestine to establish: **Polish Rifle Corps**.				
	3rd Carpathian Rifle Division		**4th Rifle Division**		**Tank Brigade**
	1 Brigade 1st, 2nd, 3rd Battalions 2 Brigade 4th, 5th, 6th Battalions 3 Brigade 7th, 8th, 9th Battalions		Staff raised, division not manned due to ill health of evacuees from USSR. Division's cadre staff disbanded in September.		1st, 2nd Tank Battalions
August	Second evacuation arrives in Iraq.				
September	**3rd Carpathian Rifle Division**	**5th Infantry Division**	**6th Infantry Division**	**7th (Reserve) Infantry Division**	**2 Tank Brigade**
	Palestine. 1 Brigade 2 Brigade 3 Brigade	Iraq. 13, 14, 15 Regiments	Iraq. 16, 17, 18 Regiments	Iraq. 7 Brigade 22nd, 23rd Battalions. 8 Brigade (cadre only)	Palestine. 4th, 5th Tank Battalions
	Sikorski names the forces in the Middle East: **Polish Army in the East**.				
November	Transferred to N. Iraq. 3 Brigade disbanded.	3 Brigade 10th, 11th, 12th Battalions 4 Brigade 13th, 14th, 15th Battalions Division named **Wileńska** in Dec.	6 Independent Rifle Brigade 16th, 17th, 18th Battalions 2 Tank Brigade 4th, 5th, 6th Tank Battalions	7 Brigade 22nd, 23rd Battalions 8 Brigade (cadre only)	Transferred to Iraq and incorporated into 6th Division.
1943					
March	1 Brigade 1st, 2nd, 3rd Battalions 2 Brigade 4th, 5th, 6th Battalions	5 Wilno Inf. 13th, 14th, 15th Battalions 6 Lwów Inf. Brigade 16th, 17th, 18th Battalions. Division renamed **Kresowa**.	Division disbanded.	7 Brigade 22nd, 23rd Battalions 8 Brigade (cadre only)	4th, 5th, 6th Tank Battalions
July	Above formations grouped into the **Polish II Corps**, 7th Div. providing Base facilities.				

the crime the Polish were in league with the Nazis. To prevent further discord in the Allied camp, Foreign Secretary Anthony Eden was tasked by Churchill with persuading the Poles to accept the line that the Katyn report was German propaganda. Sikorski knew he must do so for the cause of Allied unity, but many exiled Poles believed he had become a yes-man to the West and should have protested more strongly, not only over Katyn, but also the citizenship issue, the refusal of the Soviets to allow more Poles to leave the USSR and the future post-war boundaries of Poland. General Pownall felt the matter required further attention; having already demanded the suppression of anti-Soviet sentiment amongst the Corps it was also necessary to bring Anders under tighter political supervision, especially with regard to his future orders of the day. To this effect the two generals met on 2 May, and Lieutenant General Pownall wrote to Anders:

> *I should be made aware, before you publish them, of further Orders of the Day which you may wish to issue from time to time.*
>
> *Let me say at once that this is not because I have any lack of confidence that you may go beyond my recent instructions to you on the subject. But as you are aware the political situation is now very delicate indeed and it is most important that nothing should appear, either in London or here, which might prejudice negotiations now going on.*
>
> *I am kept fully informed from London of the line that is being taken there in regard to all published statements. We must follow suit here. It is for this reason, to ensure that we do not step off the path, that I now ask you to let me see, in future, any Order of the Day which you may wish to publish which can have, however indirectly, any political flavour.*
>
> *Yours,*
> *H. R. Pownall*[3]

The Polish soldiery were far more politically aware than the troops of other Allied contingents, and the Poles knew full well that their long-term future depended more on politics than any military action. Rumours abounded that Anders and the Polish Army in the East were becoming increasingly dissatisfied with Sikorski's handling of the Soviets and desired to see a new head of the exile government. The issue was compounded by some members of the Polish Government expressing concern that General Anders was in command of a larger force in the Middle East than that commanded by Sikorski in Britain. Indeed the Polish Army in the East was frequently referred to as

'Anders' Army', a title the Polish Government disliked intensely. Anders was seen as a potentially powerful political figure, able to count on the loyalty of his men, and one who might even have ambitions towards the Polish Government. This potential for a split in Polish loyalties was unacceptable to the British, who urged Sikorski mostly strongly to travel to the Middle East and assert his authority over Anders and the Army to bring them back into line. Sikorski recognized that the present situation of the Polish forces in the Middle East was becoming difficult to handle. Indeed the bickering between the two Polish generals tried the patience of Churchill: 'Here we have all the elements of instability which led Poland through many centuries in spite of the individual qualities and virtues of Poles. In my view, no countenance should be given to subversive movements in the Polish Corps... we have armed and are feeding these Polish troops and they begin their usual Polish fissiparous subversive agitation.'[4]

Despite these deep grievances the training and organization of the Polish Army continued at pace during April, with Lieutenant General Pownall writing to all Allied formation commanders under his command stating that thorough and realistic training was of the utmost importance. He wrote to Anders on 30 April with his appraisal of their progress, emphasizing the importance of training higher commanders and the Corps Headquarters:

> *In connection with the training of the staff, it is most important that the Corps Headquarters should be given as early as possible the opportunity to work and train as a team, unencumbered by the many distracting affairs of the Base and Lines of Communication. I would like the Corps Headquarters, therefore, to open at KIRKUK by the 3rd May, 1943.*
>
> *You should delegate as much as possible of your rearward matters to a deputy and decentralize to heads of services authority to deal with administrative matters at the Base, so that you yourself will be free to give your almost undivided attention to the training of the Polish Corps for battle and battle maintenance.*[5]

Major General Klimecki approved these measures and the separation occurred with the 3rd and 5th Divisions, armoured brigade and supporting arms and services forming the Army Corps moving north to the Kirkuk-Altun Kupri region from late April, leaving the Base and rear units at Khanaqin and Qizil Ribat. On arrival in Kirkuk the Poles took up guard duties at strategically important installations, coming under attack several times from bands of Kurdish militants who had been stirred into action by Kurdish-speaking German agents parachuted into Iraq near Mosul. These agents were soon captured, being readily distinguished from the locals by their far higher levels of personal hygiene. The 3rd Carpathian Rifle Division took up positions near the town of Altun Kupri from 6 May, in an inhospitable locale the Poles nicknamed the 'Valley of Hell'. The sun-parched landscape consisted of steep rocky hills vegetated with thistles, dry desert weeds and cacti, all covered in dust blown in from the desert sands, which blanketed everything and everyone. Even in early summer the temperature was reaching 50°C and the nearest water supply was 12km away, with water collections made twice daily. The harsh climate took some getting used to and the men longed for a transfer to anywhere else.

The Soviets were still enraged by the Polish response to Katyn and launched a major propaganda campaign directed at the Polish Army by radio and newspaper distribution throughout Iraq. Anders was furious that the Soviets could distribute such material freely in Iraq and wrote to Lieutenant General Pownall on 22 May:

> *I have issued orders and used my influence to preserve calm, and calm is kept unreservedly... Lately there are being distributed in Persia, Iraq and Palestine Bolshevist propaganda newspapers in Polish... of course not any kind of Bolshevist proposals will have any effect on our men, who have suffered enough in the Bolshevist paradise, and having seen many thousands of their own killed, mistreated and dying of hunger in Russia. The fact alone, that such papers are allowed to be sold and distributed freely, has an irritating effect on my soldiers and is deeply resented by them.*
>
> *This is why I am taking the liberty of asking you to give your kind attention to this matter in order to find perhaps a way to suppress this harmful and detrimental propaganda.*
>
> *Yours sincerely,*
> *W. Anders*[6]

The matter was taken up immediately by PAIC, with Major General Baillon replying five days later:

> *You asked me to take up the question of suppressing the 'Wolna Polska' in Iraq. Investigations have necessarily taken a little time owing to the irregular way in which the paper comes into the country and is distributed.*
>
> *I am anxious to do everything I can to help you maintain the morale of your troops and, although there has been nothing in the paper so*

> *far which is likely to affect their morale, I agree that we should try to prevent copies of it getting into their hands.*
>
> *Unfortunately, the matter does not lie entirely in our hands, for although British influence is great in Iraq we cannot suppress this paper, any more than any other, without the agreement of the Iraqi administration. I have discussed the matter with the Ambassador, who advises that to approach the Iraqi Government might lead to just those political repercussions here and elsewhere which we want to avoid in the interests of Polish-Soviet relations.*
>
> *While it is impossible, therefore, to ban the paper and stop it coming into the country, arrangements have been made to reduce its distribution. Since, however, this cannot be 100 per cent effective, it would greatly help if you took steps to ban its circulation among your troops, and I should be grateful for your co-operation in this way. By those two methods we should be able to ensure that any harmful effects the paper may have on them will be reduced to a minimum.*[7]

Sikorski was busy at this time attempting to resolve the many complex political issues that stemmed from the influx of Poles from the Soviet Union, which had brought forth many fragmented governmental bodies; it was the direct coordination of government activity in the Middle East that Sikorski saw as necessary to bring political unity to the Army. Sikorski presented the Polish Government with a proposal to create a delegate to the Middle East. This was approved by the Council of Ministers on 17 May, empowering the delegate to coordinate all local governmental bodies. These pressures weighing heavily on him, Sikorski met with Anthony Eden on the morning of 24 May. Eden noted: 'When General Sikorski came to see me this morning he spoke of his anxiety to secure that his troops were employed in battle. He did not know what our plans were and he did not ask... if our eventual entry into the Balkans was to be via Italy, he begged most earnestly that Polish troops should be employed, in the Italian venture. It would be depressing for the morale of his troops if they had no opportunity to take part in the forthcoming operations.'[8] Eden minuted that he understood the General's position, but could not give any commitment at that stage.

To initiate these changes in both governmental and military organization Sikorski departed for the Middle East to handle matters in person, a move that was strongly supported by the British Foreign Office. After landing in Cairo on 27 May and following preliminary discussions, General Sikorski was convinced that the position of delegate should be filled promptly, since much work needed to be done. The post required one who could speedily bring about change and also work effectively with the local British authorities. Sikorski's choice was Ambassador Tadeusz Romer, who had recently arrived in Cairo from the USSR; his choice was approved by the Council of Ministers on 4 June.

The major element of Sikorski's Middle Eastern tour was his inspection of the Polish forces from the 1st to 17th June, during which he presented his organizational plans to Anders and the formation commanders. Anders was quick to dispel rumours about the ousting of Sikorski and indeed, Sikorski was most impressed by the professionalism and loyalty of the soldiers he reviewed. He called a conference of all senior officers in June, for discussions covering not only military matters such as organization and postings, but also the political situation and the activities of the Polish Government in London. Sikorski stressed that in negotiations with the Soviets there had been no compromise at all on the eastern boundaries of Poland, that the future of Poland lay with the Western Allies, it was not subject to deals with the Soviets, and to that end it was necessary for the Polish Government to maintain an attitude of self-restraint and calmness so as not to jeopardize the initiatives of Britain with the USSR over the Polish question.

Sikorski then announced his decisions on organizational and personnel matters related to the expected use of the Polish Army in the Mediterranean. The deployment would consist of two divisions of infantry, a tank brigade and supporting services, a total that corresponded to the formation of a corps, as opposed to an army. For this reason Sikorski intended to restore his Army Corps organization as planned in 1942, with the base, and field training schools being united into a separate command subordinate to the London authorities. There was no requirement for the role of Army Commander. This proposal did serve to answer Lieutenant General Pownall's concerns over the Poles' organization for combat, although in his opinion, the base and Army Corps would be best served under a single overriding commander as at present. The scheme inevitably led to differences of opinion between Sikorski and Anders over the organization of the Army and of Anders' powers as Commander.

Lieutenant General Anders recognized the need for uniformity in total command of the armed forces in the Middle East and sought to preserve the existing leadership of the Army. His arguments were based on the political prestige of an army-sized Polish contingent, the morale of the troops, continuity of administration and coordination of base activities. Anders' and Pownall's position prevailed during the discussions, following which General Sikorski agreed to the temporary maintenance of the Army until the time of commitment at the front of the Army Corps, when General Anders would take command of the latter. This left a current lack of Corps Commander. Accordingly, on 16 June, General Sikorski created the position of Deputy Commander of the Army Corps and appointed Major General Bohusz-Szyszko, who was to direct preparations and training until the Army Corps was ready for action as part of a higher operational Allied formation. At such time Anders would take direct command of the Army Corps, to be named the Polish II Corps (Polish I Corps was based in Britain and was destined for action in northwest Europe).

In connection with this reorganization General Sikorski foresaw a number of personnel changes being required, which he discussed with Lieutenant General Anders in Cairo. Principal amongst them were that the commander of the base, Major General Wiatr, should have much greater autonomy, that command of the 3rd Carpathian Rifle Division was entrusted to Major General Kopański, command of the 5th Infantry Division was to remain with Colonel Sulik, Major General Przewłocki was appointed Chief of Staff of the Polish Army in the East, and Colonel Wisnowski became Chief of Staff of II Corps, with Colonel Skowronski as Quartermaster. In addition, Colonel Okulicki, commander of the 7th Reserve Infantry Division was placed, along with his division, at the disposal of the General Staff in London. The essence of these appointments reflected the gradual winding down of the Polish Army in the East coinciding with the emergence of II Corps.

These changes afforded the base formations greater autonomy from the fighting formations, while simultaneously gaining stronger affiliation with the governmental authorities in London. Sikorski saw the separation as necessary given his objectives for the Base. The Base Commander had two main tasks to perform, the first being to enhance the fighting effectiveness of II Corps by supplying training and instruction facilities and reinforcements. The second was a far more political role, to provide skilled personnel for the future reconstruction of post-war Poland. To realize the latter the Base Commander was to oversee and facilitate the work of the central government in such areas as providing education up to university level, along with civilian, social and welfare concerns.

Of concern to all Polish commanders in the region was the poor health of the men and their arduous existence in the heat of the Iraqi desert. In addition to guard duties, the major units conducted a number of large-scale exercises at brigade and division level, in order to familiarize the men with their weapons and the staffs with the organizational methodology to coordinate them. These culminated in June with a vast war game organized by Major General Selby of PAIFORCE. The tropical heat of Iraq during June and July necessitated military exercises being restricted to 2–4 hours per day. Even so, the summer climate was almost intolerable for the Polish soldiers. Heat and the effort expended during intensive training led to a renewed outbreak of malaria – some 5,000 were affected. The hospitals were overloaded, and it was necessary to create special malaria camps, with the total number of patients reaching 8,000. In addition there were numerous deaths resulting from severe sunstroke. These circumstances resulted in the Polish Corps not meeting the May deadline which was subsequently reset to 1 August 1943.

Having experienced the climate first hand, General Sikorski sought to acquire better conditions for his men and in late June gained approval from General Wilson, the British Middle East Commander, to transfer the Polish units to a more hospitable Mediterranean region. The exact territory the Poles would be stationed in was not yet decided; Anders was adamant the Corps should be located in Syria or Lebanon – he wished to steer clear of Palestine in order to avoid any complications that might arise from the 4,000 Jewish soldiers in the Corps choosing to settle in the numerous Polish-Jewish communities in Palestine, a possibility that could significantly reduce his manpower. The British shared these sentiments, since the ethnic and religious balance of Palestine was on a very fine balance to preserve peace and the influx of 4,000 Jewish soldiers could have major consequences for stability in the region; the British authorities were very keen not to let such a situation arise.

A major challenge now presented itself in numerous incurable cases of malaria. Throughout the summer the Polish hospitals had been sending such unfortunate individuals to hospitals in Tehran, a situation that was undesirable for the Persians, who succeeded in persuading the Foreign Office in London to stop all such transfers from 13 July. This left 380 cases in the hands of the Polish hospitals in Iraq, that General Pownall insisted should be treated in a dedicated facility at the Polish Base. The British authorities were in agreement with the Poles that incurable malaria cases had to be transferred out of Iraq – not only was the climate disadvantageous for them, such patients took up valuable space in military hospitals required for regular sick and casualty cases of the Polish Army. The ultimate fate of these men remained undecided.

Further diplomatic difficulties arose with the Persians when the Poles sent to Ahwaz 100 soldiers discharged for alcoholism and for possessing criminal records. Neither the Polish camp at Ahwaz, nor the local Persian authorities had the facilities to deal with them and the Persians resented having such men at large. Lieutenant General Pownall took up the issue, writing to Anders on 13 July:

> *In the circumstances, I have no alternative but to request you to arrange for their return to Khaniqin or Qizil Ribat, and for their retention there in military custody. Will you therefore take the necessary action to this end?*
>
> *The ultimate disposal of these men presents a very difficult problem. As they have not been sentenced to imprisonment or detention they*

cannot under our laws be held in imprisonment in any British establishment whether in a theatre of war or overseas. I feel, therefore, that the only solution is for the Polish Army to form a small detention unit, using personnel not fit for normal military service, and to hold these men in custody in the Polish Base. I should therefore be grateful if you will cause your staff to submit, in the normal way, an establishment for this purpose.[9]

Sikorski was determined to establish greater governmental control over the Polish forces in the Middle East and established a Military Department at Romer's offices on 29 June, headed by Colonel Adam Szymanski who answered directly to Sikorski. The department was the size of, and functioned very much as a military mission to the Polish Government in the Middle East, providing Sikorski with up-to-date information on the progress of the war and the disposition of Polish forces. The Military Department was to receive and effect the orders of the Council of Ministers and the Commander-in-Chief through liaison with British and American staffs. Colonel Szymanski was to keep in constant contact with the Polish Army in the East to ensure full cooperation between Anders and the Government.

On 3 July, General Sikorski, together with Major General Klimecki, other staff officers and his daughter flew from Cairo to London, saying their goodbyes to the civilian and military authorities at Cairo airport. On his return flight to England General Sikorski stopped off at Gibraltar to visit his friend Major General Mason-MacFarlane who was now commander of the territory's garrison, bestowing upon him the prestigious Order of Polonia Restitua, First Class. Sikorski boarded his plane for the flight to London, but shortly after take-off his aircraft crashed into the sea and all on board were killed. Mason-MacFarlane was inconsolable at losing such a friend, especially in his own command area, for him the red ribbon of the order of Polonia Restituta would forever be tainted with the blood of General Sikorski. The funeral was held at Westminster Cathedral on 15 July and the British delegation as noted by General Sir Alan Brooke were struck by the 'sad picture of Poland's plight: both its state and its army left without a leader when a change of the tide seems in sight.'[10]

Sikorski held a degree of respect and prestige among the British establishment that no other Polish politician or soldier could equal. It was clear that no one in the Polish General Staff or Government would be able to hold the combined posts of Prime Minister and Commander-in-Chief, a feat Sikorski had managed through force of personality, ability and not least his stubbornness. The British partly wished to see the two positions separated because the combined role reflected strongly the inter-war influence on Polish politics wielded by the Army. The Polish President Władysław Raczkiewicz also saw it was necessary to create a more democratic framework, not only to ease British apprehensions but also to elevate the legitimacy of the Polish Government in Exile amongst the other Allies, in particular the USSR, who were now openly questioning the legitimacy of the London-based Poles.

To achieve these goals the President set about creating a cross-party cabinet incorporating ministers and officers from across the Polish political spectrum. This new political inclusivity by design brought opposing characters together and inevitably conflict ensued, none more marked than that between the new Prime Minister, Stanisław Mikołajczyk and the Commander-in-Chief, General Kazimierz Sosnkowski. Sosnkowski was popular with many of the Polish soldiers, having had the distinction of winning the only major victory over the Germans in 1939 at the Battle of Lwów. Many of them hoped the new Commander-in-Chief would continue his military success and be a strong defender of Polish interests. The same view was not held for the new Prime Minister and his cabinet, especially amongst II Corps. Hearing of the appointments Anders radioed London: 'This government is utterly bereft of our trust and our view of it is decidedly negative.'[11]

Sosnkowski and Mikołajczyk did not want to serve with each other and there persisted a strong antipathy between them, notably over foreign policy and military strategy; Mikołajczyk wished to continue Sikorski's agenda whilst Sosnkowski saw that the course of the war was changing and that a new strategy was required. Sosnkowski was also a controversial choice with the British, Churchill in particular disliking his appointment as the General was perceived to be anti-Soviet and a fascist. Anthony Eden wrote to President Raczkiewicz on 6 July, objecting to the nomination of Sosnkowski. It was evident that Sosnkowski's tenure as Commander-in-Chief would not be smooth.

Despite a bout of illness Lieutenant General Anders proceeded to implement Sikorski's organizational plans and on 6 July issued his orders for the new command arrangements, which in effect amounted to a near unaltered army command under the new title of II Corps. The plan for the base also proceeded, although the diversity of its mission was narrowed to place strong emphasis upon supporting the combat operations of II Corps. The organization of the individual formations was left unaltered, the new order of battle coming into force on 21 July.

General Anders was by now very keen to meet Sosnkowski and clarify the new Commander-in-Chief's aims and objectives, but his state of health denied Anders the opportunity to travel to London, so his deputy Lieutenant General

Tokarzewski went in lieu. The most pressing matters to be discussed were the command personnel changes that would have to be made following the death of General Klimecki, which left the position of Chief of the General Staff open. Sosnkowski now appointed Major General Kopański to this role, with command of the 3rd Carpathian Rifle Division passing to Major General Duch. Major General Paszkiewicz, 2 Armoured Brigade's commander was also transferred to London, being replaced by the Chief of Staff of the Army, Major General Rakowski. Anders remained Commander of the Polish Army in the East overseeing II Corps, which was under the daily stewardship of II Corps Deputy Commander, Major General Bohusz-Szyszko and also the base under the command of Major General Wiatr.

The new Commander-in-Chief's views on military strategy were soon made clear. Especially illuminating is a memo submitted by the Chief of the Polish General Staff, Major General Kopański entitled 'Aims and Principles Regarding the use of Polish Forces Abroad'.[12] Kopański, while noting the main objective was to contribute to an Allied victory, questioned Sikorski's strategy of seeking a major independent military contribution. The memo asserted that Poland's contribution was small in comparison with the other belligerents and that the continuity of the country's fight was largely symbolic. In view of a lack of reinforcements – the bane of any exile army – this contribution could only decrease, especially if committed en bloc or in an independent area of operation. Kopański proposed the Polish forces should be committed in no more than divisional strength. The proposal did not state that forces should be held back, but neither was it enthusiastic for the opposite. Sosnkowski painted a dark picture that offered little opportunity for the employment of forces; he had no illusion that the future looked other than bleak. His recommendation was to increase the tempo of operations against Germany, to monitor events in the Balkans and to seek clarification of the Allies' plans, then to commit forces at the decisive climax of the war.

Sosnkowski's plans for II Corps emerged in August: firstly the reorganization of the Polish Army in the East into II Corps had to be accomplished; secondly, plans for the incorporation of the Corps into the Allied armies as a fighting force needed to be finalized. Whilst Sosnkowski wished to take stock of Allied plans, the British wanted action, and soon. Anthony Eden was well aware that the recent disgruntled rumblings emanating from the Poles in the Middle East stemmed predominantly from their lack of action and natural bent towards political intrigue. They had idled in the desert for too long and in their frustration were lashing out at those perceived to be holding them back from their cause – principally Sikorski and subsequently Mikołajczyk. The Polish Army in the East would have to be put to a productive purpose with haste;

indeed on 13 July during a planning meeting for the invasion of Italy, Churchill had noted: 'The Polish troops in Persia should be brought to Egypt for this task. These Poles wished to fight... and once engaged will worry less about their own affairs, which are tragic.'[13] This point he also conveyed to the Americans: 'I will in no circumstances allow the powerful British and British-controlled armies in the Mediterranean to stand idle. I am bringing the very fine Polish Army from Persia into Syria, where it can participate.'[14]

The issue was resolved during the Anglo-American Quebec Conference held during August 1943, when the broad Allied strategy for prosecuting the war was agreed. As part of the discussions on the Mediterranean theatre held from 10 August it was decided to deploy the entire Polish II Corps in the forthcoming Italian Campaign, Churchill informing Lieutenant General Ismay, his Chief of Staff on 13 August.

British relations with the new Polish Commander-in-Chief commenced with a meeting of Sosnkowski and his British counterpart, General Sir Alan Brooke on 22 July 1943. Sosnkowski's principal aim was to prevent Polish soldiers being used as cannon fodder for Allied offensives, mainly by seeking for them a specialized capacity, in particular armoured formations, as well as independent command arrangements. General Sosnkowski also proposed a massive increase in the size of the Polish Army in the United Kingdom, which included the formation of a new armoured division entailing a doubling of the number of soldiers, changes that would mean the transfer of a large contingent from the Polish Army in the East (which was by now predominantly a reserve and garrison body) and its subsequent complete reorganization. This force would then form the nucleus of the post-war Polish Army. The plan could possibly delay deployment of II Corps but would enable reinforcement of the units stationed in Britain that were destined for fighting in northwest Europe.

Sosnkowski had no plans to deplete II Corps and supported its deployment to Italy; however, he urged that the force be reorganized through the creation of an armoured division, a move he saw as necessary given the developments in warfare that rapidly evolved during the years of raising the Polish formations. However, this reorganization would entail the near disbandment of one of the infantry formations, the 5th Infantry Division, and would call into question the operational readiness and timescale for deployment of the Corps. Sosnkowski felt it would lessen the possibility of large numbers of Polish soldiers being killed in mass infantry assaults on well-fortified strongholds, sacrifices that would achieve little for Poland. The aim was for as many of these soldiers as possible to survive the war and join with the Polish forces in the UK and northwest Europe to form the post-war Polish Army.

Sosnkowski was adamant that Polish soldiers should not be sacrificed to afford politicians in London a greater bargaining force with the major Allies. The Army to was be a professional non-political body and political considerations were not to dictate military thinking at any level. This was a complete turnaround in the utilization of the Army and was far from universally well received, notably when it came to the Prime Minister and Lieutenant General Anders, both of whom still wanted the endeavours of the Army to be used to further the political cause of post-war Poland. General Sir Alan Brooke was not won over by Sosnkowski either and commented in his diary for that day: 'He is definitely not up to the standard of his predecessor but quite a nice individual to meet.'[15] Once again British attention would turn away from the Polish Commander-in-Chief towards Anders, in relation to deploying II Corps.

In Iraq, news of the transfer of II Corps to the Middle East arrived by letter to Anders on 17 July:

> *It is probable, I understand, that a decision will shortly reach this HQ that the Polish Corps is to move to Middle East, commencing with the 3rd Carpathian Div in early August. I understand from Middle East that it was originally intended that the Polish Corps should go from here to SYRIA. Owing to the dangers of malaria however, it has been decided that the Polish Corps cannot be located in SYRIA until mid-October. In consequence, the 3rd Carpathian Div will proceed initially to PALESTINE, and be located in the GAZA area, probably until the end of September, when they will go to SYRIA for intensive training. They will remain in SYRIA either until they are required for operations or until winter. If they are still in SYRIA when winter comes they will return to GAZA. The same procedure will be applicable to the remainder of the Polish Corps.*
>
> *It was, I know, your desire to avoid contact between the Poles and the Jews in PALESTINE, and this was the reason why you did not wish the Polish Corps to be located in PALESTINE. In the GAZA area, however, there are few Jews and towns are remote, so that it should be possible to avoid such contact.*[16]

Lieutenant General Pownall officially informed General Anders of the approval to transfer the Polish Army from Iraq to Palestine on 21 July. This was supplemented the following day when General Wilson wrote Anders a letter expressing his pleasure at having the Polish II Corps again under his command and saying, 'I have assured the military authorities in England that I consider your Corps will be completely ready for any operations after the 1 January 1944.'[17]

The transport schedule for relocating the Poles was formulated by General Pownall's staff officers and issued to Anders on 26 July. II Corps was reassigned to the British Ninth Army under Lieutenant General William Holmes, transferring to the umbrella of the British Middle East Command. The relocation realized Sikorski's earlier insistence on moving the Polish Army to improve its health and conditions and came as relief to the soldiers – at last the searing deserts of Iraq were behind them and the troops found themselves in the far more hospitable Mediterranean climate of Palestine, with its abundant citrus groves and of course myriad holy sites to visit. The soldiers' morale rose sharply and the Corps greatly benefited from the climate, which assisted many recoveries from malaria. With a clear fighting purpose the serious business of fighting a war took its rightful precedence, while at the same time political agitation waned considerably.

It was during the summer of 1943 that II Corps relocated to Palestine, where it was clustered to the south of the territory, the Corps Headquarters being located near Gaza at Kilo 89 Camp, while the 3rd Carpathian Rifle Division was based at Julius in northern Palestine. The arrival of the Poles was well observed by Middle East Command: 'The task for the Poles, helped by their mentors, was to change themselves into up-to-date soldiers of the war's fourth year. Mechanization was part of the change, and another was to foster in Polish commanders an interest in administration to match their liking for plain fighting. Polish officers were inclined to view administration, and even training, as the concerns of subordinates.'[18]

On arrival in Palestine, II Corps' formations were numerically close to establishment strength, with training well underway. The activities to be undertaken included the completion of specialist training, namely 1 Carpathian Rifle Brigade was to head to Amioun in Lebanon for mountain warfare training and to attend the Ninth Army Ski School, and the conducting of large-scale corps manoeuvres, namely Operation Virile. Final establishment strengths were to be achieved through the continued cannibalization of non-front-line units, a necessity that revealed the Achilles heel of the Polish war effort – there were no reinforcements and no more recruits.

6
Ready to Fight

Near the end of July 1943, the Allies were actively looking toward the Italian mainland as their next objective, with General Alexander's 15th Army Group coordinating the build-up. A campaign on the mainland, no matter how short, was perceived as requiring between six and twelve divisions drawn from the British, American and French armies. Planners anticipated the Germans would not oppose Allied landings in southern Italy but would instead form strong defensive lines to hold Rome and the north. The Allied leaders met in Quebec during August for the Quadrant Conference, that included in its agenda discussing options for offensive actions in Italy. General Eisenhower foresaw that the immediate build-up in Italy was likely to be slow and that the Allied forces might face prolonged and bitter fighting.

The Allied leaders however saw no reason to increase the resources already provisionally assigned to the Italian campaign; they expected the Germans to offer relatively little opposition south of Rome. Indeed, the theatre command was now to withdraw seven divisions and send them to England in preparation for the cross-Channel attack, and to replace these in part by French divisions as they became ready for action after being equipped and trained. The necessity of deploying the Polish II Corps was questioned – their additional manpower was no longer envisaged as essential. There was also concern expressed over the proposed establishment of Polish recruitment centres in Italy that would, it was felt, aggravate Stalin. On the other hand, the Polish politicians felt that following the inevitable Italian surrender the war was entering its final stages and it was now absolutely necessary to deploy Polish forces in battle; their political aspirations were wholly dependent on active Polish involvement with the Allied war effort. Accordingly the Polish Government pressed the British Government to commit them to battle throughout the autumn of 1943.

The general consensus from the Quadrant meetings was that the Mediterranean theatre was to be of secondary importance to the main cross-Channel invasion of northwest Europe. Subsequently the Italian campaign would be restricted in its resources, and consequently so would the Allied build-up on the Italian mainland. Whether the Allied forces in Italy could, against any increased German opposition, muster enough troops, equipment, and supplies to drive north fast enough to make the campaign worthwhile was far from certain. But they were going to risk it.

Aware of the difficulties facing the Allies and of the Poles' own lack of reserves, Sosnkowski and the Polish military chiefs in London had by September 1943 prepared three potential alternatives for the organization of II Corps, whose essential differences centred on whether to keep the existing composition of two infantry divisions, or to create a reserve pool by converting one into either an armoured division or an independent infantry brigade and a tank brigade. Sosnkowski's final organizational plans (which also included a massive increase in troop numbers in the UK, to be drawn from transfers from the Polish Army in the Middle East and from recruiting Poles coerced into German service) were received by the War Office on 26 August and caused some unrest. From a practical standpoint the British doubted that the Poles could recruit so many Polish soldiers, and were also concerned about the long-term consequences of creating a large Polish Army outside Poland. The British leaders expressed political anxiety over the inevitable organizational delays II Corps would experience and worried that any further postponing of the Polish debut on the Italian battlefield would infuriate Stalin. The British had the upper hand – reorganization and transfer of personnel to Britain depended on their resources. Sosnkowski had to put his plans on hold.

Details for the deployment of II Corps arrived in a letter from General Sir Alan Brooke, Chief of the Imperial General Staff, on 18 September. In preparing the conditions under which the Poles would join battle in Italy the Imperial General Staff envisaged the deployment of the complete II Corps. However, Alan Brooke proposed that the state of operational readiness attained by the 3rd Carpathian Rifle Division meant this formation could be considered for deployment in Italy ahead of the remainder of the Corps, the whole then transferring to the command of Allied Forces Headquarters under General Eisenhower. Sosnkowski was not enthused by the proposal to deploy the 3rd Division alone, stressing the need to introduce the whole of II Corps to enhance the morale and prestige of the Polish armed forces by committing a large formation. However, he opined that the likely timing of the complete II Corps reaching battle readiness would be the beginning of January 1944. After a long debate, Sosnkowski agreed that in the case of real necessity by the Allies the 3rd Division could be sent to the front ahead of the main Corps, subject to the following conditions:

(a) The Corps would be used as a whole under a Polish general. The 3rd Carpathian Division could, however, be used in advance of the rest of the Corps if real necessity arose.
(b) In the event of the 3rd Carpathian Division being used in advance, the remainder of the Corps would join it as soon as ready for battle. On no account would the Corps be split for operational purposes.
(c) Divisions would not be used in initial assaults from the sea.
(d) Divisions would be used for operations and not as garrison troops.[1]

These measures were approved by the Polish Government on 21 September, and there followed discussions between Sosnkowski and Lieutenant General Grasett, British liaison with Allied contingents, which resulted in a deployment schedule for II Corps being ready for action by 1 January 1944.

Sosnkowski informed Anders of the Imperial General Staff's proposal for deploying II Corps in Italy on 20 September 1943. Anders however, was still adamant that deploying the Corps as a whole was vital for both Poland's military and political aspirations and to maintain morale. The independent deployment of the 3rd Division would, he felt, severely compromise these objectives. From a practical standpoint, Anders considered the deployment of the 3rd Division alone would expose the formation to greater than average losses and showed a lack of confidence from the British in the training of the remaining 5th Division. He wanted equal treatment of both formations by simultaneously introducing them to the front, and argued that his approach would also be easier to achieve. Also, Anders set about convincing Lieutenant General Holmes, the commander of the British Ninth Army in Palestine, that the separate introduction of the 3rd Division into battle would be inadvisable, as the low state of readiness of the remainder of II Corps meant that supporting units would not be ready for deployment alongside the division if needed.

Anders insisted that the Corps as a whole required further training, including specialist mountain training for the 5th Infantry Division, and that full corps-level training could only practically be achieved by retaining the 3rd Division within II Corps for the duration. He recommended that another Allied division in lieu of the Carpathian should be considered for rapid deployment to Italy if necessary. Thus the issue of separating the 3rd Division was postponed, but the issue did bring to the fore a vital point: that battlefield losses in contemporary warfare were likely to be on a scale larger than previously expected. This raised much disquiet amongst the London authorities as the Polish command did not have an adequate pool of reserves. The question of finding reserve manpower for II Corps became a frequent topic of debate between Anders and Wilson, with Anders raising the possibility of recruiting Poles who had been forced to serve in the German military. General Wilson expressed his doubts about the notion, but agreed to defer judgement until a later review of the Polish forces.

The neighbouring territories of Lebanon and Syria were now used extensively for mountain warfare training in preparation for the invasion of Italy. Following the successful training of the 1 Carpathian Rifle Brigade, the 5 Infantry Brigade now received specialist training at the Middle East Mountain Warfare School in Amioun, Lebanon and qualified as expert rock climbers. Such specialized preparation was very much to General Sosnkowski's liking, making the division an asset to the British that they would be unlikely to waste. The remainder of the 5th Infantry Division was also brought up to full strength, receiving its full complement of heavy weapons and equipment and undertaking a rigorous training programme, bringing it to the level of a fully operational assault division. The 16th Infantry Battalion was now faced with the unusual and difficult task of surrendering their mascot, a Syrian brown bear named Michał (after the Polish Lieutenant General Michał Karaszewicz-Tokarzewski of the former 6th Infantry Division), which had been gifted to the battalion by the Shah of Persia. Michał's behaviour became increasingly aggressive as he matured, and indeed he became infamous for fighting the popular Wojtek, so he was handed over to the Tel Aviv Zoo that September.

Now 2 Tank Brigade embarked upon a period of extensive war preparation. In the late summer of 1943 the brigade's tanks were loaded on to trains for Basra and subsequent shipping to Palestine. The 4 Armoured Regiment was the first to arrive in Palestine during late September, enjoying a relatively smooth journey. The other regiments did not fare so well; a lack of motor transport obliged the 5th Tank Battalion's personnel to march the full 1,249 km from Iraq, whilst the 6 Armoured Regiment was delayed at Basra awaiting sufficient motor transport and only arriving at Nuseirat, near Gaza, just before Christmas. It was in Palestine that the 4th Tank Battalion was renamed the 4th Armoured Regiment and the 5th Tank Battalion officially adopted the title of 1 Krechowiecki Lancers Regiment on 1 December, with the entire brigade being renamed 2 Armoured Brigade later the same month. At Nuseirat, Major General Bronisław Rakowski was appointed Brigade commander and the regiments were fully equipped with modern M4A2 Sherman III medium tanks.

Pursuant with Anders' insistence on the Corps being deployed as a whole, General Holmes arranged for the Corps Headquarters and those of the major formations to receive additional training in Corps-scale combat operations and headquarters activities. These were all put to the test in one of the largest wartime manoeuvres to take place in the Middle East, held in Palestine between 22 and 30 October 1943. The exercise, Operation Virile, involved the Polish

II Corps – assigned the title Philistine Army – attacking the rest of the British Ninth Army, termed the Levant Army. The battle area was inside a triangle roughly drawn between Tel Aviv on the Mediterranean coast, Jerusalem to the southeast and to the north Tiberias on the western shores of the Sea of Galilee. The area enclosed most of central Palestine, the terrain comprising rugged hills with sparse infrastructure. Amongst the nationalities serving in the Levant Army were British, Indian, Greeks and Senegalese.

The battle simulation provided much needed vigour and purpose to the Poles who undertook their attacking role with gusto, commencing with the rapid overrunning of a Greek position, unleashing a deafening barrage of mortar and machine-gun fire that sent the defenders fleeing in disarray. The Poles took many Greek prisoners and the British referees had to restrain the Poles' advance so as not to draw the exercise to a premature conclusion. The cities of Latrun and Nazareth fell to the Polish soldiers, who proceeded northward to capture the hill-top Church of the Transfiguration that surmounts Mount Tavor, moving quickly onwards to Safed, passing the Sea of Galilee en route. The exercises culminated with the Polish troops assaulting and capturing Mount Hazzar (Hill 425 near Tiberias) held by the Free French and their Senegalese troopers, who put up the toughest and most spirited defence the Poles had encountered. The French commander congratulated the Poles on their victory by sending them bread and wine, a courtesy that went down very well. The Poles were glad to meet Allied soldiers they could converse with and aided by wine, conversation and stories were shared and friendships made. Virile was a success; the Polish divisions greatly improved their battle readiness and much credit was given to the many drivers who proved adept at negotiating the serpentine mountain tracks by day and night at breakneck speed.

On completion of the exercise, Lieutenant General Holmes found II Corps to be fully ready for future combat deployment. General Wilson observed the exercises and was greatly impressed with the progress the Poles had made since the previous winter, both in training and the physical state of the troops, who had now thrown off the malaria they brought out of the Soviet Union. The manoeuvres were followed by a training spell in Palestine, during which the gunners of the Army Group Polish Artillery went through intensive training and practice firings, supported by the survey directorate practising their field tasks of artillery position fixing. The Polish II Corps was well equipped with artillery, fielding over 600 guns of varying calibres. The Polish Army possessed its own terminology for the naming of artillery regiments, having abolished the term field artillery before the outbreak of war they now classified artillery solely by calibre as light, medium and heavy. The corresponding terms in the British Army were field, heavy and super heavy and led to some confusion. These

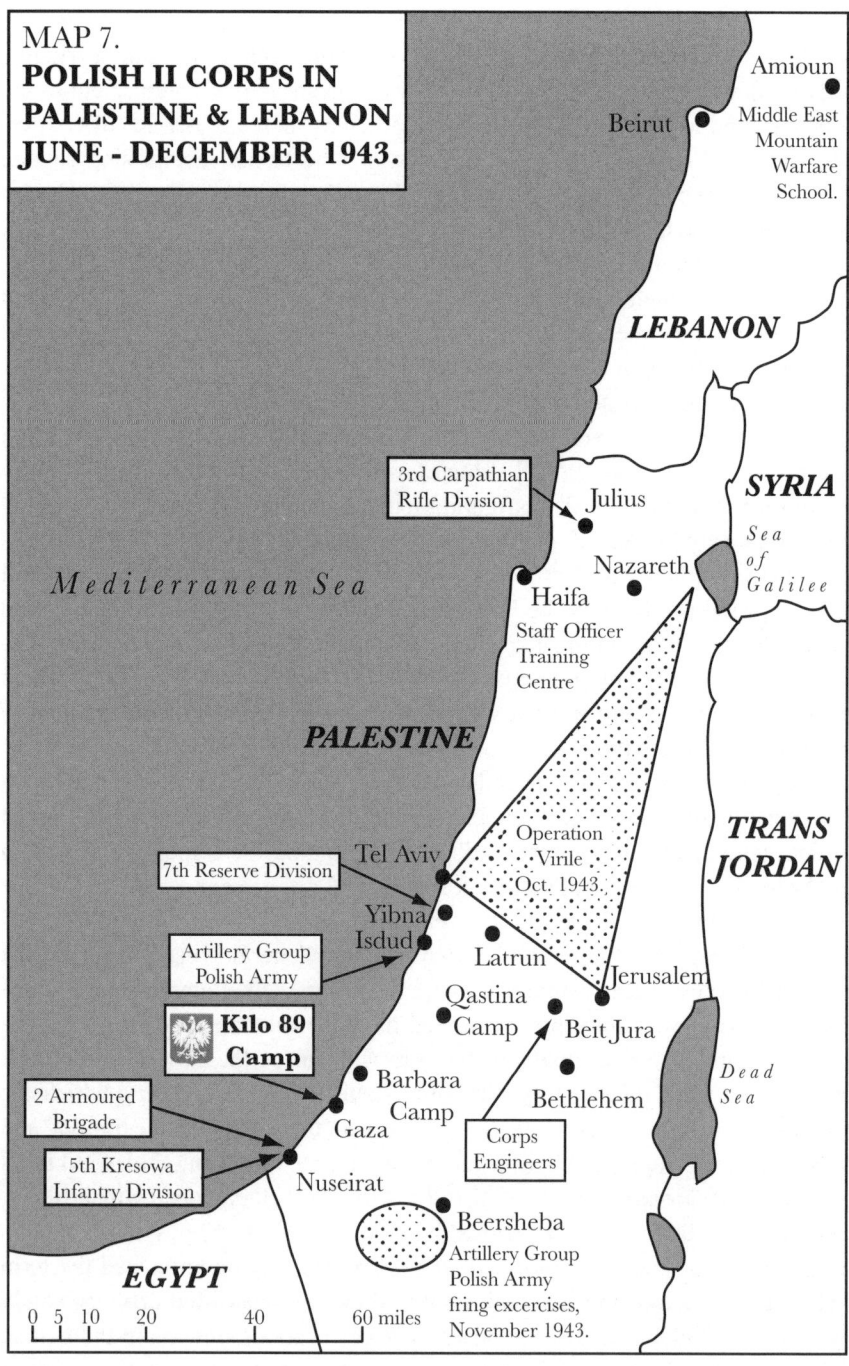

artillery exercises culminated on 26 November, at the range near Bersheba, where the entire II Corps artillery passed their firing examinations before Generals Sosnkowski and Patton and a huge crowd of spectators.

By the close of 1943, 2 Armoured Brigade was fully equipped with modern vehicles, although training still had to be conducted. With these achievements in training and equipping, Lieutenant General Anders had achieved the goal of preparing the Corps for operational readiness by the deadline of January 1944.

The strategic situation in the Mediterranean was developing fast – by late 1943 the Allied armies were advancing deeper into the Mediterranean, capturing Sicily in August and landing on mainland Italy on 3 September, nearly four years to the day since the Germans invaded Poland. Initial progress was promising, the Italian surrender largely mitigating any concerted defence. The Allies consolidated their foothold in Italy as the American Fifth Army landed at Salerno and occupied Naples on 30 September, whilst the British Eighth Army occupied the heel area around Taranto and Bari. However the Germans, although few in number in Southern Italy, mounted a calculated and effective fighting withdrawal that successfully delayed Allied progress and crucially denied the Allies the space to deploy more formations to exploit their successes. The American forces came up against the brunt of organized German defences at Salerno and received a thorough mauling at their hands. This was not going to be a short campaign against minimal opposition; Eisenhower's earlier warning of a heavy, protracted engagement was now unfolding. Instead of a rapid thrust up through the Italian mainland the Allies were now bottlenecked in the south and the Germans were taking stock of the situation and noting the strengths and weaknesses of their opponents, in particular the Allied troops' reliance on heavy artillery preparation and air support as preludes for daring thrusts. This reliance grew greater as the fighting dragged on and the men became weary – that was when more ships on the horizon were necessary, more men, more artillery, and more supplies in follow-up convoys were required, but were not there. The soldiers knew the reinforcements were not there. They began to fight for survival, rather than victory and the campaign began to get bogged down in a war of attrition.

The issue of involving troops from various national contingents began to rear its head in the autumn of 1943. The campaign so far had been an Anglo-American joint operation, but with the requirement for more troops to make progress, combined with the transfer of formations to England and strategic emphasis upon cross-Channel preparations, the Supreme Commander had to look to the 'minor allies' for more manpower. The British stance changed as they became embroiled in a costly march up the boot of Italy and they were now eager to bring in the sizeable Polish contingent in the Middle East to fight there. Most important were Anders' 3rd and 5th Infantry Divisions. Anders could now feel confident that II Corps would soon go into battle as a single cohesive Polish force. Eisenhower saw the unity of the Allied force as being paramount to success, but he was now discovering that the British and US concepts of the role of the Supreme Commander differed when it came to the degree of control the Allied Commander-in-Chief had over troops of nationality other than his own.

Eisenhower resolved that all contingents adhere to a policy of deploying their resources for the common good. This focus on the final, collective objective was key to the US leader, who was frustrated by the individual agendas of minor allies who were, he felt, characterized by 'pious aspiration thinly disguising the national jealousies, ambitions and recriminations of high-ranking officers, unwilling to subordinate themselves or their forces to a commander of different nationality or different service.'[2] The various national contingents would have to focus their efforts on the immediate conflict and not upon the post-war political environment, and the commanders would have to adapt their outlook and strategy to fit in with Eisenhower's plans, or be left out of the Allied equation altogether. General Eisenhower made this known to all contingents in a series of meetings held in early November at Algiers, and the French found themselves on the receiving end on 5 November, with Eisenhower demanding the commanders drop their rivalries and political agendas and get on with the war. The French were brought to heel, with the bickering Generals De Gaulle and Giraud having to make public display of their newfound unity.

Throughout the autumn Sosnkowski had devoted as much attention and time to II Corps as he could manage. This culminated with his decision to inspect the troops in Palestine that autumn, following visits to the Middle East and North Africa for conversations with the Allied commanders about the terms and organization on which II Corps would enter the Italian front. Meetings were scheduled with the Free French, then with the Supreme Commander of the Allied Forces in the Western Mediterranean, General Eisenhower in Algiers, then on to the commander of the Italian fronts, General Alexander, in his field headquarters in Italy and finally to Cairo to meet with Generals Wilson and Anders before reviewing the troops.

The purpose of these visits was to examine the desirability and feasibility of either deploying the existing Corps structure, or reorganization in the light of operational experience. The blunt reality was that the Corps as it was structured did not possess the strength to operate independently; there was an insufficient number of infantry organized into two divisions of two brigades each, which did not allow full, deep and prolonged exploitation of tactical success.

The available artillery could not provide full support for an infantry advance and there was little thrusting power, due to the small potential afforded by the one, weak armoured brigade. All Allied commanders involved with the deployment of II Corps being aware of these challenges, the scheduled series of meetings sought to bring the topic to the fore and find workable solutions to the deployment and structuring of the formation.

At the first of these meetings, on 6 November, General Eisenhower confirmed that reinforcements for II Corps were the paramount issue. Reserves totalling one-fifth of the Corps strength were required, whereas the Poles' resources to cover losses amounted to 2,000 soldiers, or about one-quarter of the required amount. Hence, Eisenhower proposed the reduction of the Corps to one infantry division of three brigades, a tank brigade and a number of corps units, and stressed that the Commander of II Corps would not always be able to exercise command over all of those forces.

Sosnkowski immediately informed the Polish cabinet and his staff in London, who, considering the foregoing analysis, agreed to the reduction of the Corps if that was the stipulation for its front-line deployment, but preferred a composition of one infantry division of two brigades, one armoured division and the necessary types of corps-level units. Such a change, the command felt, would provide an additional 4,000 soldiers for the reserve, whilst still affording the Poles a command of corps size with its attendant prestige. According to optimistic assessments the reorganization of the formations could be accomplished within six weeks. Both the staffs in London and Sosnkowski realized that once deployed in Italy, the Poles would come under full British control and their ability to steer II Corps' course would be greatly reduced; now would be the last chance to maintain II Corps as a viable, independent Polish command. However, Eisenhower stressed the need to focus on combat operations on the Italian front, in particular the value and need for infantry formations. To the US Supreme Commander, this was just another example of national agendas compromising the overall Allied strategy. Eisenhower was aware that reorganization would cause a delay, but in his directive for the prosecution of the Italian campaign issued on 8 November he stipulated that having occupied 'a general line, we will have to pause in order: (a) To reorganize and regroup our forces. (b) Thoroughly to repair communications and reserves in the forward area adequate for another big advance.'[3] He was anticipating this line being north of Rome, but the Germans were not planning on being so obliging and were hard at work creating a fortified chain across Italy south of Rome, named the Gustav Line.

While Sosnkowski and Eisenhower agreed on the need to establish adequate reserves, the two remained divergent over the resulting organization of II Corps. The question was passed on to the Polish and British staffs who were present, to jointly consider the benefits and shortcomings of both plans and present the resolution to General Alexander. Intense deliberations that day concluded that neither of the two proposals offered a more sustainable force than the other, and that to facilitate the rapid entrance of II Corps to the Italian front its existing composition and organization should remain unchanged.

News of these discussions was not well received by the British politicians in the Middle East. Anthony Eden was deeply concerned about what he believed were Sosnkowski's proposals and he telegrammed Churchill and Harold Macmillan immediately on 6 November, expressing great concern about breaking up II Corps:

> *I have just heard that General Sosnkowski who is believed at present to be at AFHQ Algiers, is arriving in Cairo within the next 24 hours or so with a proposal to break up the Polish Corps in the Middle East in order to provide material for building up the second armoured division in the United Kingdom. This would completely upset the balance of the Polish forces as at present organized in the Middle East and it has been suggested that it would probably make it impossible for the remaining Polish troops to be moved to Italy... General Anders appears to have no idea of what is contemplated and I know that the Allied liaison staff here are apprehensive of the proposal if carried out, both on General Anders and the Polish troops. Polish Corps have just completed a final exercise which was most successful, and are keen I understand to get to grips with the Germans... What really disturbs me, is the probable effect on the Russians if the entry into action of the Polish troops is still further delayed... I fear that, if General S.'s proposal is carried through and there is further delay in getting them into action, the effect in Moscow will be deplorable... I have already expressed my misgivings to the Commander-in-Chief Middle East who has inspected the Polish Corps and considers that they should be sent into action as soon as possible so as to maintain their training and morale.*[4]

Further confusion ensued when Harold Macmillan, the resident Minister in the Middle East, upon reviewing Eden's telegram felt that the Foreign Secretary had made an error in understanding the plans of General Sosnkowski. The General's plan was to convert the structure of the Corps into one infantry division and one armoured division so as to create an adequate pool of reserves to sustain combat losses, not to transfer soldiers out of the Corps to Britain.

The next meeting on Sosnkowski's Middle East trip was with General Alexander on 9 and 10 November. Sosnkowski was assured that the II Corps would comprise an independent Polish Corps of the Eighth Army, on its own stretch of the front. Alexander stated that in the initial phase of the Polish commitment to battle the force would be used in the mountainous area of central Italy, and that no part of the Corps would be detached and used separately, except if deemed truly urgent and indispensable to Allied operational needs. The only Polish formation that would be delayed in its entry to the Italian front was the armoured brigade, that would not join the Corps until the spring after completing full training.

Discussion then turned to Eisenhower's proposals. Alexander agreed with Eisenhower's proposed reorganization of II Corps – of reducing the Corps to one infantry division of three brigades along with an armoured formation, whilst retaining the title of a corps. Alexander, like Eisenhower previously, believed that the three-brigade division would be more effective at the front, calling on support from other Allied units as required, citing the achievements of II New Zealand Corps which had a near-identical structure to that proposed for the Poles. This notion did not meet with General Sosnkowski's approval; it was not the independent command he had been insistent upon and after lengthy discussions, General Alexander made a second proposal – the formation of one infantry division and an armoured division, very similar to the previous plan Sosnkowski had presented to Eisenhower, but with the proviso that if it was necessary to reinforce the infantry formations, such reinforcements would be drawn from the armoured units which would correspondingly reduce in size.

Sosnkowski then raised the findings of the Polish and British staff's deliberations in Algiers – that the lack of any tangible benefits from restructuring strongly supported retaining the Corps' existing structure during the initial phases of deployment, and that only if and when operational needs required should any restructuring or organizational changes be made. Alexander agreed to the transportation of the Corps to Italy in its existing structure, but he considered their subsequent reorganization to be necessary. In the latter part of the meeting Sosnkowski addressed the British politicians' fears by clearly stating the expected transfer of around 2,000 men to the Polish Air Force in Britain was to be taken from the 8,000 soldiers comprising the Polish Army in the Middle East, and not from any formations of II Corps and that in the future Polish reserves would be obtained from the recruiting of interned Poles in Germany and Switzerland. Sosnkowski stressed that II Corps should not be used to spearhead major breakthroughs in the German lines that would doubtless result in massive and unsustainable casualties. He went on to raise the long-term plan for II Corps, to become the nucleus of the Army for the post-war independent Poland, in light of which Sosnkowski would prefer its battle engagements not to include protracted attritional fighting, in order to preserve as much of its structure as possible.

General Alexander listened to these arguments and sympathized with them, but he could not rule out using II Corps for major offensive actions. A second meeting was held the next day during which Alexander confirmed that, as per the existing September plan, the Polish II Corps would be attached to the British Eighth Army under Lieutenant General Bernard Montgomery and that it was destined to be deployed on the Italian front for combat duties. The 3rd Carpathian Rifle Division, with its specialist training in mountain warfare, would be the first unit deployed to the Eighth's front on the River Sangro.

Sosnkowski's next meeting was held in Cairo on 13 November with General Wilson and Air Chief Marshal Douglas, with Anders also in attendance. Sosnkowski relayed to them that he considered it possible to adopt the final draft proposal of Alexander (that the Corps would ultimately consist of one infantry division of three brigades and an armoured division), along with the transfer of almost 2,000 soldiers from the Polish Army in the East in order to bolster the Polish Air Force in Britain. Wilson was in agreement with Sosnkowski's stance that the Corps should not be deployed in individual units but as a whole and offered to retrofit Polish units lacking heavy weapons once they were in theatre. However, Wilson was absolutely set against any immediate reorganization that would only delay the deployment of the Corps. He sent telegrams to the War Office and the Imperial General Staff stating that it was not feasible at that time to reorganize II Corps, owing to the fact that priority for new equipment was with the forces engaged in Italy, and that 'the Polish troops were fully prepared for battle, in excellent fighting spirit, and an asset that should not be wasted by delaying their departure to the front.'[5] Wilson also objected to the transfer of Polish soldiers out of his command to Britain, as this loss of manpower would weaken his forces in the Middle East. General Wilson preferred to put aside a final decision on these organizational changes pending the advent of appropriate guidance from London.

That Wilson was at divergence with Eisenhower and Alexander reveals the difficulties and strains he was under, as Brigadier Molony pointed out: 'He seems to have lost touch with the realities of war during his successive tenures of command in Persia and Iraq and in the Middle East.'[6] These tenures had also seen him preside over the creation and training of Polish II Corps and Wilson took pride in the achievement – restructuring it now would cast a shadow over his ability, at a time when that ability was coming under increasing scrutiny from the British General Staff and also the Americans. To defend the organization of II Corps was also to defend Wilson's position and reasoning. Eisenhower and especially Alexander were by contrast immersed in the current land combat of the Italian campaign and fully understood the need to update the organization of II Corps for it to succeed on the contemporary battlefield.

Later that same day, 13 November, Sosnkowski conducted several debates attended by Anders and the commanders of the major Polish units to discuss the proposed reorganization, future manpower replenishment and the rationale behind the plan. Sosnkowski voiced his view that Polish influence with the Allies could only wane as the war progressed and that his deep devotion to his soldierly duty to preserve Poland drove him to urge against fanatical heroics and partisan politics that were not, he stressed, going to achieve anything but self-destruction. Sosnkowski now proceeded upon his inspection of the soldiers in their encampments, where he made time to speak to individual soldiers and explain the situation Poland was facing. On 14 November Sosnkowski delivered a patriotic speech to II Corps, calling for their steadfast discipline and professional commitment to the Army in such difficult times for Poland and saying that the soldiers of II Corps were to uphold the traditions of heroism and valour on the battlefield. The men now knew for certain they were going to battle and as the largest Polish armed force, much would be expected of them.

In light of the reshuffling of the military hierarchy imposed by the new Polish government and Sosnkowski's choices for London appointments, Anders now forwarded his nominations for commanders of the principle formations of II Corps: Major Generals Zygmunt Bohusz-Szyszko as Deputy Corps Commander, Bronisław Duch to command the 3rd Carpathian Rifle Division, Nikodem Sulik the 5th Kresowa Infantry Division and Bronisław Rakowski the Armoured Brigade. These candidates met with Sosnkowski's approval, indeed the appointment to Corps Chief of Staff, Colonel Wiśniowski, was one of Sosnkowski's closest associates from the time he spent as Inspector of the Army and commander of the Polish southern front.

Sosnkowski now held another briefing, on 16 November for senior Polish officers at II Corps' Headquarters, where he tabled the proposals made by Generals Eisenhower and Alexander. Much lively and spirited discourse ensued. It was agreed to make the transfer of 1,900 troops to Britain, but that these should consist only of junior soldiers from non-line units, women volunteers and cadets. Much anger was expressed over the continued depletion of the Polish forces in the Middle East – more than 12,000 soldiers had been transferred to Britain during the period 31 May 1942 to 8 September 1943 and these transfers were directly to blame for the lack of reserves and the considerations of reducing and restructuring the Corps again. Sosnkowski then turned to the discussions he had undertaken with the Allied commanders in the Mediterranean concerning the necessity, in the absence of infantry reserves, to adopt the proposals of General Alexander – to thin out the Corps' front-line formations, and to do so as soon as possible to avoid delaying the entry of the Poles to combat. Any hold-up might lead to the Allies imposing even more severe changes that the Polish leadership would be unable to object to once the Corps was deployed in the operational area. Anders firmly opposed any further alteration to the Corps, which he intended should join combat with the Germans as soon as possible to counter the increasingly anti-Polish propaganda emanating from the USSR.

The conclusion of this final meeting was a foregone conclusion for Sosnkowski, as on 15 November the Polish Minister of National Defence, Major General Marian Kukiel sent a telegram informing him that both the Polish Prime Minister, Stanisław Mikołajczyk and the British Foreign Secretary, Anthony Eden, had intervened on the issue of accelerating the Polish II Corps' entrance into the Italian campaign, both men wishing to see the Corps deployed in combat. The British Government clarified that there would be no reorganization prior to deployment and no reduction in strength. The intervention was largely to counter accusations made by the Soviets that the Western allies were not pulling their weight in fighting the Germans. In late October Molotov had raised the fact that the communist Polish Division was already fighting with the Red Army on the Soviet front and had won a major engagement at the Battle of Lenino, to which Anthony Eden responded that he hoped the Polish II Corps would soon join the fighting in Italy. Molotov then claimed that General Sosnkowski's plans for the Army demonstrated he did not want the Poles to enter battle at all, but Eden defended Sosnkowski and reiterated that the Polish troops would definitely be used. He acknowledged 'it was partly our [the British] fault that they had not been in action earlier'.[7] On 16 November, Winston Churchill complained to General Sir Alan Brooke that he had contributed to the failure to rebuild the Polish II Corps and that shortly both Polish divisions would be sent to the front even if their states were incomplete, because of Soviet dissatisfaction with the Polish war effort.[8]

Sosnkowski fully appreciated the need for a rapid appearance of II Corps at the front; his enthusiasm was only tainted by the prospect of the Corps failing to sustain itself in the future. He proceeded at once to make arrangements for deploying the Polish troops to Italy. On the same day as the final conference with Polish officers, 16 November, he requested that Anders convey to General Wilson the message that he had no objection to the Corps maintaining its current organization as this would expedite the advent of Polish troops in battle. Wilson was delighted, exclaiming 'Everything for the front!'[9] and recommended a further conference once Sosnkowski had prepared his final guidelines for deployment.

On 25 November Sosnkowski published his guidelines for the deployment of the Polish Army in the East, the Army was to be divided into three echelons, the first comprising II Corps and the advanced echelon of the Polish Army in the East providing the Corps' base, which formed a cohesive entity readily capable of integrating into the British Army in Italy. The second echelon comprised Army Headquarters and units not in II Corps, and the third Army units remaining in Palestine, Syria and Iraq providing administration, supply, training and civilian support. Sosnkowski's guidelines delineated the shape of the Polish forces in the Middle East as had been proposed earlier by Sikorski, specifying that II Corps would be detached for combat operations with Anders as Corps

Table 5
Polish Order of Battle in the Mediterranean Following General Sosnkowski's Organizational Plan, November 1943.

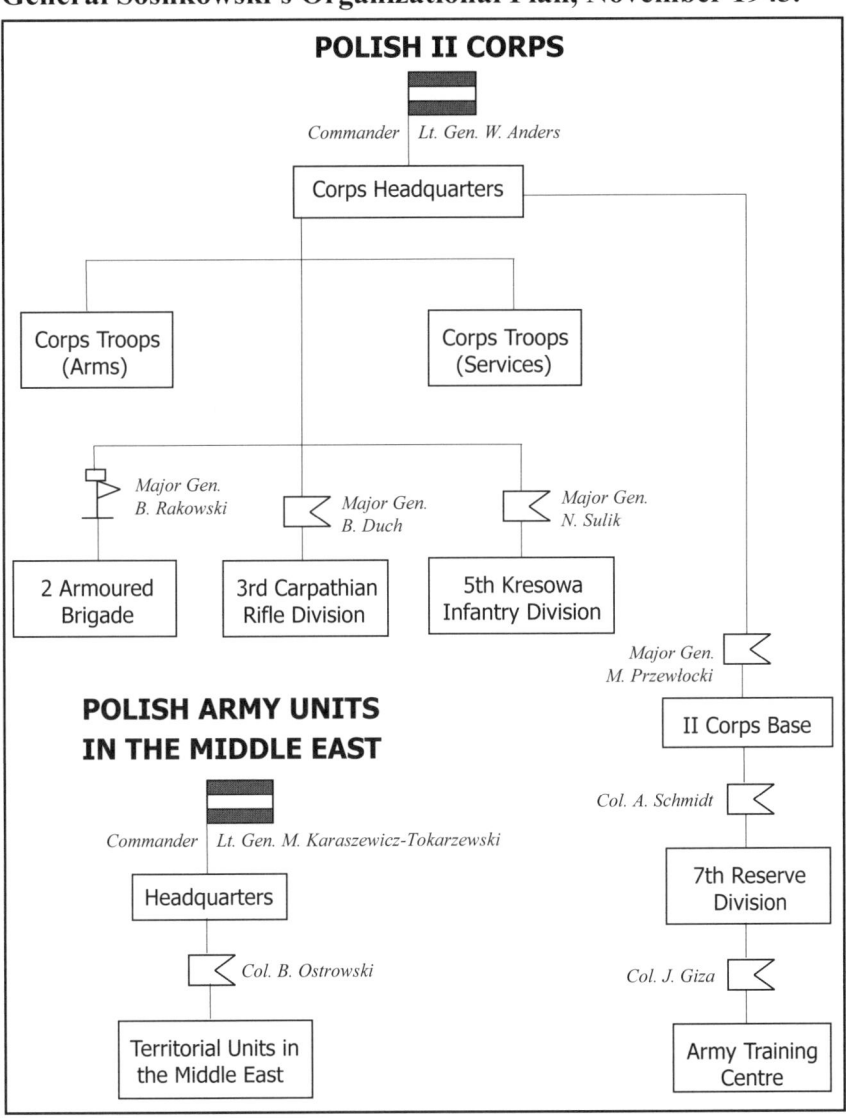

Commander. Sosnowski went further and named Anders as commander of both II Corps and the Polish Army in the East as a whole, officially confirming the role he already conducted.

The Big Three Allied leaders now conferred in Cairo, Tehran and once again in Cairo. The initial meeting ran from 22 to 26 November and broadly agreed the Anglo-American objectives and strategy for defeating Germany and Japan, the second in Tehran from 28 November to 1 December involved Stalin and Soviet views. On the return of the Anglo-American staffs from Tehran a third meeting in Cairo ran from 3 till 7 December 1943, an Anglo-American affair to iron out the details of strategy including operations in the Mediterranean. In attendance was General Sir Alan Brooke, who informed Anders and Sosnkowski of current developments over lunch on 4 December.

With Sosnkowski's plan now formalized it was ready for presentation to General Wilson, the British commander in the Middle East, who was delegated by London to finalize the deployment of II Corps. Anders and Sosnkowski met with General Wilson in his headquarters on 7 December, where the three discussed details of the transfer of II Corps to Italy and the reorganization of the Polish Army in the East. Consistent with his earlier stance General Wilson confirmed II Corps would be transferred to Italy without any further changes to the existing structure. This was a great relief to the Poles in the Middle East, who had feared their hard-won Army would be greatly reduced in strength on the eve of battle. The existence of a large Polish formation also kept alive Poland's dreams of freedom, as in the words of Harold Macmillan it was 'more than a military formation, it was a crusade.'[10] Wilson did not rule out however the possibility of restructuring the Corps as per Alexander's proposal if necessity required it. Principle in this regard General Wilson again expressed to Anders his concern as to how II Corps would gain reinforcements in the event of sustaining heavy casualties, and Anders reiterated his proposal that Poles forced to serve in the German Army would cross over the front to join II Corps at the first opportunity.

General Wilson listened patiently to Anders' suggestions and then informed him that there were already 750 of such Polish soldiers currently held in Allied prisoner-of-war camps in Italy. Anders expressed his desire to incorporate these men into II Corps, however it was beyond the remit of General Wilson to approve this, consent for such a plan must be received from London. Finally, Wilson stated that 2 Armoured Brigade would remain in Egypt until completion of its training before deploying to Italy in March, and that Sosnkowski's request for additional personnel to be sent to Britain would be actioned upon. Following this conference Wilson conferred to Anders that he would provide all possible assistance to the proposal to incorporate former Polish soldiers who had been coerced into German service.

On 8 December General Sir Alan Brooke met with Sosnkowski informing him of the principal outcomes of the Allied conferences at Tehran and Cairo. In connection with the transfer of the Poles to Italy, General Sir Alan Brooke relayed the logistical matters and in particular the provision of Landing Ship Tanks needed to convey heavy tracked vehicles that were in short supply and high demand in every theatre of war. As such the infantry formations would be the first to embark for Italy in conventional shipping, followed later by the armoured brigade as Landing Ship Tanks became available. The build-up of II Corps in Italy was therefore likely to take several months, during which time the infantry and support units could expect to be deployed on passive defence at the front pending the arrival of 2 Armoured Brigade and subsequent corps strength participation on the main front. The 7th Reserve Division was included in the order of battle to provide numerous base and training facilities in Italy, thus enabling the Corps to become an autonomous tactical and administrative component of the British Eighth Army. As a result of this, the division's 8 Rifle Brigade that had been turned into the Army Reserve Centre remained in the Middle East, largely to assist in the processing of Poles forced to serve in the German Army. Sosnkowski was satisfied with the proposal as he sought a gradual commitment of the Corps to the front line. This would allow time for the separate Polish command to become established in the country, thus becoming able to assert greater autonomous control over the Polish troops. Sosnkowski even secured a promise from Alexander to consult on the deployment of the Corps in combat – in fact all Allied commanders associated with the deployment of the Polish II Corps to Italy were (for the first time) in agreement with the plan.

Not all in II Corps were delighted with the news of imminent combat deployment as the chronicle of the 3rd Carpathian Division noted in its entry for 21 October.[11] The last delay to the Polish Army in Palestine was brought about by the desertion of Jewish soldiers. There had already been sporadic cases of individual Jews deserting throughout their period in the Middle East, but by late October 1943 the character of the desertions had changed into almost organized desertions involving a great many more men. The problem became more noticeable following Sosnkowski's speech and orders issued on 14 November, that the 3rd Division would be sent to the front line. The largest single instance took place on Sunday, 21 November, when upon returning from mass, the soldiers found a great number of Jews had deserted during their absence. The division lost 601 Jewish soldiers between 15 November and 10 December and in total II Corps lost an estimated 2,000 Jewish soldiers during this period.

The desertions were a highly contentious issue in Palestine and the British security and police forces set to searching for them, searches which also controversially included looking for illegal arms. Polish Military Police units were deployed alongside British detachments and almost immediately heated confrontations sparked outrage from the raided Jewish settlements of Ramat Hakovesh and Hulda. In response the British authorities issued the following:

> OFFICIAL COMMUNIQUE
>
> Highly tenacious accounts of the search which took place on the sixteenth of November at Ramat Hakovesh have been given wide publicity, calculated to mislead and inflame public opinion.
>
> The actual facts are as follows:-
>
> It was reliably reported to the security authorities that certain deserters from the Polish Army were harboured by Ramat Hakovesh and moreover, that at this settlement was a training camp for a unit of an illegal armed organization, and that illegal arms were concealed in the settlement.
>
> Ramat Hakovesh was accordingly searched on the sixteenth of November by a police unit acting in conjunction with Polish Provost personnel and Imperial military units.
>
> Certain military equipment was found in a camp within the perimeter of the settlement and the occupants were arrested. The Mukhtar and members of the settlement refused to co-operate in the search for Polish deserters and by their attitude rendered it impossible for the Polish authorities or police to ascertain whether any deserters were present in the settlement.
>
> The settlers further endeavoured by acts of violence to prevent the police from carrying out their lawful duty and generally subjected them to extreme provocation. Not withstanding the missiles and force to which they were subjected the police maintained the utmost restraint and carried their task to completion with a minimum of force.
>
> No shots were fired until on the withdrawal of the police party the violence of the settlers reached a hysterical pitch and the officer commanding the party, who was in charge of the rearguard, was obliged in order to secure the personal safety of the rearguard to fire two shots from his revolver at the feet of the aggressors, wounding one man but not seriously.
>
> Thirty-five persons were taken into custody.[12]

At Hulda the Polish provost initiated the search of the settlement for deserters, followed immediately by British authorities searching for hidden illegal arms, the latter resulting in the destruction of several settlers' property. The following trials in Jerusalem of the settlement's defence committee yielded nothing in favour of the British authorities, and no Polish deserters were discovered, although at the trial concerning Ramat Hakovesh three Jews were given lengthy custodial sentences.

Under the circumstances, the Polish military authorities in Palestine felt compelled to halt their raids on Jewish colonies from 9 December due to the bitter resentment among the population. Jewish spokesmen had made the charge that the raids were merely camouflage to enable the British police to hunt for arms without bearing responsibility for initiating the searches. Carried out on the pretext of searching for deserters from the Polish Army, the raids had not uncovered any such individuals and had merely proved that the Jewish settlements were not sheltering them. The Polish authorities indicated that they were inclined to discontinue their searches in the Jewish colonies, not wishing to become involved in local politics; the searches were the affair of the local administration. Where the deserters had gone remained a mystery.

Not all Polish Army units were to be deployed as part of II Corps for duty in Italy; a considerable number of administrative, supply and army-level units remained in the Middle East according to General Kazimierz Sosnkowski's 'Guidelines for the Organisation of the Polish Army in the East' issued on 25 November 1943. This directive divided the Army into three echelons as described earlier; the second and third of which were to remain stationed in the Middle East. The second echelon of the Polish Army in the East was redesignated as the Polish Army Units in the Middle East (its Polish title abbreviated to JWŚW) on 7 May 1944, with its headquarters based in Cairo. It was under the command of Lieutenant General Karaszewicz-Tokarzewski, the former commander of the 6th Infantry Division, with Major General Jozef Wind as his deputy and Colonel Stanisław Künster as Chief of Staff. The JWŚW included in its staff 1,700 women under the command of Colonel Antonina Płońska. The women worked in the storage depots, warehouses and canteens, and provided clerical and administrative assistance. Women also played a prominent role in the medical facilities, post offices, education and entertainment sections.

The JWŚW operated throughout Egypt and Palestine providing administrative, support and welfare services. The Transport and Supply section comprised 317 General Transport Company of the Polish Women's Auxiliary Service (which embarked for Italy in November 1944) and 320 General Transport Company under Major Jan Wrona. These companies conducted base and stores movements amongst the supply and ordnance depots in Egypt. Medical facilities included 4 General Hospital in Cairo that was deployed to Italy in June 1944, with hospital No. 5 being raised to take its place. The cadres of 8 Infantry

Brigade formed an Army Reserve Centre also based in Cairo that gave welfare and support to those soldiers permanently disabled from injuries or illness. A Civil Administration Training Centre was established to prepare garrisons and officials for the tasks of interim military government in Italy.

The wide range of civilian affairs gathered under the aegis of the Polish Army in the Middle East were administered by the headquarters of the Territorial Units based in Cairo and commanded by Colonel Bolesław Ostrowski. Mainly staffed by women of the Polish Women's Auxiliary Service, the command operated numerous small units including the Base Kit Store that looked after superfluous gear – the things officers were not supposed to take into the field, including bulky personal effects, souvenirs, trophies, musical instruments and other items collected during II Corps' period in the Middle East. The 15th Field Court Martial was based in Palestine, along with an attendant military prison in Jerusalem. Numerous administrative centres were established throughout Egypt, Palestine, Syria and Iraq that assisted in local government and in coordinating the welfare of displaced Polish civilians in the region, notably providing schools for the children. The Polish Red Cross and YMCA also continued to give valuable support to the Polish children and civilians in the Middle East.

Much concern had been expressed as to the education of young Poles below the age for military service who had been evacuated from the USSR. In response, Colonel Ignatius Bobrowski established the Junior School Command in Palestine from June 1942, based at Bashit, where a specially prepared youth camp began receiving boys from various Polish state schools across Persia and Iraq from July. All schools were transferred to Army control in November 1942, the boys' institutions being combined into the Junior Cadets School. A Junior Special School was established to cater for those children suffering from malaria and other infections acquired during their periods of captivity and transportation. The inclusion of children into the Army received no support from the British authorities but was funded by the Polish soldiers, who accepted their pay being reduced to the rank below that which they held, with the difference used to finance the schools and civilian welfare programmes.

The Junior School established at Bashit in August 1942 was for boys only, providing a general education with numerous additional military classes alluding to the traditions of the pre-war Cadets Schools of Lwów, Chelmno and Rawicz. The boys wore military uniform and were divided into five companies, the youngest in the first and the eldest in the fifth company. Classes commenced in September of that year and were predominantly taught by women from the PWSK, along with elderly soldiers, nuns and a handful of teachers from pre-war Poland. Materials for the schools were hard to come by, in particular Polish language text books, but Polish Jews living in Palestine from before the war were able to supply a limited number and the Army Printing and Publication Section then set to reproducing them for the schools. The tented accommodation and barrack room facilities at Bashit were not ideal and the school relocated to Qastina military camp in October 1942, before moving to its final location of Barbara Camp near Nazareth in July 1943. Over 1,500 boys were taught between 1942 and 1947, and upon leaving they had the option of joining the Army or attending high school or one of the mechanical schools which specialized in engineering, signals and aviation. These establishments were set up with the assistance of the British Army's Young Soldiers Battalions.

Girls were taught at the separate School for Young Volunteers initially based at Bashit, before it was relocated to Nazareth, to its new home in the Franciscan Monastery adjacent to the Basilica of the Annunciation. A smaller school for girls was established at Ain Karem, also in a Franciscan Monastery. For girls choosing to continue their studies after completing school, as opposed to volunteering for the forces, a higher level of vocational education was offered by the Gymnasiums and Lyceums in Nazareth, which from September 1943 ran courses in economics, business, administration and other skills regarded as essential for a functioning post-war Poland. The various schools operated until 1947 and the withdrawal of British forces from Palestine pending the creation of the state of Israel.

7

The Move to Italy

From December 1943 through to January 1944, the Polish II Corps was transferred from Palestine to the vast transit camp at Qassasin on the banks of the Suez Canal, awaiting deployment to Italy. Final unit training and personnel appointments were now made with 2 Armoured Brigade taking part in further exercises, this time at full brigade strength, following which the Brigade received orders to prepare for action from March. The American, General George Patton, reviewed formations of II Corps and met with Anders on 17 December 1943 in Cairo, where Patton noted in his diary that the Polish general was 'very much of a man… He has been hit [wounded] seven times… He told me, laughing, that if his corps got caught between a German and Russian army, they would have difficulty in deciding which they wanted to fight the most.'[1] Such comments sat well with Patton, but for the British staffs showed again that Anders was not prepared to hold back in criticizing the Soviets and that II Corps could be as much of a political hindrance as a military ally. But the Polish troops were needed in Italy and all efforts were now focused upon their dispatch.

The Polish formations would not be deployed directly to the front line; they would instead be concentrated in the rear base areas as the men and their equipment were shipped to Italy in convoys. Once fully regrouped, the formations would be assigned to the front as operations dictated. The Poles were to be concentrated in a base area near to the port city of Taranto. Base areas such as this were pivotal to the support of the Allied armies in all expeditionary theatres. The British established long-term, large depot facilities termed bases at all theatres of operation, the main function of which was to be the Rear Maintenance Area receiving, holding and distributing the vast quantities of materiel and stores required by a modern mechanized army, as well as the holding and training of reinforcements, the provision of medical care for casualties, and entertainment facilities for troops on leave.

To fulfil the function of base for II Corps it was initially planned to transfer all units of the Polish Army in the East to Italy along with II Corps, but the practicalities of sending so many supporting and ancillary formations by sea meant this could not be achieved. Instead only those elements immediately required to maintain II Corps as it disembarked and regrouped in southern Italy were despatched. The advanced echelon of the Polish Army in the East began arriving at Taranto from December 1943. It quickly became evident that this organization would have to be fully employed on the sole task of supporting II Corps and it therefore became subordinated to that formation, coordinating the supply of materiel and reserves along with the training of new personnel and formations. The organization adopted the title II Corps Base from May 1944, and from August adopted the same insignia of II Corps, the mermaid crest of the city of Warsaw named *Syrenka*, except it was on a blue not red background.

The movement of II Corps to Italy was organized by the British authorities as they possessed the means of transport and provision of maritime convoys. Polish merchant and naval ships were heavily involved, among them the merchant vessels *Batory* and *Puɫaski* transporting troops, and the warships *Krakus* and *Śląsk* escorting the convoys. The British authorities determined the quantity, order and composition of each convoy. Organization of the transport was not based on the size and disposition of the Polish units, but upon the availability of shipping and what units could be accommodated on whatever ships became available. This resulted in the transportation of the Corps' personnel and equipment taking from early December 1943 to mid-April 1944.

Thus II Corps' formations were transferred to Italy over a period of four months, five large convoys arriving at the port of Taranto more or less at intervals of two weeks – delivering 34,000 soldiers. None of the convoys carrying troops were attacked either from the air or sea, but a collision between two ships from the second transport in February resulted in the death of one gunner. There were a larger number of smaller convoys, especially those carrying equipment, most of which also landed at Taranto. Equipment and hardware was also shipped to the ports of Bari and Brindisi on the heel of Italy. Ships from Alexandria took 2 Armoured Brigade's tanks, vehicle commanders and drivers to be landed at Taranto, whilst the remainder of the personnel boarded troop ships in Ismailia and arrived in Naples on 14 April, moving eastwards shortly afterwards to the region Cardito–Cardittello.

Shipment of II Corps to Italy began with the 3rd Carpathian Rifle Division, and the bulk of the division's troops and forward detachments of the service branches – some 8,600 soldiers – departed from Port Said in Egypt on 21 December 1943, bound for Taranto. They were later followed by additional drivers and vehicles, and finally the last of the small units and remaining staff from Egypt. Units of all sizes arrived with their personnel and light equipment first, followed by their heavy equipment in separate convoys as shipping availability permitted. This resulted in vehicles and support equipment arriving sometimes in bulk or on occasion one vehicle at a time, accompanied by the specialist staff. There was no set order of precedence for the arrival of equipment, some branches opting to send all personnel together on the first transports and unaccompanied equipment afterwards. The time difference between the arrival of the personnel and the landing of equipment was up to two months. This had the result of delaying the specialist training of many services who were without their equipment and was a particular problem for the ordnance and electrical-mechanical engineering branches that were heavily dependent upon the tools of their trade. The remaining equipment and smaller units were transported amongst the numerous smaller convoys from Egypt, until all were installed on the Italian mainland by 16 March 1944.

The organization of convoys for the corps-level formations was to be conducted differently. These troops, especially the artillery and mechanized regiments, were divided into several transports, accompanied by groups of 200 personnel. The transport of personnel from these branches was not conducted by moving complete formations, but by filling ad hoc shipping availability with any troops from any branch who could be accommodated. The first to be despatched were forward command staff and advanced echelons of selected branches, who arrived on 8 January and commenced the organization of the disembarkation points and staging areas for the forthcoming convoys. These first branches comprised the Guard Battalion, detachments of signals, engineer and military police formations, along with the Field Map Section, field bakery, two transport companies, part of the Ordnance Supply Depot Company, Medical Stores Depot and the Technical Inspectorate. The next transport to Taranto on 25 January, delivered II Corps Headquarters and the first detachments of the corps-level troops; the Carpathian Lancers Regiment, light and heavy artillery of the artillery group along with its command staff, part of the 10th Corps Engineers Battalion and the 11th Corps Signals Battalion. The Corps' service branches also began arriving with 21 Transport Company and 30 Independent Transport Platoon Workshop, followed by the remainder of the electrical-mechanical engineering branch (PEME). II Corps Headquarters was up and running immediately and was issuing organizational orders the day following its disembarkation, 26 January 1944.

The remaining corps detachments from Egypt arrived in two convoys on 8 and 21 February. These included the remaining elements of the anti-tank and anti-aircraft artillery regiments, engineer and sapper formations and remaining command staff. Amongst the last units to be mobilized were the Reserve Tank Battalion under the command of Major Zygmunt Chabowski and Major Stanisław Siciński's 7th Reserve Reconnaissance Squadron. The 5th Kresowa Infantry Division also landed in Italy on 21 February and was fully installed by 16 March. By the end of March nearly all the Corps' accompanying equipment was in country. The convoy on 16 March carried the last remaining branches of the 3rd Division and corps-level units, and two new formations – the field surgical and blood transfusion units. Additional elements for the Base infrastructure were also landed.

126 *From Warsaw to Rome*

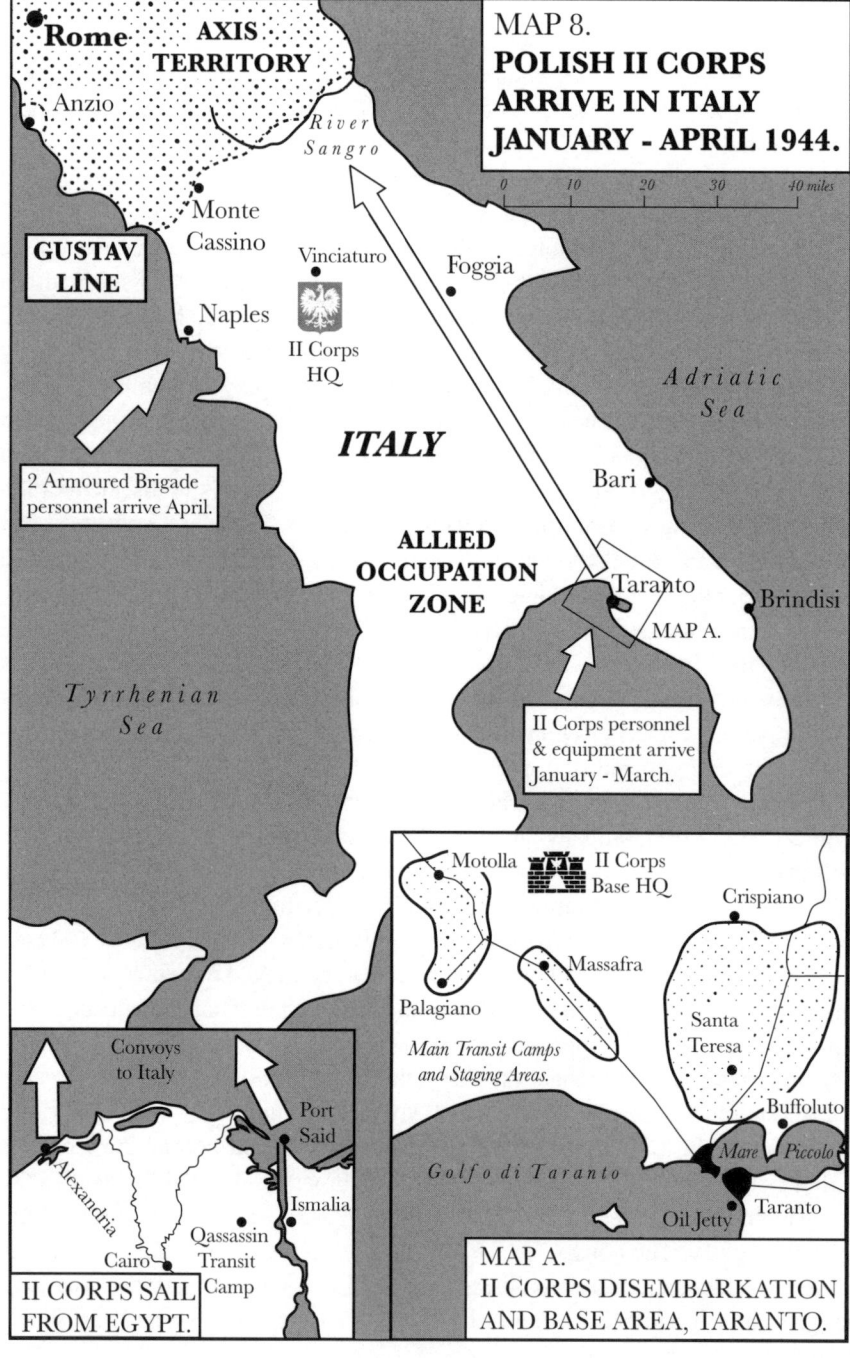

Ships carrying soldiers and their luggage to Taranto most frequently docked at the Oil Jetty berths 1–5, with equipment docking at Tossi and Porto Mercantile and even in a few cases discharged directly from the ships anchored in the lagoon Mare Piccolo, and at the quay in Bufflauto. The discharge of cargo proved to be a prolonged and complicated operation. As the troops of the 3rd Carpathian Rifle Division disembarked they marched on foot, carrying their light equipment to their allocated accommodation in tented encampments in the Santa Teresa area. Troops that landed at the Oil Jetty were fortunate enough to be driven into the city of Taranto, where they departed on foot to their billets. Formations whose accommodation was located in the more distant garrison towns of Mottola, Palagiano and San Basilio, were transported by truck. Vehicles were also used for the distribution of departmental equipment, heavy luggage and for soldiers unable to march.

Alongside the men and equipment were a great number of women serving in the Polish Army, who were also arriving. From December 1943 volunteers were recruited from the PWSK to serve in Italy in support roles; some 1,500 women volunteered, the remaining 1,700 continuing their work in Palestine and Egypt in the hospitals, schools and training centres under Colonel Antonina Płońska. The women who volunteered to accompany the Army into Italy performed administrative, clerical, hospital, and transport duties predominantly operating in the Base areas. The administrative and clerical staff became typists, translators and office workers, the economics branch operated the catering facilities, armed forces shops and warehousing/stores dumps. There was also a welfare and educational section which played a prominent role in cultural activities, having in its ranks three theatrical ensembles who would give concerts of music and dancing on Polish national holidays for the wounded in the base hospitals and convalescent home. Volunteers served in the casualty clearing stations, field and general hospitals alongside the military and Red Cross nursing staff. A detachment of volunteers also served on the British hospital train evacuating casualties to the base areas; these women assisted the doctors in care of the wounded and acted as translators.

The PWSK fielded 316 General Transport Company, and 318 Field Kitchen and Mobile Library Company. Other female detachments worked in 312 Map Section of 12 Geographic Company, where they assisted in the production of the finished maps. Signals-qualified women staffed telephone exchanges, radio stations, telegraph offices, cipher offices and operated the tele-printers. These companies also assisted in providing the base post office network (it was the women in the signal sections who were victims of the earlier mentioned underwear-stealing brown bear incident at the Qizil Ribat Camp, Iraq, in 1942). The PWSK formations moved to Italy in stages, the first to arrive being the medical staff, between January and March, the canteen, signals and entertainment units in February, 316 General Transport Company in April/May and the Inspectorate staff in June.

The disembarked II Corps was concentrated in the area surrounding Santa Teresa, in a sprawling complex of encampments named Robertson, Dowler, Alexander and Tucker. These lay on an east–west axis, slightly off the beaten track, and to the northeast of them, on the road to Monopoli, was O'Connor Camp. All these camps were exclusively accommodating the Polish forces. The area was well chosen, the hillsides protecting the camps from onshore storms and the dense olive groves providing a veil against aerial observation. The cultivated, well-maintained soil was easy to dig into and establish camp. The close proximity of the camp complex to the port of Taranto was a definite advantage also. Troops arriving on the ships could march to their accommodation without requiring valuable motor transport, and a plentiful supply of foodstuffs was obtainable from the nearby British 53 Detail Issue Depot. Only the ordnance sections had much further to travel, their work being conducted in Bari at the British Army's 500 Army Ordnance Depot, which was problematic in view of arranging transport between Bari and their accommodation.

In these five camps were accommodated all branches of the Corps ashore in Italy before 8 February. Only II Corps Headquarters and its attendant formations were based outside the camp complex, in the hilltop town of Mottola. From Mottola's elevation the entire bay of Taranto could be observed, by then a raft of merchant and naval vessels. The continuous influx of new transports resulted in constant relocation of the formations within the encampments. By the beginning of February, after the arrival of more corps units, the principle formations were based as follows: Camp Robertson was the hub for most artillery units, Camp Alexander housed the Corps Engineers, Camps Dowler and Tucker the troops and service establishments with anti-aircraft artillery based at Dowler, and Camp O'Connor, lying on the Monopoli–Taranto road, housed the Corps' supply and transport branches, along with the medical stores depot and 1 General Hospital. The Carpathian Lancers Regiment was based outside San Basilio. This order lasted until the arrival of the 5th Kresowa Infantry Division, whose numbers demanded a reorganization. To keep the divisional units together Camp Robertson was made available by transferring the artillery units to San Basilio in the second half of February, along with the artillery sections of 327 Detail Issue Depot.

In the garrison area of Santa Teresa, 32 Field Hygiene Platoon identified eleven water points, but only one of them on the road running to Taranto had water safe to drink. To prevent possible shortages of water, a daily allowance was set at one gallon per man. To allow bathing for the men weekly transports to the military baths in Taranto were arranged. There was however, no shortage of naturally available water; the weather was undoubtedly the most unpleasant surprise for the troops arriving there. The wet, cold and raw winter was the very antithesis of the sunny Italy of tourist brochures. The soldiers quartered in tents had a particularly miserable time in the wind and rain. The weather, combined with rampant venereal disease and typhoid fever amongst the civilian populace, soon began to affect the men's health. Typhoid bacteria as well as dysentery were detected in a number of water points around the camp area.

By April the base was host to 6,000 personnel under the Base Commandant Major General Marian Przewłocki, with Colonel Wilhelm Wilk-Leśniak as Chief of Staff, Lieutenant Colonel Stanisław Żelaski as Quartermaster, and Lieutenant General Bolesław Szarecki, Chief Hospital Inspector. Principal base units included the 7th Reserve Division, Army Training Centre, hospitals and the Santa Teresa transit camp, all of which were dwarfed by the vast stockpiles of equipment and supplies offloaded from ships in the ports of Bari and Brindisi to feed the ever-growing demands from the front. The Poles now found themselves once again in an active war zone, surrounded by endless columns of soldiers and equipment flowing towards the front whilst the air above was filled with the roar of aircraft.

Throughout December, Major General Bohusz-Szyszko had held a series of talks with Lieutenant General Leese concerning the immediate deployment of the 3rd Carpathian Rifle Division that was projected to be battle ready by 25 January 1944, ahead of the main body of II Corps. The Poles were against the idea of separating the division and the issue was finally resolved at a meeting between Leese, Bohusz-Szyszko and Duch, where it was agreed that the Carpathian Division would indeed proceed to the front as soon as possible with movement orders being issued in the first week of January. With the dispersion of the troops to the front the business of replacing the tented facilities with more permanent structures to house the various administrative, training and maintenance establishments began. The large programme of building work and general construction projects in the base and line of communications area were executed by the Artisan Works Company and the Garrison Engineers, both based in Mottola. Construction underway at this time included the military prison, and extensive workshops for heavy engineering maintenance including the servicing of tanks and lorries.

The principal Polish base establishment in Italy was the 7th Reserve Division that performed the role of Corps Reception Camp and Reinforcement Holding Group, receiving and training new soldiers in establishments based around the town of San Basilio. The 7th Division included two Reinforcement Holding Units; the 23rd and 24th Infantry Battalions together forming 7 Infantry

Brigade. The Reinforcement Holding Units collected soldiers from both the Santa Teresa Transit Camp and the Reception Centre, quartering them whilst arranging their onward transfer to the various branches of the Corps. Over the coming months, 7 Brigade gradually expanded its role to include driver training, mortar, anti-tank and chemical warfare instruction. To facilitate this training process, 26 British Liaison Unit, previously titled the Military Mission, continued in its role of mentoring the Polish officers in the latest facets of modern mechanized warfare, in particular the importance of army administration and logistics. Numerous interpreters were employed and the working language was frequently French.

Alongside 7 Infantry Brigade, the division had a similar organizational layout to a standard infantry division, whose training regiments provided instructors in specialist areas including artillery and signals, with the units' headquarters providing demonstrations and equipment displays, all of which supported the training provided by the Army Training Centre. The 7th Mixed Artillery Regiment for example, had a staff of 91 instructors and comprised a headquarters, 1 Mixed Battery of field and heavy artillery, 2 Anti-Tank Battery and 3 Anti-Aircraft Battery. The remainder of the division's companies were similarly arranged into training cadres with small staffs such as the 7th Machine Gun Company with 22 instructors. The 7th Division commenced training operations in March 1944 and by May the monthly total for those completing training was 807.[2]

The separate Army Training Centre provided training establishments for new recruits and soldiers who were being transferred to different branches. The centre was composed of two branches of the Chief Instructor's Office – Arms, and Services. The arms section included Special Courses, Infantry School, Artillery School, Signal School and the Wireless School, while from May onwards Engineers were trained at Capua in the Polish Wing of the British Engineering Training Centre. The services section included Transport and Supply, the Ordnance School, Electrical & Mechanical Engineers School, and the Administration School.

By the time of the Battle of Monte Cassino the Supply & Transport Corps comprised over 5,000 personnel, making it the largest of the supporting formations. Instruction was provided for motorcyclists, truck drivers, car and jeep drivers and for more specialist vehicles such as the Diamond-T tank transporters. The training of PEME and Supply and Transport troops was largely conducted by front-line units, owing to the lack of equipment in the base area. The Army Training Centre also housed the Polish Women's Auxiliary Service Officers' and Cadets' School for female volunteers, with Captain M. Musztak-Olechowicz commanding the Warrant Officer Driving School. Tactical and PEME training was conducted at the British Central Mediterranean Training

Centre and Army Tactical Centre. Polish soldiers under British instruction remained subordinate to the administrative command of the Polish Army Training Centre staff, but were subject to the authority and syllabus of the British training centres.

The Army Training Centre began running training courses in Italy commensurate with the 7th Reserve Division in March 1944, with the first batch of 27 trainees completing their courses in May, 138 more in June (from when the centre became permanently attached to the 7th Reserve Division) and 280 in July.[3] The various military schools located around San Basilio provided specialist instruction and training with the assistance of the divisional elements of the 7th Reserve Division.

The armoured formations required their own specialist base units and these began transferring to Italy from March. The first armour support unit to land was the 7th Reserve Reconnaissance Squadron, arriving in Taranto on 22 March before being based at San Basilio as part of the 7th Reserve Division. The Reserve Tank Battalion arrived at Naples on 12 April, its equipment landing at Taranto. General Anders subsequently ordered the restructuring of these armoured training and replacement units on 15 April to allow them to integrate fully with the British system of organization. To this effect, the two formations were merged into the Armoured Training Centre from 12 May, that was detached from the Polish base organization and operating instead as the Polish Wing of the British 1st Armoured Replacement Group (Central Mediterranean Force) at Frigento, 50 miles east of Naples. The centre was tasked with the supply of tanks, armoured cars and self-propelled guns, complete with crews, to the armoured, reconnaissance and artillery regiments. Due to vehicle shortages training was often conducted in tanks that had been knocked out in combat and had been repaired to a serviceable, if not combat-fit state. The graduates from the schools were sent to the Forward Armour Delivery Squadron for assignment to the fighting regiments.

The training of non-English-speaking units, both in the operational area and also in the rear was greatly assisted by the work of the Printing Section. The latter published thousands of pamphlets, translations, manuals and other printed materials, as well as novels, prayer books, calendars and diaries. Up to the cessation of hostilities the Printing Section had published: of 52 different manuals, a total of 228,109 copies; 302 pamphlets totalling 96,120 copies; 143 school text books and novels, totalling 362,981 copies – adding up to 479 publications with 687,210 copies printed in all.[4]

Numerous units of the Polish Women's Auxiliary Service were deployed in the base areas around Taranto, with 316 General Transport Company arriving at Taranto on 4 May 1944, under the command of Lieutenant Colonel Maria

Trojanowska; all the women had volunteered for active service. The company's primary duty was to transport battlefield casualties received at the base railhead to the General Hospitals around Taranto, and on occasion to transport German prisoners of war to their detention camps. The company was equipped with American 3-ton Dodge trucks armed with light machine guns and the women were all issued with Thompson sub-machine guns and revolvers. The company had a strength of 324 and was based in a camp at San Basilio, on the road between Bari and Taranto. Later in the year a second women's transport company was also transferred to Italy, the 317th Company.

Other important administrative functions included managing the financial and legal branches. The Pay Corps' Chief Paymaster's Office was based at Mottola along with other administrative units. II Corps' pay office had three principal functions – handling pay and allowances and accounting for deductions, maintaining personnel records, and advising all units about accounting procedures. Agents dealt with the officers' pay, with the Pay Corps administering the allowance for married officers, while payment of the soldiers' wages was enabled by an annual grant of three and a half million pounds from the British Government. Constituent elements included Corps and Division Cash Offices, Financial & Audit Office, Command Pay Office and Transit Cash Office. Strict measures were enforced to prevent the black market exchange of currency.

The Judicial Service was administered from San Basilio by Judge Colonel Stanisław Rohm, who oversaw the operation of the field courts martial. Each formation was assigned its own courtroom, along with the 12th courtroom at Campobasso and the 14th courtroom located at II Corps Base at Mottola. Those found guilty and remanded into custody were removed to the military prison to serve their sentence, which at this time was still under construction at Mottola. Apart from this detention facility there was also a prisoner-of-war camp at San Domenico for captured German soldiers.

In addition to these military establishments the wider scope of responsibilities tasked to Polish II Corps necessitated the inclusion of several ancillary sections normally associated with formations at higher Army level. These comprised the Army Education & Welfare Section and the Army Training Centre that enabled the Corps to function as a self-contained unit, an important ability considering its remoteness from the Polish authorities in London. The Army Education and Welfare Section was tasked with stimulating morale, primarily through the early dissemination of news. This was achieved through the production of two Polish newspapers, a daily *Dziennik Zolnierza* (Soldiers' Daily) and a weekly *Orzel Biały* (White Eagle). Frequent visits were made to the hospitals and the convalescent home to provide tutoring and courses. Organized educational activities were found to improve morale in the military prison and the reinforcement holding unit (7 Infantry Brigade), and a wide range of short courses were provided on topics from woodwork to mathematics that proved very popular. Special lectures were given to soldiers recruited from German POW camps and those who had been forced to serve in the German Army, to bring them up to date with current affairs. The section broadcast regular programmes to the Polish forces and possessed a transmitter capable of reaching Poland, that Lieutenant General Anders used to address their home country on 3 March 1944.

The Welfare Service administered hotels and social and rest centres for officers and enlisted ranks on leave, along with attendant canteens and cultural services such as cinemas and libraries. The affiliated Entertainment Group provided movies, musical concerts and theatrical productions. Popular artists included the singer and dancer Elżbietą Niewiadowską, Renata Bogdańska, Leon Koller, Gwidon Borucki and Adam (Gipsy) Hauersztok. The wealth of Polish cultural and educational facilities led to the base area being nicknamed Little Poland. In addition to military activities, it provided personnel trained to assist with the civil administration of Italian towns and districts, maintaining public services and order. These units comprised Civil Administration Teams and interim town mayors wherever there was an absence of effective local authority.

The development of the Polish Base proceeded at a speed and came to embrace the training and organizational elements for an army scale formation, which the Poles hoped would go on to become the basis of their new Army in post-war Poland. Though this ultimately failed to materialize, the Polish II Corps was nonetheless constantly maintained with the required volume of ammunition and equipment, which given the challenging terrain of Italy was a considerable feat accomplished only by coordinated inter-service cooperation. This administrative aspect was one of the key elements of modern warfare that the British training staffs imparted to the Poles; its application greatly enhanced their fighting potential. The establishment of Polish welfare and educational units throughout the Middle East went hand-in-hand with the goal of providing a generation of young people with the varied skills needed to rebuild post-war Poland, so education and training in civilian administration were very much to the fore. Sadly, these plans never came to fruition and the young men and women were dispersed along with the service personnel across the world after the war.

The Polish II Corps of the Second World War was not the first Polish exile army to fight in Italy – from 1797 to 1803 a Napoleonic Polish Legion campaigned in the Lombardy Republic. Poland had disappeared from the map of Europe in 1795, following the third partition of Poland by Austria, Prussia and Russia, but Napoleon Bonaparte recognized the fighting potential of the many displaced Polish soldiers and promoted the creation of a Polish Army in Italy to attack their common enemies. To this end, Napoleon summoned the greatly respected cavalryman General Jan Henryk Dąbrowski to Paris in 1796, to raise legions from exiled Poles and those who had escaped from partitioned Poland, to form part of the army of the newly created Lombardy Republic. General Dąbrowski launched a manifesto to recruit these men and commissioned a song, the 'Anthem of the Polish Legions in Italy', to rally the troops – it is now the national anthem of Poland. Some 7,000 men responded to the call and from these Dąbrowski created a disciplined army, complete with Polish uniforms and insignia, with the concessions to epaulettes in the colours of Lombardy and a tricolour bow. The Legions began fighting alongside Napoleon from May 1797 and continued until the beginning of 1803, notably entering Rome in May 1798 and being at the Battle of Tresia in June 1799. General Dąbrowski was highly decorated, receiving amongst others the award of the Orders of Militari Virtuti and the French Légion d'Honneur during his military career.

Unfortunately the Polish Legions never managed to fight their way through to liberate Poland from the Russians, as they dreamed of doing. Instead, following the 1803 peace treaty between France and Russia the Legions were dispersed, Napoleon fearing that growing disappointment amongst the Russian-hating Poles could lead to a rebellion in the Army. To prevent this he despatched 6,000 Poles to the Caribbean island of Haiti, to suppress a local rebellion. Only 300 returned. Many Polish soldiers of II Corps drew parallels between their situation and that of the earlier Polish Legions, and references to this are frequently encountered amongst the contemporary Polish-language literature of the period.

(*Above left*) Polish anti-aircraft gun and equipment abandoned after attack by German aircraft, Battle of Bzura, Poland, September 1939. The German Blitzkrieg assault based on close cooperation between army and airforce proved a devastatingly effective new means of attack. (Source: ww2db.com, no picture credit available)

(*Above right*) The partition of Poland, Brest, 21 September 1939. Red Army Commander Vladimir Yulianovich Borovitsky (in leather coat) leans over a map of central Poland to face German General Heinz Guderian, to finalize the demarcation of the German–Soviet border following their joint invasion of Poland. (Source: ww2db.com, from German Federal Archive, Bild 101I-121-0010-11)

(*Left*) The German invasion of Poland was one of the most aggressive assaults ever launched and appalled the world through the deliberate targeting of civilians. Here, a 10-year-old Polish girl Kazimiera Mika mourns the death of her sister, gunned down by a strafing German aircraft, near Warsaw, 13 September 1939. (Source: ww2db.com, photo by Julien Bryan)

Polish prisoners of war captured by the invading Red Army being marched into captivity. (Source: Wikimedia Commons, uploaded from Soviet newsreel September 1939, also Czerwony Sztandar (Lviv newspaper) September 1940, by unknown TASS war correspondent.)

(*Above*) Major General Alexei Panfilov, Head of the Soviet Mission to the Polish Army. A victorious tank commander against the Japanese, Panfilov was assigned to the General Staff in Moscow and placed in charge of the Red Army reserves, including the Polish Army. (Source: Polish blog, http://postacie.ovh.org/panfilow.htm no picture credit available)

(*Above*) General Władysław Sikorski, the Polish Prime Minister and Commander-in-Chief, a statesman held in the highest regard by the Allies. His untimely death in 1943 deprived the exiled Poles of a leader highly experienced in the complexities of international politics. His successors never commanded the same respect or influence. (Source: United States Library of Congress LC-USW33-019087-C)

(*Left*) Lt. Gen. Władysław Anders shortly after his release from Soviet detention and appointment as commander of the Polish Army in the USSR. Having shared the same hardships as the rest of the army detained in the USSR, Anders commanded the near fanatical allegiance of his soldiers. (Source: ww2db.com, original from Anders, Władysław, *Bez ostatniego rozdziału*, Warsaw, 1990)

Polish policemen and civilians being forcibly marched out of Poland by Soviet Internal Security Troops, the NKVD, 1939. These, and hundreds of thousands of other Polish civilians were banished to the remotest regions of the USSR for use as hard labour and farm hands. The death toll was catastrophic. (Source: ww2db.com, no picture credit available)

(*Above*) Cavalry of the Carpathian Lancers Regiment, Polish Independent Carpathian Rifle Brigade on parade in Palestine, 1940. These soldiers had escaped from Poland after 1939 and joined the French Army of the Levant in Syria. Following the defeat of France in 1940 the Brigade marched out of Vichy-controlled Syria and into Palestine to continue the fight alongside the British Army. (Source: Wikimedia commons)

(*Above*) General Georgi Zhukov of the NKVD, Political Commissar of the Soviet Mission to the Polish Army. Zhukov had the full confidence of Stalin and he subsequently commanded great executive authority within the Soviet system. (Source: Author collection, no picture credit available)

(*Left*) Major General Kopański, commander of the Independent Carpathian Rifle Brigade and subsequently the 3rd Carpathian Rifle Division. Following General Sosnkowski's appointment as Commander-in-Chief, Kopański was recalled to London to serve as the Polish Army's Chief of Staff. (Source: ww2incolor.com, no picture credit available)

(*Below*) Soldiers of the Polish Independent Carpathian Rifle Brigade parade before British and Polish dignitaries in Palestine, 1940. (Source: Wikimedia commons)

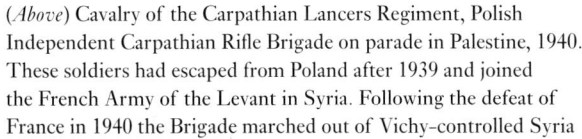

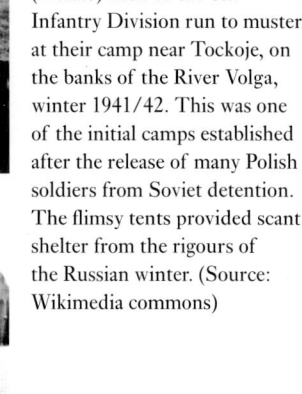

(*Above*) Signing of the Mutual Friendship Pact between Poland and the USSR, Moscow, 4 December 1941. From left: Lt. Gen. Anders, General Sikorski, Stalin, Molotov. (Source: Wikimedia commons)

(*Middle*) Men of the 6th Infantry Division run to muster at their camp near Tockoje, on the banks of the River Volga, winter 1941/42. This was one of the initial camps established after the release of many Polish soldiers from Soviet detention. The flimsy tents provided scant shelter from the rigours of the Russian winter. (Source: Wikimedia commons)

(*Left*) Inspection of the Polish Army in the USSR by General Sikorski (far right) in December 1941. To the left of the podium stands Lt. Gen. Anders, Col. Okulicki and a Soviet officer. (Source: Wikimedia commons)

The snow-clad steppes of the border with China and Afghanistan – a bleak and inhospitable environment that became the Polish Army's second and final base in the USSR. General Anders sits in the snow during a training exercise as Soviet officers (in peaked caps) maintain a watchful presence, early 1942. Note the Polish soldiers are now wearing British Army uniforms and helmets. (Source: Wikimedia commons)

(*Above left*) General Sikorski with Lt. Gen. Anders (behind) review women volunteers to the Polish Army in the USSR, December 1941. Creating military roles for women greatly facilitated their release from Soviet detention. (Source: ww2incolor.com, image 621349. No picture credit available)

(*Above right*) A cargo ship loaded with Polish evacuees arrives at Pahlevi, Iran, having sailed across the Caspian Sea from Krasnovodsk, USSR. The open deck is crammed with soldiers and civilians. (Source: ww2incolor.com, image 626158, no picture credit available)

The brutality of Stalin's dictatorship; the decaying body of a major of the 1st Light Horse Regiment. Taken prisoner by the Soviets in 1939 he was shot through the head by the NKVD in 1940 near Katyn. The bodies of several thousand Polish Army officers were discovered by the retreating German Army in a mass grave, all were found with their hands tied behind their backs and all killed with a single pistol shot to the back of the head. By publicizing the discovery Goebbels delivered a propaganda coup that almost destroyed Allied unity. (Source: Wikimedia commons)

(*Left*) Lieutenant General Sir Edward Quinan, Commander-in-Chief of British Troops in Iraq until August 1942. (Source: *PAIFORCE: The official story of the Persia and Iraq Command 1941–1946*, prepared for the War Office, 1948, HMSO, Crown Copyright)

(*Above*) Lieutenant General Sir Henry Pownall, Commander-in-Chief of Persia and Iraq Command, March to September 1943. Pownall oversaw the creation of II Corps out of the Polish Army in the East. A hard taskmaster, he moulded them into a modern fighting formation of British outline and ordered Anders to follow the Allied stance over the Katyn massacre and to rein in anti-Soviet agitation amongst the Polish soldiers. (Source: *PAIFORCE: The official story of the Persia and Iraq Command 1941–1946*, prepared for the War Office, 1948, HMSO, Crown Copyright)

(*Above*) General Sir Henry Maitland Wilson, Commander-in-Chief of Persia and Iraq Command from August 1942 to February 1943 and subsequently Supreme Allied Commander Mediterranean. Wilson was a strong advocate for the Polish Army and greatly facilitated their development. His physical bulk led to the near-official nickname 'Jumbo', and even his command was assigned an elephant as its formation sign, which he took as a compliment, pointing out that elephants are renowned for their intellect. (Source: *PAIFORCE: The official story of the Persia and Iraq Command 1941–1946*, prepared for the War Office, 1948, HMSO, Crown Copyright)

(*Below*) Carpathian Lancers Regimental HQ at Mena Camp, Palestine 1942. Note the pennon flying in the foreground; the chequered square contains a block of colour for each of the four squadrons, whilst the trailing banner is in the red and blue colours of the Regiment. (Source: Author's collection, photo by Lieutenant Henryk Siemiradzki)

(*Left*) Valentine tank of 2 Tank Brigade during training exercises in the Middle East, 1943. Training of tank crews took place in Egypt and Iraq before moving to Palestine with the whole of II Corps in late 1943, where the Brigade was outfitted with modern Sherman tanks. (Source ww2incolor.com, image 477842, no picture credit available)

(*Right*) Lieutenant General Karaszewicz-Tokarzewski, commander of the 6th Infantry Division and subsequently Deputy Commander-in-Chief Polish Army in the East and following Sosnkowski's organizational plan, commander of Polish Army Units in the Middle East, the JWŚW. Photographed in Jerusalem, 1942/43. (Source: United States Library of Congress, LC-M33-12965-C)

(*Above*) Marmon Herrington armoured car of the Carpathian Lancers Regiment on patrol in the Palestinian desert, a lonely activity. (Source: Author's collection, photo Lieutenant Henryk Siemiradzki)

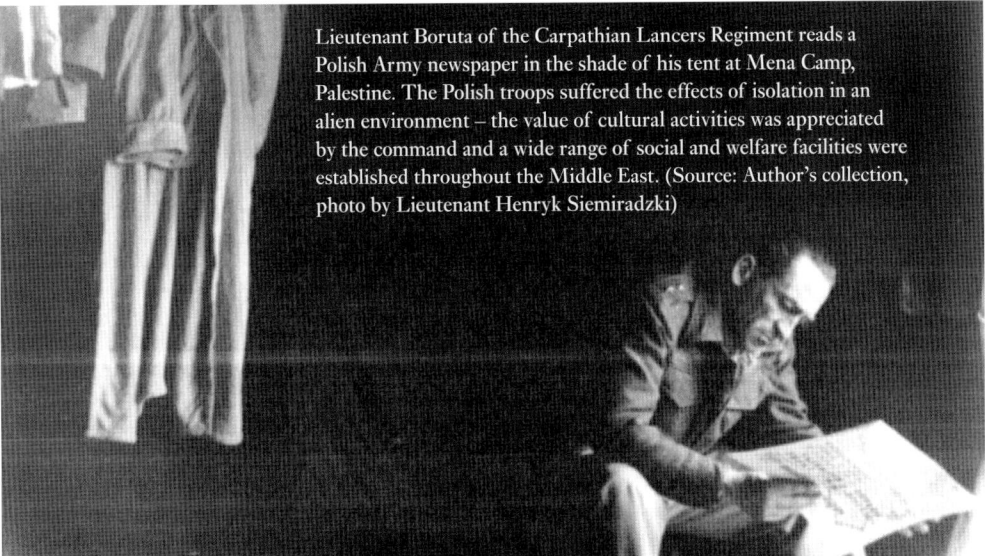

Lieutenant Boruta of the Carpathian Lancers Regiment reads a Polish Army newspaper in the shade of his tent at Mena Camp, Palestine. The Polish troops suffered the effects of isolation in an alien environment – the value of cultural activities was appreciated by the command and a wide range of social and welfare facilities were established throughout the Middle East. (Source: Author's collection, photo by Lieutenant Henryk Siemiradzki)

(*Above*) Two transport companies of II Corps were staffed entirely by women – 316 and 317. Photo taken in the Middle East, either Iraq or Palestine, note the RAF roundel painted on the cab roofs for recognition from the air. (Source: ww2incolor.com, image 62882081, no picture credit available)

General Patton exchanges formation insignia with Lt. Gen. Anders during Patton's inspection of Polish forces in the Middle East in late 1943. The American General was greatly impressed by the toughness and fighting zeal of Anders and his soldiers. (Source: ww2db.com, no picture credit available)

(*Right*) Lt. Gen. Anders and Master Zygmunt Deyczakowski on the deck of MS *Batory* during the sea passage from Egypt to Italy, 1944. Convoys of Polish merchant ships such as this liner, escorted by Polish naval vessels, ferried Polish troops across the Mediterranean for five months to establish II Corps in Taranto, Italy. (Source: Wikimedia commons)

(*Below*) Allied generals deliberate their plans, from left: Lt. Gen. Leese, Eighth Army Commander, Lt. Gen. Anders, II Corps Commander and Maj. Gen. Duch, 3rd Carpathian Infantry Division Commander. River Sangro sector, March 1944. (Source: Divisional photo album of 3rd Carpathian Rifle Division in Italy, 3 *Dywizja Strzelców Karpackich w Italii, Firenze*, 1945, published by the division's own press, all photos by Polish Army photographers. This photo by J. Fuks)

(*Above*) Supply and logistics was a vast undertaking, moving a large mechanized army and the provisions to keep it running through the Apennine Mountains was a tortuous and time-consuming endeavour. (Source: Łoziński, Marian, *Przechodniu, Powiedz Polsce…*, Kraków 1972, many editions before 1994)

(*Above*) Observation post of the 12 Podolski Lancers on the Capracotta sector. Observation and harassment of the enemy were the mainstay of operations during the winter months on the Sangro River front. (Source: Divisional photo album of 3rd Carpathian Rifle Division in Italy, 3 *Dywizja Strzelców Karpackich w Italii, Firenze*, 1945, published by the division's own press, all photos by Polish Army photographers. This photo by W. Domański)

(*Left*) Infantry battalions sent out regular patrols, here soldiers of the 3rd Carpathian Rifle Division complete with winter camouflage move out across the snow-covered slopes of the Sangro valley. (Source: Divisional photo album of 3rd Carpathian Rifle Division in Italy, 3 *Dywizja Strzelców Karpackich w Italii, Firenze*, 1945, published by the division's own press, all photos by Polish Army photographers. This photo by J. Siemek)

(*Above*) Patrol of the 3rd Carpathian Rifle Division begins the climb up one of the region's many mountains. The terrain and climate were as much as a challenge as the Germans. Small patrols such as these were regularly sent out to set ambushes and probe enemy positions. (Source: Łoziński, Marian, *Przechodniu, Powiedz Polsce…*, Kraków 1972, many editions before 1994)

(*Middle*) Monte Cassino monastery in ruins, Italy, February 1944. This desolate scene of destruction was to become the terrain on which the Polish II Corps would fight to secure mastery of the strategic hills, possession of which was pivotal to enable the charge to Rome to begin. (Source: ww2db.com)

(*Right*) 40mm Bofors Anti-Aircraft Gun and crew from a divisional artillery regiment await H Hour and the commencement of battle. With little enemy airforce action anticipated such guns were used to fire tracer rounds over the battlefield to delineate lines of advance for the troops. Many anti-aircraft gunners were re-assigned to mortar batteries and as stretcher bearers for the battle. (Source: Anders, Władysław, *Bez ostatniego rozdziału. Wspomnienia 1939–1946*, Warsaw 1989, many editions before 1994)

(*Left*) Artillery observation posts were established as far forward as possible to identify enemy gun positions and report on the accuracy and effect of the Polish artillery fire. The German guns proved to be too well dug in to be engaged and the 25pdr Field Gun equipping most Polish artillery regiments lacked the power to destroy fortifications of rock and concrete. (Source: Anders, Władysław, *Bez ostatniego rozdzialu.Wspomnienia 1939–1946*, Warsaw 1989, many editions before 1994)

(*Right*) An artilleryman from the Carpathian Rifle Division checks the lay of his 25pdr Field Gun under cover of a camouflage net. The artillery regiments were positioned on the flat valley floor beneath the monastery, totally exposed to enemy observation and fire. Movement was restricted to a minimum, and only by night. The gun positions of the 6th Carpathian Artillery Regiment were suspected by the Germans and shelled relentlessly prior to the battle. The Poles did not return fire as that would have confirmed their presence. (Source: Wańkowicz, Melchior, *Monte Cassino*, Warsaw 1989, many editions before 1994)

(*Below*) Polish infantry take cover behind a ridge as their artillery engage German positions ahead of them. (Source: Anders, Władysław, *Bez ostatniego rozdzialu.Wspomnienia 1939–1946*, Warsaw 1989, many editions before 1994)

(*Right*) Polish soldiers hug the ground as phosphorus rounds hit German defences ahead of them. (Source: Anders, Władysław, *Bez ostatniego rozdziału. Wspomnienia 1939–1946*, Warsaw 1989, many editions before 1994)

(*Left*) Hill 569, here raged one of the fiercest engagements during the Monte Cassino battle. (Source: Divisional photo album of 3rd Carpathian Rifle Division in Italy, 3 *Dywizja Strzelców Karpackich w Italii*, Firenze, 1945, published by the division's own press, all photos by Polish Army photographers. This photo by W. Domański)

(*Below*) Polish infantry advance through the smoke of a preceding artillery barrage to engage German paratroopers dug in on the hillside above. It was an exceptionally difficult task and cost the Poles heavily in casualties. (Source: Anders, Władysław, *Bez ostatniego rozdziału. Wspomnienia 1939–1946*, Warsaw 1989, many editions before 1994)

Polish infantry throw grenades at entrenched German positions on Hill 593. (Source: Wańkowicz, Melchior, *Monte Cassino*, Warsaw, 1989, many editions before 1994)

Polish troops scaling a rock face with ammunition crates, Monte Cassino, Italy, May 1944. (Source: ww2db.com, no picture credit available)

(*Right*) Hill 593. Much of the terrain at Cassino consisted of bare rock and scree slopes, with no cover, nowhere to dig in and no shelter from shrapnel –the only survival strategy was to kill the enemy and the fighting became fanatical and ferocious on both sides. (Source: ww2db.com, no picture credit available)

(*Below*) Dead soldiers of the 6th Battalion, 3rd Carpathian Rifle Division lie strewn at the foot of Hill 593. (Source: Łoziński, Marian, *Przechodniu, Powiedz Polsce…*, Kraków 1972, many editions before 1994)

(*Above*) Polish infantry cautiously approach a seemingly deserted German machine-gun post, the soldier in the foreground is manoeuvring a demolition charge on a length of stick to make sure the position is clear. (Source: Wańkowicz, Melchior, *Monte Cassino*, Warsaw, 1989, many editions before 1994)

(*Left*) With the Polish flag flying above the ruins of Monte Cassino Abbey, Bugler Lance Sergeant Karol Czech sounds the *Hejnal Mariacki*, a traditional Polish piece played daily from the cathedral tower in Kraków. The Battle of Cassino won, the next Polish attack, on the neighbouring town of Piedimonte and the mountains to the east was about to get underway. (Source: Łoziński, Marian, *Przechodniu, Powiedz Polsce…*, Kraków, 1972, many editions before 1994)

(*Right*) The remains of an upturned Polish Sherman tank along the Polish Sappers' Road, a tortuously narrow and steep supply track to the front line. Numerous vehicles fell into the ravine below or in the case of breakdowns had to be pushed over the edge to clear the road. (Source: Wańkowicz, Melchior, *Monte Cassino*, Warsaw, 1989, many editions before 1994)

(*Above left*) Lieutenant Colonel Bobiński, deputy commander of 2 Armoured Brigade and commander of 'Group Bob' that was tasked with the assault on Piedimonte. (Source: ww2incolor.com, no picture credit available)

(*Above right*) View from Highway 6, the hilltop town of Piedimonte just ahead, and behind the hills lead to Passo Corno and Monte Cairo in the distance. The Abbey of Monte Cassino is just out of shot to the right. (Source: Wańkowicz, Melchior, *Monte Cassino*, Warsaw, 1989, many editions before 1994)

(*Left*) Polish soldiers man their machine gun amidst the rubble and disabled tanks that lay scattered around the town of Piedimonte. (Source: Wańkowicz, Melchior, *Monte Cassino*, Warsaw, 1989, many editions before 1994)

(*Below*) Tank crews of the 6 Armoured Regiment deliberate on the best course of action to take. Tanks were totally unsuited to the terrain and the regiment lost nearly all the vehicles it deployed – as a result the dismounted tankers assumed the role of infantry and attacked the Germans on foot. (Source: Wańkowicz, Melchior, *Monte Cassino*, Warsaw, 1989, many editions before 1994)

(*Above*) The upturned tank of Warrant Officer Średnicki that toppled from one of the steep escarpments leading to the town of Piedimonte. (Source: Wańkowicz, Melchior, Monte Cassino, Warsaw, 1989, many editions before 1994)

(*Right*) British Generals Alexander and Leese decorated with Polish Virtuti Militari Cross awards, Italy, July 1944. (Source: ww2db.com, no picture credit available)

Polish II Corps preparing to embark for the voyage from Italy to the UK and their subsequent processing into the Polish Resettlement Corps and onwards to civilian life. (Source: Wikimedia commons, photo by Benon Tuszyński)

8

Mountain Warfare and the Defence of the Sangro River

The military formations of all combatants, Allied and Axis, had greatly increased both in size and in the level of mechanization during the years between the wars. They were however designed for warfare on the open plains of central Europe; the mountainous terrain of Italy dictated a different approach, requiring specialist mountain expertise and such formations were in very short supply in the British Army. Mountain warfare had become regarded as a sideline, a skill for local colonial troops to exercise. Lieutenant General Leese's Eighth Army was therefore largely unprepared for what lay ahead, containing only a few mountain-trained formations of any size – the Indian 4th, 8th and 10th Infantry Divisions, whose men were naturally acclimatized to mountain warfare. Thus, 1 Brigade of the Polish 3rd Carpathian Rifle Division along with 5 Brigade of the 5th Kresowa Infantry Division, with their extensive mountain training in Lebanon and Syria would be a real asset to the Eighth Army.

The Allied forces in Italy were facing a protracted campaign of mountain warfare posing many tactical and administrative problems that, especially in the winter months, were difficult to overcome. It was not just the German Army that was stalling their progress; it was the mountains that denied any rapid advances. Invariably, good roads through mountain passes were rare and side-roads amounted to little more than rough tracks. The landscape of the mountainsides was universally steep, punctuated with rough crests and serrated ridges that required little development by the Germans to create formidable defensive lines. This was the environment the men and machines of the Eighth Army were expected to conquer. Typical of the British-administered forces the formations of the Eighth Army were large and generously equipped. They were totally reliant on motor transport for their deployment and success. The rugged terrain would push the physical abilities of both man and machine to the limit.

Mountain warfare is a specialist skill and most of the Allied soldiers in Italy were novices in it. Only a few formations possessed any real understanding of the terrain, its hazards and advantages. For the majority the transition from field to mountain was painful and exhausting; life had to adapt to allowances of water, food, shelter and warmth that were far below what they were accustomed to in training or other campaigns. Along with having to acquire greater physical endurance the initiative of individuals and small groups of soldiers became pivotal to success, as communications between commanders and men were practically impossible. Once committed to action the soldiers had to think constantly for themselves, with their commanders in no position to control the action, a far cry from the highly coordinated methodology typically employed. Such skills were not learned in an instant and those who did attend the few mountain warfare courses available often had their instinctive aversion to mountain fighting reinforced.

This aversion to action in mountainous regions was not confined to the men actually conducting the fighting; the commanders, from brigade level to General Leese himself, considered the mountains to be obstacles best circumvented or if they must be tackled as a necessary hardship to enable their main plans to proceed. As such, there was little regard to using the mountains to advantage; rather, British battle plans concentrated on pushing as many formations as possible through passes and along valley floors, features that were inevitably confined amongst mountainous terrain and therefore failed to allow the troops and equipment committed to them to manoeuvre in any effective way. No attempt was made to streamline the size, quantities of heavy equipment or the dependency on road vehicles, to suit the terrain. Instead it was just accepted that movements and supply would be drawn-out cumbersome affairs. By contrast the Germans fully understood the strong natural defences the mountains offered and utilized the terrain to their full advantage. The British approach to planning was quickly understood and the Germans responded by preparing massive defences in depth and in good time. Stout fortifications covered the main routes through the passes and elsewhere the mountains themselves formed natural, strong defences.

Faced with such effective German resistance the Allies did not adapt their approach, instead intensifying it by committing ever larger formations to capture strongpoints in predictable set-piece attacks. They had little success and the Germans developed ever more effective defences against them. The mountainous terrain made the assaults mainly infantry work; a long slog on foot up slopes and crest and along ridges, with actions fought by small groups spread thinly over the ground. The Germans responded by making deadly use of light machine guns and mortars in well-prepared positions. The infantry brigades in the British divisions amounted to half the division's manpower and this proved barely adequate in the rough terrain, which though steep covered a very large ground area through crests and gullies. Even large commitments of men achieved far less than anticipated, as they were spread thinly, with poor communications. By contrast the geographical features assisted the defenders, allowing them to infiltrate the attacking formations and to outflank and envelop them.

With the infantry struggling through the terrain, the supporting arms were ever more relied upon and artillery support became lavish. Unfortunately the masses of artillery guns available did not yield the devastating results desired, since they also were thwarted by the terrain. The narrow ridges and crests did not suit saturation shelling and the prepared strongpoints were of such immense structure and so well concealed as to often escape detection or neutralization. Immense artillery programmes, moreover, consumed equally vast amounts of ammunition and to bring such quantities through mountainous country was a difficult business. There were other disadvantages. Heavy artillery support required a long time to arrange and the infantry soon became unwilling to try to advance without it. This resulted in the tempo of attacks becoming slower and momentum spasmodic. Tanks were of little help, because the ground denied them mobility and forced upon them the role of self-propelled guns. When tanks were used to attempt a breakthrough, want of space to deploy reduced them to an immobile, armoured mass. Direct support from the air suffered much the same disadvantages as the artillery.

These factors coupled with atrocious winter weather, meant the Italian front had fought itself to a standstill by the close of January 1944. Several attempts to breach the German winter defensive line had not succeeded; the American II Corps achieved limited success in the Monte Cassino area in January, also in that month amphibious landings were made behind the German lines at Anzio with the objective of striking on to Rome. The operation, although initially successful, did not achieve the envisaged breakout from the beaches and these troops, isolated in their pocket behind enemy lines, were in a difficult situation. Allied efforts on the Italian front were accordingly concentrated first on Anzio and second, Cassino. The New Zealand II Corps launched an assault on Cassino in February, with little success on the ground, but it did cause the Germans to transfer the bulk of their formations to that sector, leaving only two infantry divisions to cover the 75km front stretching from Ortona on the Adriatic coast to Alfedena, following the course of the Sangro River. This was the area to which the Polish II Corps was assigned for acclimatization to the Italian front and for gaining combat experience before engaging in offensive action.

The dramatic Sangro River valley is flanked by steep mountains, scoured with deep gorges and fierce watercourses, and the region is dotted with ancient hilltop towns and villages. The winter of 1943/44 was particularly harsh; prolonged temperatures below zero and deep snowdrifts compounded the difficulties in occupying the region, with its rocky alpine peaks encrusted in ice and the limited road network making them almost impassable. It was in this environment that the first Polish soldiers saw combat in Italy. The Polish 6 Troop of 10 Inter Allied Commando travelled from Scotland to Italy in late 1943, arriving in Italy at Taranto on 1 December. The troop was assigned to the British 2 Special Service Brigade of Brigadier Tom Churchill. As they had not been in action before, Brigadier Churchill was anxious that the Poles should obtain some battle experience as soon as possible, so approached Lieutenant General Dempsey of the British Eighth Army's V Corps to see if they could operate on his Corps' front to obtain their 'baptism of fire'. Dempsey replied that there would be a role for them carrying out fighting-reconnaissance patrols in the rugged mountains overlooking the Sangro River on the enemy's front. Accordingly, from 13 December 1943, 6 Polish Commando Troop became established on the Sangro front at the remote but picturesque ski resort of Pescopennatro, on the right flank of the British 56th Reconnaissance Regiment, in atrocious and bitter winter weather.

Patrols were sent out daily with the first being led by Major Władysław Smrokowski on their first day. The fighting patrol moved through Castel del Giudice before crossing the Sangro River and upon approaching a farm they made contact with a German patrol, losing one man. On 20 December, the Poles learnt that two mountain-trained Jäger companies were planning to attack a British field artillery battery near Capracotta the following night. The Polish commandos deployed to thwart the Germans, but despite the efforts of the gunners firing on the San Angelo river crossing, the Germans pushed forwards and within the hour the Poles were surrounded. The commandos held their position and fought a nine-hour battle in the village – they got away with just three lightly wounded, but inflicted heavy casualties upon the Germans.

The Poles felt disadvantaged against the Jägers as the latter possessed skis and white winter camouflage smocks, equipment they did not have. After negotiations with the local mayor, several pairs of cross-country skis were procured. Two days later a patrol, dressed in the white flowing robes worn by local men at funerals, skied to a mountain plateau. There they encountered an Austrian light mortar detachment, and coming under fire, the Poles were forced to retreat, complete with several spectacular clifftop falls. Christmas Day was celebrated with half a pig and three sheep that had been acquired during a patrol the previous day, and despite having to patrol on Christmas Day itself, a hearty meal was thoroughly enjoyed by all. On New Year's Eve the Poles moved to San Pietro

Avellana, with heavy snowfalls the next day trapping them in the village – it was only after one of their number skied to Capracotta on 5 January that supplies were dropped to them by parachute. Five days later the Troop retired to a rest area.

The Troop's next mission was to cross the Garigliano River alongside 169 Infantry Brigade from the 56th Infantry Division, with orders to pass through the forward troops and disrupt the German rear with ambushes near Carceri. At 1800 hrs on 27 January, the Troop, under the cover of heavy shelling, crossed the river under intense enemy fire; they then followed a white tape laid by the leading battalion through the minefields until it stopped near an orange grove. Continuing their advance, they entered the orange grove, where four Poles were wounded by mines, but nevertheless by 0330 hrs the troop had reached the proposed rendezvous with British infantry of the Queen's Royal Regiment for an attack on the ridge above Sciullo. The British did not make the rendezvous and the Poles were ordered to seize the village alone. The Troop clambered towards the summit; when challenged, they charged into the German position and by 0430 hrs were in possession of the ridge. As dawn broke, the British infantry and 40 Royal Marine Commando arrived.

Later the same day, the Polish Troop was ordered to seize Monte Valle Martina to the northeast of Sciullo, and to patrol down the Valle Zintoni. Captain Woloszowski, the second in command, led the Monte Valle Martina patrol and captured a small German patrol. However, the firing alerted a large group of Germans higher up the mountain and the patrol found itself in serious trouble and taking casualties, including the death of Captain Woloszowski. Even with his Thompson sub-machine gun jammed, one Pole charged a group of Germans and convinced them to surrender.

Meanwhile, Lieutenant Czynski and the Valle Zintoni patrol had captured a six-man mortar team and a forward artillery observation post in a ravine, and were resting when they heard firing break out. Major Smrokowski and his Tactical Troop HQ then arrived, and both groups hurried through the trees; when they reached open ground they saw Woloszowski's patrol had taken several prisoners but had suffered casualties. Smrokowski instructed Czynski that the high ground must be held at all costs; Czynski seized the summit shortly before the Germans arrived. The enemy was determined, and hand-to-hand fighting developed in which at least one Pole drew his commando knife. However, the Poles were outnumbered, and it was only when Smrokowski committed his reserve of Lieutenant Zalewski's section that the fighting swung in their favour. By 1015 hrs the Poles had cleared Monte Valle Martina, at a cost of 4 killed and 22 wounded; the Germans left 30 dead. The troop continued patrolling until the 3rd Carpathian Rifle Division took over the sector from the British in early February, the commandos then retiring to conduct further training.

Movement of the Polish formations from the base into the Corps' operational area along the Sangro River commenced with the 3rd Carpathian Rifle Division. Movement orders arrived on 4 January and between the 11th and 16th the division and its equipment left the Santa Teresa transit camp for the front. The division's personnel transferred to the area surrounding Masseria S. Augustino, south of Barletta from where they moved north by rail, taking nine trains to complete the move. The division's vehicles were transported by sea within the same time frame, at the end of which the commander of 2 Infantry Brigade oversaw the disbandment of the division's camp at Santa Teresa.

With Polish troops now being deployed to the front Lieutenant General Anders flew from Cairo to Algiers on 30 January, for discussions with General Wilson concerning details of the deployment of II Corps in Italy – he also, taking a moment from his schedule, presented a silver Polish cap badge to Wilson's secretary, the Countess of Ranfurly. From January 1944 the command of all Allied operations in the Mediterranean theatre came under General Maitland Wilson in his new role as Supreme Allied Commander, Central Mediterranean Force. His command extended over Italy, where General Alexander's 15th Army Group coordinated General Clarke's American Fifth Army and Lieutenant General Leese's British Eighth Army, whilst troops in the Middle East were under General Paget and those in North Africa under Lieutenant General Gale.

General Wilson felt that occupying this 60km front would make it unlikely the Polish II Corps would undertake any major offensive actions and was thus limited to defending the flanks and lines of communication of the Fifth and Eighth Armies. Lieutenant General Anders formulated a defensive plan for the Corps based on analysis of the ground and the opposing German forces. Anders' plan featured three key elements; ensuring the continuity of the front, securing lateral inter-army communications and protecting the flanks of the Fifth and especially the Eighth Army.

With the Poles now committed to battle Lieutenant General Anders set foot in Italy on 10 February. However, he was depressed at the international political situation. The Red Army had crossed the pre-war border into Poland on the night of 3/4 January and was fast advancing through the country. The Soviets made it plain they were claiming all liberated territory in the east that they had first occupied in 1939 as belonging to the USSR. They were also demanding changes to the Polish Government in London to make it more pro-Soviet, as well as official Polish acceptance of the revised eastern border of Poland. In the Western Allied camp there was also a marked change in the tone of the British and American press, which began urging Poland to accept these territorial adjustments. In light of these events Anders did his best to inspire the soldiers, hoping that the Soviet occupation would be a transitory step to Polish freedom.

On 11 February, Anders reported to Lieutenant General Leese at his headquarters in Vasto for a conversation upon the organization, location and battle readiness of II Corps during which Anders broached the subject of Poland's political fate and the pro-Soviet stance adopted by the *Eighth Army News* that was proving damaging to morale. This struck a raw nerve with Leese, who was exasperated with the passions of Anders and his men, in particular their continuing vocal concerns over the future of Poland – for Leese such personal feelings and agenda had no place in the day-to-day business of war. He therefore acknowledged Anders' remarks, but soon after issued a firm rebuke to Anders in a telegram: 'In my capacity as Army Commander I have to point out to you how superfluous it is for a Corps Commander to express in public any opinions concerning the political situation, in particular at this present moment.'[1] It was not until much later in the war that relations between the two men became more amicable.

With the final organizational debates concluded, the conditions under which the Polish II Corps would be deployed were agreed as follows:

(a) A liaison mission from the Polish Commander-in-Chief would be attached to Allied Forces Headquarters to present his wishes. The mission would also represent the General Officer Commanding the Polish 2nd Corps.
(b) The corps would go into action as one integral whole after all its units had arrived in Italy. Exception would only be made in case of real emergency.
(c) The corps would be used within the British Eighth Army.
(d) The corps, under General Anders, would be subordinated directly to the commander of the Eighth Army and given an independent sector of the line.
(e) The Polish Commando unit operating in Italy would be brought under the control of the Polish Corps.
(f) The Polish sick and wounded would be treated in Polish hospitals.
(g) Polish prisoners of war from the German Army would be made available for service with the Polish forces.[2]

The last point on the list, securing reinforcements, was of vital importance for the continuation of the force as a corps level command. Alexander agreed to the recruitment of Polish prisoners of war from the German Army, who were to be sent to screening camps separate from other prisoners of war and then for training with the 7th Reserve Division. Indeed, Alexander was 'glad that I was able to reward his spirit of enterprise by making the necessary arrangements for the accommodation of this unusual accession of strength to the Polish Corps.'[3] This unique facet of Polish recruitment was achieved in practice by screening Polish prisoners of war at the forward detachment of 3 Military Draft Office based at Mottola. The facility consisted of a reception camp, selection wing and holding companies, and potential recruits were assessed by an administration officer, a medical officer and a psychiatrist. During the course of the war in Italy, a total of 35,000 such recruits were found suitable for military service and were subsequently trained by the 7th Reserve Division.

The 22nd February was to prove a dark day for the Poles. Winston Churchill delivered a statement on Polish affairs to the House of Commons in which he announced that the British Government agreed to the Soviet acquisition of eastern Poland and that Poland should be compensated with German land in the west and north. These decisions had been arrived at during the Tehran conference of November 1943, notably without the Poles being present. The news was a heavy blow to II Corps. Anders summoned a conference of senior commanders at which all agreed a great injustice had been done and that confidence in Great Britain had been badly shaken. Nonetheless, Anders was adamant that the Polish must continue the fight and performed a most sterling achievement in maintaining a united II Corps, dedicated to fighting alongside the Allies. Whilst power politics meant this Polish crusade could not succeed in delivering their freedom, it most certainly would result in the destruction of the German enemy, and without defeating Germany there could be no hope for Poland. Accordingly, II Corps entered into battle with the Germans in Italy, hell-bent on vengeance for the plight of their nation.

The 3rd Carpathian Rifle Division began relieving the British 78th Infantry Division during the first week of February, taking up positions along its 45km section of the front running north of Passo del Monte to Castel Vincenzo. The changeover period lasted until 25 February because deep snowdrifts hindered motor vehicles on the narrow, winding mountain roads. The Polish II Corps took over the sector from 13 February; the Corps Headquarters was based at Vinciaturo with initially only the 3rd Carpathian Rifle Division under its command. General Anders anticipated two possible lines of attack the Germans could launch – a direct southerly advance to Isernia or a push through the mountains heading southwest towards Venafro – both of which would if successful destroy the supply lines of the Eighth Army. The commanding officer of the 3rd Carpathian Rifle Division, General Duch, now set about organizing the division's defence of their sector centred on S. Pietro Avellana and the mountain ridges of M. Pagano–La Caprara–M. Morrone–M. S. Croce. General Duch analysed the potential lines of German attack and identified key locations that must be denied to the enemy, those being the mountains M. Morrone–M. Curval, along with the ridges and crests leading to Montenero. If the Germans were to place artillery on these features they would hold sway over the sector.

The defence of S. Pietro Avellana depended on securing the hills to both the east and west of the town, with the naturally strong defensive position of Castel di Sangro lying to the west providing an effective block to a German advance upon Isernia. Duch decided to concentrate his division's efforts on thwarting this possible line of enemy attack, deploying both infantry brigades and the reconnaissance regiment. Such a number of troops was essential due to the wide area the division was tasked with defending – even so, the manpower was thinly spread. The area was split into three sectors with the 12 Podolian Cavalry Regiment conducting reconnaissance of the most northerly boundary of the division's operating area, while 2 Carpathian Rifle Brigade would hold the northern sector and 1 Carpathian Rifle Brigade the south.

The 12 Podolian Cavalry Regiment's sector stretched for 20km and was characterized by inhospitable and inaccessible mountainous terrain (the area had earlier been held by 6 Polish Commando Troop). The regiment aimed to secure village strongpoints and patrol the many tracks and trails crossing the sector. One squadron was based in Pescopennataro, with detachments of half-squadron size assigned to Collidimezzo and Montazoli. Reserves were held in Castiglione and Agnone.

In the northern sector, 2 Carpathian Rifle Brigade was focused on the front running Castel del Giudice–S. Pietro–Castel del Sangro, but owing to severe snowfall the position of Castel di Sangro could not be fully developed. It was held by two companies who were completely cut off until 26 February, when they were relieved by three companies of the 5th Battalion. These positions would secure the right flank of the divisional area and patrol the roads leading to Rionero; the next layer of defence was provided by three companies of the 6th Battalion based in Capracotta, S. Pietro and Vastogiraidi; the last-named settlement lay at the confluence of the valleys leading from Capracotta and S. Pietro and thus would act as a break to any German thrust in that area. The 4th Battalion lay to the southeast of the sector at Carovilli.

In the southern sector, 1 Carpathian Rifle Brigade held the region Rionero–Cerro with the 1st Battalion based in Rionero and a patrol base established at Montenero that was intended to maintain a constant activity in the hills, although the appalling weather delayed such deployments. The 2nd Battalion was based in Cerro with a company assigned to Castel S. Vincenzo. The 3rd Battalion was held in reserve in the area Forli del Sannio, just west of the 4th Battalion's position.

Artillery support was vital for the troops and the 2 Light Artillery Regiment covered the northern sector being located on the southeast slope of the ridge M. Miglio– M. Pagano. The southern sector was covered by the 1 Light Artillery Regiment whilst the 3 Light Artillery Regiment covered the divisional area as a whole, with both regiments located at Rionero. Major General Duch ordered the preparation of artillery fire upon the suspected lines of German assault and the suspected forming-up areas between Scontrone and Pizzone. In addition, the 1 Rifle Brigade was assigned one platoon of 17-pounder anti-tank guns from the divisional anti-tank regiment.

The Polish formations on the front overwintered in the mountainous country along the course of the Sangro River, with resulting hardship to the Polish troops, who, after two years in the Middle East now had to adapt themselves once more to life in the frost and snow. Specialist white winter camouflage smocks were issued for wear over the standard khaki battledress, while woolly hats and gloves were eagerly sought-after luxuries. Skis were distributed. The weather strongly influenced the Corps' defensive layout – in particular it was necessary to find suitable accommodation for the greatest number of troops, since any prolonged exposure to the elements in the front line was liable to affect the health of the soldiers. This was the case in the 2nd Carpathian Rifle Battalion where 200 men reported sick following four days on the hillsides of Montenero. As many personnel as possible were billeted with local families, the first time these men had experienced family life in five years. The Poles readily integrated with the sociable Italians, enjoying the warmth of their fireplaces and their hospitality.

Activity on the Sangro River sector was largely confined to patrolling, owing to the ground conditions during the winter months. Under these conditions even patrol work was particularly difficult; soldiers had to trudge through the snow over hilly country for several kilometres before reaching the German positions, then lie in ambushes among the rocks and snow, often for forty-eight hours at a time, to intercept an enemy patrol. Enemy patrols were not aggressive and the Poles soon gained dominance over the no-man's land. This was achieved by a great effort from all units, 2 Carpathian Brigade sending out 180 men a day to patrol and lay ambushes, and they returned with detailed information on German positions and strengths.

Mountain Warfare and the Defence of the Sangro River   145

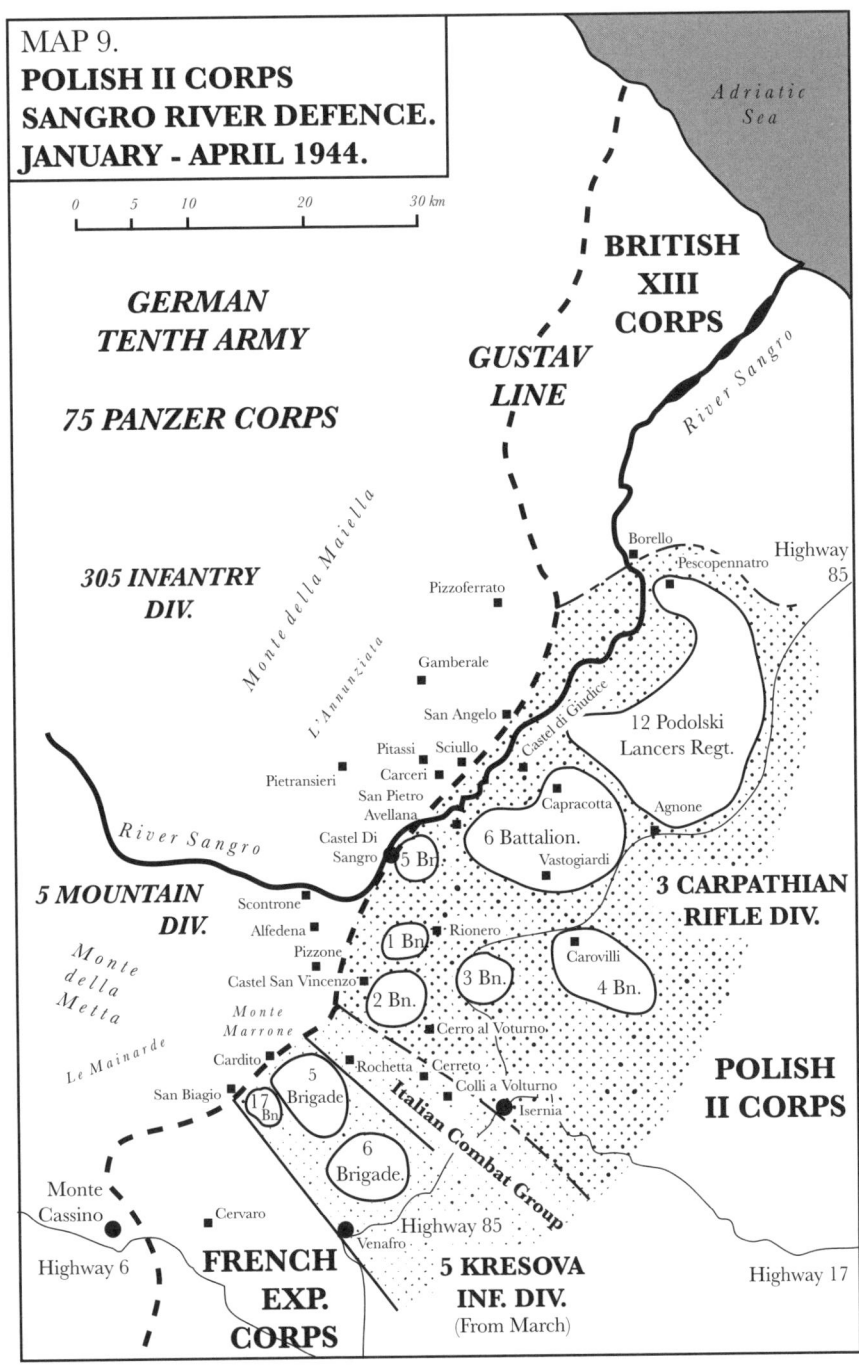

Commensurate with the Sangro River deployment was the development of the vast system of supply and replenishment for the front-line formations to sustain large-scale, intensive combat operations. The considerable task of supplying and maintaining the Army in the field was undertaken by the Corps Headquarters under the oversight of the deputy quartermasters. The various services responsible for keeping the Army supplied with the material of war, with petrol, oil and lubricants, food, clothing and necessities, effected delivery through an ordered chain of base depots, advanced depots, sub-depots and detail issue detachments. Each service branch: Ordnance, Supply and Transport, and Electrical and Mechanical Engineers had their own individually tailored supply system, but were all intermeshed to use trunk lines for transport, and at each stage in the chain the depots were organized into areas and sub-areas for administration and protection. The whole organization was referred to as the Lines of Communication and stretched from the heel ports of Bari and Taranto across the open Foggia plain, over the Apennine Mountains to the Sangro.

At first, Polish units deployed along the River Sangro were supplied directly by the British Eighth Army. The Poles soon began taking over responsibility with II Corps quartermaster's office up and running in Campobasso from 18 February. During the next fortnight the numerous service sections – supply, transport, ordnance, workshops and medical – arrived in the Corps' operational area, enabling the Polish services structure to take over the role of supplying II Corps from the Eighth Army.

From 7 March, the principal supply delivery point for II Corps was the railway station in Lucera. Trucks then conveyed goods from the railway station to the supply base at Campbasso. Here food was collected from 326 Detail Issue Depot, with the large formations collecting their provisions every alternate day: even dates for the 3rd Carpathian Rifle Division and odd dates for Corps units. In addition to these regular supply runs stockpiles of food and other staples capable of lasting twenty-four hours were established at the supply centres in Isernia, Molise, Pescolanciano and at the division's positions. Supplies of road fuels were held in the British fuel repository at Termoli on the Adriatic coast. Distribution of fuel was organized by the British mobile fuelling point in Cassaralenda, from where the Polish allocation was dispatched by the third line transport companies to the storage and distribution centre, 334 fuel section in Campobasso. Here, the fuel reserve was stored for distribution to the formations in jerry cans and also provided a direct vehicle filling service. Ammunition arrived by rail at the Polo Matese station near Bojano. Here two ammunition-handling sections were established from 5 March.

The medical service now established a line of evacuation from the front line to the base hospitals. Advanced dressing stations of the 3rd Carpathian Rifle

Division were established in Isernia, Bojano, Forli del Sanio and Carovilli. These facilities then passed on patients to 3 Casualty Clearing Station in Campobasso that housed 23 British Blood Transfusion Unit, Polish 344 Medical Supplies Depot and the American 567 Motorized Ambulance Convoy. In addition, 29 and 31 British Field Surgical Units were utilized in Isernia and in Agnone respectively. These facilities in the Corps' operational area were supported by the three military hospitals located in the base area around Taranto. The role of 3 Casualty Clearing Station was to process the evacuated wounded and sick soldiers, who were kept there up to three weeks and if their health had not improved by then they were transported to 50 British Evacuation Hospital in Termoli.

The Corps remained at the strength of a single division until March, when as a result of the large-scale regrouping of Allied formations preceding the spring offensive, the 5th Kresowa Infantry Division relieved the 2nd Moroccan Division of the French Expeditionary Force along a 14km front on the sector from Castel Vincenzo to Hill 850. Also deployed to the front was 2 Army Group Polish Artillery, supporting both divisions. The neighbouring Italian Combat Group came under the command of the 5th Kresowa Infantry Division.

With the entry of the 5th Division to the Corps area the defensive front now stretched for 60km. In light of this increased frontage and the tortuous geography of the region, Anders reassessed his strategy on 19 March; the Corps could only perform a defensive role guarding the flanks of, and communication between the Fifth and Eighth Armies. Anders foresaw possible offensive German action being focused on either a southerly push towards Isernia, potentially cutting the Allied armies in Italy in two, or more likely an attack through the mountains to Cardito and on towards Venafro, thus paralysing the supply lines to Monte Cassino. What Anders saw as inevitable was that the Germans would attempt to reinforce and consolidate their positions along the Sangro River, capturing as much high ground as possible to afford them extensive observation posts whilst simultaneously increasing their threat to the eastern flank of the Eighth Army. The vital task was to hold and protect Highway 85, the principal communications route from Isernia to Venafro that was pivotal to the supply and maintenance of the Eighth.

Anders devised his defensive strategy to achieve complete mastery of the mountains, dominating the vital lines of communication to the Allies by focusing the actions of II Corps in two regions. The northern section would hold the plateau between San Pietro and Rionero along with the heights in the Montenero area by securing the track between Rivisondoli and Villetta, along with the establishment of strongpoints at Monte Migli, Monte Pagano, Montagnola, Monte Marrone and Monte Curval. The southwestern section would block any route of advance towards Cardito and hold the rugged peaks and gorges between Monte Casale–Monte Passero and La Falconara. Thus Anders divided the Corps' area into two parts in his orders of 19 March 1944:

(a) The northern sector was to remain in the hands of the 3rd Carpathian Rifle Division whose task was expanded to encompass:
- The defence of the sector of the Sangro River from Borrello to the ridge southwest of Montenero and Castel S. Vincenzo, its main efforts being to focus upon the routes to Isernia, securing the roads Alfedena–Castel San Vincenzo and Zittola–Rionero and defending the ridge Rionero–Monte Sitaccario;
- Defence of the divisional boundary focused on Castel San Vincenzo;
- Establishment of a reserve brigade (minus one battalion) at Vandra.

(b) The southwestern sector was entrusted to the 5th Kresowa Infantry Division which was assigned the Italian Combat Group to bolster its defence. The formations were spread out to the southwest of Castel San Vinzenco, where one company was based to secure the division's boundary with the 3rd Division. The front of this sector ran along the ridge Monte Castenuovo, Le Mainarde, then through Cardito and along the southern edge of the road to the village of San Biagio, skirting the peaks of Monte Sante Croce, Colle dell Arena and Hill 1019, and finally bordering on the French Corps along elevations 850–1000.
- The core of the defence was the ridge Monte Passero, Monna Casale and further to the east of La Falconara. The division established a reserve in the area of Colli al Volturno, again formed of one brigade minus one battalion.
- The Carpathian Lancers Regiment also formed part of the Corp's reserve.

The role of the Carpathian Division was largely unchanged, its original plan proving well capable of the defence of a wide front. The division was bolstered from 25 March through the arrival of the 15 Poznan Lancers Regiment in the area of Capracotta. This addition enabled the 6th Battalion to be assigned as the divisional reserve whilst elements on the 2 Brigade's front were strengthened by two infantry companies. Simultaneously the division's artillery was bolstered by the advent of one battery of the 10 Heavy Artillery Regiment. The Carpathian Lancers Regiment remained in the division's reserve until 25 March, after which it transferred to Corps command but remained in the same location of San Massimo – one half-squadron was left assigned to 1 Carpathian Rifle Brigade.

The defence of the 5th Kresowa Division's sector was much more involved. In order to hold its rugged sector the Italian Combat Group was placed under its command, boosting the number of soldiers by 7,000, whilst the division's organic 15 Poznan Lancers Regiment was transferred to the northern sector. Artillery support was provided by the Artillery Group Polish Army comprising the 11 Heavy Artillery Regiment, one battery of the 10 Heavy Artillery Regiment and the 7 Horse Artillery Regiment. These regiments had the principal role of providing counter-battery fire and for shelling the possible lines of German advance, thus the main focus was upon the San Biagio sector since it was the most probable direction of German attacks.

Major General Sulik, commander of the 5th Division, reviewed the challenging task presented to him. In the event of a major German attack Sulik foresaw the main axis would follow the highway running Biagio–Cerasuolo, with supporting assaults being launched from the area Monte della Metta towards Rochetta to threaten the southern flank of the division. Sulik decided to divide his operational area into two sections:

(a) The northern sector 'Mare' would be assigned to the Italian Combat Group tasked with the defence of Monte Mare–Colli al Volturno in order to prevent the enemy from launching strong thrusts from Pizzone–Monte Mare to the south and southeast, and also securing the slopes of Regione Valle di Mezzo.

(b) The southwestern sector of San Biagio was held by 5 Wilenska Brigade, tasked with blocking the main direction of German attack on the wide belt along the axis running east of Cardito–Hill 1029–Cerasuolo.

In the northern sector, the alpine massif and pathless ridges of Le Mainarde and Colle S. Pietro constituted strong natural defences. Sulik saw the numerous gorges and valleys that cut through the mountains as making good paths for counter-attacks against German advances. The Italian Combat Group assigned to this sector comprised two battalions of the 68 Infantry Regiment, 29th and 33rd *Bersagalieri* Battalions, Alpine Battalion, *d'Arditi* (commando) Battalion, 5th Anti-tank Battalion, two batteries of the Italian 11 Light Artillery Regiment and the 5th Engineering Battalion. The northern flank of this group secured the boundary with neighbouring 3rd Carpathian Division in the area of Castel San Vincenzo, with two companies occupying the southern and central parts of the ridge Monte Castelnuovo and the projection stretching to the southwest. A further kilometre to the south, two and a half companies barred any possible attack from the slopes of M. Mare. Reserves were held in the towns of Rochetta and Scapoli and also to the north at Colli a Volturno and Fornelli. Artillery support was bolstered by a battery of the Polish 4 Light Artillery Regiment located west of Cerasuolo.

The southwest sector was characterized by high mountains and deep gorges that would challenge any German advance. Deep gullies amongst the hills to the west of Cardito offered strongpoints from which to launch counter-attacks against loss of the high ground running through Hill 1029 and Colle dell Arena. Sulik opted for a strong defence of the southern sides of Le Mainarde combined with securing the valleys and roads running south and finally holding the peaks of Hill 1029 and Colle dell Arena. The addition of 17th Lwów Infantry Battalion that was based in San Biagio and two heavy machine gun companies bolstered 5 Brigade. The three battalions of 5 Brigade each formed a base of defence: one was sited in the area Le Mainarde–Colle San Pietro, covering the approaches and road to Cerasuolo, another held the hills surrounding Cardito to thwart assaults from Monte San Croce, and the third Colle del Arena, marking the boundary of the left flank. All three bases were located close to the front line, only two to three kilometres distant, with local reserves of a strength of one or two companies a further kilometre behind. Artillery support was provided by the 6 Light Artillery Regiment (less one battery) located on the southern slopes of Monna Casale.

Meanwhile, the natural elements continued their assault on all in the region, with blizzards and snowdrifts hampering communications between strongpoints and company positions frequently out of touch. This entailed the keeping of considerable reserves of stores, for example on the Capracotta sector, there was always a reserve stock for twelve to fourteen days, dumped to meet an emergency. The mountaintop roads were also particularly exposed to snowdrifts and ice, notably on the night of the 25/26 March when a column of 31 mules and 25 Indian muleteers became buried in the snow in the Pescopennataro area, several of whom could not be saved. Considerable attention was therefore given to the problems of keeping the roads clear of snow.

Great attention was also paid to the preparation and improvement of the defensive positions. During the 5th Kresowa Division's stay in the sector, 180 tons of barbed wire and 220,000 sandbags were used on such work. Throughout the Corps' area 74km of roads were repaired, 282m of Bailey bridge were laid and the Pagano tunnel, 3km long, was cleared of rubble, mines and booby traps and adapted for motor vehicle traffic. These efforts provided secure communication with the defended locality of Castel di Sangro and reduced the fifteen to twenty casualties per day from German artillery fire to an average of five. Defensive construction work included digging trenches, gun emplacements and smaller fortifications from the mountain stone, the creation of observation posts for coordinating artillery support, mine laying and the establishment and protection of telephone lines and exchanges. These works proved very useful in subsequent operations, allowing the Allies to man the sector with weak but mobile units, concentrating the bulk of their forces on the anticipated May offensive against Rome.

With the prevailing weather conditions and the rugged terrain, combat activity was restricted to patrolling, particularly on the 3rd Carpathian Division's sector where units were thinly spread in its area coupled with the considerable distance that had to be covered to encounter the enemy. Nonetheless, as mentioned earlier, 2 Brigade sent out up to 180 men a day, always with artillery observers and with good preparation. The resulting Polish dominance over the no-man's land are confirmed by the casualty figures – the Poles suffered 3 killed, 7 wounded and one missing, against German losses amounting to 35 killed and 26 taken prisoner.

The principal objective of the 3rd Carpathian Rifle Division was the reconnaissance of the strategic high ground of Montenero, with the aim of denying this terrain to the Germans who could then have threatened the eastern flank of the Eighth Army. From as early as 8 February, patrols were being sent out with the 1st Company of the 2nd Battalion patrolling for two days in the Alfedena region, while other units established camouflaged positions on Monte Curval. The next significant action was Patrol Foxtrot, sent out by the 2nd Battalion on 17 February and supported by a battery of artillery. This formation advanced through Colle Alto–Il Calvario to the railway station at Alfedena, where they destroyed the German defences and inflicted significant losses on the enemy. Further Polish patrols gained dominance over no-man's land as far as Colle Gallina. Numerous smaller patrols were active on the south slopes of M. Curval and M. Fosse, these culminated in the final occupation of the latter hill on the 2 April. Some of the reconnaissance patrols penetrated as far as the area of Pizzone and Monte Mattone. The aim was to deny the Germans access to favourable forming-up positions at the source of the Sangro River.

Frequent clashes and exchanges of fire occurred between the Polish strongpoints of Capracotta and San Pietro Avellana on the one side and the German positions on the rising ground to L'Annunziata on the other. The Germans attempted to push south towards the Sangro River from their advanced strongpoints located south of the village of Gamberale, and from neighbouring strongpoints. In spite of deep snowdrifts and sleet showers, the Poles launched a series of ten patrols and raids in February and six in March towards Gamberale, Checo, Pitassi and along the gorge east of Cle Checo towards Pietransieri and M. Toceo, that prevented the enemy from reaching the Sangro. One particularly successful patrol from that action was conducted against Gamberale on 19/20 February, when they reconnoitred towards Colle Bucci searching for German observation posts on Monte dell Ellera. The patrol succeeded in capturing several prisoners and threatened to surround the garrison at Gamberale.

Reconnaissance actions of the 12 Podolski Lancers Regiment stretched between Colle di Mezzo and Pescopennataro. The regiment had to reckon with not only a large geographical area, but also numerous minefields strewn throughout the valleys and hillsides of this stretch of the Sangro River. Sabotage action by Italian Fascists was widespread in this region, as were fierce incursions especially in early March. Faced with such challenges combat activity was limited to diligent observation of the enemy's front, with patrols only being sent forward to investigate suspicious sightings. The regiment deployed more aggressive patrolling during 21–23 March, launching successful attacks upon Pizzoferrato and Gamberale.

The 15th Poznan Lancers Regiment took over the Capracotta strongpoints on 6 April, continuing their predecessors' patrolling activity and maintaining control of their sector of no-man's land. From 13 April a particularly successful two-day reconnaissance action was conducted by two sections of the 1st Squadron in extremely difficult rocky terrain, with snow up to the waist, when the detachment succeeded in climbing the southern slopes of Hill 1613 and there destroying a five-man strongpoint.

In the 5th Kresowa Infantry Division's sector, in view of the nearness of enemy defensive positions, patrolling was much more difficult, but seven major patrols were sent out exclusively by night. Apart from this, ambushes and listening posts were established with good results. The main patrol areas were the hills to the north of the Cardito–San Biagio road where patrols were sent on average every third night, the area south of the same road but on a less frequent basis, the southern slopes of Monte Carella on average three or four times a week, and Monte S. Croce every other night. The patrols were effective at eavesdropping and setting ambushes – several combat clashes ensued with a patrol on Monte Carella attacking a German position on the night of 3/4 April, scattering fifteen Germans.

During the first days of 5 Infantry Brigade establishing itself on the front there was considerable aggressive action from the enemy: on the night of 31 March/1 April a strong force of German troops attacked the 13th and 15th Battalions several times, but upon meeting strong Polish resistance they withdrew, having sustained considerable casualties. The most decisive action on this sector was a major assault conducted by the Italian Combat Group, launched at dawn on 31 March against Monte Marrone, the southernmost projection of the German defences in the Monte della Metta mountain range and a prominent observation post. The attack came as a surprise to the Germans as the Alpine Battalion Piedimonte charged up the ridge of Colle Rotondu–Monte Maronne with supporting attacks by 185th Parachute Battalion capturing the eastern end of the ridge and 33rd Bersaglieri Battalion seizing Le Mainarde. The offensive was supported by the 11 Italian Artillery Regiment with counter-battery fire provided by the Polish 2nd Artillery Group and divisional artillery regiments. The German forces quickly retreated, outflanked and under increasing artillery fire. The Italians sustained only minimal losses, and the success of the operation was largely attributed to careful planning and only weak German resistance. Not that the enemy had yet quit: a series of counter-attacks by fifty Germans were launched to regain the position, but all were thrown back and after their attempt to recapture Monte Marrone on the night of 9/10 April was repelled, the Germans made no further efforts.

The relatively quiet sector enabled intensive training of the Army Group Polish Artillery to be conducted against the enemy; special emphasis was given to training forward observers and to gunnery and target computing practice. The observers occupied extremely exposed observation posts, several at altitudes of 1,800m that could only be reached through technical rock climbing. The winter cold was intense, a far cry from the warmth of Palestine.

The *Eighth Army News* reported on the efforts of the Poles on the Sangro front, highlighting the traditional Polish bugler: 'Each day at noon a Polish Corporal, watched by local inhabitants and Allied troops climbs to the top of the municipal building in a small mountain village and sounds the call, which is carried for miles on the clear air.'[4]

9

The Monastic Fortress

The Abbey at Monte Cassino is awe inspiring in its majestic setting. The monastery surmounts a 700ft-high rock pinnacle lying on a spur protruding into the Liri Valley, at the extremity of which a projecting ridge of foothills ascend precipitously to the snow-covered peaks of the Apennine Mountains. The monastery's location dominates the surrounding Liri Valley, which is mostly flat and put to olive groves and farming. As well as having a physically imposing presence the Abbey is of great historic significance, being home to the Franciscan order of monks and in Ancient Roman times was the site of the Temple of Apollo.

Strategically, the massif of Monte Cassino commanded the vital Highway 6, the only major road leading through the Apennine Mountains to Rome, 85 miles to the north. This important feature had to be captured before the Allies could advance further. The dominating mountain was the 5,400ft Monte Cairo that afforded the enemy a perfect view of the Allied positions, along with outposts on the lesser mountains of Passo Corno and Monte Castellone. The Germans boasted about the impregnability of the fortress of Monte Cassino and its surrounding hills – the German term fortress referring specifically to defences constructed of steel and concrete, including strong bunkers and overhead cover, supported by heavy weapons well dug in. The Germans were well established, occupying all vantage points, giving them the best possible defence, and so far the position had indeed proved impregnable. The region was garrisoned with elite formations of paratroopers and mountain troops supported by numerous artillery emplacements, all with commanding positions over the battlefield.

Monte Cassino was proving to be a real headache for the Allies. What had been envisaged as another stepping-stone towards Rome had become a solid wall halting any advance up the Italian peninsula. The Germans' stubborn defence led to a four-month battle, during which the Allies launched four major assaults. The first of these was conducted by the US Army and succeeded in crossing the River Rapido, which coupled with attacks from the French to the northeast of the monastery enabled them to advance as far as Albaneta Farm, only 1,000 yards from the Abbey, before grinding to a halt by 12 February in face of the entrenched German defences. The second attack was launched by the 4th Indian Division and the 2nd New Zealand Division, whose casualties were so high that they had to be withdrawn on 18 February. The third offensive followed a massive air raid that obliterated the town of Cassino and the monastery. The Americans, Indians and New Zealanders then launched an attack that was repulsed by 26 March, largely due to the difficulty of advancing through the utter devastation wrought by the aerial bombardment. After months of fighting all that remained of the monastery was a gruesome pile of rubble, with one corner wall still standing; the town of Cassino lay in ruins, completely destroyed, the picturesque olive groves were now just leafless trees, burned by shellfire.

The length and ferocity of the battle had led to a war within a war, and the combatants on both sides saw it as symbolic of the entire struggle – the fate of Cassino would be the fate of the war. Cassino became an obsession and its participants fanatical. Hitler was adamant that Cassino must be held, his generals fielded only their best troops and despite a winter of devastating Allied artillery and aerial bombardment they held fast, enduring massive casualties in the process. The defenders developed a mystique of their own; they held the impregnable fortress and would never surrender it. In this respect the battle was hugely significant for Germany, it was the last rock they could cling to in the turning tide of the war – to abandon it would mean the death of their already-waning belief in German invincibility.

For the Allies, Cassino had become the ultimate test of self-worth. They had suffered appalling casualties from three failed assaults – to vindicate such sacrifice it must be taken. The capture of a rock surmounted by a Franciscan monastery now held more significance than the campaign's absolute objective of Rome. The capture of Cassino, not Rome, would decide the fate of the Italian campaign. That it was going badly for the Allies was infuriating, especially after their successes in North Africa; the reputation of the Eighth Army had to be regained by seizing the seemingly impregnable fortress. Victory at Cassino would be the first step on the final path to Allied victory in the war; they had everything to prove. The battle was inevitably going to be fierce and protracted.

The fourth and decisive Battle of Cassino was described as 'General Alexander's masterpiece: an operation in C major with full orchestra.'[1] For the first time in the Italian campaign Alexander was able to mount an offensive at a time and place of his own choosing, instead of being precipitated into action by events and pressures elsewhere. Also for the first time summer weather would make it possible to deploy large formations: the new offensive would be fought, not by companies and battalions, but by massed divisions. There would be a greater superiority in guns and machines than ever, but this time there would also be a preponderance of infantry. As Alexander himself remarked, quoting Nelson: 'Only numbers can annihilate.' This time there would be numbers. It was to be the vindication of Churchill's Mediterranean strategy, the justification for the long winter agony, the triumphant salute of the Mediterranean veterans to the new armies poised to strike across the English Channel and open the final chapter of the war. In the grand design of the war as a whole, the summer offensive in Italy was the prelude to the finale. But it was also a climax in its own right.

As long ago as 22 February, shortly after the second Cassino battle, Alexander had redefined the strategy of the campaign: 'To force the enemy to commit the maximum number of divisions to operations in Italy at the time Overlord is launched.'[2] This could not be done by merely pushing the Germans back another few miles, the enemy had to be drawn into a major battle and destroyed. Alexander's plan for achieving this had a classic simplicity. The new strategy developed in early March would concentrate all Allied fighting units on the Cassino and Liri Valley front on the west coast, all but abandoning the Adriatic east coast push. Operation Diadem would hurl every available Allied soldier and weapon against the Gustav and Hitler Lines, in the largest battle yet fought by the Western Allies. With this restructuring of Allied divisions for the assault on Rome the entire Eighth Army including the Polish II Corps would have to be called into action for the assault on Monte Cassino.

In view of the intended use of the Polish II Corps on the Monte Cassino sector in the large-scale Allied Spring Offensive, an order had been issued on 2 April advising the formations of their anticipated relief by the British X Corps during the period 8–17 April. The reliefs were effected without incident on 15 April; the 3rd Carpathian Rifle Division moved to the area Carpinone–Froslone–Sessano, the 5th Kresowa Infantry Division to the area Prata–Sannita–Capriati a Volturno, and the Artillery Group transferred to the staging area by the 'Bridge of 25 Arches' on the River Volturno. Total casualties for the Sangro River defence had mounted to 17 officers and 182 other ranks.

Following Leese's February meeting with Anders the former had necessarily sought guidance on the 'Polish problem' from the resident British minister, Harold Macmillan, who briefed him on the current state of Polish affairs and agreed to liaise with Anders on political points, thus reducing some of this extra burden on Leese, and certainly it would prove a boon until relations between Leese and Anders improved.[3] Protocol would require the Polish Commander-in-Chief, General Sosnkowski, to consent to the operation, but as Alexander was now more aware of the Polish situation he felt sure that Sosnkowski would not agree to deploying the entire Corps in a major assault. Anders would be far more likely to accept the challenge and accordingly on 24 March, when

General Leese called off the New Zealand Corps' offensive, he wasted no time in summoning General Anders and his Chief of Staff, Colonel Wisniowski to his headquarters. Sosnkowski was due to arrive in Italy to inspect the Polish troops within the week, so speed was of the essence to secure full Polish commitment to the coming battle.

Lieutenant General Leese got straight down to business, informing his visitors of the new plan to open the road to Rome with a full-scale Army Group operation. This would still entail, however, the taking of Monte Cassino and the massif, and the battle for these strongpoints was to be, he said, 'in Polish hands'. Then he added: 'But if General Anders does not agree to undertake the mission I will have to rely on another Corps, and I will use the Poles on a different axis. Would you kindly think about it for ten minutes and let me have your decision?'[4] The Polish generals went into a huddle and quickly went over the five considerations that were uppermost in their minds:

1. Monte Cassino was known throughout the world as the major obstacle barring the way to Rome. The battle, therefore, would have international impact.
2. The attack would be the first face-to-face contact with the Germans since 1939.
3. If the Poles were to take Monte Cassino this would give the lie to Soviet propaganda and prove that the Polish Army was willing to fight the Germans.
4. While giving due consideration to the possible casualties it was doubtful they would be much lighter even if the attack were made on another axis, across the Rapido for example.
5. The role of the Polish troops would have great significance for the future of the Home Army in Poland.[5]

Even before the ten minutes were up they had agreed to take on this mission. Leese thanked them and asked them for the time being not to share the news with more than a handful of other senior Polish commanders. Lieutenant General Anders and the Polish II Corps would have the task of capturing Monte Cassino and operating onwards towards Piedmonte San Germano. These were the key strategic features of the Gustav and Hitler Lines; their capture would bring about the collapse of the Germans' defensive systems spanning the breadth of Italy. Anders accepted the task, having faith in the ability of his troops to prevail. He was well aware that success would bring fame once more to Polish forces and elevate the spirit and reputation of his nation. On the other hand there was a risk that the entire Corps might be lost in one action, and this concerned many of the London Poles, prominent amongst whom was General Sosnkowski.

It was noted by the British that in Anders' brief deliberations with his generals on the topic of committing the Corps to battle, their five principal considerations involved scant regard for the battle itself, and intimated that the decision-making criteria of the Polish Corps did not operate according to quite the same strictly military criteria that would have governed the decisions of other Eighth Army commanders. The political ramifications of the engagement were far more to the fore in II Corps' priorities and this difference of approach was to become even more pronounced as the battle neared, and notable across all ranks of the force, causing the British authorities much concern.

Sosnkowski arrived in Italy on 26 March, his intention to negotiate the best possible terms on which II Corps would enter the fighting. He was most perturbed to discover that Alexander and Anders had already made these decisions and also by the manner in which they were made – none of the parties involved informed him until after Anders had committed II Corps on Alexander's terms. Sosnkowski was furious that the British had pushed the issue through before his arrival, especially after the assurances he had gained from Alexander and Wilson the previous autumn that he would be consulted upon the Corps' deployment. He took stock of the situation and wrote the following letter to Anders on 12 April:

> *General Anders*
> *Top Secret*
>
> *In connection with the intended use of the 2nd Corps for action in the Cassino fortress area, the most important considerations are the diligent and detailed preparation of the actions, on which depends not only the reputation and vindication of the 2nd Corps, but that of the whole Polish struggle, both politically and socially. A botched offensive could utterly destroy the Corps.*
>
> *General, make the fullest possible use of my following suggestions:*
>
> 1. *The task of the 2nd Polish Corps is the most important in the whole 15th Army Group.*
> 2. *The Corps must therefore enter into action duly supported and reinforced by the Allies. It must also have its own shortcomings in hardware addressed (especially the provision of heavy mortars). Corps Artillery should be bolstered by the inclusion of British heavy artillery in appropriate numbers.*

3. The Corps action can be most effectively engaged by the enemy's artillery fire concentrated in the regions:
   (a) From the PNC(north); ATINA - VILLA LATINA - BELMONTE CASTELLO
   (b) From the west; AQUINO - PONTE CORVO

   This artillery would have to be silenced by aerial bombardment and our own artillery. Of course, the most reliable guarantee of success would be to capture the positions:
   (a) Our own actions should be aimed at mastering the region Belmonte-Atina possibly combining operations with 10th Corps and the mountain group, ascending to Atina via the massifs Monte Mare and Monte Cavallo;
   (b) By a preceding attack by the French Expeditionary Corps and 10th Corps achieving mastery of the PNC.-WEST slopes of the MAJO massif.

4. The 2nd Corps actions will undoubtedly be hampered by the impact of direct tactical fire, (and possibly counterattacks) from the Germans on both flanks (from Monte Corno and Monte Cassino). Especially upon MONTE CORVO, the dominant terrain feature over which the Corps will attack, if the enemy is able to fire upon this, at the critical time of our initial advance we will suffer significant losses. That is why it must be regarded as a pivotal action to control Monte Corno. The Corps formations will need to be reinforced by the inclusion of a British infantry brigade to achieve this task, and an appropriate amount of artillery. The simultaneous capture of MONTE CORNO and ATINA will result in breaking the Hitler Line. Monte Cassino is too difficult to assail from the eastern face and therefore should be engaged by the British units, located on the left side of our Corps. Monte Cassino will best be neutralized by aerial and artillery bombardment.

5. It does not seem that for the reasons of terrain it was possible to clear the field by the earlier attack of 13 Corps. However, to compel the enemy to disperse his artillery fire and pull partly off the section of our attack ensure simultaneous commencement of the 13 and 2 Polish Corps.

6. Finally, too early a take over of Cassino sector by the 2nd Corps could work against us by exposing our intentions to our opponent, thus negating the surprise factor. Our entrance to the field should be made only 2-3 days before the start of the action, this will allow sufficient familiarization for the unit commanders prior to attacking their objectives. At higher levels of organization, reconnaissance teams have to set to work as early as possible.

> *I regret that this, such a major offensive operation, is to be undertaken by the 2nd Polish Corps, this development displays a u-turn from what had been agreed with General Alexander during November last year, and was decided upon just before they announced my arrival to Italy, which has deprived the Chief of the Polish General Staff the opportunity to express his opinions in advance, and thus exert the proper influence proportionate to the using of the Polish Army to seize the principal objective.*
>
> *I authorize you, General, to produce this letter in English translation for the Eighth Army commander.*
>
> Supreme Commander
> Sosnkowski
> General.[6]

Launching an all out assault in a major attritional battle was precisely the type of scenario Sosnkowski wished to avoid, according to Anders: 'I told him of the task that had been assigned to the Corps in the coming offensive, but he did not form a favourable view of the plan, which he considered would be both very costly and fail in its objective. He thought an attack should be made across the mountains, leaving Monte Cassino on the left flank.'[7] Anders and Sosnkowski argued over the decision, but ultimately Sosnkowski resigned himself to accepting that since it was already made and could not be reversed, his resolve would now be to secure the best possible terms of engagement. He was successful in gaining British heavy artillery support, although his call for a brigade of infantry could not be spared. Sosnkowski then turned his attention to gaining as much information from Italian commanders on the terrain and tactics that would benefit the Corps.

The terrain of the six-square-mile battlefield is that of a crumpled conglomeration of bare stone-strewn hillsides, jagged rock outcrops and steep ravines, in which false crests abound and the divergence between maps and reality makes it difficult to describe accurately. The ground is characterized by two parallel ridges running southwards from Mt Castellone and from Colle Majola, separated by a steepish valley tapering into a gorge at the southern end of which, at that time, stood the large ruined buildings of Albaneta Farm on a small plateau. The principal feature of the western ridge was a spur known as Phantom Ridge and on the eastern ridge the tangled rock outcrops around Point 593 and the D'Onifrio Ridge. The ridges were far from hospitable terrain, largely rough broken ground with ridges, knolls and hollows jumbled together. Huge boulders were scattered everywhere, deep clefts and sheer rock faces abounded, and the numerous gorges were filled with dense thorn bushes. To attacking troops the ground posed an endless succession of tactical puzzles. This or that knoll or ridge might seem to be promising objectives but would turn out to be commanded from an unlikely direction by another knoll or ridge or indeed by several. A line of approach might look as if it would 'go' but would turn out to be blocked by some impassable obstacle. Both sides were aware that the advantage of the ground lay wholly with the defenders.

The distribution of enemy units was thought to include about seven German battalions holding the area, with the monastery, the south and west of the massif, and part of the town still held by Heidrich's paratroopers, whose key strongpoints were located between Colle Sant' Angelo–Point 706–Monte Castellone (3 Parachute Regiment and the Ruffin Kampfgruppe from the 5th Mountain Division); in the monastery and the upper reaches of the town (4 Parachute Regiment and the Parachute Machine Gun Battalion); and on Points 593 and 569 and around Massa Albaneta (1st Battalion, 3 Parachute Regiment). In reserve was the 1 Parachute Regiment, around Villa Santa Lucia and the reverse slopes of Colle Sant' Angelo. All these positions were as strong as ever although Allied reconnaissance and intelligence believed erroneously that they must have been considerably weakened by the earlier battles. Heidrich's division still had a generous allocation of artillery under command, including the 242nd Assault Battalion, 525th Anti-Tank Battalion (the latter equipped with self-propelled 88mm guns), four ordinary artillery battalions from Tenth Army, and one from the 90th Panzer Grenadier Division. Also in the line was the 71 Werfer Regiment disposing of forty 15 and 30cm mortars held near Pignataro, as well as thirty 15 and 30cm mortars at Villa Santa Lucia. The Division's firepower was considerable. Further to the north, the 5th German Mountain Division held the sector up to Monte Cairo. It was thought that the German artillery could bring at most 230 guns to bear on the area and 130 at the least, combined with a great many mortars and *Nebelwerfer* rocket-launchers.

Both the dominant ridges housed numerous defensive positions that were capable of providing covering fire for the other; the system resulted in interlocking arcs of fire and was largely responsible for halting the Allies' previous assaults. A complex network of similar defences covered the approaches to the monastery. The German defences had been very much improved and consisted of a linked and mutually supporting system of foxholes, sangars, bunkers and pillboxes in steel or concrete, combined with barbed wire and anti-personnel mines. The advantages of the ground lay wholly with the Germans, who also enjoyed almost perfect observation from their heights.

Armed with this intelligence Anders now appraised the battlefield, flying over the area, and conducting as careful a reconnaissance as was possible from the bullet-swept Allied positions on the slopes of Mt Castellone, Colle Majola and the D'Onifrio Ridge. He also collected every scrap of relevant information from those who had fought the earlier battles of Mt Cassino, particularly from the 4th Indian Division. Planning for the attack on Cassino was conducted using aerial photography as a principal reconnaissance tool, patrolling on the ground being kept to a minimum so as not to alert the enemy to the coming offensive. As a result, it was not possible to carry out as full an appraisal of the battlefield as was desired, with a particular lack of appreciation of the physical terrain from the infantry's perspective.

Anders decided that there were four dominating points or 'natural' objectives, from right to left the S. Angelo Hill–Point 575–Point 593 and the Abbey. Anders examined and dismissed the possibility of scaling the bare and excessively steep southern and eastern slopes of Monastery Hill. He also dismissed the idea of attacking the Abbey and the saddle from the D'Onifrio Ridge, as the 4th Indian Division declared the deep gorges which had to be crossed were impassable, due to the appalling ground, dense scrub and risk of sweeping enemy crossfire. An attack from the northwest on a broad front from Colle Maiela and Monte Castellone to Point 593, Point 575 and Colle S. Angelo, along the main ridges of the Cassino mountain spur would enable the capture of the high ground of Mass Albaneta and Albaneta Farm without mountain climbing and with concealed forming-up areas. The high ground could be used to drive out German mortar positions in the valley below and as an area for launching tank assaults towards the Abbey. This plan would allow for three of the objectives to be attacked almost simultaneously, thus neutralizing to some extent the advantage held by the Germans due to their mutually supporting defences.

Anders produced an outline plan of attack that was presented at a conference on 6 April. His intention was to ignore the town of Cassino and the monastery, instead breaching the enemy defences from the high ground to the northwest along the axis of Colle Maiola–Mass Albaneta, capturing and holding the southwest slopes of the high ground (northeast of Highway 6) in order to gain observation over the Liri Valley. This would enable the supply and reinforcement routes to the monastery to be kept under fire, thereby isolating Cassino and Monastery Hill, which could fall of their own accord or if necessary could be attacked from the northwest. The 5th Kresowa Division was to attack on the right and capture the high ground of Phantom Ridge–Colle S. Angelo and Point 575 and then to effect junction with units of the British XIII Corps. The 3rd Carpathian Division was to attack on the left and capture the southern end of Snakeshead Ridge and Massa Albaneta. On the capture of divisional objectives, the 3rd Carpathian Division was to be prepared to continue their effort and attack over Hill 444 to take the monastery. These operations were to be covered on the flanks by dismounted reconnaissance regiments holding the ridge of Monte Castellone on the right and the slopes of Monte D'Onifrio on the left. The plan offered no magic formulae. Both divisions' assaults were directed into the teeth of the German defences, where they would be subjected to the deadly arcs of fire and would inevitably sustain high casualties.

The divisional commanders, Major Generals Duch and Sulik, were then able to study the ground and make their plans. Anders held his final coordinating conference on 25 April, when the views of the commanders were considered. The resulting plan differed from the original in only two points: each division was to be allotted a squadron of tanks that were to be used first on Mass Albaneta and then on the monastery. Apart from the attack on Mass Albaneta, the Kresowa Division would have first call on armour. Secondly, the advance of the Kresowa Division was to be halted at Phantom Ridge so as not to expose the division's flanks. When the divisional and brigade commanders began making their appraisals of the forthcoming battle plans the English observers were once again astounded by the Polish eagerness to enter the fray. According to Brigadier T. P. D Scott: 'Their attitude towards this battle was unusual… . One Brigadier rose to his feet and asserted with much vigour that his men had fought at Tobruk, were seasoned warriors and would therefore lead the attack. The other Brigadier at once rose to his feet and said No, he was the senior, therefore his brigade would do the attack… Such a display of keenness to attack in our Army might be misinterpreted.'[8] The issue was eventually amicably resolved and in both the Carpathian and Kresowa Divisions it was decided to attack with only one brigade up.

Anders' plan committed all the infantry of his two-brigade divisions, leaving him without a reserve. He therefore withdrew an infantry battalion from the 5th Kresowa Division, replacing it by the Carpathian Lancers Reconnaissance Regiment, dismounted from their vehicles, and arranged to withdraw a battalion from the 3rd Carpathian Division after the capture of Albaneta Farm. The want of a proper reserve of infantry was unfortunate but could not be avoided if he was to secure all the mutually supporting features simultaneously. General Sosnkowski had managed to negotiate with Alexander the inclusion of the Polish Commando into II Corps for this operation, providing a much needed boost to assault troop numbers in the 5th Kresowa Infantry Division. The whole attack was to be supported by the firepower of over 300 artillery guns. The attack by the Polish II Corps against the high ground of Monte Cassino was to be combined with an attack by the British XIII Corps along the bordering Liri valley. Further to the south, the French Expeditionary Corps was to attack over the Aurunci Mountains, infiltrate and then outflank the German defences. The American II Corps was to attack along the coastal road.

Table 6
II Corps Organisation for the Battle of Monte Cassino

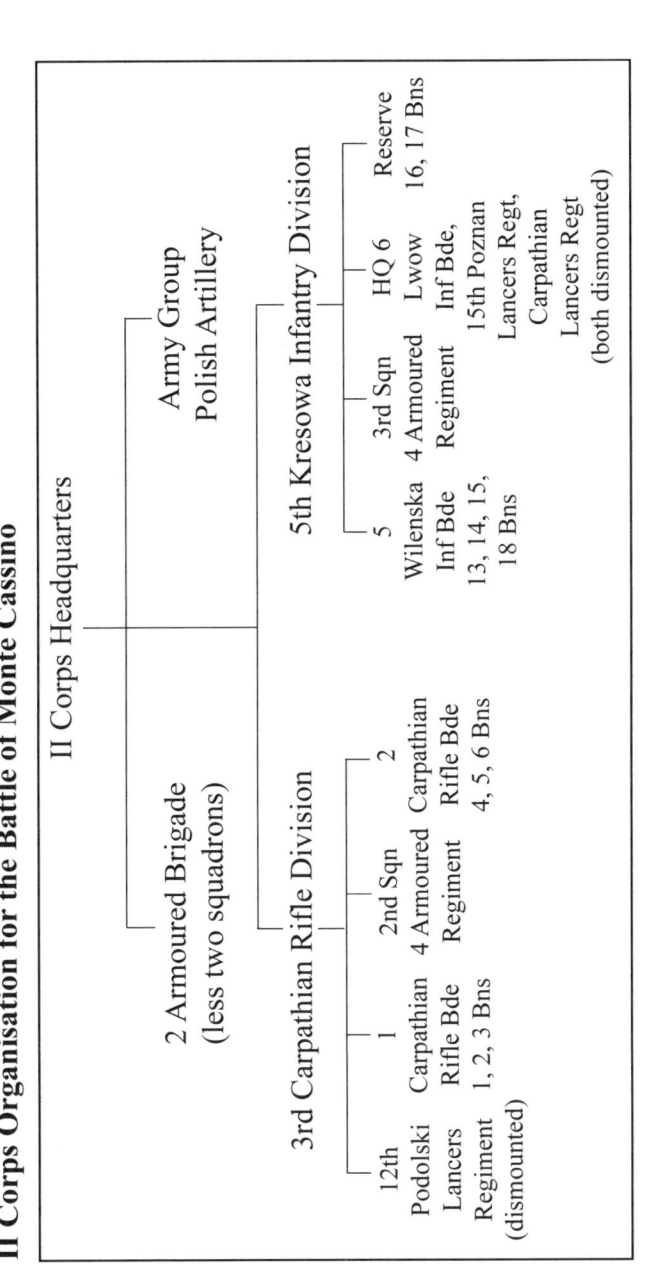

10

Preparations for Battle

To coordinate the preparation and operations for the assault on Monte Cassino, a Tactical Headquarters was established in the area east of San Vittore on the western slope of feature 687, on 18 April. The Tactical Headquarters moved to the Passo Annunziata Lunga slope on 3 May for better cover, while the original site was used as a forward observation post by the formation commanders. The Tactical Headquarters was a small base containing only the personnel needed for the command organization, namely the Corps Commander and his personal staff, Lieutenant Colonel Jan Lachowicz's Headquarters Defence Company, signals and other essential services. Lieutenant General Anders' aide de camp was Captain Prince Eugeniusz Lubomirski, a diplomat who had served in the Polish Embassy in Paris as chargé d'affairs before the fall of France. His linguistic and diplomatic skills were much in demand. The Main Headquarters was much larger and located further behind the lines – here the Chief of Staff coordinated the detailed planning and staff work concerning operations. The Rear Headquarters was established in the Mutteo area from 18 April and accommodated the quartermasters and associated service branch chiefs dealing with the detailed and extensive work of supplying and maintaining the Corps.

Harold Macmillan visited the headquarters on 24 April and was greatly awed by the spectacle, for it was not merely a field command post but a miniature recreation of an entire country, complete with rituals, one of the most memorable being the distinctive sounding of the trumpet at noon each day. This reenacted the historical call to the people of Krakow to muster against the Tartars, in that the performer always ends on a broken note, the originally trumpeter having been shot through the neck with an arrow as he played. Such cultural expressions of their history of struggle against oppressors reinforced their determination to continue the fight against the Germans and also served to remind them that the coming engagements would result in loss of life. It was becoming apparent to all Allied visitors and personnel assigned to the Polish headquarters and formations that the Poles were going to display a very different attitude to the battle than the other Allied contingents.

Between 24 and 27 April, Polish troops began taking over the Cassino sector, relieving the British 78th Infantry Division, whose soldiers were taken aback by the intensity of Polish feeling towards the Germans. One officer wrote: 'They hated the Germans, and their military outlook was dominated by their hate. Their one idea was to find out where the nearest Germans were and go after them... They thought we were far too casual because we didn't breathe blind hate all the time.'[1] With their passionate motivation for the fight the Poles were largely disappointed by what they deemed to be the mundane professionalism of the Eighth Army, contrasting Polish heroism against the British sense of duty, a national characteristic the Poles interpreted as a reluctance to fight to the death. The ordinary British soldiers were simply bemused by the Poles' intensity and the reckless behaviour that was often the result. Of their resolve there could be no doubt. According to an officer in the Irish Brigade: 'Their motives were as clear as they were simple. They only wished to kill the Germans and they did not bother at all about the usual refinements when taking over our posts. They just walked in with their weapons and that was that.'[2]

The most important of the 'usual refinements' was trying to avoid being seen or heard by the enemy, but this did not seem to interest the Poles at all. For them, these enforced lulls in the fighting were merely a tedious delay, and passively manning the line was not something to which they had given much thought. However, from the moment of taking over the sector the soldiers had to live in their defensive positions under constant enemy observation from many directions. Movement was really only possible by night, as movement by day brought down enemy infantry and artillery fire. During daylight the men had to stay in cramped, uncomfortable positions in shallow hollows scraped in the rocky ground, without adequate cover against enemy fire. The idea of cowering out of sight of the Germans for days on end was particularly distasteful and many Poles took extraordinary risks in demonstrating their impatience with this sort of hole-and-corner warfare, frequently leaving their shelters to openly taunt the Germans with foul language and gestures.

The crews of 2 Armoured Brigade were reunited with their tanks at Pignataro before moving to the Corps' staging area of Capriati on the River Volturno. The tanks were carried by Specialist 'Diamond-T' tank transporters of the Eighth Army's 4 Tank Transporter Company by road; these massive articulated lorries were highly specialized vehicles, boasting 21 gears and towing a 22-wheeled low-loader trailer. The winding mountain roads leading towards the front were frequently little more than glorified mule tracks, and combined with blacked-out night driving required the drivers to be highly skilled. The tanks were unloaded in the Corps' operational area and handed over to the 9th Forward

Delivery Squadron that delivered the tanks to the armoured regiments' encampments around the village of Prata. This squadron also supplied tracked vehicles for the artillery and engineer formations including self-propelled guns, gun tractors, bridging tanks and tracked recovery vehicles. New armoured vehicles for 2 Armoured Brigade were held east of Naples by the 7th Reserve Tank Battalion vehicle-holding section, where the vehicles were assembled and crews readied for despatch to the front.

At Capriati, training and familiarization with the infantry divisions was conducted, establishing methods of cooperation, a system of codes and signals agreed and personal contacts formed. The tanks of the platoon commanders were now outfitted with additional radio equipment and all 52 Shermans of the 4th Armoured Regiment received additional armour plating. In this staging area the regiment was subject to a German air raid that caused little damage and no casualties. The 4th 'Skorpion' Armoured Regiment, named for the many scorpions that shared the training camps with the tank crews in the Middle East, was assigned to provide armoured support for the forthcoming battle. The 2nd Squadron was assigned to the Carpathian Rifle Division and the 3rd Squadron to the Kresowa Infantry Division. The 1 Krechowiecki Lancers Regiment did not participate in the fighting at Cassino, being based from 24 April in Cardito, 10km north of Naples. The 'Children of Lwów' 6 Armoured Regiment was held in the Corps' reserve.

The extent of the earlier attack by the New Zealand Corps was delineated by their trio of knocked-out Sherman tanks. On 28 April the Polish tanks relieved the Canadians in all their forward positions. Lieutenant Bobaka's platoon immediately moved to the forwardmost positions, observing German activity around the gorge and performing other tasks as required by the commander of the 14th Infantry Battalion, with whom they were in constant radio contact. Lieutenant Bobaka's men mounted the immobilized New Zealand tanks under fire from the German artillery and mortars. The tanks had suffered damage to their weaponry, steering, batteries and engines that the platoon set themselves to fix, creating a list of all damaged components that night. The commander of the 14th Infantry Battalion had forbidden all vehicle traffic to the front, so every night the crews ran back and forth to San Michele, with mule columns to carry the heavier parts, and over the coming days and nights were able to fully restore the three tanks to combat readiness, the noise of the engine tests being masked by artillery fire. The tanks were nicknamed Adam, Barbara and Celina and were to play a full part in the upcoming battle. On 1 May, the 3rd Squadron sent forth four of their own tanks from the 1st Platoon to the 'car park' area on Cavendish Road to cover the area Villa–Caira, coming under the operational command of 6 Lwów Infantry Brigade. The crews fulfilled this role, under constant fire, until 11 May. These and Lieutenant Bobaka's platoon were the first Polish tank teams on the front line in Italy.

The Polish artillery had by May 1944 grown to its largest size yet in the period of exile. Their commanders placed great confidence in the decisive effect this firepower could provide on the battlefield, based on the experiences of the North African campaign. However, the nature of the fighting and the terrain of Italy were far removed from the rapid advances and vast open spaces of North Africa. The weapons and tactics that were so effective in that earlier campaign would prove far less decisive in the fighting to come. At Cassino the Polish artillery had to be established sufficiently far forward to provide support for the infantry attacks. Unfortunately this entailed siting the guns in the flat Rapido Valley beneath German observation posts on Monte Cifalco, Monte Cairo and Monastery Hill, and under enemy artillery attack from the area Belmonte–Atina (north of Monte Cifalco). A strict control was maintained over all artillery activity so that the total volume of fire each day never varied, and the Germans could have no suspicion that many new batteries were being moved into position. These new guns were always moved into sites that had been previously camouflaged.

The example of the 6 Lwów Light Artillery Regiment is representative of the conditions encountered by the gunners crammed into the valley floor beneath Cassino. The Regiment moved into position on 22 April, relieving the Free French artillery. The position was not favourable as it was bisected by a major supply road which attracted much attention from German observers and received constant shelling – on 29 April, eighty 105mm shells landed on the second battery alone. Due to the need to preserve secrecy there was a lack of direct reconnaissance of the terrain prior to the battle that led to the guns being positioned to less than maximum effect. Further difficulties were encountered with the emplacement of the guns that had to be made in the gorges of streams in the immediate vicinity of roads due to the lack of tracked vehicles. The gorges seldom ran at the optimum angle to the line of fire and they were too few and far between for the artillery to keep in range with the infantry advance. The exposed artillery positions on the valley floor therefore had to be extremely well camouflaged and had to remain silent until the actual assault began. The supply of the positions also posed a major challenge. All stores for the artillery were brought to the eastern side of the Rapido Valley by truck and were then transferred to jeeps and mules for delivery to the positions at night.

Previous Allied assaults at Monte Cassino had revealed that artillery alone gave the infantry insufficient close support and that high-angle weapons were also needed to engage the enemy's prepared emplacements. In light of this, the Polish divisional anti-tank regiments were issued seventy-two 4.2in. heavy mortars and sixteen flamethrowers between them. Unfortunately this new equipment did not arrive in time for their crews to receive adequate training, so the mortars and flame-throwers were not employed in a close support role as envisaged, thus greatly reducing the advantages anticipated for their deployment. To assist with counter-artillery and mortar battery fire, 3 Battery of the 8 Heavy Anti-Aircraft Artillery Regiment was assigned to II Corps, providing eight guns in the ground support role sited in the vicinity of the Inferno Track. The guns' high rate of fire and air-burst shells proved particularly effective; the flat trajectory was however a limitation in that only targets in line of sight could be engaged. Resulting from these combined difficulties the corps level heavy artillery had to be used for direct support, though the dispersion was too great to allow for adequate synchronization with the movements of the infantry.

The Signals Corps was busy laying over 70 miles of telephone and telegraph cables, fitting 2,300 field telephones, installing 220 switchboards and establishing a network of couriers. When the Polish II Corps relieved the British 78th Infantry Division a strict radio silence was imposed on them, so their language would not give away the fact that they had now come into the line. If they had to use radios they employed English signallers attached to them for the purpose. Signals and communications were pivotal to organizing the assembling army, and German observers were keeping a close watch on the cable routes, bringing down artillery and mortar fire upon them during the night when it would be most difficult to locate and fix the line breaks.

The vulnerability of the telephone network was highlighted a few days prior to the battle by an incident at San Pietro. Whilst searching for a break in a cable a signalman of the Line Maintenance Section found the line becoming slack near a garden shed. Tugging at it, unsuspecting, he pulled the pin out of a grenade tied to the end of the cable, which exploded twenty or thirty metres ahead of him. Following this incident the Carpathian Signals Battalion headquarters received a telephone call from an unknown person with a German accent. 'What's the time?' the startled operator was asked, and the caller went on, 'Are you not yet tired of repairing such damage? Because we do not get tired of causing it.'[3] The Germans constantly hacked into the telephone network, concealing their attached wires with artificial pigeons. Their operatives would then call up Polish positions claiming that they had lost their codebooks, and could they reply by sending a plain text message. To counter this threat frequent patrols guarded the telephone lines, regularly firing machine-gun bursts to scare away the birds, any still sitting would indicate German agents had been at work. Such frequent incidents highlighted the importance of using coded messages at all times. A section of messenger pigeons were attached to each division as an emergency communications back-up.

Signals sections at the Corps Headquarters played a pivotal role in liaising between ground formations and their supporting aircraft. Requests for aerial artillery spotting were passed on to 651 RAF Artillery Air Observation Squadron, where five dedicated spotter aircraft identified enemy artillery positions, with one aircraft for each division, two for the Army Group Polish Artillery and one free. The pilots and observers would radio in their sightings to the Air Support Signals Unit, who in turn relayed them to the Army units. Requests for aerial reconnaissance were forwarded in the same manner, the Air Support Signals Unit contacting 318 Polish Air Force Squadron. Photographs were sent from the airfield by motorcycle dispatch rider to the Corps Intelligence Headquarters, where the Army Photographic Interpretation Unit analysed them in detail.

The engineers had a great variety of tasks to perform during the build-up to the battle. A special supply track named the Polish Sappers' Road had to be reconstructed, under fire from the Germans, to allow the transportation of infantry, tanks, and equipment to the front. This route became crucial for the carriage of ammunition and for the evacuation of the wounded. Numerous artillery positions had to be constructed in hilly terrain, which frequently entailed digging in and positioning guns on hillsides with slopes of over 45 degrees, all of which had to be achieved under camouflage to conceal the preparations as much as possible from the Germans. The level terrain of the Rapido Valley floor posed a different set of problems, the land was waterlogged and swamp-like and subsequently a hotbed of infectious disease. Over one million sandbags were laid to assist in the draining of the land, as the result of a cholera or malaria outbreak would have been devastating.

The engineers worked closely with the Intelligence Section's camouflage units, frequently setting up smoke screens to conceal movements and construction work. Effective as these were, they inevitably had a short duration and more permanent screening of fixed locations was needed, especially from Luftwaffe observers. The huge stockpiles of ammunition and supplies had to be kept concealed and the dispersement of the stores to numerous smaller dumps facilitated this, some being ingeniously disguised as rocky outcrops, while stockpiles of petrol cans were concealed beneath olive groves. The artillery and mortar positions also had to be well camouflaged in their exposed positions on the valley floor. Some batteries were located in new positions not used by the previous formations, the new roads delineated by lime and rock piles. Others sited their gun positions in the shell craters that pockmarked the previous regiment's position. Roads were also hidden from enemy observation, the 1,500ft approach to the Carpathian division's headquarters being concealed by curtains, as were the entry to the Kresowa division's headquarters, the half-kilometre road to the mules' watering station and the route to the gun emplacements of the 7 Horse

Artillery Regiment. Movements were also strictly regulated – at the headquarters of the Carpathian division, amongst dense olive groves, moving across the open glades was forbidden, to conceal any activity from the Germans, who could readily observe the area from the monastery. The camouflage arrangements were highly successful, aerial photographs showing barely a trace of the 15,000 tons of ammunition, petrol and stores dumped amongst the olive trees north and east of Venafro.

The Poles fielded three engineering battalions at Cassino, one for each division and one at corps level. The Corps Field Park Company was based west of Venafro, some 20km from the front, along with the divisional engineers' main field parks, sharing the same location as the Graves Registration. The Carpathian engineers' advanced store was the 'San Michele Dump', located 4km behind the front and occupying some 80,000m², while the Kresowa engineers' advanced store was sited in Inferno Gorge. The Corps' 1st company worked extensively preparing the Polish Sappers' Road along with the 6th Kresowa Engineers Company, while 4th and 5th Companies maintained the roads in the Inferno Track supply dump area and also along the entire length of that route from Acquafondata to Portella. The 1st Carpathian Engineers Company was tasked with assisting the evacuation of battlefield casualties and maintaining the lines of communication. At this time, 2 Armoured Brigade had no dedicated engineers, the 2nd and 3rd Companies of the Carpathian and Corps Engineers being detailed to support the advance of the tanks of 4 Armoured Regiment. Italian Pioneer Companies installed and operated 18,000 smoke candles to conceal the Polish artillery positions, along with camouflage constructed from 4,000 nets, 5,800 gallons of paint, 1,500 yards of hessian and 50 coils of steel wool.[4]

The supply and maintenance of II Corps was a vast task. To reduce this extra burden on the command staff a separate Sub Area Headquarters was formed at Venafro to organize the supply lines in the Corps' operational area. The brunt of the distribution work fell to the Supply and Transport Corps. Supply was the coordinating element responsible for the supply depots and arranging the distribution of food, water, domestic stores, lubricants, disinfectants, medical supplies and fuel for cooking, heating and lighting. The transport section was solely tasked with the responsibility for delivering the supplies along with the vehicles, their maintenance and the provision of drivers. The organization was equivalent to the British Royal Army Service Corps. A separate Ordnance Corps organized combat equipment and ammunition supplies, frequently utilizing the Supply & Transport Corps organization for final delivery and distribution to the end users.

II Corps' operational area around Monte Cassino lay some 240 miles north of the base area in the heel of Italy and to achieve efficient re-supply all deliveries were divided into several stages. The largest link in the chain, the line of communication zone, stretched from the base areas in southern Italy to the distribution centres serving the numerous corps at the front and was administered by the British Eighth Army. The Eighth delivered all supplies and equipment for II Corps by train, principally to the railhead at Vairano and its surrounding depots, each train delivering on average 2,500 tons of goods. From these centres the Polish authorities took responsibility for distributing and delivering supplies and ammunition to their formations. The destination for all stores movements was 401 Forward Maintenance Centre, 20km away at Venafro, from where stores of all kinds were collected and distributed. This sprawling facility contained supply detachments from all the branches and services of the divisional and Corps formations and acted as a channel through which munitions, food, transport and reinforcements were able to reach the forward units. Vast stockpiles of stores of every kind were built up in preparation for the battle of Monte Cassino, including 395,000 gallons of petrol and 339,000 food ration packs with the transport sections carrying 16,000 truckloads of ammunition, 4,000 of food supplies and 4,000 of war materials.[5]

Ammunition arrived in Italy at 557 Base Ordnance Depot at Bari and thence to 14 and 16 Base Ammunition Depots that despatched trains to Advanced Ammunition Depots 3 and 501 at the respective railheads of Vairano and Mignano. Depot 3 at Vairano was capable of handling 2,000 tons of stores per day and 501 Depot at Mignano had a daily capacity of 900 tons. The unloading of these trains at Vairano was conducted by 350 Ordnance Railhead Company, dividing the stock into useable quantities and preparing these for loading onto trucks for delivery to a holding point, 401 Forward Ammunition Depot, from where ammunition was distributed to the formations assisted by the inclusion of two Eighth Army Ammunition Rates held in the depot. A reserve stock was kept at the Vairano railhead and on the eve of the attack the dump held 4,463 tons of shells. In total over one million rounds of artillery and mortar bombs were stockpiled for the battle. Daily ammunition expenditure during the build-up to the battle reached 1,000 tons.[6]

The delivery of vehicles to all Allied armoured formations in Italy entailed sizeable logistic challenges, stemming from the ever-growing distances between the base vehicles parks and the front line. The Eighth Army delivered all vehicles to II Corps operational area at the Eighth Army Forward Vehicle Park, while engines, spare parts and gun barrels were delivered to the Eighth Army Ordnance Field Park at Riardo. From these depots the Polish 37 Corps Troops Ordnance Field Park collected the vehicles and spares to their staging point on the banks of the River Volturno.

The organization and control of this sprawling transport system was a considerable administrative challenge. Responsibility for movements within the Corps' operational area lay with the headquarters' Movement section that devised the delivery schedules. These were then passed to the military police's Traffic Control section that provided advice on the capacity and adequacy of roads, the degree and type of traffic control required and on whether existing resources would prove adequate. The Traffic Control companies of the formations then ensured that troop and supply convoys reached their allotted destinations at the required time, largely through the use of checkpoints and signposts with motorcycle MPs maintaining order on the roads and directing traffic flow.

The Corps' operational area was itself subdivided into three stages: the third-line supply and transport units collected goods from Vairano and other Eighth Army depots and transported them to 401 Forward Maintenance Centre. At this depot complex the second-line supply companies of the divisions and tank brigade broke down the bulk supplies into the quantities and type required by the front-line units, at Detail Issue Depots 326, 327 and 328, where enough stock was held to last for two to three days. Food and water were distributed daily to the formations with food rations dispatched from 326 Supply Depot by second-line transport units to the divisional maintenance areas and thence by first-line transport companies to the forward positions, frequently by means of mules and jeeps.

The infantry division's second-line transport companies used their own dedicated routes for the delivery of supplies from Venafro. The Carpathian division used Highway 6, with the village of San Michele as its staging area, utilizing their tracked Universal Carriers to transport stores. The Kresowa division was supplied through the mountains to the north using the same route as the New Zealand Corps in the adjacent sector, this being from Pozzilli to Acquafondata and thence by the Inferno Track to the divisional dump in Inferno Gorge near the village of Portella. This route was limited to seventy vehicles per day due to the slow, rugged nature of the track; additional stores deliveries were routed along the 3rd Division's supply line. Most supply convoys were sent out in the hours of darkness under cover of smoke screens, as the German artillery had a commanding view over the main roads in the vicinity of Monte Cassino and had prepared accurate fire plans to disrupt them. The road haulage capacity of the Poles was boosted by the assignment of several British and American units; three British General Transport Companies were assigned for the build-up to the battle, along with a Tipper Company for road construction and maintenance. The US Army allocated a Motor Ambulance Convoy to assist with the carriage of wounded soldiers.

The first-line transport companies in the divisional area collected stores from the brigade dump and delivered them to the front line. Delivery was made by truck, jeep and trailer, by mule and by porters, almost exclusively by night to avoid detection by the Germans. Each infantry brigade was assigned two British Royal Army Service Corps platoons of 33 Jeeps with bantam trailers. The jeeps were fitted with chains over their tyres and were able to access positions in the most rugged terrain. These jeep platoons made their first appearance during the winter of 1943 and proved to be highly effective; the Poles referred to them as Light Transport Companies and each Polish brigade retained one platoon each on a permanent basis, the second platoon returning to the British after the conclusion of the assault on the Gustav Line. On the front, 2 Armoured Brigade's units were supplied from the brigade dump established at Pratta, close to the railhead at Vairano that was kept stocked by Captain Skarsynski's 9th Supply Company. Willy's Jeeps and Stuart light tanks effected the final delivery of water, fuel, food and ammunition to the front line.

The execution of all these movements required a vast quantity of fuel, with each infantry division allocated 49,000 gallons of petrol per day. Petrol was pumped via a pipeline from Naples to 18 British Petrol Filling Centre at Mignano, where road tankers of 78 British Bulk Transport Petrol Company forwarded it to 12 British Mobile Petrol Filling Centre 3km south of Pozilli, that acted as a filling station for road vehicles. Those formations that could not reach the filling station were supplied by 334 Petrol Depot where the fuel was transferred into containers for distribution to the end users. The depot also dealt with diesel and lube oils. The adjacent 335 Firefighting Team provided firefighting units for the rear areas, in particular the petrol depots, ordnance and stores parks as well as all other military and civilian locations.

The precipitous terrain around Monte Cassino limited motor vehicles to basic movements between depots and the forward staging posts. To deliver the supplies to the front line necessitated in many circumstances the use of mules. The Cyprus Regiment of the British Army operated all pack transport companies for the Eighth Army, with the Cyprus Pack Mule Group established to provided mules for the assault on the Gustav Line. Five mule companies were dedicated to supplying Polish troops on the slopes of the Monte Cassino massif; the Carpathian division was assigned three mule companies, the Kresowa two. Troop sergeants were responsible for overseeing the loading of the mules, during which process the animals were tethered, each mule being loaded in 4–5 minutes. Every night between 700 and 1,200 mules would set off in single file along the treacherous mountain paths, branching out to reach the divisions' positions. An infantry battalion would on average require 50 mule loads per night, each animal carrying over 180lbs of supplies. On their return journey the mules carried the wounded to medical aid posts. The animals' hooves were wrapped with cloth to reduce the noise of metal shoes on stone, although the sound of dislodged rocks was enough to bring German mortar fire down on the tracks, the locations of which the Germans were well aware. Injured and sick mules were treated by the veterinary section of the Polish medical corps, who wore distinctive collar patches of mauve edged in dark green and additional care was provided by 1 British Veterinary and Remount Section and 803 British Cavalry Mobile Veterinary Section.

The care of the wounded was a priority task that in the difficult Italian terrain necessitated much close cooperation between the operational and administrative branches. To achieve as rapid a system of evacuation as possible the process was divided into many stages from the battlefield to the hospital (see Table 7). Casualty treatment began in the field, all soldiers being trained to provide elementary first aid and to administer morphine. Every soldier was issued with a first field dressing to be kept in a specially provided pocket on the right leg of the battledress trousers, while a larger shell dressing was often stowed under the camouflage netting of the helmet. A medical platoon was assigned to each infantry battalion headquarters, providing immediate front-line care for the wounded at the Battalion Aid Post staffed by a medical officer, usually a captain from the assigned ambulance company. Assisted by a medical orderly he would assess which casualties could be saved and which were beyond all hope of survival – such men were read their last rites by a chaplain. The brigade's assigned ambulance company would then evacuate the wounded from the battlefield to the Advanced Dressing Station by hand, or on jeeps specially adapted with a framework that could carry up to four stretchers. Men drawn from the anti-tank and anti-aircraft artillery regiments supplemented the ranks of the stretcher-bearers. The armoured regiments operated a similarly structured system, but mechanized, with turretless Stuart tanks evacuating the wounded. Those casualties able to walk from the battlefield were to make their way to the Walking Wounded Collection Post for transportation to the Advanced Dressing Stations.

The Advanced Dressing Stations' primary role was to stabilize the most seriously wounded before their onward journey. Here they were given some immediate treatment, anti-tetanus injections were administered to them and their personal records collected. The operating tents were dug into the ground, as the Advanced Dressing Stations were well within range of enemy artillery. From here the ambulance company transported the casualties onwards to the Main Dressing Stations located at the Ambulance Company Headquarters. At these tented facilities casualties were rapidly assessed by a medical officer who sorted the cases according to whether resuscitation and urgent operation was required, or for onward evacuation. The walking wounded were transferred to a large holding tent, where dressings could be adjusted and from where they could be rapidly loaded into ambulance cars or trucks. The Polish Women's

Auxiliary Service and the Red Cross provided canteens that maintained a constant supply of hot drinks and light meals. Those whose injuries were not severe were then moved to the Rest Station and Convalescent Depot at Acquafondata prior to rejoining their units.

The most serious cases, including casualties with abdominal wounds that required immediate intervention, were taken to the attached surgical teams. Field surgery units were located at each Main Dressing Station, Casualty Clearing Station and the Field Hospital, and were composed of two surgeons, usually specialists in abdominal surgery, with their attendant staff. Major Mieczysław Bieleckiego headed II Corps' surgery units, that were supplemented by four units from the British Royal Army Medical Corps. These field surgery units were a new concept trialled for the first time at Cassino, operating from under canvas awnings extending from the sides of specially equipped lorries. Each active Main Dressing Station was assigned a field transfusion unit as part of the surgery unit, which proved invaluable for the resuscitation of serious cases and also for enabling their onward travel to the casualty clearing station. The blood was provided from British Royal Army Medical Corps supplies and was kept refrigerated, so it could be stored for up to three weeks. For the most serious cases transfusions were arranged to continue in transit by means of frames and clamps improvised by the engineers' workshops. On 8 May, tragedy struck when the Main Dressing Station of the 6th Ambulance Company was destroyed by German artillery fire.

From the Main Dressing Station, casualties requiring further treatment proceeded to the Clearing Stations in motor ambulances of the Supply & Transport Corps' 29 Motor Ambulance Convoy. The convoy consisted of seventy-five ambulances, predominantly Austin K2s, along with Bedford Mk1 heavy ambulances, unarmed half-tracks and modified jeeps. The unit was based at 3 Casualty Clearing Station at Venafro, transporting casualties from the Main Dressing Stations along a route running Portella–San Michele–Cervaro–San Vittore–Pietro–Infinie–Venafro. The American 567 Motor Ambulance Convoy was equipped with Dodge ambulance cars based at 5 Casualty Clearing Station and performed the same role transporting casualties on a different route to the north, running Portella–(Inferno Track)–Acquafondata–Pozzilli–Venafro. These US soldiers were immediately recognizable, all being African-American recruits.

Both Major Dr Leon Kehle's 3 Casualty Clearing Station (CCS) and Lieutenant Colonel Dr Stanisław Sikora's 5 CCS shared the same allocation of resources, principally a medical team headed by a surgeon – Captain Dr Adam Jakabowski at 3 CCS and Captain Dr Donat Massalki at 5 CCS, assisted by eight nurses and numerous supporting staff. The facility could cater for 200 wounded, with 50 beds and space for 150 stretchers. The casualty clearing stations comprised several tented facilities and wards. The medical officer on duty at reception decided whether patients required operation, admittance to a ward or onward travel to a more specialized facility. Those deemed to require immediate surgery were sent direct to the pre-operative ward, where blood transfusions and other resuscitation aids were provided along with X-rays. From there they were taken by stretcher to the operating theatre – a large structure made from two tents laced together. An ambulance was stationed at the theatre to transfer patients to the wards immediately after their operation. Most other wards were of large square tarpaulin tents. Beds were available in only one of the surgical wards, in the other patients lay on stretchers. The staff slept in their wards or in bivouacs close by. The all-important canteens of the Polish Women's Auxiliary Service maintained a steady flow of food and drink, Łomnicka canteen serving 3 CCS and Bronianowska 5 CCS.

The two casualty clearing stations alternated admission days, so only one would receive the wounded each day. This gave the staff twenty-four hours to prepare patients for onward travel and evacuate them to 6 Field Hospital, ensuring the station had all its beds and facilities ready for the next day's admissions. Those successfully treated were discharged and marched to the troop transit camp at 401 Forward Maintenance Centre. Those fit to return to the battle zone were placed in the reinforcement pool and so rejoined their previous unit. Those who needed more time to recover were transported to the local convalescent depot at Acquafondata. Drivers of the motor ambulance convoys transported the patients from the casualty clearing station to hospital.

Major Dr Stanisław Krzywański directed 6 Field Hospital, where wounds requiring more surgery than the Casualty Clearing Station could provide were operated on. This facility was the Polish Field Hospital during the battle, being located just outside the town of Pozzilli, 24km from Monte Cassino. The hospital was newly established on 24 April with base hospital personnel from the Convalescent Home with the addition of the British 9th Field Surgery Unit. Casualties requiring further extensive medical attention were transported by the 31st Corps Ambulance Company through Bojano to 2 General Hospital at Campobasso, where there were 600 beds.

All preparations for the battle were completed by 8 May with zero hour set for 2300 hrs on 11 May. The soldiers in the line now had to wait in their positions' shelters, though some became reckless living amongst such constant bombardment and had to be reined in before their carelessness caused injury. Many found the best way to handle the fear was to sleep whenever possible; for all it was a bitter test of self-control.

The short distance between the opposing forces meant that even the smallest movement would draw down German fire, as the whole area was under close observation. This in turn meant that no food could be prepared

Table 7
Line of Evacuation for Battlefield Casualties

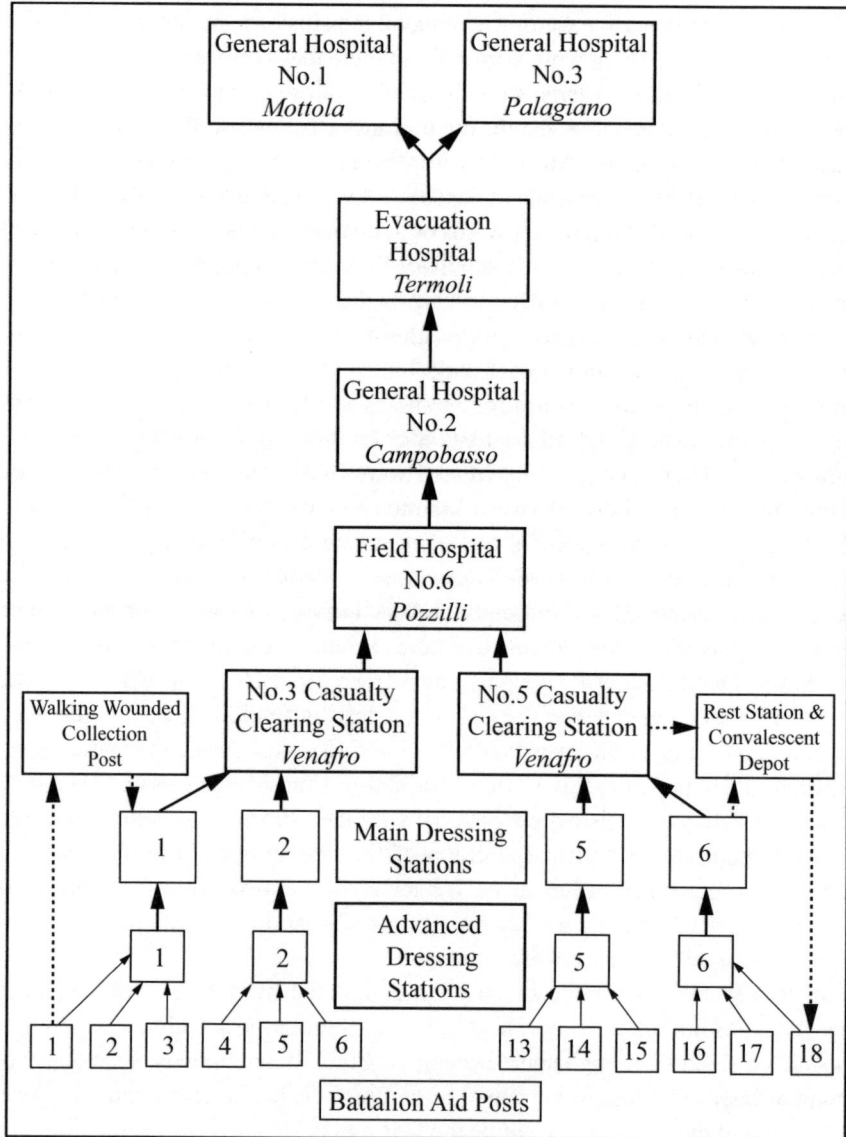

or brought up; the men existed purely on dry rations and water, the latter a scarce commodity frequently carried by heavily laden mules. Not that many of the men had much of an appetite with all the decaying corpses around, especially as the bodies were engulfed by flies during the day and gnawed at by rats through the night. With little movement possible during the day, the business of defecation was effected by the use of empty ration tins. These were then hurled over into the German lines accompanied by a string of expletives.

The stealthy transfer of the Eighth Army and its Polish Corps to the Cassino sector was a complete success. In those six weeks of spring and early summer between the end of the third battle on 24 March and the launching of the fourth offensive, the whole Allied front presented a daily picture of half-hearted defence. There were sporadic exchanges of a few shells, an occasional round or two of mortar. But there was no noticeable change in the landscape, no new roads or discernible gun positions, no troop movements. There was nothing to indicate that the approaches to the Rapido could now handle considerable volumes of traffic, that some mountain tracks could now bear tanks, that the number of artillery pieces between Cassino and the sea had swollen to 1,600. As late as the second day of the battle Kesselring estimated that the Allies had six divisions against the four with which he was defending the Cassino front – in fact there were thirteen. Alexander had achieved the three-to-one local superiority ratio that had been accepted as essential to a major breakthrough against modern prepared defences.

11

Assault on the Gustav Line

Lieutenant General Anders' order for the day of 11 May opened: 'Soldiers! The moment for battle has arrived. We have long awaited the moment for revenge and retribution over our hereditary enemy.'[1] Generals Leese and Alexander must have raised their eyebrows at such words; the passionately expressed hatred of the Germans was like that of no other Allied contingent and there could be no mistaking the savagery of the fighting to ensue. Indeed, the Eighth Army's attempts to buoy them up before the battle were far from being so evocative, with Leese's address concluding, 'We address our special greeting to the Polish Corps which fights now at our side for the liberation of its beloved country. I appeal to you all. I wish to see in your eyes the eagerness for battle. To arms! Every man must do his duty in the struggle ahead but final victory will belong to all of us.'[2]

The difference between the addresses of Anders and Leese clearly showed the Poles as being motivated by passion and the British by a sense of duty – indeed Leese and his staff appeared to be oblivious to the fact that the Poles viewed the coming battle as vengeance for the plight of their homeland. These men had lost everything and it was clear to them that the end of the war would not mean the end of their troubles but the beginning of new ones. There was a cold fury in their demeanour. More than any other soldiers on the Allied side they had good reason to hate. They had come a long way and endured a great deal to fight the men who had ravaged their country in 1939, and there would be no half measures about the way they went into the attack. The British Military Liaison to the Polish II Corps also seemed to miss the mark, with a rallying speech that left the Poles with a sense of being inadvertently embarrassed and patronized. The only emotional contribution made by the British was in their christening the Polish attack with the code name Operation Honker, a name the Poles believed likened them to a flock of geese homeward bound. The British, for their part, wondered whether the intensity of the Poles might not sometimes be their undoing and perhaps cost them many lives. For modern war is a skill as well as a test of courage, and bravery is not enough. Assault had to be cunning not merely fanatical. What was certain was that these men would give everything. They had willingly taken on the unpleasantest of the many unpleasant tasks this offensive entailed – the scramble across the vicious ridges that were now strewn with nearly as many corpses as boulders.

The preceding days had been sunny but the morning of 11 May was dull and it remained so all day; a little rain fell and by afternoon there was a haze over the valley. Summer had arrived and the valley floor erupted with wild corn and poppies that flourished undeterred by the salvos of artillery. The winter fighting had taken a huge toll on the mountainsides – where there should have been groves of acacia, olive, orange, vine and oak stood only lacerated stumps. The shattered remains of the monastery still stood on high, in noble defiance of the passing battle, a fleeting though destructive episode in its long history. The early morning sun would burst through the dawn haze, bathing the blue-grey mountain and honey-coloured ruins of the Abbey in a glow of gold and pink.

That day the plan was for the Allied artillery to cease firing before nightfall and the day's light firing programme petered out altogether during the afternoon to create a low-key atmosphere, a calm before the storm. Almost simultaneously the German guns also ceased firing and a strange silence descended on Monte Cassino and the valley. Prior to this the guns of both sides had fallen quiet only once that year, on Easter Day, and in the prelude to the offensive the silence was uncanny and oppressive. The Poles in their forming-up positions were aware this was to be no ordinary battle; their thoughts during these long hours varied according to each man's temperament. Probably all felt the weight of the occasion, unless war-weariness had filled their minds with apathy and resentment. The men experienced every emotion and thought from exhilaration to acute fear, and states of mind succeeded each other, or passed only to return, or most strangely occur almost simultaneously.

The sun set at a quarter past eight to the singing of nightingales, and as darkness fell fireflies took to the calm air. The night was warm, with some mist forming in the valleys of the Gari and Liri and in pockets on the higher ground. Looking up the commanders were relieved to see a bright starry sky and to know they would not be deprived of the services of the late moonrise.

At 2300 hrs, half an hour before moonrise, the artillery of the entire Eighth and Fifth Armies sprang to life, tearing the night sky to pieces in a blaze of gun flashes and a cacophony of destruction. Throughout the first forty minutes, in positions from Acquafondata stretching as far east as the Tyrrhenian coast, over 1,000 guns of the Eighth Army concentrated their fire on known enemy artillery and mortar positions in the area of Atina–Belmonte, Villa S. Lucia and the Liri valleys, 'Mortar', Wadi, Passo Corno and the area of Terelle. This counter-battery fire was of particular importance to the Polish II Corps' operations, owing to the right-angled bend formed by the front line in the area of Monte

Cairo, which enabled enemy artillery from Belmonte–Atina to fire into the rear of attacking Polish troops. At the end of this 40 minutes, that is after 2340 hrs, the bulk of the artillery was directed against enemy infantry positions on the objectives of both Corps' attacks, while at the same time the harassing of enemy artillery and mortars continued.

The majority of Polish artillery guns were located in the valley floor beneath the monastery and thus were firing at targets unseen to the gunners, relying totally on the accuracy of the observers' radio reports and preceding artillery-mapping surveys. Amongst the many gunners involved was Captain Bronisław Sokołowski, Commander of 4 Troop, 2nd Battery, 9 Light Artillery Regiment, which commenced firing at 2305 hrs and continued non-stop all night. From his sandbagged command post, nicknamed the Stork's Nest, Sokołowski relayed target coordinates received from headquarters to the gunners by a one-way phone link, the gunners using hand signals to acknowledge receipt of the orders. During the following morning Sokołowski had to leave the command post to visit one of his gunners who had apparently not acknowledged the receipt of an order. He was only ten paces from the Stork's Nest when it was destroyed by German artillery fire. This counter-fire from the Germans inflicted many casualties amongst the artillery positioned on the flat valley floor beneath the hills. Despite the Corps' gun positions being concealed by a smokescreen over a belt of ground 7km wide for the whole period of the attack, the German artillery began shelling their positions once they had been revealed during the preceding firing. However the smoke did prove successful in hampering the accuracy of this counter-battery fire.

In preparation for the attack the Sherman tanks of the 2nd and 3rd Squadrons, along with two tanks from the regimental headquarters and two batteries of self-propelled anti-tank guns (Wolverines), moved out from San Michele at 2300 hrs. The 1st Squadron along with the 17th Lwów Infantry Battalion was held as a corps reserve around San Michele. To avoid unnecessary complications between the tank squadrons and the infantry brigades, coordination of the tanks, Wolverines and engineers was overseen by Captain Iwanowski. The 3rd squadron's 1st platoon based in the car park was the first to make the start line. The front could only be reached along the narrow, winding mountain track called the Polish Sapper's Road, which proved to be extremely demanding for the tank drivers. Traffic control was especially important along the single-track road and the Inferno Track, so the Military Police set up one-way systems to keep things moving. One tank driver, upon rounding a hairpin bend, was blinded by the intense artillery barrage and crashed his vehicle into the mountainside, blocking the road to all traffic. After several unsuccessful attempts to move it there was no option but to push it off the road and let it roll down the mountainside.

Artillery preparation on II Corps sector continued until 0100 hrs on 12 May, then the infantry of both divisions, 1 Carpathian Brigade and 5 Wileńska Brigade, began to cross their start lines. From the 1 Carpathian Brigade the 2nd Battalion was to launch an attack from the area of Point 596, along the ridge toward Snake's Head Ridge with the objective of its capture and also of Point 569. The 1st Battalion to the right of the 2nd Battalion attacked with its four companies one behind the other, with the aim of first capturing the Gorge and then Albaneta Farm. The northern flank was to be protected by a troop of tanks using the track running from Colle Majola to Massa Albaneta, supporting the 1st Battalion, supplemented by two self-propelled guns, a machine-gun company and the dismounted 12 Podolski Lancers reconnaissance regiment.

The 2nd Battalion stormed Snake's Head Ridge at 0130 hrs and through the sheer fury of their first onslaught had by 0245 hrs liquidated most of the enemy pillboxes on the hill; further, some infantry elements overran the northern part of Point 569. However, the Germans were now beginning to recover and Polish casualties had already been severe. Under the intense German counter-fire the Polish instinct for bravado kicked in, much as the British had feared. One Polish officer recalled: 'Most of us were content to huddle ourselves in the holes and hollows we had found, but some soldiers, in my opinion, were stupidly reckless. Many were killed through their carelessness. I noticed that the Germans very wisely stayed under cover at all times, whereas our men would suddenly stand up to hurl defiance at the enemy. They paid dearly for these and similar acts of bravado.'[3]

The 1st Battalion was suffering heavy casualties in the gorge, as the Germans had arranged its defence with frontal and flanking machine guns. It was not until dawn and after further artillery 'softening' of the area that the 1st Battalion, supported by tanks, could attack the gorge and several infantry sub-units managed to struggle through to the northern slopes running up to Albaneta, although these troops in turn became pinned down by increasingly heavy artillery fire. The supporting tanks of the 4 Armoured Regiment were having a hard time. At 0430 hrs the two regimental headquarters' tanks, four tanks of the 3rd Squadron and fifteen from the 2nd Squadron advanced along the track to meet Lieutenant Bobaka's platoon before the gorge. The gorge had not been cleared of mines and the whole area was under constant observation from the German positions high upon Mount Cairo. At 0500 hrs Lieutenant Białecki, Commander of the 4th platoon, with an additional two tanks from the regimental headquarters squadron pushed forward into the gorge. Enemy artillery and mortar fire concentrated on them and in a matter of minutes Lieutenant Białecki's lead tank suffered a direct hit to its ammunition magazine. The resulting explosion blew the turret clean off the tank's hull, killing three of the crew instantly. Covered in flames Lieutenant Białecki managed to jump out of the tank, as did one other crewman, who died of his burns and injuries on 19 May – the day after victory at Cassino. The remaining tanks in the gorge were now without radio contact with headquarters and the infantry; trapped by poor visibility they were forced to a halt under the heavy German fire.

Elements of the 1st Battalion managed to advance beyond the gorge, but lacking tank support were forced to withdraw under heavy fire from Mass Albaneta and Point 575. The gorge had been heavily mined and the sappers engaged in clearing a path for the tanks suffered such heavy casualties that they were unable to continue their work; eighteen out of the twenty men were either killed or wounded. The battalion was now at a standstill and efforts to restore momentum to the attack were not helped by an almost total breakdown of radio communication. The Brigade Commander thus received only sporadic and indirect reports that made the position obscure to the commanders. With the tanks unable to hold their forwardmost gains, Captain Iwanowski decided to pull back and ordered all vehicles to fall back to their start lines on the night of the 12/13 May.

At the same time the enemy artillery and *Nebelwerfers* held the approaches to Point 593 and the gorge under such heavy and continuous fire that any communication forward, including the bringing up of ammunition was out of the question. As the Polish advance slowed so the Germans, true to form, began to launch savage counter-attacks upon Point 593, supported by overhead machine-gun and mortar fire from the monastery and by enfilade fire from Colle d'Onofrio. The first was driven off, as was a second an hour later. A third counter-attack again failed to rout the Poles and seize the crest, but this time the attacking Germans went to ground in craters or behind boulders on the southwest slopes and began to snipe at the Polish positions only a few yards away. When darkness fell the German commander ordered yet another counter-attack and the paratroopers crept right up to the Polish perimeter under cover of a mortar bombardment. The mortars proved devastatingly effective on the bare rocky ground and virtually obliterated the entire 2nd Battalion, who could find no cover. As soon as it ended the paratroopers rose up and rushed forward. After bitter hand-to-hand fighting, the few surviving Poles were either captured or forced to retreat back along Snakeshead Ridge. On the southern slopes of Point 593 only one officer and seven men were found alive, and even next morning, when the stragglers had come in, the 2nd Battalion numbered no more than a few dozen men. The companies of the 1st Battalion on the northern slopes of Point 593 also suffered casualties from artillery and mortar fire, particularly artillery fire from the area Atina–Belmonte falling in their rear, coupled with machine-gun fire from San Angelo and Point 575.

The two assaulting battalions of 5 Wileńska Brigade advanced from their forming up areas at 0100 hrs; the 13th Battalion on the right was detailed to capture the northern parts of Phantom Ridge and the 15th Battalion on the left, the southern face. The attack was preceded by sapper patrols for mine clearing and marking the route. The 18th Battalion of 6 Lwów Brigade was in the second echelon behind the 15th Battalion, and was to leave its forming up area later, passing through the leading battalions to capture the ridge. The 14th Battalion was to hold the start line; with 6 Lwów Brigade providing a diversionary attack on Passo Corno and protecting the right flank, the left flank covered by 2 Carpathian Rifle Brigade. To help keep the advancing infantry on course, light anti-aircraft guns fired tracer bursts to mark the edges of artillery barrages, and the attack was supported by mortars, machine guns, tanks and engineer sections equipped with flamethrowers.

The diversion was successful; however, progress made by the leading battalions of 5 Wileńska Brigade was unexpectedly slow. They were scheduled to commence their assault against Phantom Ridge at 0145 hrs, but the forward elements did not reach the ridge until 0230 hrs. The delay was caused by heavy enemy artillery and mortar fire that began immediately the infantry left their forming-up areas. The massive opening artillery barrage had achieved little more than severing the telephone lines amongst the German gun positions; as these were quickly repaired German artillery commenced heavy coordinated bombardment on the advancing infantry. The forward battalions suffered approximately 20 per cent casualties in their advance towards Phantom Ridge. In addition, this artillery fire was severely disrupting communications between the assaulting troops and the Brigade Commander, Colonel Kurek, with the majority of wireless sets having been smashed up or their operators killed and the impossibility of dispatching runners.

Two companies of the 13th Battalion, moving on the extreme northern axis, reached the top of Phantom Ridge, where they met concentrated enemy artillery and mortar fire with both frontal and enfilade fire from enemy automatic weapons. Because of the radio failure the Polish gunners had little idea of where their own men were or what parts of the German line should be saturated. The Germans had few such problems and began bracketing the whole eastern face of Phantom Ridge with the most terrible rolling barrage, moving up and down and destroying everything. The troops had no means of fighting against it and were struck down or forced to seek cover behind rocks that afforded them no protection. Under this heavy fire the companies were quickly whittled away. The two rear companies of the 13th Battalion also reached the top of Phantom Ridge, but after clearing pillboxes on its northern sector were pinned down by intense fire that made further movement impossible. Again it was impossible to coordinate the actions of these companies and platoons because of the almost total breakdown in communications.

In the meantime, at 0200 hrs Lieutenant Trejdosiewicz, tank commander of the 1st Platoon, 3rd Squadron, moved onto the slopes of Phantom Ridge. Despite their heroic efforts, the 3rd Company of the Corps Engineers had been unable to clear the area of mines and in the first hours of fighting had lost six men killed and thirty-eight wounded carrying out mine clearance and demarking the cleared routes. The tanks suffered losses as well; enemy artillery fire had destroyed two and a third had become wrecked in a crevasse. During the night the forward medical facilities of the 4 Armoured Regiment were housed in dugout shelters further protected by the bulk of parked-up Valentine bridge-laying tanks. All four of the doctors working at the station were wounded but refused to be evacuated, choosing to remain and tend to the incoming casualties. The Kresowa Division's assault sappers were fully engaged supporting the attack on Phantom Ridge, during which action engineer Second Lieutenant Jerzy Gradosielski won the Polish Militari Virtuti and British Military Cross.

In the south, the 15th Battalion charged to the top of Phantom Ridge and engaged pillboxes there, a difficult task owing to the thick undergrowth, rocky ground and the darkness. Two companies of this battalion managed to force a way between the enemy pillboxes to reach Point 517 before coming under intense enemy fire. Upon finding himself out of touch with the flank units and completely isolated, the commander of these two companies withdrew to Phantom Ridge, where he started mopping up enemy positions that had been overrun.

At 0300 hrs, the 18th Battalion arrived at its forming-up location alongside the 14th Battalion's defences, but all communications forward and with the Brigade Commander were broken. The Battalion Commander, seeing elements of the 15th Battalion passing over Phantom Ridge, assumed that this ridge was completely in Polish hands and ordered his men to advance. By 0630 hrs, the 18th Battalion reached Phantom Ridge and its troops joined with the men of the 15th Battalion in mopping up enemy pillboxes. By this time, the narrow and exposed piece of ground was congested with Polish troops and after daybreak casualties began to mount as the Germans began picking them off. At dawn, an enemy counter-attack was hurled back, but no attacker could hold out for long on the exposed slopes by day. They could not be reinforced, nor could they be supplied. They were on their own and continued to fight as best they could. Major General Sulik reviewed the progress of the battle and although the formations were without signals and had incurred heavy casualties the intermediate objective was in Polish hands. He therefore decided to commit the 16th and 17th Battalions in a second attack at 1500 hrs.

It was not signalling communication alone that had been lost with the attacking formations; the dust and smoke from the artillery barrage resulted in the battlefield being enveloped by a thick impenetrable cloud through which it was impossible to view the conflict. Even the forward artillery observation officers with their elevated positions could not see what was happening. There was general consternation that the Germans had not only survived the initial artillery bombardment but that their infantry were counter-attacking with ferocious success, supported by devastating artillery fire. The reality that this was to be a savage fight to the death now began to sink in, although many could not believe the resolve of the Germans and instead convinced themselves the artillery fire could only be coming from their own Polish artillery. The result was a chaotic and panicky scene, as Lieutenant Dębicki of the 6 Light Artillery regiment recalled: 'Suddenly a major from one of the units under fire runs up roaring at me: "You son of a bitch you're killing my boys! Stop it! Now! Now!" I manage to answer: "They're not our guns, major sir. They're the Germans'!"...Now he is pulling a gun on me!... Slowly, very slowly, the poor fellow turns away and vanishes into this terrible night.'[4]

The heavy fighting on Phantom Ridge continued until 1300 hrs, when the 18th Battalion's commander decided that it was simply not possible to continue the attack and the holding of ground would only lead to greater casualties – indeed the leading battalions of 5 Brigade, the 13th and 15th, had been virtually destroyed. No men in those battalions escaped injury, the broken bodies of those killed tumbled down the mountainside to collect in heaps in the valley below, amongst which was almost the entire complement of Captain Jurowski's company. Unable to establish liaison with Brigade headquarters the 18th Battalion's commander realized that he must withdraw to the start line. In the confusion of the German artillery bombardment a number of the exhausted troops from the 13th and 15th Battalions mistook this withdrawal as a general retreat and fell back, leaving only the forward companies, totally isolated and without communications, to hold Phantom Ridge.

During the morning of the 12th Anders decided at first to mount another attack at 1500 hrs, using his sparse reserves. But as the morning passed and as he learned more of the casualties amongst his troops and their subsequent disorganization, coupled with the seemingly unhindered German artillery, Anders decided to withdraw to the start line. Indeed the opening artillery barrage had not succeed in silencing the German guns as during the morning of 12 May the German artillery regained its ascendancy, forcing the withdrawal of the infantry from their recently captured positions and simultaneously inflicting heavy casualties in the rear areas of the Polish infantry divisions. This was largely due to the German artillery and infantry both being protected in heavily entrenched, concealed bunkers on the reverse hill slopes and were thus inaccessible to the Polish guns. The equipment of the light artillery regiments, the 25-pounder gun, which was so effective in the desert campaign, proved to be of too light a calibre, lacking the destructive power needed to destroy the strong German defences built into the solid rock. As a result the Polish infantry were forced to pull back as the German guns were able to fire upon them unhindered. The concentrated fire from the Polish artillery in stage two of the barrage did succeed in inflicting heavy casualties amongst the German infantry and served to clearly delineate the enemy positions.

During the afternoon the commander of the Eighth Army, Lieutenant General Leese arrived at Polish Corps Headquarters and both commanders reviewed the situation. Polish losses had been severe; half of each division had been crippled and no ground had been gained. However, the Germans had been badly mauled and by the sacrifice of the Poles on the mountain heights they had succeeded in easing the burden on the British troops in the Liri Valley. The Generals agreed that the attacks by the Polish II Corps and the British XIII Corps were too widely separated, that the Germans might be prepared to lose some ground in the Liri Valley and that by shifting their fire and reserves onto the Polish sector the Germans might attempt to destroy it by making full use of their advantage of high ground. Anders initially planned to reorganize for an attack during the night of the 12/13 May, however Leese decided that the Polish II Corps would require extensive reorganization following its heavy losses and would not be called upon to attack again until the complementary encirclement of Cassino through the Liri Valley had made more decisive progress. This would shorten the distance between the two advancing forces, preventing the Germans from maximizing their fire manoeuvreability, and it was agreed to reschedule the attack for 15 May. The retirement of Polish combat units took place that night, the 1st Battalion being the last unit to withdraw at 1300 hrs the following day. The battle had so far cost the Poles some 1,800 casualties, and once again the combination of the Cassino position and the resilience of the German paratroopers proved unbeatable.

The attack of the British XIII Corps succeeded in forcing the river and establishing a small bridgehead on the western bank of the Gari, beginning at its confluence with the Rapido and extending to the village of San Angelo – these gains were pivotal to achieving the encirclement of Cassino. As most of the enemy fire was concentrated on the defence of the high ground of Monte Cassino, the troops met comparatively lighter artillery and mortar fire. By the evening of 12 May, units had pushed forward at several points to a maximum distance of 1km from the river. Progress was slow owing to the difficulty of getting heavy equipment across the river. The Allied commanders had hoped for more success yet no one was discouraged and all were planning to continue their attacks or to mount fresh ones. General Alexander summarized the situation in a message to Sir Alan Brooke: 'On the whole the battle has gone fairly well considering the stubbornness of the opposition. This is the Poles' first battle... . I saw both my army commanders this morning and they are reasonably satisfied with the opening stages of the battle, but there is no doubt that the Germans intend to fight for every yard and that the next few days will see some extremely bitter and severe fighting.'[5]

12

A Brief Respite

Lieutenant General Leese had intended the Polish Corps to attack Monastery Hill again on 15 May, however 13 and 14 May saw developments that changed the tactical situation. Whilst the 1st Parachute Division was holding fast to Monte Cassino, the muddle of German units down on the floor of the Liri Valley were being driven from their positions. Furthermore the American and French forces were making powerful inroads through the German XIV Panzer Corps' sector. The situation had developed into almost the complete opposite of what Leese and others had thought – what was prevailing was the advance of XIII Corps in the Liri Valley and this was now strangling the German grasp on Monastery Hill. In light of this Leese ordered the British 78th Infantry Division to press on up the Liri Valley and delayed the deployment of the Polish Corps once again, issuing his orders for the next phase of the battle on 15 May. The objectives were to achieve the complete isolation of Monastery Hill and to clear and open Highway 6. This was to be done by XIII Corps pushing up the Liri Valley, coupled with the Polish II Corps attacking the Cassino positions and subsequently linking up with the British. The Canadian Corps was to push forward along the southern side of the Liri Valley. At 1030 hrs on 16 May, Leese informed his commanders that the attack would begin the following day at 0700 hrs.

The four days that passed between the Polish Corps' first and second attacks were spent reorganizing the battered assault formations for the next round of fighting. Activity against the Germans was maintained through constant patrols by day and night, and arranged salvos by the artillery and machine guns in the hope of provoking the Germans into replying, thereby disclosing their defensive fire plans. Casualties amongst the infantry had been far higher than anticipated during the first assault on the Cassino massif, particularly in the 5th Kresowa Division where 5 and 6 Infantry Brigades were drastically reduced in numbers by the intense fighting, which also consumed all existing reserves. Faced with a shortage of infantry for the second assault the division's commander, Major General Sulik, created four scratch-infantry battalions on the night of 16/17 May each consisting of two infantry companies of three platoons fielding a total of around 250 men in each battalion. These improvised units were formed from all branches of the division's personnel and were to be deployed as reserves and for mopping-up operations following the main infantry's advance. They consisted of:

(i) 1st Scratch Battalion commanded by Captain Ludwik Szamocki; raised from two batteries of the 5 Anti-Aircraft Artillery Regiment plus one company from the 5 Anti-Tank Regiment.

(ii) 2nd Scratch Battalion commanded by Captain Marian Kuniewicz; raised with elements from each of the division's artillery regiments with the second company raised from the rear elements of the division's headquarters, medical, camouflage and security sections, drivers, 5th Heavy Machine Gun Battalion, 15 Poznan Cavalry Regiment, and divisional artillery regiments.

(iii) 3rd Scratch Battalion commanded by Major Stanisław Maculewicz comprised the 4th and 5th companies of the division's engineers who served as additional stretcher-bearers.

(iv) 4th Scratch Battalion commanded by Major Stanisław Małecki's was formed from further elements of the 5 Anti-Aircraft Artillery Regiment into an infantry formation of two companies charged with the evacuation of the wounded and the supply of ammunition.

(v) Major Smrokowski's Group was formed by amalgamating the Commando Company with the Assault Squadron of the 15 Poznan Cavalry Regiment.

For everyone in the line the whole of Cassino had now become a vision of a hellish other world, one characterized by the crescendo of explosions that shook the ground, great mists of smoke creeping amongst the positions and the omnipresent reek of dead bodies. Even in the so-called rest areas it was impossible to escape the ubiquity of death. When Captain Smereczynski was sent back for a brief respite he found that he had to sleep 'more or less alongside a dead Indian... . The place was alive with rats, big, bloated creatures that scurried about with impunity while we slept. The sickly sweet smell of decaying flesh was nauseating and we could do nothing to rid ourselves of it.'[1]

A much needed and welcome sight for the recuperating soldiers were the canteens of 318 Field Kitchen and Mobile Library Company of the Polish Women's Auxiliary Service, commanded by Lieutenant Colonel Bronisława Wysłouchowa. The canteens serving the fighting formations were well within the range of the German artillery and the presence of the women volunteers, so close to the front and sharing the hardships of the troops, was a great morale boost to the wounded soldiers. The kitchens provided tea, coffee, sandwiches, cakes, fruit and writing paper, free of charge to the wounded. Care of the sick was the primary task for these platoons during battle, assisting with their onward evacuation to the hospitals and making them as comfortable as possible, and women were also detailed as stretcher-bearers to carry the wounded from ambulances into the medical facilities. The mobile library provided articles, magazines and books for the soldiers, working closely with the education sections of the PWSK and the public relations section. To supply food for these canteens and for the formations, 331 and 332 Mobile Field Bakeries at Pozilli each produced over 20,000lbs of bread per day by working a shift pattern that enabled constant production.

Wojtek the bear was also on the front with 22 General Transport Company, and he too was glad of the pause in fighting allowing him to indulge in his favourite pastimes of swimming and playing in the water. Wojtek particularly enjoyed a dip in the sea and delighted in swimming underwater and suddenly emerging with a loud roar amongst the local lady bathers – to startled shrieks! Although there was no sea for Wojtek to enjoy at Cassino he did make full use of the cold showers, learning how to operate them himself, though he took so many showers that the door to the shower hut eventually had to be locked. According to numerous accounts, during the Battle of Monte Cassino the bear helped his patrons by transporting ammunition, which he carried in his massive paws. Wojtek quickly got used to the sounds of battle and would climb tall trees during bombardments to get the best view. In recognition of his popularity, headquarters approved an effigy of a bear holding an artillery shell to be used as the company's official emblem.

The 4th Armoured Regiment remained fully active during the pause between assaults. On 13 May, Captain Iwanowski took over command of the various clusters of armoured units now consisting of the 2nd and 3rd Squadrons, the New Zealand tanks of Lieutenant Bobaka, two batteries of Wolverines and a battery of 6-pounder anti-tank guns. These formations had no supporting infantry of their own and Captain Iwanowski organized a defensive strategy that allowed them to successfully hold out against the Germans and continue to launch harassing action. With the absence of news from the front, Captain Iwanowski sent forward four tanks from the 2nd Squadron, which at 0700 hrs on 14 May reached the area of the gorge in sight of Mass Albaneta. The tanks fired accurately into the enemy bunkers, destroying several, although they could not advance further due to the dense mining of the track. The tanks were engaged in heavy exchanges of fire and began to run out of ammunition. As one of the vehicles pulled back it reversed into another, knocking it over, though Lieutenant Hopko and his crew were able to bail out relatively unharmed. The 2nd Squadron also suffered losses in the morning, including the commander of the 2nd Platoon, Second Lieutenant Zolnierczyk. The 4th Armoured Regiment was now well emplaced in the gorge area and on the southern slopes of Phantom Ridge.

On 15 May, the 3rd Squadron was joined by two platoons from the Caira –Villa area and also by three Stuart tanks from San Michele carrying engineers for the task of mine clearance. The regiment's allotted engineers, the 3rd Company of the 10th Engineering Battalion were now so reduced in numbers as to be unable to continue their duties. Colonel Glinski, the regiment's commander, issued orders and instructions concerning the attack scheduled for the following day, which was subsequently postponed to 17 May. On 16 May, at the behest of Colonel Rudnicki, deputy commander of the Kresowa Infantry Division, the 3rd Squadron deployed to Phantom Ridge to destroy bunkers and weaken the enemy's defences. The tank crews overcame the mountain obstacles and by 2200 hrs had destroyed the bunkers that had halted the previous assaults of the Kresowa infantry. Lieutenant Siczek's 2nd Platoon of the 1st Squadron took over the task of securing the Caira–Terelle direction and moved to the area of Monte Cairo. On the eve of the major assault on 17 May, the 4th Armoured Regiment's assets in the field comprised 1 tank of the Regimental Headquarters Squadron, 14 tanks of the 2nd Squadron, 10 tanks of the 3rd Squadron, 3 New Zealand tanks, 3 Stuart tanks, 4 Wolverines and 1 Valentine bridge-laying tank. Reinforcements for the tank formations were despatched by the 9th Forward Delivery Squadron that forwarded 60 non-commissioned officers from the Armour Training Centre.

The quantity of ordnance consumed during the fighting was immense, with daily artillery expenditure averaging 1,000 tons of shells and each battalion of infantry consuming over ten tons of small arms ammunition and grenades. The intense fighting led inevitably to the firing emplacements brimming over with spent shellcases. To clear this debris and make way for the next stock of ammunition the Salvage Section collected re-useable containers and small equipment that could be recycled as well as ammunition that had been unpacked but not fired. The Supply and Transport Corps collected salvage from the front on their return journey. Salvage units 371 and 372 were based in between Venafro and Pozilli, where the material collected was transferred to 370 section at the railhead at Vairano for transport to the rear areas. Salvage sections were often formed from Italian Pioneers and prisoner-of-war work details.

Luftwaffe activity during the battle had not been significant and the light anti-aircraft artillery regiments mainly engaged wandering patrols of Focke Wulf 190 fighter-bombers attempting to strike at depots and infrastructure in the Corps rear areas. The divisional Anti-Aircraft Artillery Regiments were predominantly deployed at the Inferno Gorge and San Michele dumps and around headquarters facilities. The Corps 7 Light Anti-Aircraft Artillery Regiment assigned one battery to the front providing eighteen guns of 40mm calibre sited around the vast supply dumps at Venafro, the other batteries being dispersed to provide defence in depth from low-flying aircraft throughout the Corps Troops and Lines of Communication area.

Unfortunately, the well rehearsed system of casualty evacuation could not be successfully applied at Cassino for two principal reasons: the length of time required for the initial evacuation from the front line, and the exceptionally severe nature of the wounds sustained by men in the mountain sector from shells and mortar bombs exploding at varying heights on the flint-hard rock. Those wounded on the mountainsides had to be carried down the steep, treacherous paths for more than two miles and the only way it could be done was to establish a chain of stretcher-bearer posts sited every 200 yards from the top of the valley. What with the sheer physical difficulty of the descent, and delays caused by the constant harassing of this supply route by the German artillery and mortars, the transporting of each casualty invariably took several hours. It was a difficult ordeal for a badly wounded and shocked man to have to endure. The stretcher was constantly tilted or suddenly put down as one of the bearers stumbled or slipped and both the bearers and their charges were frequently hit by enemy fire.

Many of the wounded were unfortunate enough to receive neither treatment nor evacuation, but languished in agony on the rock face or slumped in a coma. Such abhorrent scenes were beyond what the soldiers could bring themselves to deal with. These casualties were only cleared from the battlefield later and miraculously several of these horrifically mutilated men who had been left for dead, with no food or water for almost a week, managed to survive and embark upon the long road to recovery. For those fortunate enough to be evacuated their actual arrival at the casualty clearing stations was far from orderly – some crawled on their own, some were helped by friends, others slung over a shoulder. The helpers, wounded and dying were all in a frantic state of excitement, but none showed fear, only fury and rage. The Polish zeal for heroism led to many such instances of soldiers receiving multiple injuries, until they could not possibly force themselves to fight any further. Only then would they accept that they required medical care and a great many died as a result.

Cassino produced its own extra burdens in that a much higher than usual percentage of casualties sustained head and eye injuries. Previous fighting at Monte Cassino had highlighted this occurrence and in anticipation of these types of wound additional specialist British units were assigned to the Polish Medical Corps, including 1 Maxillo Facial Surgery Unit, 3 Ophthalmic Unit and 4 Mobile Neuro Surgical Unit. The reason for the high incidence of such injuries was as follows: a shell bursting on ordinary ground partly buries itself (and some of its effect) and directs its blast and shrapnel forward. A shell or mortar bomb bursting on the flint-hard slope of a mountain has a much more damaging effect, the fragments of metal and rock flying further and less predictably. In addition the troops were denied the normal cover of trenches, as these could not be dug into the rock. Their only protection was the sangar; a breastwork of loose stones. A concentration of shells bursting above them could strike straight down into the heart of these inadequate sanctuaries. In such conditions shrapnel could kill or wound at a range of a hundred yards or more, and many serious injuries were caused, not by the shells themselves, but by the sharp pieces of rock they sent flying in all directions. In addition, the Germans used glass anti-personnel mines and when these devices were exploded components were shot vertically into the air, embedding themselves in the faces and eyes of nearby soldiers.

As hospitals 2 and 6 became full it was necessary to send casualties to the rear hospitals in the base area around Taranto. The severely wounded from Monte Cassino were moved on to 50 British Evacuation Hospital at Termoli on the Adriatic Coast where four hospital extension units each of 100 beds were attached to provide Polish sections at this facility. From Termoli, the wounded travelled southwards by British hospital train to Bari, Brindisi and Casamassima, where motor ambulances of 316 General Transport Company transported the casualties to the base general hospitals. The less severe cases were driven from 2 General Hospital to Barletta and thence to the base hospitals, the journey from front line to general hospital taking on average two to three days. The wounded were moved on in this way to free up bed space in the chain for the next casualties to be treated without delay. The base general hospitals, 1 General Hospital at Mottola and 3 General Hospital at Palagiano, attended to those requiring extensive surgery and intensive care and were much larger facilities, each with up to 1,200 beds.

The ready availability of penicillin in the Allied forces saved the lives of a great number of wounded soldiers and speeded the recovery of hospitalized casualties. In fact, penicillin is estimated to have directly saved an extra 15 per cent of wounded men and was first used by the forces during the campaign in North Africa. The pharmacists would prepare syringes and serums of the new drug from powdered stock with saline solution. It was a time-consuming process, but the Germans by contrast possessed no stocks of anti-bacterial drugs so their ability to quickly treat infections was far inferior – even those who did recover took much longer to recuperate before returning to the field.

The Battle of Monte Cassino was not the only source of high hospital admittance figures that May. The beginning of the Italian summer corresponds with the advent of the malaria season. The authorities foresaw a great many hospital places being required to cater for these cases and subsequently great emphasis was placed on preventative measures and treatments – 34 Anti-Malaria Control Section was based in Bojano, and served the corps-level units with sections 3 and 5, the infantry divisions. Malaria was certainly a huge problem in the Italian campaign, killing more soldiers and civilians than the fighting, bombing and shelling combined. During May 1944 a total of 3,274 soldiers were in the care of the base hospitals, including for that month 2,122 wounded soldiers and 950 sick cases, the latter making up almost one third of the hospitalized personnel. Of these men, 202 subsequently died of their injuries or infections.[2]

13

Victory at Monte Cassino

Constant reconnaissance had given the Polish commanders an interesting picture of the layout of the German defences. They believed that two interlocking rings existed, forming a figure-of-eight plan. The northern ring included (moving anti-clockwise) Point 593–Phantom Ridge–Colle S. Angelo–Point 575–Point 505–Albaneta Farm. The southern ring included D'Onifrio–Point 569–Monastery Hill. The German strongpoints were sited on the circumference of each ring, covering the perimeter and the ground within. Attacking troops therefore would gain very little by capturing a small part of a ring; one or two German strongpoints might be destroyed but the others would prevent the attackers from penetrating more deeply or from fanning out from their breach. Moreover, dead ground inside the rings harboured local reserves for the Germans' favourite tactic of launching immediate counter-attacks, which were of a most rapid and ferocious nature. The interrogation of German prisoners captured in the first attack confirmed this analysis. The Polish commanders believed that they must capture at least half a ring in the first assault if they were to break the whole by further attacks. However the nature of the ground restricted the frontage of an attack to much less than half a ring. It was a most difficult tactical puzzle.

Anders decided that, as before, the 5th Kresowa Division would attack on the right and the 3rd Carpathian Division on the left. The 5th Division's attack was to be made by a specially organized group under the command of Colonel Rudnicki, the Deputy Divisional Commander. The group consisted of the surviving remnants of the 13th and 15th Infantry Battalions of Colonel Kurek's 5 Wileńska Infantry Brigade, the 16th, 17th and 18th Infantry Battalions of Colonel Sawicki's 6 Lwów Infantry Brigade, the Polish Commando, detachments of the 15 Poznan Lancers Regiment and the 3rd Squadron of the 4 Armoured regiment. The 7 Anti-Tank Regiment deployed its 8 Troop with the 3rd Carpathian Rifle Division and 9 Troop with the 5th Kresowa Infantry Division, both detachments equipped with M10 Wolverine self-propelled guns to provide bunker-busting fire for the infantry and the 4 Skorpion Armoured Regiment.

The infantry were to attack in waves of battalion strength, to capture in succession the northern part of Phantom Ridge, Colle S. Angelo, a northern hump known as Little S. Angelo, and Point 575. In more detail, the 16th Battalion was to capture Phantom Ridge, while the tanks protected its left flank. Next, the 17th Battalion would pass through to capture Colle S. Angelo, its right flank protected by the Polish Commando. The 13th Battalion would help in taking Point 575, or would exploit success. The 18th Battalion was held in reserve. The attack was to begin at 0700 hrs on 17 May and was to be preceded by a twenty-minute counter-battery and counter-mortar barrage from the Corps' artillery, followed by forty minutes of concentration on the German positions. The plan was brutally simple and resembled the storming of a breach in eighteenth-century warfare.

The opening artillery barrage for the second assault ran for an hour from 0600 hrs. Immediately following the intense bombardment the infantry of the 5th Kresowa Division launched their attack. Earlier, during the night of 16/17 May, a company of the 16th Battalion, sent to reconnoitre Phantom Ridge, captured a number of posts of the 3rd Parachute Regiment on the northern parts of the ridge. The battalion commander at once sent other companies forward and by 2300 hrs the whole 16th Battalion was securely posted on Phantom Ridge, the division's first objective. The 5th Light Artillery Regiment provided fire support for the 16th Infantry Battalion with the forward observation officers of the regiment, 2nd Lieutenants Grobicki and Kazinierczak (codenamed Cyklop 2) positioned on the slopes of Point 706 with a commanding view of the action, only 100 metres from the Germans. The pair successfully called in artillery strikes to destroy German bunkers and machine-gun emplacements.

The 17th Battalion, after leaving their forming up areas at 0710 hrs, advanced quickly past Point 706, reached Phantom Ridge and, passing through the 16th Battalion, stormed Colle S. Angelo. It was largely due to the speed of their advance that the major part of this battalion escaped enemy defensive fire, which came too late and only engaged the tail-end of the battalion consisting mainly of ammunition porters, stretcher-bearers, wireless operators, etc. This battalion was successful in mopping up the northeast slopes of Colle S. Angelo, but on its western slopes a series of pillboxes continued to be tenaciously defended by the Germans. Here, the fighting was waged with the utmost ferocity as the Germans counter-attacked. Heavy casualties were sustained from enemy positions along the southern slopes of Passo Corno, coupled with particularly accurate mortar fire from the valley of Villa S. Lucia. The troops of the 17th Battalion, having expended all their ammunition, were unable to either move forward or to effectively drive off enemy counter-attacks that reached their climax at 1400 hrs, when the Germans recaptured the southern slopes of Colle S. Angelo.

Victory at Monte Cassino 203

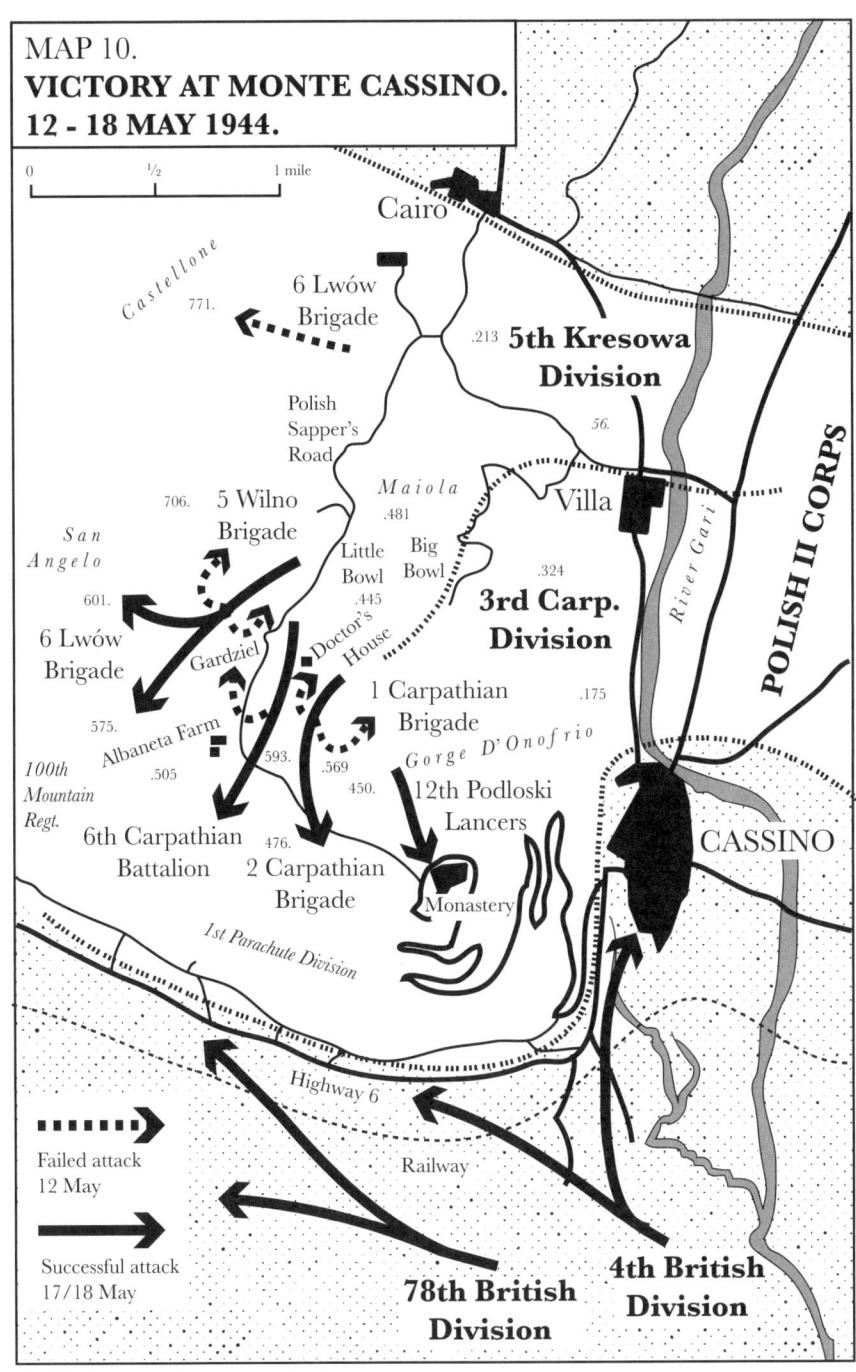

During this time the battalions in the second wave and assembly areas were under constant German artillery and mortar fire that prevented communication with the rear. In response to these counter-attacks, a heavy concentration of fire was put down by the Polish artillery and mortars for an hour from 1500 hrs, after which the infantry of the 15th Battalion, instead of attacking Point 575, had with the 16th Battalion to join the 17th in a concerted attack to recapture S. Angelo, which combined with the Polish Commando Company succeeded in mopping up the hill's southern slope up to the summit. The attempt to extend the attack to the northern slopes of Colle S. Angelo and Point 575 was halted due to the stubborn German defence, the exhaustion of the Kresowa Division's infantry and lack of adequate artillery support. The situation had become critical; casualties were enormous, ammunition stocks almost depleted and the platoons and battalions had become hopelessly intermixed. The situation remained unchanged until the morning of 18 May.

The 4 Armoured Regiment's 3rd Squadron was detailed to advance upon Phantom Ridge, to hold the area and provide fire support for the infantry attacks on Point 575 and San Angelo. The 2nd Squadron was to advance through the gorge, capture Mass Albaneta and provide covering fire for the infantry of the Carpathian Rifle Division. The 3rd Squadron attacking Phantom Ridge had to advance over very steep, boulder-strewn terrain under heavy mortar and machine-gun fire from several undamaged bunkers. Second Lieutenant Besser, commander of the 1st Platoon was killed by machine-gun fire and several tanks were damaged. The tank of Second Lieutenant Kochanowski rolled over on the steep slope; the crew all escaped from the overturned tank and continued the assault on foot. The 3rd Platoon reached the summit of Phantom Ridge at 1100 hrs, without the support of infantry or engineers. The dismounted tank crews attacked the remaining bunkers with hand grenades, taking several German prisoners. The tanks upon the ridge attracted much artillery fire and were under constant bombardment until dark, where they remained, covering the attack against Colle S. Angelo.

In the 3rd Carpathian Division's sector, the 6th Battalion began to advance through the gorge towards Albaneta Farm whilst two companies of the 17th Battalion moved along the western slopes of Point 593 towards Mass Albaneta. The Carpathian Division's assault engineers were in the first wave of attack, clearing obstacles, mines, and destroying bunkers, operating in positions completely exposed to enemy fire. The tanks of the 2nd Squadron were then able to advanced into the gorge, the squadron commander, Captain Władysław Drelicharz, pushing forward metre by metre, to the foreground of Mass Albaneta, picking their way through the densely laid mines. There the tanks fired heavily onto Point 593 – the crews were now in sight of their objectives of Mass Albaneta and the ruined farm buildings, and beyond to the Monastery of Monte Cassino. The tanks now proceeded along a narrow ridge that could barely accommodate two vehicles side by side. Close cooperation between the tank crews and engineers enabled their advance to continue under heavy fire, although several tank crew were wounded and one killed. Further movement of the squadron was halted by the difficult tasks of mine clearance and route marking, which the engineers were able to complete during the night of 17/18 May.

The previous assault on these positions had revealed that the Germans possessed strong machine-gun and mortar positions concealed behind the remaining eastern and southeastern walls of the monastery, that were able to wreak havoc on the troops attacking Points 593 and 569. The commander of the Carpathian Division's artillery, Colonel Lakinski, decided that the only means of neutralizing these emplacements was to deploy an anti-tank gun on the heights to engage them directly. To achieve this a 6-pounder gun was manoeuvred during the night along the Polish Sappers' road and onto the heights providing clear observation of the monastery, a feat that the men involved likened to moving one of Hannibal's elephants over the Alps; the effort was rewarded however, as the gunners could now deal with enemy machine guns firing from the basement windows of the Abbey.

The approach to Mass Albaneta itself was very hazardous on account of the thickly sown mines in the open ground before the buildings. By the evening of 17 May, the infantry of the 6th Battalion had approached to within 150 yards of the ruins of Mass Albaneta. The capture of this stronghold necessitated more mine lifting which could not be done before dusk. The infantry were unable to support the tanks through the night, as they were exhausted from the day's fighting. Colonel Glinski therefore raised a volunteer section from reserve tank crews and vehicle recovery patrols, who arrived from 2000 hrs to guard the tanks. German artillery and mortars shelled the tanks' positions throughout the night. At the request of the commander of 2 Armoured Brigade, Colonel Glinski sent eight tanks from the 1st Squadron to the gorge that evening, to assist and extend the operational capabilities of the 2nd Squadron. With the reserve from San Michele now being deployed in the field, the base area was to be held by the 3rd Squadron of the 6 Armoured Regiment.

The 4th Battalion carried out its first assault against Point 593 at 0923 hrs on 17 May. The German position was heavily defended by machine-gun fire and the defenders succeeded in driving back the forward attacking company. The company commander repeated the assault for a second and third time, suffering appalling casualties. His company was compelled to halt and was pinned down by heavy fire. The battalion commander, Lieutenant Colonel Fanslau, threw further companies into the assault, but all with the same result; Point 593 changed hands repeatedly following attack after counter-attack. At 1430 hrs, and after further preparations, yet another assault supported by the whole of the artillery was launched. Lieutenant Colonel Fanslau led his men personally; he was killed by a burst of machine-gun fire that cut down the first wave of attacking troops. This assault too fell short and broke down on the southern slopes of Point 593, fifty yards from the heavily defended enemy machine-gun positions. The men were by now utterly exhausted and on the verge of complete nervous and physical collapse. At 1535 hrs the 4th Battalion passed over to the defence with the task of holding the captured positions.

Anders issued fresh orders at 2100 hrs on 17 May. The Kresowa and Carpathian Divisions were to hold the ground that they had won, to reorganize, and to patrol. The following day the Kresowa Division was to capture Point 575 and the Carpathian Division was to seize Albaneta Farm.

The broader assault of the Eighth Army was advancing steadily, making deep inroads up the Liri Valley whilst the French Expeditionary Corps made such remarkable advances that the whole Gustav Line, including Monte Cassino, was no longer holdable for the Germans. Late on 17 May, Heidrich was ordered to pull his 1st Parachute Division back. The paras reluctantly accepted the order and began slipping out of the bunkers and pillboxes they had held since February towards Piedimonte and the Hitler Line defences, but being sure to leave covering rear guards in the pillboxes on the heights.

By dawn on 18 May the tanks of the 1st and 2nd Squadrons were already attacking from the area of the gorge towards Mass Albaneta. On clearing the gorge, the two leading tanks, those of platoon commander Second Lieutenant Białkiewicz 'Pirat' and of Sergeant Machowiak 'Pazur' were immobilized by enemy mines. The explosions stunned the crews, but no one was injured and the tanks continued to shell bunkers around Mass Albaneta and the other objectives of the Carpathian infantry. The remainder of the 1st Squadron's tanks moved past them, the 2nd Squadron firing upon the monastery while they advanced towards the ruins of Albaneta farm. There the 1st Squadron fired deep into the German rear positions and shelled the retreating Germans as they fell back to Piedimonte. Patrols of the 6th Battalion found the Albaneta Farm deserted, the 4th Battalion repeated the assault against the enemy positions on the western slopes of Point 593 and this time succeeded in taking the hill completely. The 3rd Squadron again took firing positions upon Phantom Ridge, supporting the infantry of the Kresowa division during their final assault on San Angelo.

The fighting lasted until 0700 hrs after which the battalion began to storm Point 569; it was captured at 1000 hrs. The Polish troops overran the remaining Germans in their defences, and moved towards the monastery that had fallen silent. So weary were the Poles that when they first intercepted the German radio message giving the orders to withdraw from the monastery they were unable to find any infantry with enough strength to clamber up to it. Eventually word was sent to the 3rd Carpathian Division's reconnaissance regiment, the 12 Podolski Lancers, who sent forward a patrol that entered the abbey at approximately 1015 hrs, accepting the surrender of the German commander and about thirty men, while another hundred or so Germans made their way down the slopes of Monastery Hill and surrendered to the British. The patrol then hoisted the Polish flag above the ruins. The mopping up by the 3rd Carpathian Division of scattered pillboxes lasted until 1400 hrs.

Down on the floor of the Liri Valley, the 78th British Infantry Division were contemplating tackling Highway 6 and were frustrated by being forbidden to cross it. The reason was that the road was the boundary between the division and the Polish II Corps and at that time the positions of the Poles were not known. It was not until the early hours of the 18th that the 78th Division was ordered to send a patrol to make contact with the Poles across Highway 6, two miles west of Cassino. By this time the junction of the two wings of the Eighth Army was not a military operation but a formal ceremony. Rising to the occasion, the commanding officer of the battalion concerned nominated three corporals, all holders of the Military Medal, to make the journey and convey the compliments of the 78th Division to the Poles. Later that afternoon a patrol of the 5th Battalion made contact with units of the 78th British Division on Highway 6.

Enemy artillery fire nonetheless continued to be threatening and effective. In the afternoon Captain Iwanowski gathered the squadron commanders to discuss the situation when they came under an artillery barrage that killed Iwanowski and Lieutenant Bartnowski and wounded Captain Drelicharcz, the medical officer Dr Dudek and two other men. Captain Antoni Dzięciołowski subsequently took command of the armoured units. The three squadrons were ready to pull back to the San Michele area but enemy activity necessitated that they remained in position until 19 May.

The commander of the 5th Kresowa Division continued operations on 18 May, but having no fresh troops he committed improvised companies formed from men of the Anti-Tank Regiment, Divisional Defence Company, spare drivers, etc. By morning, Colle S. Angelo was completely mopped up and the troops advanced to the foot of Point 575. The fighting for this hill continued until the evening, owing to the impassable nature of the ground, the steep walls and numerous crevices and fissures in the rocks, made good use of by the German paratroops as dugouts. Hill 575 was eventually secured on the night of 18/19 May. General Anders described the savage fighting at Phantom Ridge as 'une bataille acharnée'. The Polish II Corps' tenacious assault upon the Monte Cassino Abbey inspired General Alexander to address the II Corps: 'Soldiers of the 2nd Polish Corps! If I were given the right to choose among any soldiers, the ones I would like to have under my command, I would choose You – the Poles.'[1] Both sides had fought hand-to-hand to the death, as epitomized by the scene of a dead Polish soldier still grasping his rifle, with its bayonet impaled in the body of the German who shot him.

14

Breaking the Adolf Hitler Line

With the seizure of Monte Cassino the II Corps could embark upon the second stage of the offensive, that of making contact with the Adolf Hitler Line north of Highway 6. Lieutenant General Leese had identified the township of Piedimonte San Germano as the Corps' closest target on this defensive line. Piedimonte was a small medieval walled town on top of a steep hill rising abruptly from the valley floor, accessible only by a single winding road. The location was naturally defensive and offered commanding views over the Liri Valley. Anders had decided on 30 April that his preferred plan to capture Piedimonte was to gain the adjoining high ground of Passo Corno and Mt Cairo before attacking the town from the valley floor. Capturing these high features would deny the Germans direct observation of the unfolding battle in the Liri Valley and hinder their ability to call in accurate artillery fire. The considerable losses incurred during the recent fighting limited the number of troops for the assault on Mt Cairo. Anders selected formations that had held the defensive sector of Mt Castellone during the fighting for Cassino, principally the 15th Poznan Lancers and the Carpathian Lancers, and placed both under the command of Colonel Witold Nowina-Sawicki, Commander of 6 Lwów Infantry Brigade. A preceding artillery barrage was to be delivered by the 6 Light and 11 Heavy Artillery Regiments.

The operation commenced on 19 May at 1330 hrs with the 2nd Squadron of the Carpathian Lancers attacking from the southern slopes of Mt Cairo. The leading platoons under Lieutenant Lickindorf were ill at ease about having to advance to the start point and then launch their assault in broad daylight, in full view of the German defenders. There was only one approach track, not only narrow but also hanging precipitously above a deep ravine. There was no alternative to this route and the Germans could observe their movements precisely. The men had all patrolled the area recently and had come under fire – they hoped Colonel Rudnicki possessed intelligence that the Germans had abandoned their defences, but still expected the worst. The heat of the summer sun beating down on the steep mountain slopes was intense and after making a dash to the last area of natural cover before the start line the men were wringing with sweat. Many of the troops in this leading group stripped down in the scorching heat – and at this moment the Germans opened fire. Heavy machine-gun and mortar fire rained down upon them and their only course of action was to advance and destroy the enemy positions, they could neither fall back nor dig in.

Lickindorf lead the assault but was quickly cut down by flying rock splinters that severed his femoral arteries, while others in the leading group were hit in the face and suffered shattered arms and hands. The chaplain, who was also the medic, was overwhelmed by the quantity of blood and the cries of the wounded as he tried in vain to save Lickindorf's life. The squadron commander, Captain Stryjewski took over the assault, dividing the force into two groups to attack the left and right flanks of the bunkers ahead. Speed was essential, they had to get out of the German fire as fast as possible or be wiped out. Stryjewski also called down supporting fire from the 6 Light Artillery Regiment that proceeded to tear the mountain apart. The bunkers were so well concealed that locating them was proving elusive amid the turmoil of the battle. Trooper Kuc was the first to identify and engage the bunker with rifle fire and under his cover the attached British mortar advisor crawled up to it only to be knocked into unconsciousness by an exploding grenade. Captain Stryjewski's two flank groups then surrounded the bunker and, despite sustaining heavy casualties, laid relentless fire from every available weapon upon it until it was destroyed. The remains of the squadron pushed on uphill into the dense smoke of the preceding artillery barrage, and captured the next bunker, its defenders giving up and fleeing uphill to the next line of defence. Within half an hour the Carpathian detachment had succeeded in capturing one of the foothills to Monte Cairo, Point 720, and although under direct fire from German strongpoints began to prepare themselves for the assault of Monte Cairo from this new base line.

By 1515 hrs the Carpathian squadron had pushed forwards and neared the intermediate summit of Feature 852, here regrouping on a hummock to attack and strike from the northern and eastern slopes against the leading German defences. These were arranged in two lines, about fifty metres distant from each other and were covered by bunkers built from concrete and the mountain stone. The first line was covered by four bunkers and presented a perfect location for the Germans to launch a counter-attack. This was prevented by the British soldier who had now come round and with bursts of submachine-gun fire on the flank held the Germans at bay. As the smoke grew deeper and visibility deteriorated further, this man twice got to his feet and stood amidst the turmoil to fire accurate bursts at the Germans. On his third burst he was shot in the face and fell dead to the ground. The fighting lasted until 1545 hrs, taking the form of individual assault actions on each separate strongpoint until all the bunkers were seized and the area secured. Meanwhile the squadron of Poznan Lancers overcame the defenders' obstacles on the southern slopes of the folds of Hill 852 and began consolidating their positions. Hill 852 was now in Polish hands.

Further assaults up the precipitous and exposed slopes were made and then repelled by devastating German artillery, mortar and machine-gun fire. The Poles were sustaining heavy losses and the men were rapidly growing fatigued. On the southern flank a squadron of the 15th Poznan Lancers made some headway along the southern slope of neighbouring Hill 710 before, at 1420 hrs, being diverted to support the beleaguered Carpathian squadron in a combined effort towards Hill 893. The remaining units of these regiments had to be utilized for carrying ammunition and evacuating casualties on the steep mountainsides, where nothing other than porters could traverse the wild, pathless slopes.

The Germans however, remained firmly ensconced in their second-line defences on Hill 893, from where they unleashed a heavy bombardment. After a short break to catch their breath, the two Polish squadrons began at 1610 hrs to try to advance further. The fighting was very hard and when ammunition stocks became depleted the struggle continued with hand-to-hand combat as long as the men could muster their strength. Ultimately, the German positions were breached at 1630 hrs. Hill 893 was then dominated completely, and the Carpathian Lancers sent forward patrols to chase towards the next hill, 912, on the ascent to the ultimate objective of Passo Corno. Still, the Germans were regrouping and at 1715 hrs came forth a German counter-attack on Hill 893 from the west. But the attack broke down and 893 remained in Polish hands. The enemy did not attempt any more counter-attacks, concentrating instead their defences on Hills 945 and 912.

At 1800 hrs Major Kiedacz, commander of the 15 Cavalry Regiment, took over the whole offensive. He originally planned to carry out assaults on Hill 912 by nightfall, but the state of exhaustion among the forces of both squadrons necessitated delaying the execution of this to the following day. To strengthen the Polish position the commander of 6 Brigade sent forward the second squadron of the 15 Cavalry Regiment during the evening. The squadron arrived on the battlefield after dark and at midnight relieved the heavily fatigued and depleted Carpathian Lancers squadron on Hill 893. In the fighting of 19 May the advancing squadrons inflicted significant damage to the enemy (30 killed, 23 prisoners), but also experienced significant casualties themselves (especially the Carpathian Lancers) – 28 killed, 61 wounded. It was a sacrifice, however, that provided the Allies with near mastery of the underlying terrain of the Liri Valley.

The next day, 20 May, the attack was repeated by the two squadrons of the 15 Poznan Cavalry Regiment towards the summits of Hills 912 and 945, but without clear results. After an initial success against 912, the Germans launched a strong counter-attack in the evening from 945, which forced the

Poles to retreat to the plateau of Hill 893. The third squadron of the 15 Poznan lancers arrived at the front during the night and at 0330 hrs sent patrols forward to reconnoitre the slopes of Hill 912. With strong artillery support the patrols made significant advances but were too few in number to drive home the offensive and were forced to withdraw. The assault was relaunched at 1330 hrs by the entire squadron, with the collaboration of artillery, and this time they succeeded in capturing 912 and struck forwards up towards Passo Corno. By 1500 hrs the squadron was in full assault of the pass, where a heavy German counter-attack forced the Poles back down to Hill 912 and after nightfall back further again to Hill 893.

At this stage Lieutenant General Anders gave orders at 1600 hrs to halt the attack on Passo Corno and to concentrate on tying down enemy formations in that area, the emphasis now shifting to the Polish assault on the town of Piedimonte in the Liri Valley. The Hitler Line was proving difficult to assail by the Allies, with British 78th Infantry Division embroiled in the attack on Aquino and the Canadian 1st Infantry Division battling hard between Aquino and Pontecorvo. The Germans used this pause to resupply and strengthen their defences and both opponents carefully observed each other.

The attack upon the town of Piedimonte commenced on the 20 May. The Germans had spent the previous five months fortifying the town and incorporating it into the Hitler Line defences. The approaches to the town were covered by six steel machine-gun emplacements with a strong anti-tank screen about 100–150 yards behind. The main defence line lay further up the slopes of the hill on the perimeter of the town. This consisted of five very strong bunkers hewn out of the rock near the town wall and of fortified houses on the outskirts, the whole covered by extensive minefields. The Germans had converted the town into a stronghold, fortifying nearly every building, with many of the houses in the town itself being turned into strongpoints.

Task force Group Bob conducted the attack, a specially formed composite force drawn from the few remaining combat assets in II Corps, under the deputy commander of 2 Polish Armoured Brigade, Lieutenant Colonel Władysław Bobiński. It comprised the 6 Armoured Regiment, 5th and 18th Infantry Battalions, one squadron of the 12th Podolski Lancers, Corps Headquarters Defence Company, 3 Battery of 9 Light Artillery Regiment, 4 Light Artillery Regiment, one troop of self-propelled guns of the 7 Anti-Tank Regiment, 10 and 11 Heavy Artillery Regiments, one platoon of the 10th Engineer Battalion, and a platoon of 4.2in mortars from the 5th Kresowa Division, with signals equipment and transport provided by 2 Armoured Brigade headquarters.

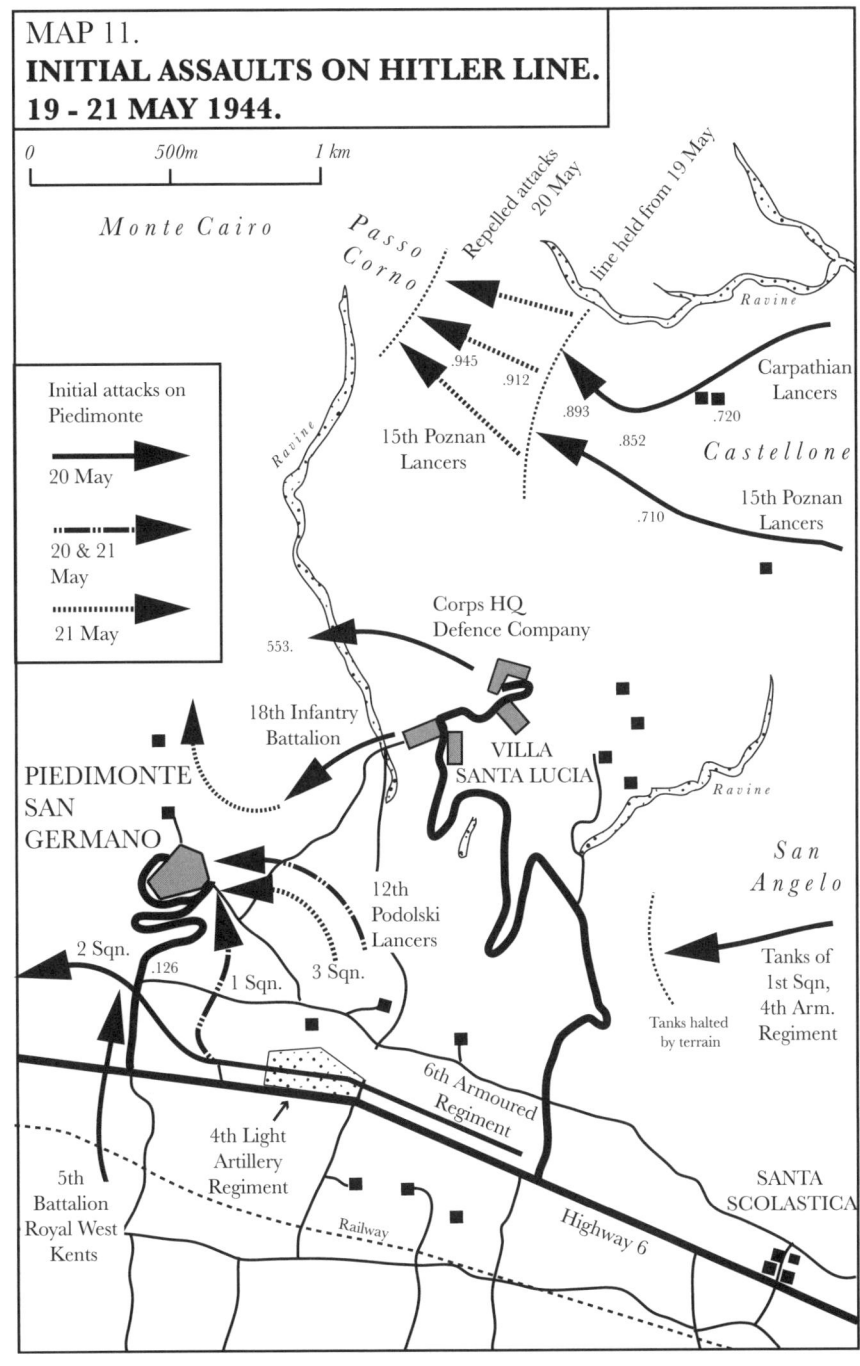

Many of these units had been seriously weakened by the previous heavy fighting for Monte Cassino, in particular the infantry; the 18th Battalion alone had been reduced to less than a third of its original strength. The troops were exhausted, most of them having been in action almost continuously since the opening of the offensive, nevertheless morale was high. The conditions for artillery support were not easy either. The locality lay at the extreme range of the Corps' guns, so that in order to ensure adequate direct support for Group Bob, the 4 Light Artillery Regiment had to be moved forward, taking up positions in completely open ground north of Highway 6, from Massa Romano to Feature 86.

The Eighth Army Commander, Lieutenant General Leese was well aware that the battle of Piedimonte was being fought by a II Corps already much depleted from the fighting at Monte Cassino. Consequently Leese conversed with Anders on 20 May, and at 1130 hrs the tasks of II Corps were defined as follows:

1. Maintain constant contact with the enemy;
2. Create the appearance that attacks on Passo Corno and Piedimonte would be launched at any moment;
3. When the enemy withdraws from Piedimonte, pursue the Germans towards Castrocielo.

What was essential was that Villa Santa Lucia must remain in Polish hands.

General Anders assigned Group Bob the task of covering the right flank of XIII Corps in the area of Piedimonte–Villa S. Lucia, to capture Piedimonte, and after its capture to patrol towards Castrociele. Lieutenant Colonel Władysław Bobiński issued his orders during the afternoon of 19 May for the assault the following day. The plan involved attacking the town frontally, from the southwest with tanks. Simultaneously the 18th Infantry Battalion would approach from the northeast, covered by fire from the direction of Villa S. Lucia. The attack was to be preceded by an assault to the south of Piedimonte by 21 Indian Brigade supported by the 2nd Squadron of the Polish 6 Armoured Regiment and to its right the 1st Squadron. This force was to advance along Highway 6, then head towards the northern side of Hill 126, south of Piedimonte. Initial infantry support would be provided by the 5th Battalion, The Queens Own Royal West Kent Regiment attached to 21 Indian Brigade.

At 0300 hrs Polish artillery began shelling Piedimonte and half an hour later the 1st and 2nd Squadrons of the 6 Armoured Regiment set off from the staging area of Santa Scolastica, followed by the 18th Infantry Battalion advancing from the western edge of Villa S. Lucia – all to converge on Piedimonte.

The assault of the West Kents made good progress and succeeded in securing its objectives without much difficulty by 1615 hrs. The West Kents now consolidated their positions and awaited the arrival of the Polish tank squadrons before advancing further. Inspired by their success Colonel Bobiński committed his force to battle.

The Polish tanks set off with Captain Ezman commanding the 2nd Squadron, with Lieutenant Jadwisiak's 1st Squadron to his right. Both squadrons adopted the same formation of two lead tanks followed by the commander's tank, HQ tank platoon and the remainder of the tank platoons. It was not long before the tanks sighted infantry ahead and opened fire on the move. As Second Lieutenant Młotkowski's lead tank closed to fifty metres from the infantry ahead he shouted, 'Cease Fire!'[1] across the radio – the Poles were actually shelling the West Kents at the rendezvous point. Fortunately no one was hurt. The combined force then turned off Highway 6 on to the dirt track leading to Piedimonte and here the commander of the West Kents chose to halt his advance, being well aware of the presence of many concealed German fortifications in the vicinity. Captain Ezman, who was keen to achieve success before nightfall and prove the 6 Armoured Regiment's worth, did not share this cautious approach. The 2nd Squadron continued its advance – without infantry support.

As the lead tanks drove along the track, passing a distinctive red-painted cottage, the Germans opened fire. They had driven straight into an ambush and the German gunners, aware the tanks were without infantry support, had the perfect opportunity to engage them at close quarters, unleashing the full ferocity of their anti-tank weaponry upon them. The lead tank of Sergeant Baran was halted in its tracks by a barrage of shells exploding before and upon it. Baran bailed out of the tank, his overalls caked in the blood and flesh of his radio operator and tried to open the driver's hatch without success; luckily the wounded driver crawled free, though the gunner died in the vehicle. Next to be hit was Ezman's tank, sustaining a direct hit to the turret that spun it through 180 degrees. Ezman attempted to dismount but was shot down; one crewman did escape but was machine-gunned as he ran, and the remainder of the crew burned inside the vehicle. The driver almost escaped, managing to drag his body halfway out of the hatch before succumbing to the flames.

Now the third tank in line began to issue forth smoke, though not from a direct hit. The vehicle had grounded on an obstruction, possibly a stone wall, and the engine compartment had sustained serious damage which led to the crew compartment filling with exhaust fumes. The vehicle's commander, Second Lieutenant Hołszczuk, opened his hatch and the smoke began to clear, so that the horror of the scene was unveiled before him. Hołszczuk knew his tank would be next and took an immediate decision – he and the crew bailed out and escaped. Three tanks were now lost and the remainder of the squadron, held back from advancing up the slope, proceeded to shell the vicinity of the red cottage. Things began to get even worse for the 2nd Squadron as through the smoke of their barrage could be seen the forms of men moving; the German infantry were counter-attacking, and without their own close infantry support the tanks were sitting targets.

With the 2nd Squadron halted in its approach to the town Bobiński issued further orders that a patrol should be sent out to reconnoitre further along Highway 6 to disclose additional German positions. Following the death of Captain Ezman, Lieutenant Masztak took command and detailed Lieutenant Hoff to lead the patrol. However Hoff's vehicles were almost out of fuel, the crews topping them up from jerry cans during pauses in the fighting. The smaller, faster Stuart light tanks were best suited to the task, although the terrain they would operate in, that of dense scrub and wooded thickets would be ideal for German anti-tank guns to set ambushes. Nevertheless the tanks struck out northwards in the direction of Aquino.

Meanwhile Lieutenant Jadwisiak's 1st Squadron was making much better progress towards Piedimonte by virtue of its route possessing better natural cover, and also due to the rearrangement of the leading tanks from two up front to three and to moving the tanks forwards individually in bounds, so as not to block the progress of the following vehicle. The Germans were not expecting two head-on tank assaults and this, combined with intense shelling from the Polish gunners, meant that the infantry ahead of the 1st Squadron were broken. As Jadwisiak's tanks rounded a smoke-clouded hairpin rise along the road into the town they were met by a column of thirty Germans marching towards them with white flags flying. The prisoners were handed over to the West Kents and the Poles pushed on, though not quickly or easily as the track ahead had been blown up and a lengthy detour had to be made to reach the town. This setback was compounded by reports from Second Lieutenant Tymieniecki's leading tank platoon that fuel supplies were running out. Lieutenant Jadwisiak made the decision to press on regardless and the platoon prepared to go.

Upon hearing these radio communications the 6 Armoured Regiment's commander Lieutenant Colonel Świelicki, who was well aware that the traffic-jammed roads meant that fuel could not get through, issued direct orders to Second Lieutenant Tymieniecki – that he should consider his task done and return to his squadron. This he duly did and began to pull back, upon which the Germans unleashed an artillery barrage that persisted for two hours. Amidst the crescendo one tank was able to identify an anti-tank gun firing on them from the left-hand side of a house. Immediately twenty tank guns and twice as many machine guns rained fire on the area; in response the Germans increased their mortar barrage upon the neighbouring West Kents. In turn, the tanks turned their fire at the suspected mortar positions and the anti-tank gun took the opportunity to reopen fire. Fortunately all the rounds flew high and exploded around Highway 6. Tymieniecki ordered his men to engage the anti-tank gun position instead of the mortars and this renewed intense barrage saw the German crew attempt to flee. One was machine-gunned down as he emerged from behind the building, another stumbled to within 50m of the nearest tank and its nervous commander, instead of firing his machine gun fired his main gun, the blast at close proximity rocked the tanks and the German was no more.

The German anti-tank guns were for now silent, but from the hilltop town poured forth a torrent of machine-gun fire upon the infantry of the West Kents lying next to Nóżka's tank platoon. The infantry had only limited cover to the north of the town, and these men on the western side were completely exposed. The Germans proceeded to decimate them with machine-gun fire, cutting them down in swathes with the surviving men desperately trying to drag the wounded to relative safety – there was none. Everywhere the Polish tank crews looked was strewn with the bodies of wounded and dying men. Nóżka's two tanks took the initiative and drove themselves forward of the infantry, turning themselves side-on to the incoming German fire to act as shields for the infantry. The tanks' sides were relentlessly strafed and heavily dented, with one turret-mounted machine gun destroyed but no other damage.

The West Kents were able to recover their wounded and were now focused upon destroying the German gun positions, but how were they to communicate with the Polish tank crews? Fortunately Nóżka could speak English and was able to coordinate his gunfire with the infantry. Dolinski in his tank was not so fortunate, he was not proficient in English and improvising what he thought sounded like English, popped his head out of the turret and shouted 'Ki spik Frencz?' then quickly ducked back down before the next burst of German bullets. Dolinski tried shouting again but with no response from the infantry, he looked on frustrated as he could see his colleague Nóżka blasting buildings to pieces in the town. The third time Dolinski opened his hatch, shouting out 'Ki spik Frencz?', an English lieutenant shouted back 'Je parle Francais!'[2] With a working language of French the infantry were able to guide the fire of Dolinski's tank and further gun emplacements in the town were destroyed. However, the curse of the German anti-tank gunners returned and with their first round they scored a direct hit to the front of Lesiak's tank. Fortunately the crew and vehicle survived, the front of the tank having been copiously reinforced by spare lengths of caterpillar track fixed across it, and these had taken the full blast of the explosion and were shot from the vehicle.

Meanwhile the Polish infantry were attacking from the northeast. Two companies of the 18th Infantry Battalion supplemented with one platoon of the Corps HQ Defence Company under the command of Major Osmakiewicz struck out from Villa Santa Lucia, heading for the northeast edge of Piedimonte. The attack lacked surprise and adequate numbers but did manage to reach the edge of the ravine along the town's eastern edge without great loss. Further assaults advanced only 150m before the troops were halted by intense machine-gun fire from two steel pillboxes constructed from the turrets of Panzer Mk I light tanks. These protruded only a foot above the ground and were covered with turf, they proved extremely difficult to identify and both survived the battle intact. Halted in its progress the 18th Battalion clung to its position in the leading ravine at the edge of Piedimonte, in readiness for further action. The platoon of the Corps HQ Defence Company focused its assault upon Hill 553, which lay to the north of Villa Santa Lucia and to the east of Piedimonte and was in the hands of German infantry. The platoon advanced up the slopes through the olive groves but got pinned down as they passed the treeline by machine-gun fire from the summit. The hilltop remained in German hands that day.

To cover the eastern attack on the town by the 18th Infantry Battalion, the 1st Squadron of the 4 Armoured Regiment who were in position around the monastery was ordered to pass through Albaneta and descend the mountain ridge in the direction of Villa Santa Lucia to support the infantry in their offensive. The 1st Squadron reconnoitred the terrain from Mass Albaneta towards Highway 6 via Casalina, and the steep mountainsides, numerous ravines and poor roads were found to make the area impassable for tanks; however the squadron remained in the area providing covering fire for the infantry until after dark.

During the evening of 20 May, Group Bob was bolstered from 1930 hrs by the advent of an improvised squadron of the 12 Podolski Lancers Regiment consisting of 70 men drawn from across the regiment and led by Lieutenant Dziewicki. With these new forces Lieutenant Colonel Bobiński relaunched the infantry attack, joining the action himself alongside the Headquarters Platoon. The 12th Podolski Squadron advanced in line with Second Lieutenant Teklinski's platoon leading, followed by the Headquarters Platoon and the platoons of Second Lieutenants Koczy and Śniechowski. As they moved through the dusk towards Piedimonte they passed an impressive relic of the German defences – a Panther turret fortification. This consisted of the turret of a Panther tank mounted on a subterranean concrete bunker so only the turret was visible. It boasted a powerful 75mm gun with a 7.5 metre-long barrel. It was a formidable anti-tank position and thankfully for the Allies it never fired a shot, the underground compartments having been destroyed with demolition charges by the retreating Germans.

At about 2000 hrs, the squadron reached the eastern fringes of the town; they had surprised the Germans completely. The squadron approached stealthily with Teklinski's platoon creeping around the final steep hairpin bend before the town. The platoon advanced further in pairs, the men disappearing into the darkness as they entered the town. Lieutenant Colonel Bobiński and Lieutenant Dziewicki, unable to wait for news from Teklinski, decided to push forward. Eerie silence reigned as they neared the medieval buildings. Teklinski's platoon advanced deep into Piedimonte, to within 20m of the church in the main square that dominated the town. Now the German machine-gun fire opened up on them. Cries of wounded Poles and gunfire sounded as if they came from all around, it was impossible to tell who were Poles and who Germans in the dark and the pandemonium. The platoon was surrounded by heavily defended buildings, linked with through passages that helped the Germans outflank the Lancers. Bobiński and the remaining platoons took cover, there was only mayhem ahead and they could not even discern in what direction the Germans might be. Bobiński sent Second Lieutenant Śniechowski to scout ahead and report back. Nothing was heard for almost half an hour, then suddenly out of the darkness charged Śniechowski, Tekliński and his platoon!

The squadron of the 12 Podolski Lancers then pulled back from Piedimonte, discovering as it did so an underground shelter to the southeast of the town that had housed the thirty-odd prisoners who had surrendered earlier that day. The platoons now made full use of this cover and occupied it for the night. Kocki's Platoon took up forward position on the road to Piedimonte, whilst Second Lieutenant Śniechowski and his men spent the night in the neighbouring ravine.

Meanwhile, the 2nd Squadron's reconnaissance towards Aquino drove only half a kilometre forward before again becoming engaged by German anti-tank weapons, self-propelled anti-tank guns and mines – two of their tanks were set alight. Faced with such fierce resistance the commander was forced to halt the attack and reconnoitre the axis of the German defences, with one platoon led by Second Lieutenant Nowak in the direction of Highway 6 and another northwards that was halted by heavy fire, resulting in one tank knocked out. Nowak's tank platoon had patrolled nearly 4km along Highway 6, as far as the airfield at Aquino without coming under attack. Most probably the German anti-tank guns had decided not to engage the small force, wishing to retain the secrecy of their positions for a larger engagement. The remainder of the squadron now began to bombard the positions of the German anti-tank defences in the area between Highway 6 and the western Panther turret emplacement. Further advances of the 2nd Squadron were limited to reconnaissance.

Finally, with the tanks running out of fuel as well as lacking infantry support and with the fast gathering dusk, the two squadrons were withdrawn at 2115 hrs and 2230 hrs to positions at their forming-up areas southeast of Piedimonte, between Monte Cassino and Highway 6. As they withdrew the tanks of both squadrons continued to suffer further losses from well-camouflaged anti-tank weapons, and one tank slipped over the tattered edge of the road into a ravine. Back in their positions they were concealed from the enemy by folds in the terrain and by 0400 hrs had refuelled and rearmed. The first day's action had been costly for the 6 Armoured Regiment – two tanks were destroyed, and four were heavily damaged wrecks and three lightly damaged, while the 1st Squadron's Commander, Captain Stanisław Ezman was killed with seven other men, and two wounded.

The attack on 20 May did not achieve mastery of the fields to the south of Piedimonte nor the disgorgement of the Germans from the slopes of Hill 553. The assaulting tanks could not overcome the rocky terrain and narrow winding streets while the infantry lacked the numbers to be decisive. The Polish artillery had nonetheless bombarded the town, reducing it to a pile of rubble. Analysis of the fighting had revealed that weak points of the German defences lay to the north and west, and subsequent attacks were to be focused on that zone. For now, both sides rested and the night was quiet.

By the morning of 21 May the Germans had recovered their balance and called down defensive fire. The forward Polish positions were subjected to constant heavy artillery and mortar fire that seriously impaired preparations for a renewed attempt to clear the town. Most heavily bombarded were the positions of the 6 Armoured Regiment whose command post was destroyed, fatally wounding the commanding officer Colonel Świetlicki. Despite the German resistance and shelling delaying offensive action in the morning, Lieutenant Colonel Bobiński was determined to re-launch offensive action in the afternoon, confident that the previous day's gains could be extended and the town seized.

The second attack was launched at 1130 hrs, by fourteen tanks of the 3rd Squadron advancing from the southeast in two groups. The right-hand group linked up with the 12 Podolski Lancers squadron and advanced past the knocked-out panther turret emplacement, suffering two tanks damaged and immobilized at the foot of the hill. At 1600 hrs the tanks and cavalry launched a joint attack clambering through piles of rock and rubble to proceed along the southern approach road, where on the hairpin bend two more tanks were damaged and hung over the steep slopes. The ensuing combat was street fighting at the closest quarters. The tanks moved forward and neutralized two of the bunkers that had been hewn out of the town wall, while self-propelled guns and artillery destroyed another strongpoint situated in the church crypt. The cavalrymen were engaged in sequentially clearing the buildings, driving out the anti-tank units and locating targets for the tanks to engage. Further advance into the centre of the town slowed to a halt as the narrow maze of mined streets proved impassable for the tanks, two of which became stranded on the parapets between terraces. Subsequently the tanks were ill positioned to engage the deeper German defences. The tank group on the left was tasked with covering the assault on the southeast of the town by providing covering fire from the southwest. The tanks advanced along the northern side of Highway 6, and again fell into fierce anti-tank fire that knocked out three of the six, the surviving vehicles managing to provide some covering fire for the assault.

At 1630 hrs Lieutenant Colonel Bobiński sent forward three more tanks from the 1st Squadron to support the attack on the southeast of the town, but they fell foul of anti-tank guns and one was destroyed and the other two set alight. The last four tanks held in reserve were now sent out to provide covering fire from the positions of the 18th Battalion. The Corps Headquarters Defence Company held their positions on Hill 553 and the 18th Battalion managed to capture further positions on the southern slopes of the hill and reconnoitre along the German lines, revealing the Germans had a network of positions leading back to Passo Corno.

The fighting in the town had made slow progress and by 1700 hrs only two streets leading to the market square had been cleared. With the arrival of dusk the Podolski squadron was once more withdrawn and took up position in line with the tanks just in front of the town wall, along with supporting tanks which during the night were subjected to heavy German anti-tank fire.

The assaults on Piedimonte had been unsuccessful and all chance of surprise had been lost. With such strong German resistance and the lack of progress, Lieutenant General Leese insisted that it was not necessary to continue the costly attempts to capture Piedimonte. Absolute mastery of the position was no longer crucial as XIII Corps was advancing further into the Liri Valley and the position at Piedimonte would soon become isolated and undefendable. Consequently, Polish action here should be that of reconnaissance in force and maintaining constant contact with the enemy.

At 2000 hrs on 21 May Lieutenant General Anders issued new orders for Group Bob, to contain the enemy rather than pursue their struggle to capture the town with the limited resources available. The group was reinforced with Colonel Karol Piłat's relatively strong 5th Battalion of the 3rd Carpathian Division taking over the positions of the 18th Battalion in the ravine to the east of the town, while the 18th Battalion was now tasked with providing static covering fire from the area of Villa Santa Lucia. To the left of the 5th Battalion lay the assault squadron of the 12 Podolski Lancers and eight tanks on the outskirts of the town. On the right of the 5th Battalion, the Corps Headquarters Defence Company on Hill 553 was relieved by one of the 5th Battalion's companies, as was the position held by the 18th Battalion on Hill 124, 1km south of Villa

Santa Lucia. At the same time artillery support was strengthened, with Group Bob receiving direct support from the 1, 3 and 4 Light Artillery Regiments. Reliefs were carried out during the night of 21/22 May.

Despite orders to cease wholesale offensive efforts to seize Piedimonte, Lieutenant Colonel Bobiński was convinced of the imminent collapse of the German garrison and that one more push would yield success. What was to be avoided was any delay that would allow the Germans to reinforce and resupply their forces and jeopardize the forward Polish positions. The third attack on Piedimonte was to be performed by the 5th Battalion assaulting from the north and southeast with the support of two tank squadrons of the 6 Armoured Regiment. The infantry on the northern front would deploy one company to finally capture Hill 553. The remaining squadron of tanks was tasked with providing covering fire from the south.

The morning of 22 May saw German artillery fire focused on the command post of Lieutenant Colonel Bobiński and nearby artillery positions. The shelling caused only light damage but did result in the preliminary supporting Polish artillery barrage being only partially completed before the third attack commenced at 1400 hrs. The main burden of the attack fell on the troops positioned the previous day on the slopes southeast of Piedimonte – the companies of the 5th Battalion, a squadron of the 6th Armoured Regiment, and later the assault squadron of the 12 Podolski Lancers who occupied Hill 144 and provided a supporting fire role.

One company of the 5th Battalion, supported by tanks, advanced along the serpentine approach road leading into the southeast of the town. Upon reaching the upper hairpin bend, assault groups split off from the left and right flanks to reach the town centre in a pincer movement. The tanks made good initial progress and the infantry fell in behind the vehicles and advanced in their tracks, moving forward in a single column along the canyon leading to the east of the town. However, as the tanks emerged one by one out of the ravine and on to the terraced fields leading up to Piedimonte they were relentlessly harried by German anti-tank fire and impaired in their movement by the rocky ground and stone walls of the terraces. The accompanying troops of the 5th Battalion, now penetrating the town, were deprived of the support of tanks, and in the ensuing street fighting could not call in the help of artillery and mortars due to their close proximity to the enemy, so found themselves in a difficult position. Major Tarkowski, deputy commander of the 5th Battalion, attempted to support the embattled infantry with reinforcements, but the German fire intensified with the development of the fighting and further movement proved impossible. Whilst leading one of these attempts to bolster the infantry battling in the town streets, Major Tarkowski was himself killed.

Breaking the Adolf Hitler Line 223

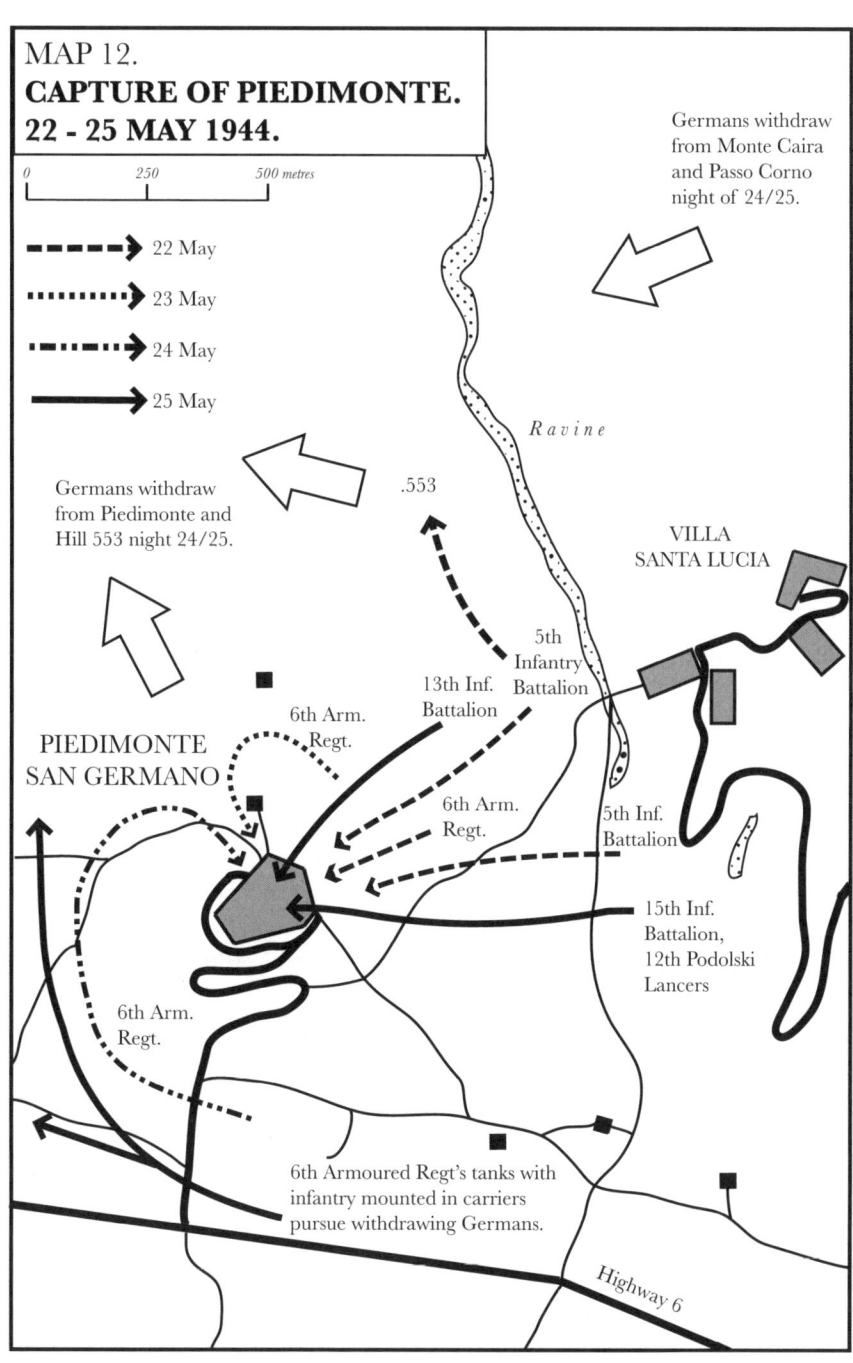

The separated group of infantry in the town had to fight on by themselves, and clearing the steep, narrow alleys of the southern part of town they were capable of making only momentary gains. The troops fought in three clusters: one group broke through the German perimeter defences but came under fire in the streets and took heavy losses, amongst them their commander, and they then fell back. The same fate met the next, smaller group, while the third succeeded in reaching the church in the town square where they became pinned down by German fire.

The two squadrons of tanks had made good initial progress along the ravine to the east, but as they emerged onto the approaches to the town they came under heavy fire. This became ever more damaging as those tanks that were able to move forward were caught in a kind of traffic jam, being funnelled into bottlenecks in the narrow approach road and urban streets. By evening the road was completely blocked after a mine wrecked a tank. Only one platoon of tanks made it past this succession of obstacles to reach the entrances to the town, where they were greeted by a devastating barrage of anti-tank fire including the Allies' first encounter with shoulder-launched anti-tank rockets known as *Panzerfausts*. There was nothing these lead tanks could do and those still capable of moving retreated to the forming-up areas to refuel and rearm. Twelve tanks remained semi-operative in the field and these formed a defensive cluster for the night around a collection of captured outbuildings. That night was intensely cold and made worse by torrential rain. The Germans added to their misery by accurately locating and destroying the 6 Armoured Regiment's ammunition dump. The tank crews were now growing accustomed to the smoke and soot of their fighting vehicles, the acrid smell of burnt powder and the discomfort of parched lips that craved water – in scarce supply. The infantry of the 5th Battalion pinned in the church fought their way out of town during the night, taking advantage of a barrage of heavy artillery that tied down the Germans.

The other squadron of the 6 Armoured Regiment numbering eight tanks struck out at 1400 hrs towards Piedimonte along Highway 6, to outflank the bastion to the southwest. The tanks began bombarding the town from the ravine to the west of the town, but again the German anti-tank defences opened fire with heavy machine guns and self-propelled guns. Two tanks were destroyed and the duel dragged on until dusk. Under the veil of darkness the squadron withdrew towards the regiment's staging post, covered by a rear-guard platoon. The Germans retained control of the western approach to Piedimonte and once again frustrated Polish attempts to advance. The lot of the 5th Battalion's company to the north was no better. Without the support of heavy weapons the company could only send out patrols to consolidate the gains on Hill 553, but these became pinned down by intense coordinated machine-gun fire that resulted in heavy casualties. The day's attack had been a near-total failure.

Late in the evening of 22 May, Lieutenant Colonel Bobiński was planning to switch to the defence in the absence of reinforcements in sufficient strength to achieve success. This position was consistent with the orders of General Anders, who would not push his forces to breaking point to acquire Piedimonte. On the morning of the following day however, Bobiński decided to renew aggressive action, despatching a squadron of tanks at 2100 hrs to take control of the northern access roads leading into the town. The tank platoon managed to break into the town but the lead vehicle became stranded on rocks whilst mines disabled the second and third tanks. The attack broke down and the remaining three tanks were ordered to withdraw, but descending the hill from Piedimonte one tank slipped into a ravine and became stranded. The driver managed to jump clear but the remainder of the crew were trapped. Great efforts were made to rescue them and the squadron commander Captain Alfred Kuczuk-Pilecki was himself killed by flying shrapnel as German machine-gun and mortar fire was directed upon the the rescuers.

On the slopes to the southeast of Piedimonte remained sixteen immobilized tanks that the crews managed to keep in action as static artillery to cover the troops of the 5th Battalion. During the night of 22/23 May a fierce battle raged, as the Germans counter-attacked to destroy these tanks, but the crews prevailed and drove the Germans back into the town, shelling the buildings throughout the night. The losses during the actions of 22 and 23 May were for the 6 Armoured Regiment, 6 dead and 19 wounded, whilst the 5th Battalion had 30 dead and 9 wounded. The Poles were not alone in suffering checks by the Germans – during the period 19–21 May the other Allied forces in the Liri Valley were also being stalled by stubborn German resistance. The Hitler Line was decisively breached by the Canadians on 23 May, but the Germans continued to hold onto their positions north of Highway 6.

On 24 May the combined squadrons of the 6 Armoured Regiment (ten tanks) were supplemented by the regiment's Defence Headquarters Company, three self-propelled guns and a platoon of Engineers. Their task was to reconnoitre the region to the west of Piedimonte where the action had taken place previously, proceed along Highway 6 and then approach the town from the north. This force made significant progress, with close cooperation between the branches resulting in the destruction of several German machine-gun and anti-tank-gun bunkers during eight hours of fighting from 1100 hrs.

On the night of 24/25 May, the 5th and 18th Battalions were scheduled for relief by the 13th and 15th Battalions and the Corps Headquarters Defence

Company. Patrols on Hill 553 made further progress and captured a number of prisoners who testified that the Germans were withdrawing from the entire Piedimonte area. Bobiński immediately ordered three detachments to pursue them; the 13th Battalion captured Hill 553 by 0600 hrs, the 15th Battalion along with the assault squadron of the 12 Podolski Regiment and dismounted tank crews fighting on foot, cleared the town an hour later. With the German garrison in full retreat Bobiński formed and led a pursuit detachment of a squadron of tanks with a platoon of infantry mounted on universal carriers. The detachment set off at 0900 hrs advancing almost a mile up Highway 6, harassing the retreating enemy until they were halted at 1100 hrs by a minefield; they then turned back bringing a few prisoners and some captured equipment. By the evening of 25 May, Group Bob had achieved its objectives and consolidated its position, the group was then disbanded with the units returning to their parent formations. During the engagement the 6 Armoured Regiment comprised 49 Sherman and 11 Stuart tanks, of which 10 Sherman, 1 Stuart and a scout car were destroyed, and a further 17 Shermans were abandoned wrecks.

15

The Aftermath

On 26 May the advances of X Corps on the right and XIII Corps on the left began pinching out the Polish II Corps. That evening it was reported that Polish troops were no longer in contact with the enemy anywhere in their sector. The breaking of the Gustav and Hitler Lines successfully realized the Allies' plan for opening the road north, and Rome was liberated on 4 June 1944. On 27 May the Polish II Corps began withdrawing towards Campobasso, the movement of units to this area commencing on 29 May and the last formation to fall back being the 5th Kresowa Division. In the Campobasso area the Corps rested and began reorganizing for the next offensive campaign up Italy's Adriatic coastline.

The Poles suffered heavy casualties during the battle – out of the commanders of three attacking brigades, one was killed and one wounded; of the commanders of nine attacking battalions, two were killed and two wounded; casualties amongst company and platoon commanders were in proportion much heavier. In one of the attacking battalions all the company commanders were casualties. The casualty total for the Polish II Corps in the battle against the high ground of Monte Cassino, Piedimonte and Monte Cairo came to 307 officers and 3,892 other ranks, comprising 923 killed, 2,930 wounded and 345 missing.[1] Enemy losses were also heavy. After the massif had been captured about 900 unburied German dead were found. The number of wounded during the first attack is not known, but it was certainly proportionally higher. The fact that this battle took place in an area measuring just over six square miles shows how fierce the fighting raged.

The high casualty figures stemmed largely from the earlier lessons of mountain warfare being learned but not applied, making the campaign a toilsome, slow business for the Allies. The mountain fighting brought forward an old truth that had been lost sight of: infantry is the decisive arm on the battlefield and there is no substitute for it. All the setbacks of the Poles at Cassino were predictable and could have been avoided by imaginative leadership. Leese's set-piece bludgeoning offensive strategy strongly influenced all the commanders; in particular there was a lack of appreciation of the terrain for troops and its effects on communications. The rigours of the natural terrain were further exacerbated by the excellent defensive positions established by the Germans, against which the use of massed artillery proved ineffective, as did tanks. Supporting arms came more to the fore; the engineers becoming vital front-line assault troops relied upon to clear obstacles for the infantry. The tank served little practical use beyond that of a self-propelled gun. Yet the mystique and prestige which hung about armour was so great that British and Polish commanders persisted in thinking of it as a decisive attacking arm instead of seeing it for what it was in Italy, a crawling monster which produced little other than congestion, confusion and delay. Flexibility of mind and organization along with a fostering of improvisation rather than relying on doctrine would ultimately prove to be the key to success.

Concurrent with the victory at Monte Cassino breaking the Gustav Line, the Allied divisions trapped in the Anzio beachhead finally broke out and along with the American Fifth Army pushed northwards up the coast towards Rome. The American commander, General Mark Clark was then presented with two options: encircle and destroy the battered German Tenth and Fourteenth Armies or make a triumphal march into Rome. Clark chose the latter and the Fifth Army entered the vacated city on 4 June, becoming the first Allied general to occupy an enemy capital. The decision won him much publicity and resulted in minimal American casualties, although it did permit Kesselring to withdraw his armies and consolidate them further north in a series of defensive lines that held until the end of the war.

The Polish achievements at Cassino were widely praised by the British Army from rank and file to the overall commanders, Generals Leese and Alexander – the latter personally decorated Lieutenant General Anders with the Order of the Bath. Lieutenant General Sir Oliver Leese regarded Anders as one of his most successful corps commanders and the men he led as being of exceptional fighting material. He wrote to Anders prior to the Poles relocation for the next offensive, passing on his congratulations: 'To yourself and to the whole Polish Corps for its magnificent achievements in the present battle and in particular for its capture of Monastery Hill. This notable feat will, I believe, go down in history as a major achievement of Polish arms, and it will certainly figure in our own military history as one of the outstanding successes gained by the Eighth Army.'[2] The British press also heralded the victory and the prominent role the Poles played in seizing the fortress of Monte Cassino.

The military establishments of Britain and Poland felt vindicated in their struggle to raise and deploy a Polish army in exile; it was a hugely successful endeavour and the victory a rallying point for the Polish nation that has stood the test of time. Politically, it achieved nothing and the Polish Government in Exile quickly slid into oblivion as anticipated by General Sosnkowski – indeed more has been commented and written upon the demise of Polish politics than on the success of Polish soldiers, and there were a great many more soldiers than statesmen. The remainder of the war saw II Corps engaged in numerous fierce battles along the eastern seaboard of Italy, culminating in the capture of Bologna on 21 April 1945 and the subsequent surrender of all German forces in Italy on 29 April. The battle for the post-war survival of the Polish II Corps now began.

The Yalta conference in February 1945 had cemented Poland's post-war fate: the Soviet Union would appropriate all of Eastern Poland that it had occupied in 1939, whilst German land to the west would be ceded to Poland. Churchill defended his actions during a three-day parliamentary debate commencing on 27 March, that culminated in a vote of confidence. The debate was volatile, with many MPs openly criticizing Churchill over Yalta and voicing strong loyalty to Britain's Polish ally. The Prime Minister was not oblivious to the magnitude of the situation; the Poles had served Britain and now he had signed away their country. He lamented: 'His Majesty's Government will never forget the debt they owe to the Polish troops who have served them so valiantly… . I earnestly hope it may be possible to offer the citizenship and freedom of the British Empire… we should think it an honour to have such faithful and valiant warriors dwelling among us as if they were men of our own blood.'[3] The debate saw twenty-five MPs risk their careers by drafting an amendment protesting against Britain's tacit acceptance of Poland's domination by the Soviet Union. The amendment failed and the Member of Parliament for Norwich, Henry Strauss, 1st Baron Conesford, resigned his seat in protest at Britain's treatment of Poland.

As the vast majority of the II Corps originated from eastern Poland they now knew for certain they had no home to return to, their Poland had gone forever. The new Poland of communist subservience to the Soviet regime held no appeal for them; they had experienced the Soviet system first hand and knew they would be convicted as traitors who had abandoned the Soviet-German Front. The worst fear of these Polish soldiers now was that they would cease to be Polish at all, that the plebiscites the Soviets held following their invasion in 1939 now had international endorsement, that all the population of that region could technically be declared Soviet citizens, and the USSR was demanding repatriation of all its people displaced by war.

Fortunately neither Anders nor the British authorities were prepared to countenance such a notion. The Polish II Corps remained in Italy on garrison duty to assist the interim Allied Military Government. Churchill had wanted to deploy them on such duties in Germany as it would have quickened the demobilization of the British Army, but the political agitation it would have caused Stalin to share the occupation of Germany with Anders' Army was deemed too inflammatory and II Corps stayed put in Italy. To determine what opinion the Corps held on repatriation to Poland, a plebiscite was conducted during September in all units of II Corps at British request. The answer was a resounding no to repatriation.

They were fortunate; no other Polish citizen had the luxury of a place to belong, even if transitory, the entire population was on the move. In the zone annexed by the USSR all Polish nationals were displaced and forced west to the new borders of Poland to make new homes and lives for themselves, whilst in the west the people took no time in expelling all Germans from their newly acquired territory and set about colonizing the area. Added to these movements, there were vast numbers of Poles who had been displaced all over Europe during the German occupation and who were now of immediate concern to all post-war authorities.

Following years of forced labour and internment, the released Polish prisoners of war from 1939, Home Army prisoners taken after the Warsaw uprising, and a multitude of forced labourers were all of the opinion that to return to Poland would be a death sentence and that joining II Corps in Italy was by far the preferable option. Almost 20,000 such persons made their way to the recruitment centres for the Polish Army in Italy, many making the journey on foot. Despite orders from General Alexander to limit numbers to 80,000, the Corps had grown to 110,000 by January 1946 and in addition there were thousands of dependent civilians and servicemen's families throughout Italy, Africa and India. Repatriation to Poland was Britain's preferred strategy for dealing with these numbers and in total some 14,000 soldiers from II Corps did return home. These men were almost exclusively post-war recruits and personnel of the former Independent Carpathian Brigade in North Africa, none of whom had experienced the Soviet way of life. Of those who had survived their ordeal in the USSR and followed Anders throughout exile, only 310 chose Poland. The total number of Polish military personnel serving in the West who went home numbered just over 105,000.[4] The remaining soldiers of II Corps stood their ground in Italy to see what fate had in store.

By far the biggest risk Anders took to ensure the freedom of Polish soldiers who served in the German forces involved the 14th SS Grenadier Division 'Galicia', formed from Ukrainians of Polish nationality. This formation ended the war in northern Italy and it fell to II Corps to administer their prisoner-of-war camp. The Soviets were adamant that they wanted this division repatriated to the USSR but all knew they would be destined for the Gulag at best. Anders flatly refused to yield to Soviet pressure to hand them over and went so far as to threaten direct military action against any Soviet personnel who attempted to remove them. A Soviet contingent to assist the repatriation of Soviet citizens 'held prisoner' by Anders was despatched to Italy soon after VE Day – it achieved nothing but stirred up Italian communists and resulted in open streetfighting between the Poles and the socialists. It was an unpleasant but thankfully short-lived episode that did serve to convince the British that repatriation to Poland was not going to be a success, nor did it endear the new socialist government of Italy to the Polish cause. Following a screening process, 176 men of the 14th SS Division were found acceptable for service in II Corps. This decision only strengthened the Soviet notion that the exiled Poles had been in league with the Germans and that any Polish soldier returning to Poland would have to be vigorously vetted and cleansed of association with the West.

Anders' political rationale has come under much criticism from many sources but what cannot be denied is his utter devotion to soldiering for Poland and to the men under his command; the exile government came a poor second and this system of priorities caused much friction between the Middle East command and London. His frequently confrontational stance is not surprising given his hard life and career of soldiering coupled with his position as a Corps and Army commander. He worked well with the British militarily, ticking all the boxes required for a good commander: maintaining discipline, unity, and effectively sending his men into battle. His business-like approach did afford him a degree of toleration from the British with regard to his tendency to spontaneous outbursts of passion which at times threatened to frustrate the broader Allied force, notably following Katyn.

Grave reservations over Poland's political future were held by those Poles who had endured the Soviet regime or understood Stalin's intentions – they had no doubt that the Soviets would rig the free elections to suit their interests. The British Government held firm to the idea that true and fair democratic elections in Poland would deliver a government chosen by the Polish people. However, the Poles were soon to be found correct. The Soviet elections in January 1947 were a farce and resulted in the installation of a puppet regime that set about arresting all members of the resistance movement that had fought the Germans, convicting its leaders of conducting unlawful military operations. They were handed life prison sentences or executed. Western embassies reported that Polish soldiers who had served in the Wehrmacht were receiving appalling treatment upon return, with hindsight a not unforeseeable scenario. Through fear or naivety Britain recognized the legitimacy of the new communist government and simultaneously ceased its recognition of the exiled government in London. The British authorities were now struggling to come to terms with the reality that the Poles had been right all along about the horrors of Stalin's rule.

The legal status of the Polish II Corps was also unravelling; the government it served was no longer recognized, but they remained under British Army command. The situation was a total mess. It could not however, continue indefinitely and in mid-1946 a solution was found: the Polish Resettlement Corps was established in Britain. The formation was under the command of the British Army and its purpose was to retrain and educate Polish servicemen for civilian life in the UK, to repatriate those who wished to return to Poland and to aid the onward emigration of those who wished to live in the USA, Canada or Australia. Accordingly II Corps was demobilized in the summer of 1946 and shipped to the UK, along with all Polish nationals of the 14th SS Division. The formations were broken up and the men dispersed through over 200 camps around the UK. Their family dependants and numerous displaced Polish civilians were then shipped to Southampton from all over the world to join the former servicemen in the resettlement camps. With the Polish election of January 1947 installing a hostile Stalinist regime, the further repatriation of citizens to Poland was clearly the wrong thing do. The plight of these people was now taken seriously by the British Labour Government of Ernest Bevin and in recognition of their wartime service and their miserable post-war position the Polish Resettlement Act of March 1947 was passed, awarding full British citizenship to all 200,000 members of the Resettlement Corps, the first ever mass immigration legislation passed in the UK.

The Poles now had a legal home, although it was not always a very welcoming one. There was much hostility focused upon the Polish community, who were perceived as taking jobs that belonged to demobbed British servicemen and it was also thought that they were traitors to socialism for not returning to the 'workers' paradise' of communist Poland. A notable case of the difficulties faced by Poles at this time was that which befell Michail Onufrejczyk, a former teacher of Polish war orphans at Barbara Camp in Palestine. Onufrejczyk was a highly decorated warrant officer who served in every twentieth-century campaign fought by Poland. He became infamous in 1947 after being convicted of the murder of a fellow Polish soldier, ostensibly to steal his £600 Resettlement Corps grant. Onufrejczyk protested his innocence, claiming the soldier had decided to return to Poland – furthermore, there was no body. Nonetheless he was found guilty of murder and sentenced to death, a punishment later reduced to life imprisonment. His was the first case in 300 years where the accused was convicted for a murder though no body was ever found – it set a new legal precedent and such cases are still referred to by his surname. The case was hugely controversial and widely seen as an open attack on the Polish community, contrived to bring them into disrepute. Such conflicts of interest, commonplace as they sadly were, proved short-lived as the need for workers to rebuild

Britain proved vast and the reality of life behind the iron curtain became widely understood to be thoroughly miserable.

The Resettlement Corps was closed down in July 1948 as part of the post-war austerity measures, with 150,000 Polish servicemen and their dependants by then having adopted life in the UK. The final resettlement camp closed in 1970 when its last occupants moved to a specialist elderly care home created exclusively for Polish veterans, Ilford Park near Newton Abbot, South Devon, that remains in operation today under the aegis of the Ministry of Defence. By the time the camps closed the Polish II Corps had slid from public memory and the veterans lived out their lives in obscurity, their stories seldom told and even more rarely listened to. But with new generations come new mindsets and values that look at the past with a different perspective, and there is much to be rediscovered about this almost forgotten chapter in our history; a lot more could be told. Sadly but inevitably the majority of those directly involved are no longer alive to tell their own story; it is now our responsibility to make sure we appreciate and record the efforts of those who went to such extraordinary lengths to fight at Britain's side.

Notes

Introduction
1. Madeja, *The Polish 2nd Corps and The Italian Campaign 1943–1945*, p. 17.
2. National Statistics, Ministry of Defence, *UK Armed Forces Monthly Service Personnel Statistics 1st January 2016*, p. 6.
3. Central Office of Information, *PAIFORCE*, p. 130.
4. Kleczkowski, *Poland's First 100,000*, pp. 4–5.

Chapter 1: The First Blitzkrieg
1. Sheffield, de Wiart and Spears, in Keegan (ed.), *Churchill's Generals*, p. 328.
2. Teslar, *Poland Remains a Rock*, p. 23.
3. Anders, *An Army in Exile*, p. 13.
4. Carton de Wiart, *Happy Odyssey*, p. 125.
5. Ironside, quoted in Kleczkowski, *Poland's First 100,000*, p. 95.
6. Sikorski's telegram to Churchill, 18 June 1940, quoted from Kleczkowski, *Poland's First 100,000*, p. 32.
7. Kleczkowski, *Poland's First 100,000*, p. 33.
8. Danchev and Todman, *War Diaries of Alan Brooke*, p. 118.
9. Eden, *Memoirs: The Reckoning*, p. 160.
10. Anders, *An Army in Exile*, p. 125.

Chapter 2: A Polish Army in the USSR
1. Anders, *An Army in Exile*, p. 30.
2. Anders, *An Army in Exile*, p. 41.
3. Anders, *An Army in Exile*, p. 44.
4. Eden, *Memoirs, The Reckoning*, p. 272.
5. Prażmowska, *Britain and Poland 1939–1943: The Betrayed Ally*, p. 88.
6. Teslar, *Poland Remains a Rock*, p. 18.
7. Eden, *Memoirs: The Reckoning*, p. 273.
8. Ismay, *The Memoirs*, p. 223.
9. National Archives, CAB 80/29 C 518458, *War Cabinet, Chiefs of Staff Committee, 17th August 1941, Polish Forces in Russia*.

10. Major General Zygmunt Bohusz-Szyszko, quoted in Barbarski and Englert, *General Anders*, p. 10.
11. Churchill, *The Second World War*, Abridged Edition, p. 469.
12. National Archives, CAB 80/30 C 518460, *War Cabinet, Chiefs of Staff Committee, 18 September 1941, Polish War Effort in Russia*.
13. National Archives, War Cabinet WP(41)238, *October 8, 1941, Moscow Conference*, p. 11.
14. National Archives, War Cabinet, Moscow Conference, WP(41)238, *October 8, 1941, Enclosure IV, Transportation Committee*.
15. National Archives, War Cabinet, Moscow Conference, WP(41)238, *October 8, 1941, Enclosure IV, Transportation Committee*.
16. National Archives, CAB 79/14 C 518458, *War Cabinet, Chiefs of Staff Committee, 2 October 1941, Polish Forces in Russia*.
17. Kot, *Conversations with the Kremlin and Dispatches from Russia*, p. 44.
18. Kot, *Conversations with the Kremlin and Dispatches from Russia*, p. 54.
19. National Archives, War Cabinet, Moscow Conference, WP(41)238, *October 8, 1941, Enclosure VII, Re-equipment of Polish Forces in Russia*.
20. National Archives, CAB 79/14 C 518458, *War Cabinet, Chiefs of Staff Committee, 2 October 1941, Polish Forces in Russia*.
21. Nagorski, *The Greatest Battle, The Fight For Moscow 1941–42*, p. 131.
22. National Archives, CAB 79/15 C 518458, *Chief of Staffs Committee, 7th November 1941, 7. Arming of Polish Forces in Russia*.
23. National Archives, CAB 79/15 C 518458, *Chief of Staffs Committee, 10th November 1941, 1. Evacuation of Polish Forces from Russia*.
24. PISM Axii 64/1 17, *Top Secret, Note, A conversation with General MacFarlane and General Szyszko-Bohusz, 21st November 1941*.
25. Kot, *Conversations with the Kremlin and dispatches from Russia*, pp. 145–55.
26. Stalin quoted in Anders, *An Army in Exile*, p. 89.
27. Molotov quoted in Eden, *Memoirs: The Reckoning*, p. 299.
28. Kot, *Conversations with the Kremlin and dispatches from Russia*, pp. 229–30.
29. Kot, *Conversations with the Kremlin and dispatches from Russia*, p. 219.
30. National Archive, CAB 79/19 C 518460, *Chiefs of Staff Committee, 19th March 1942, 2. Evacuation of Polish Forces from Russia*.

Chapter 3: Exodus to the Middle East

1. National Archive CAB 79/19 C 518461, *War Cabinet, Chiefs of Staff Committee (COS(42) 92nd meeting), 23rd March 1942*.
2. Mosley, Leonard, Middle East Correspondent, *Aberdeen Press and Journal*, Friday, April 24, 1942.
3. Auchinleck quoted in Prażmowska, *Britain and Poland 1939–1945*, p. 133.
4. Danchev and Todman, *War Diaries of Alan Brooke*, p. 252.
5. Danchev and Todman, *War Diaries of Alan Brooke*, p. 252.
6. National Archives, CAB 80/36 C 518461, *War Cabinet, Chiefs of Staff Committee*; (COS (42) 237th meeting), *27th April 1942, Allocation of Polish Forces*.

7. National Archives, CAB 66/36/48, *Polish–Soviet Relations*, 10 May 1943, p. 8.
8. National Archives, CAB 66/36/48, *Polish–Soviet Relations*, 10 May 1943, p. 2.
9. Churchill, *The Hinge of Fate*, p. 241.
10. Biegański, *Działania 2 Korpusu we Włoszech*, p. 17.
11. Biegański, *Działania 2 Korpusu we Włoszech*, p. 17.
12. Anders, *An Army in Exile*, p. 118.
13. Butler, *Mason-Mac*, p. 139.
14. National Archives, CAB 66/36/48, *War Cabinet, Polish–Soviet Relations, 10th May 1943*, p. 4.
15. Churchill, *The Hinge of Fate*, p. 551.
16. Central Office of Information, *PAIFORCE*, p. 117.
17. Countess of Ranfurly, *To War with Whitaker*, p. 170.
18. Carton de Wiart, *Happy Odyssey*, p. 99.

Chapter 4: Along British Lines

1. Kleczkowski, *Poland's first 100,000*, p. 67.
2. Danchev and Todman, *War Diaries of Alan Brooke*, p. 300.
3. Danchev and Todman, *War Diaries of Alan Brooke*, p. 301.
4. General Bohusz-Szyszko, quoted in Barbarski and Englert, *General Anders*, p. 10.
5. General Bohusz-Szyszko, quoted in Barbarski and Englert, *General Anders*, p. 10.
6. Central Office of Information, *PAIFORCE*, p. 130.
7. Central Office of Information, *PAIFORCE*, p. 130.
8. Anders, *An Army In Exile*, p. 129.
9. Churchill, *The Hinge of Fate*, p. 815.
10. Anders, *An Army In Exile*, p. 133.

Chapter 5: A Year of Challenge

1. PISM KOL 4-2, p. 98.
2. Sikorski, quoted in McGilvray, *A Military Government in Exile*, p. 96.
3. National Archives, WO201/1395 C608708, *Letter from General Pownall to General Anders, 2 May 1943*.
4. Churchill, quoted in McGilvray, *A Military Government in Exile*, p. 96.
5. National Archives, WO201/1395 C608708, *Letter from General Pownall to General Anders, 30 April 1943*.
6. National Archives, WO201/1395 C608708, *Letter from General Anders to General Pownall, 22 May 1943*.
7. National Archives, WO201/1395 C608708, *Letter from General Baillon to General Anders, 30 April 1943*.
8. National Archive, FO /594/19B, *Conversation between Eden and Sikorski, 24 May 1943*.
9. National Archives, WO201/1395 C608708, *Letter from General Pownall to General Anders, 13 July 1943*.

10. Danchev & Todman, *War Diaries of Alan Brooke*, pp. 429–30.
11. Schwanek, 'Kazimierz Sosnkowski as Commander-in-Chief', *Journal of Military History*, pp. 755–6.
12. Schwanek, 'Kazimierz Sosnkowski as Commander-in-Chief', *Journal of Military History*, pp. 754–5.
13. Gilbert, *Road to Victory*, p. 442.
14. Churchill, *The Second World War, Vol. V: Closing the Ring*, p. 34.
15. Danchev and Todman, *War Diaries of Alan Brooke*, p. 432.
16. National Archives, WO201/1395 C608708, *Letter from J.W. Kenny PAIC to General Anders, 17 July 1943*.
17. General Wilson quoted in Anders, *An Army in Exile*, p. 150.
18. Molony et al., *The Mediterranean and the Middle East, Volume V, Part II*, p. 592.

Chapter 6: Ready to Fight

1. Armed Forces Staff College (US), *History of Allied Forces HQ December 1943–July 1944, Part 3, Section 1*, pp. 690–1.
2. CinC Dispatch, North African Campaign, MS, p. 1, OCMH files. Quoted in Pogue, *The Supreme Command*, p. 86.
3. Molony et al., *The Mediterranean and Middle East, Vol. V, Part I*, p. 383.
4. National Archive, FO/954/19B, *From Cairo to Foreign Office*.
5. Anders, *An Army in Exile*, p. 151.
6. Molony et al., *The Mediterranean and Middle East, Vol. V, Part II*, p. 836.
7. Eden, *Memoirs, The Reckoning*, p. 416.
8. Biegański, *Działania 2 Korpusu we Włoszech*, p. 52.
9. Biegański, *Działania 2 Korpusu we Włoszech*, p. 53.
10. Anders, *An Army In Exile*, p. xiv.
11. PISM, C292, *Chronicle of 3rd Carpathian Rifle Division, 3 May 1942–10 December 1943*, p. 44.
12. *The Palestine Gazette* No. 1302, 25 November 1943.

Chapter 7: The Move to Italy

1. Blumenson, *The Patton Papers 1940–1945, Vol. 2*, p. 389.
2. Madeja, *The Polish 2nd Corps and The Italian Campaign 1943–1945*, p. 25.
3. Madeja, *The Polish 2nd Corps and The Italian Campaign 1943–1945*, p. 25.
4. Madeja, *The Polish 2nd Corps and The Italian Campaign 1943–1945*, p. 33.

Chapter 8: Mountain Warfare and the Defence of the Sangro River

1. Extract from telegram sent by General Leese to Anders, quoted in Anders, *An Army in Exile*, p. 155.
2. Armed Forces Staff College (US), *History of Allied Forces HQ December 1943–July 1944*, p. 689.

3. North, *The Alexander Memoirs*, p. 155.
4. Łoziński, *Przechodniu, Powiedz Polsce...*, p. 319.

Chapter 9: The Monastic Fortress

1. Majdalany, *Cassino*, p. 223.
2. Molony et al., *The Mediterranean and Middle East, Vol. VI, Part I: Victory in The Mediterranean*, p. 5.
3. Macmillan, *War Diaries, The Mediterranean Years 1943–1945*, pp. 389, 390.
4. General Leese, quoted in Ellis, *Cassino: The Hollow Victory*, p. 313.
5. Anders, quoted in Ellis, *Cassino: The Hollow Victory*, pp. 313, 314.
6. Chocianowicz, *Bitwa Pod Monte Cassino*, pp. 14–17.
7. Anders, *An Army in exile*, p. 164.
8. Brigadier Scott, quoted in Ellis, *Cassino: The Hollow Victory*, pp. 320–1.

Chapter 10: Preparations for Battle

1. Unattributed quote in Ellis, *Cassino: The Hollow Victory*, p. 315.
2. Quoted in Ellis, *Cassino: The Hollow Victory*, p. 318.
3. Wańkowicz, *Monte Cassino*, p. 63.
4. Wańkowicz, *Monte Cassino*, p. 61.
5. Wańkowicz, *Monte Cassino*, p. 58.
6. Biegański, *Działania 2 Korpusu we Włoszech*, p. 208.

Chapter 11: Assault on the Gustav Line

1. Anders, *An Army in Exile*, p. 174.
2. Leese, quoted in Ellis, *Cassino: The Hollow Victory*, p. 318.
3. Ellis, *Cassino: The Hollow Victory*, p. 327.
4. Dębicki, *Growing up Wasn't Easy*, http://felsztyn.tripod.com/id23.html
5. Molony et al., *The Mediterranean and Middle East, Vol. VI, Part I*, p. 111.

Chapter 12: A Brief Respite

1. Quoted in Ellis, *Cassino: The Hollow Victory*, p. 331.
2. Madeja, *The Polish 2nd Corps and The Italian Campaign 1943–1945*, p. 20.

Chapter 13: Victory at Monte Cassino

1. Alexander, quoted in Macyszyn, *Bitwa o Monte Cassino*, p. 62.

Chapter 14: Breaking the Adolf Hitler Line

1. Conversation quoted in Wańkowicz, *Monte Cassino*, p. 341.
2. Conversation quoted in Wańkowicz, *Monte Cassino*, p. 345.

Chapter 15: The Aftermath

1. Biegański, *Działania 2 Korpusu we Włoszech*, p. 287.
2. Letter from Leese to Anders dated 27 May 1944, Barbarski and Englert, *General Anders*, p. 198.
3. Eade, *Victory: The Sixth Volume of Winston Churchill's War Speeches*, p. 58.
4. Statistics from the National Archive Kew FO 371/56366, quoted in Kochanski, *The Eagle Unbowed*, p. 555.

APPENDIX 1

Orders of Battle for Polish II Corps May 1944

Redrawn from original Orders of Battle held at the Polish Institute & Sikorski Museum archive; A.XI.1/14 and from Biegański, Stanisław, *Działania 2 Korpusu we Włoszech*, pp. 606–24.

242 *From Warsaw to Rome*

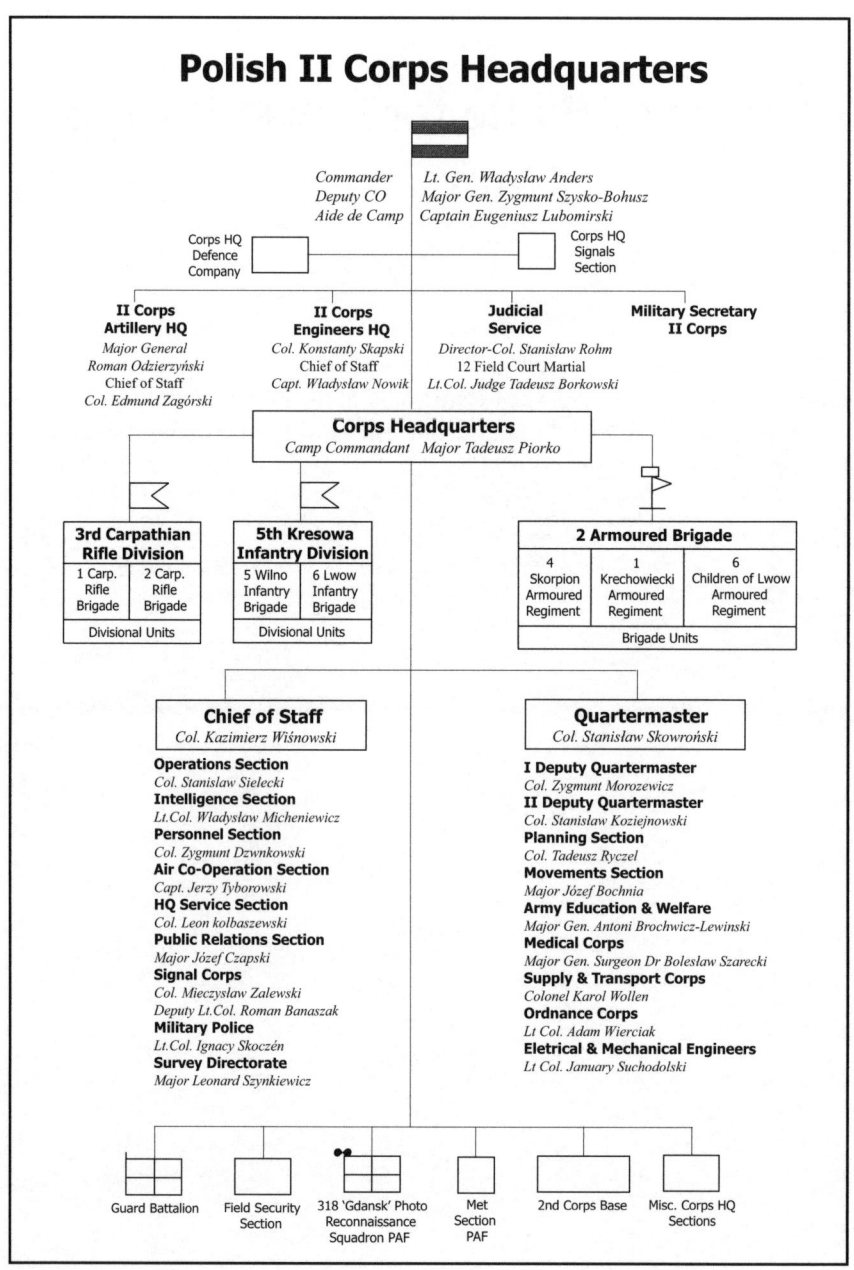

PLATE 1.

Orders of Battle for Polish II Corps May 1944 243

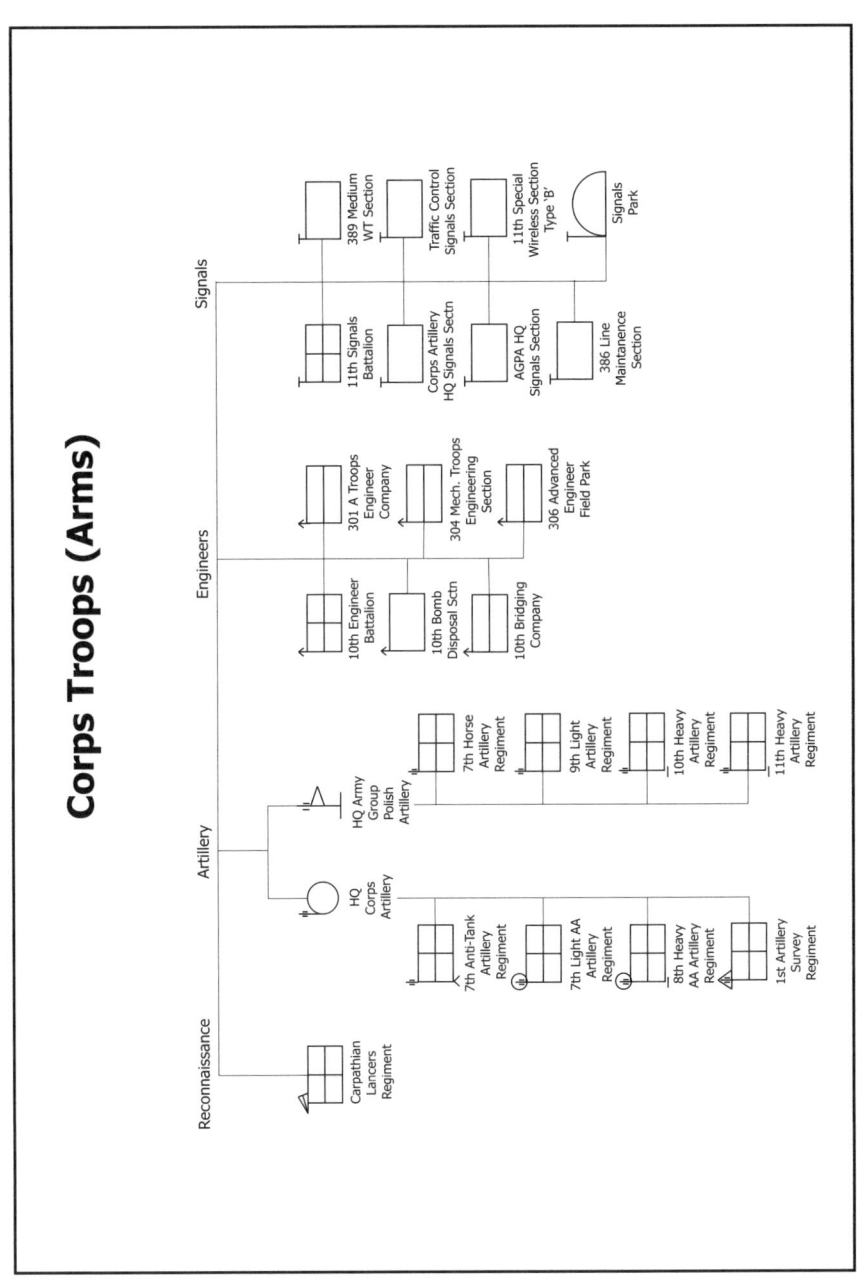

PLATE 2.

244 *From Warsaw to Rome*

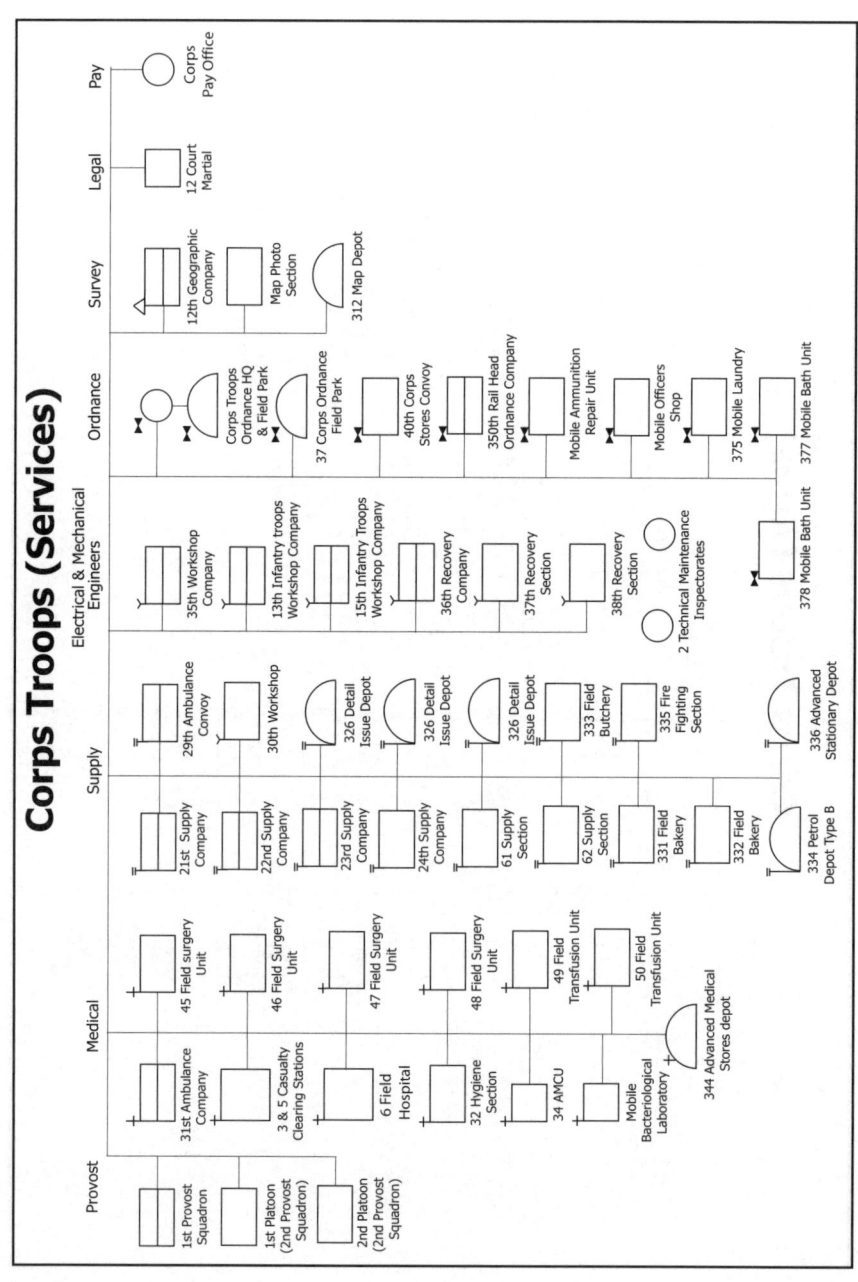

PLATE 3.

Orders of Battle for Polish II Corps May 1944 245

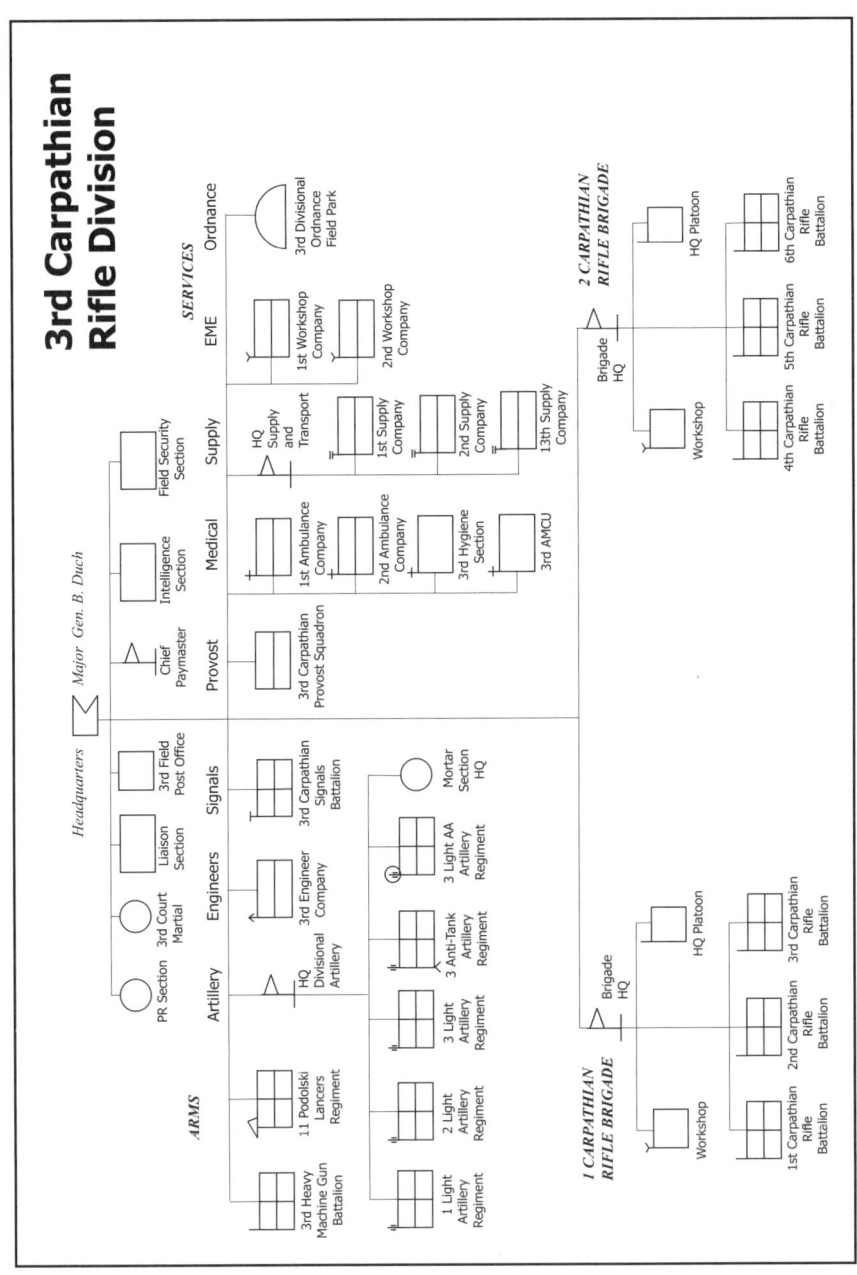

PLATE 4.

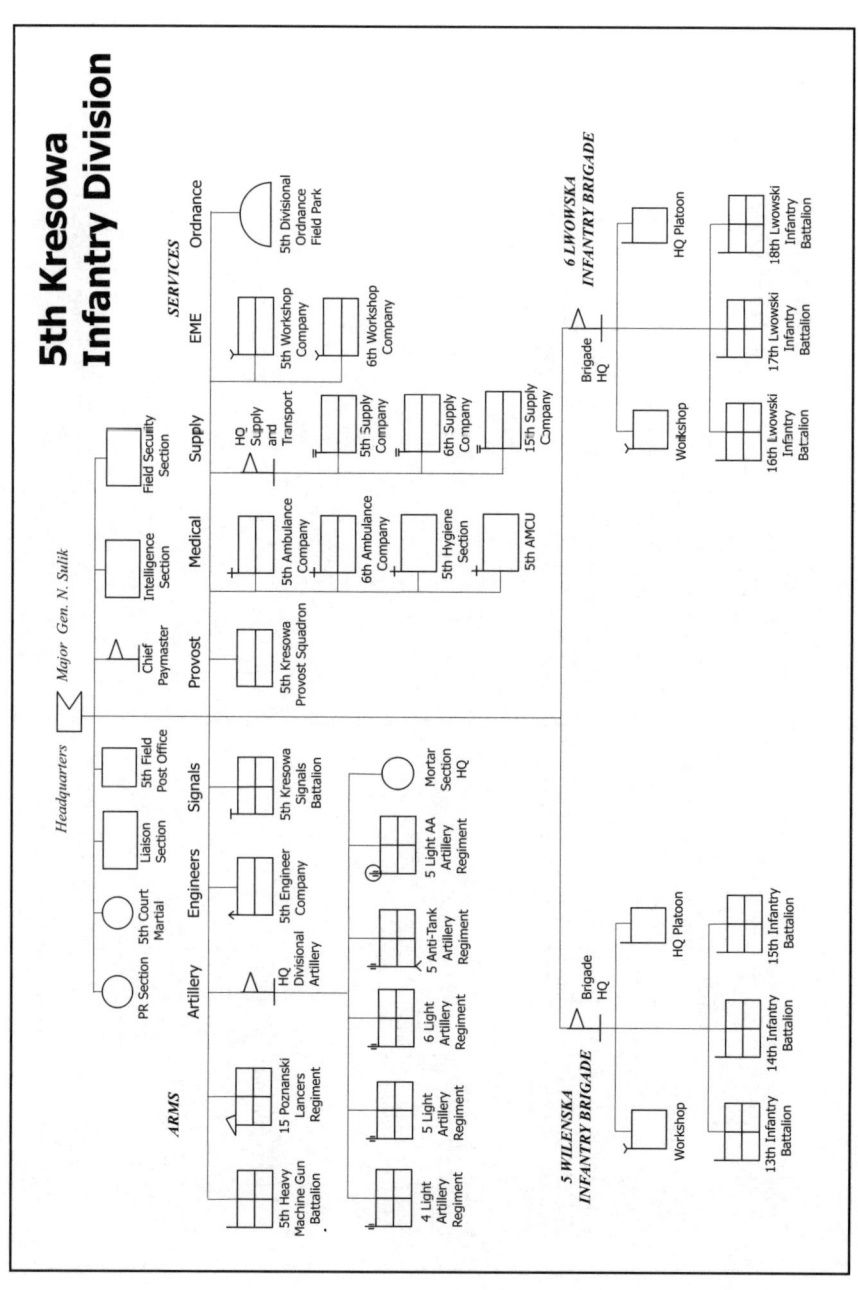

PLATE 5.

Orders of Battle for Polish II Corps May 1944 247

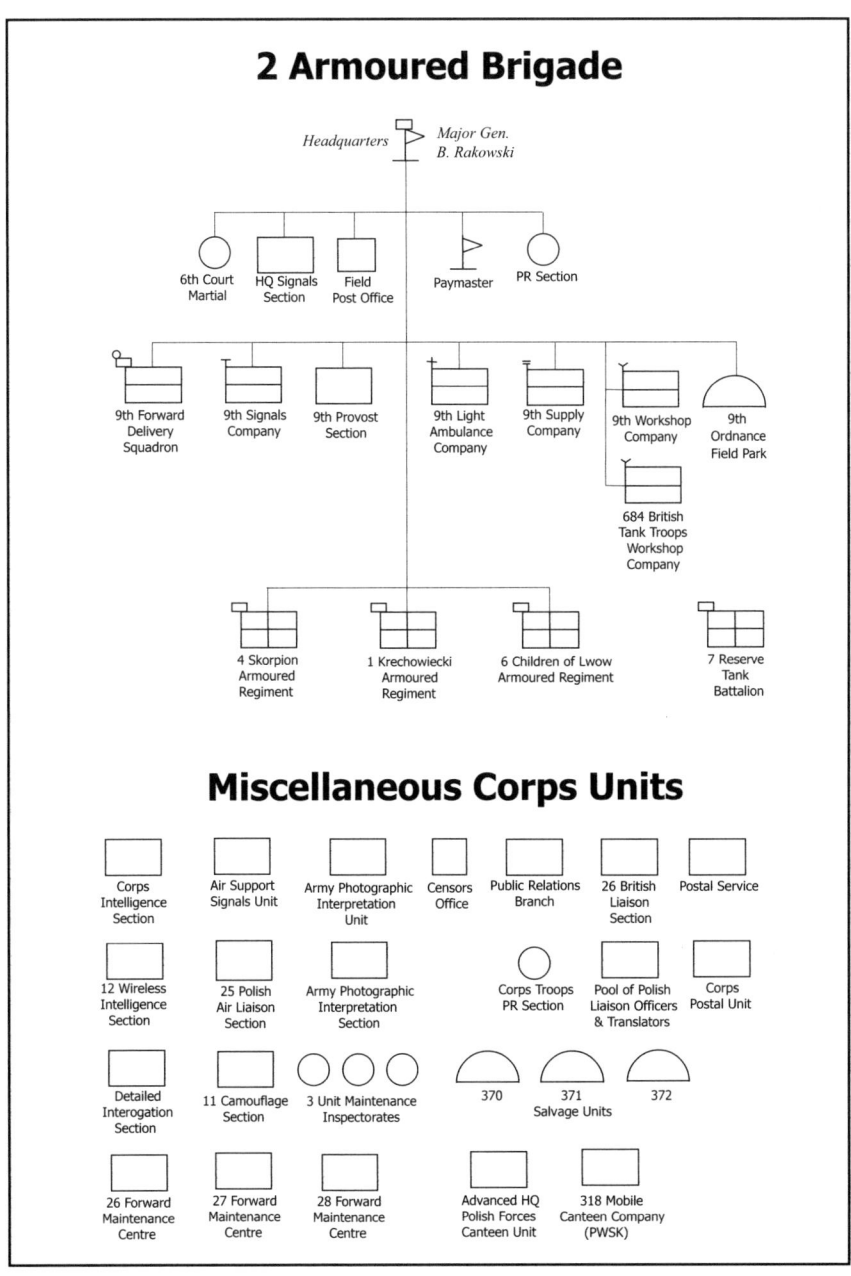

PLATE 6.

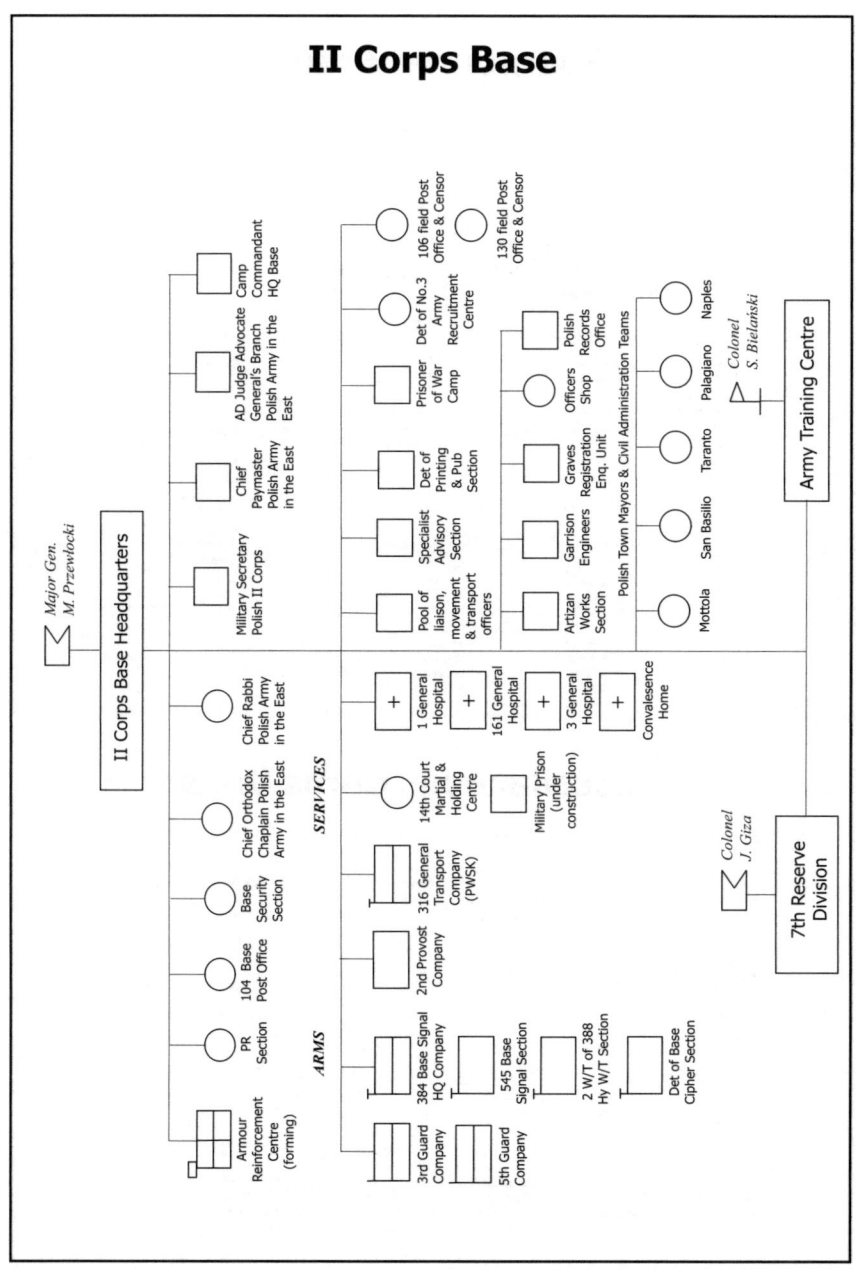

PLATE 7.

Orders of Battle for Polish II Corps May 1944 249

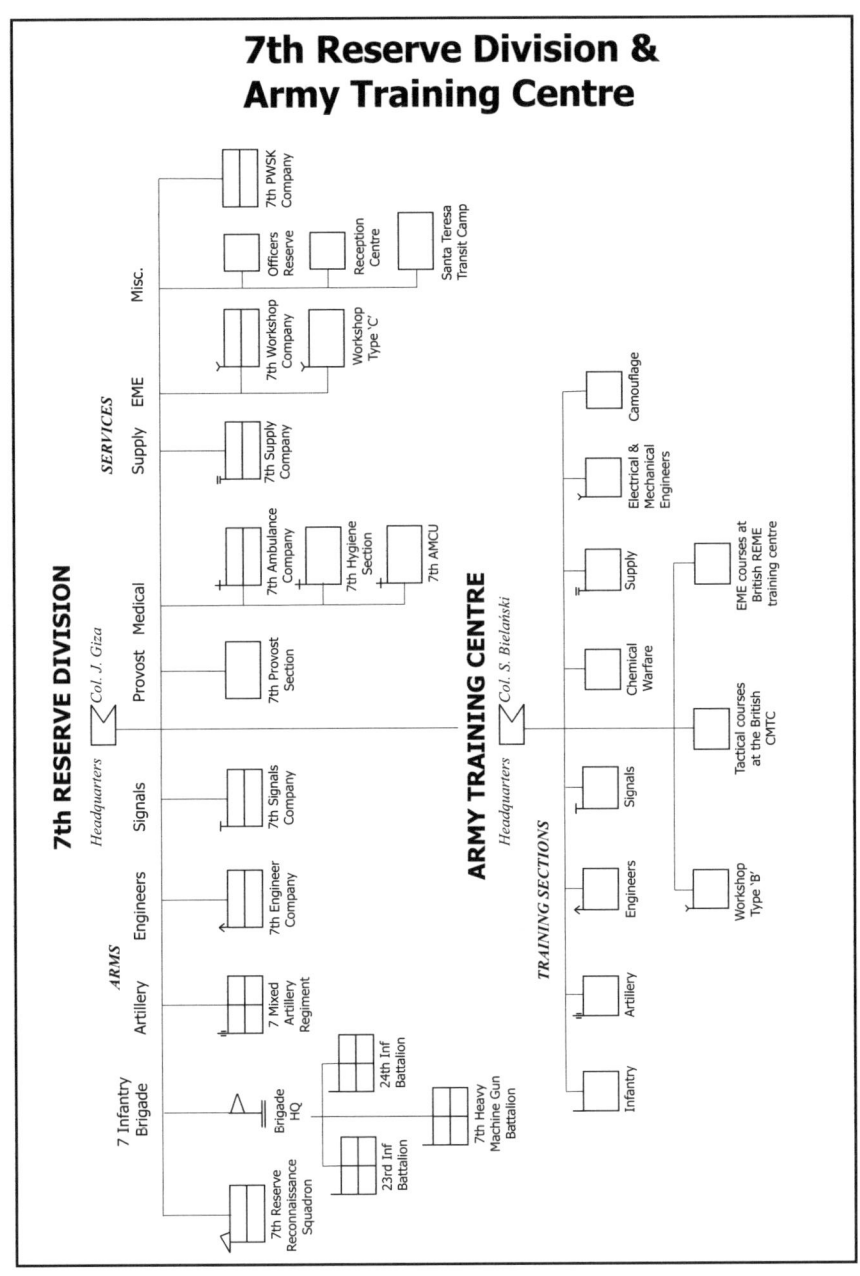

PLATE 8.

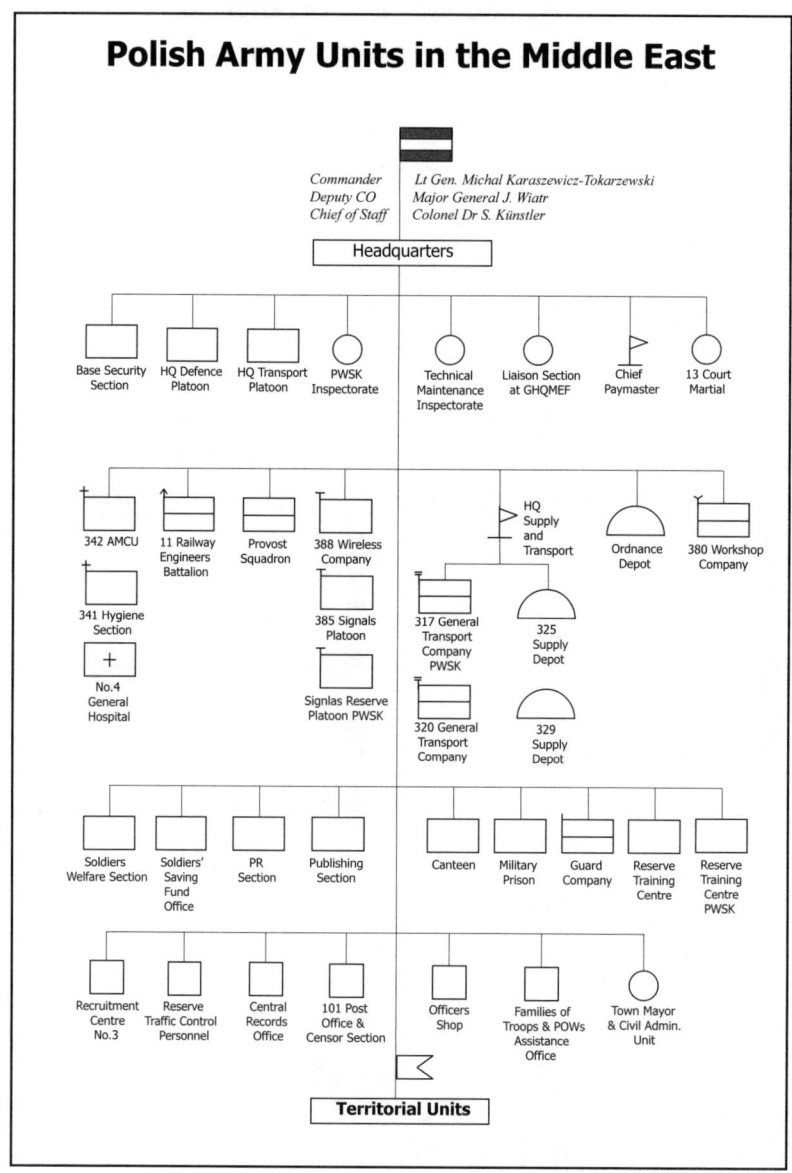

PLATE 9.

Orders of Battle for Polish II Corps May 1944 251

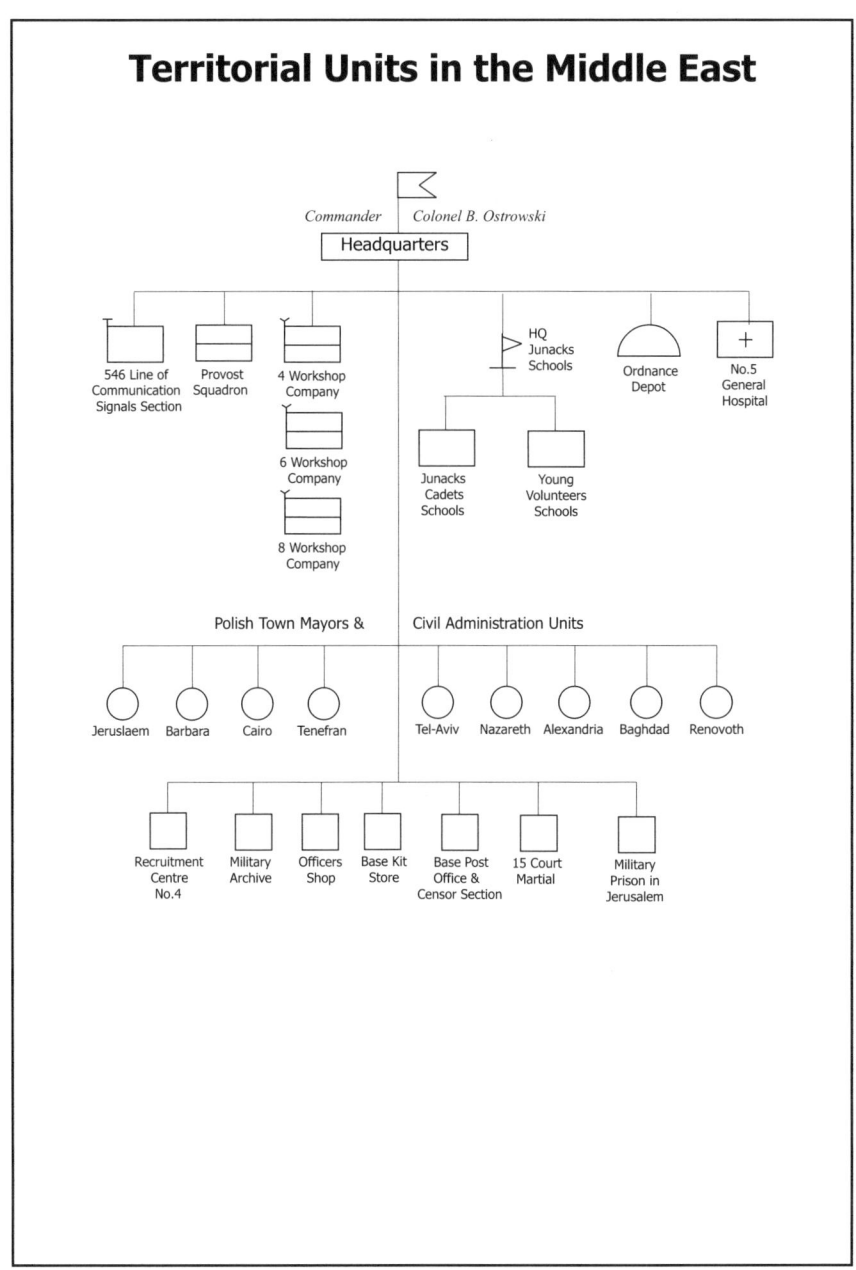

PLATE 10.

APPENDIX 2

Personnel Statistics and Equipment Holdings of II Corps

Table i
Personnel Strengths of II Corps Arms and Services, April 1944.

Arm/Service	Officers	Enlisted	PWSK
HQs	**401**	**1478**	**-**
Infantry	605	10704	-
Armour	165	2072	-
Reconnaissance	114	2186	-
Artillery	818	12036	-
Engineers	132	3680	-
Signals	100	1940	28
Military Police	20	392	-
Total Arms	**1954**	**33010**	**28**
Geographic	15	123	-
Medical	159	1938	19
Supply & Transport	205	5105	71
Ordnance	39	615	-
Workshop	79	1542	-
Judicial	19	191	-
Pay	12	26	-
Postal	3	64	-
Public Relations	19	55	-
Recovery & Salvage	3	132	-
Total Services	**553**	**9791**	**90**
Total II Corps	**2908**	**44279**	**118**

Source: Biegański, S. *Dzialania 2 Korpus we Włosch*, page 122.

Table ii
Personnel Strengths of II Corps and Base, April 1944.

Unit	Officers	Enlisted	PWSK
II Corps HQ	216	786	-
Corps Troops	847	13990	118
3rd Carpathian Rifle Division	795	13213	-
5th Kresowa Infantry Division	784	12876	-
2 Armoured Brigade	266	3414	-
Total II Corps	**2908**	**44279**	**118**
II Corps Base	**922**	**5459**	**1180**

Source: Biegański, S. *Dzialania 2 Korpus we Wlosch*, page 123.

Table iii
Vehicle Holdings of II Corps, December 1943.

Vehicle Type	Total
Tanks	160
Armoured Cars	468
Universal Carriers	392
Trucks	5297
Passenger Cars	1292
Ambulances	203
Artillery Tractors	590
Trailers	84
Motorcycles	2528

Source: Biegański, S. *Dzialania 2 Korpus we Wlosch*, page 127.

Table iv
Weapon Holdings of II Corps, December 1943.

Weapon	Per Infantry Division	2 Armoured Brigade	Corps Troops	Total
Pistols	824	1052	1305	4005
Rifles	7294	739	6920	22247
Sub-Machine Gun	4775	1290	6163	17003
PIAT	338	56	232	964
Bren Guns	752	96	466	2066
Vickers Machine-Gun	48	-	-	96
Browning .300cal MG	82	355	183	702
Browning .500cal MG	33	194	10	270
2" Mortars	196	-	26	418
3" Mortars	42	-	-	84
6pdr Anti-Tank Gun	88	-	10	186
17pdr Anti-Tank Gun	16	-	8	40
M10 Wolverine	-	-	24	24
75mm Guns	-	-	6	6
3" Howitzers	-	-	15	15
25pdr Field Gun	72	-	48	192
4.5" Artillery Gun	-	-	16	16
5.5" Artillery Gun	-	-	16	16
40mm AAA Gun	36	-	36	108
3.7" AAA Gun	-	-	24	24
M4 Sherman Tank	-	160	-	160

Source: Biegański, S. *Dzialania 2 Korpus we Włosch*, page 126.

Bibliography

Acknowledgements
Veterans' associations
The Polish Ex-Combatants Association Great Britain.
3rd Carpathian Infantry Division & Ex-Servicemen's Association.
5th Kresowa Infantry Division's Association.

Individuals
Jacek Paszkowski, Sweden
John Wright, Q&C Militaria, Cheltenham, U.K.
Gregory Dalton-Mohl, Argentina.

British National Archives (Kew)
CAB 80/29 C 518458, War Cabinet, Chiefs of Staff Committee (COS (41) 498th meeting), 17 August 1941, *Polish Forces in Russia.*
CAB 79/13 C 518458, War Cabinet, Chiefs of Staff Committee (COS (41) 290th meeting), 18 August 1941, *Telegram from No.30 Military Mission Moscow.*
CAB 79/14 C 518458, War Cabinet, Chiefs of Staff Committee (COS (41) 327th meeting), 18 September 1941, *3. Polish War Effort in Russia.*
CAB 79/14 C 518458, War Cabinet, Chiefs of Staff Committee (COS (41) 340th meeting), 2nd October 1941, *2. Polish Forces in Russia.*
CAB/66/19/11, image ref. 0001, War Cabinet, W.P. (41) 238, 8 October 1941, *Moscow Conference. Enclosure IV, Transportation Committee, Enclosure VII, Re-equipment of Polish Forces in Russia.*
CAB 79/15 C 518458, War Cabinet, Chiefs of Staff Committee (COS (41) 379th meeting), 7 November 1941, *7. Arming of Polish Forces in Russia.*
CAB 79/15 C 518458, War Cabinet, Chiefs of Staff Committee (COS (41) 381st meeting), 10 November 1941, *1. Evacuation of Polish Forces from Russia.*
CAB 79/16 C 518460, War Cabinet, Chiefs of Staff Committee (COS (41) 412th meeting), 8 December 1941, *5. Re-equipment of Polish Forces in Russia.*
CAB 79/16 C 518460, War Cabinet, Chiefs of Staff Committee (COS (41) 414th meeting), 9 December 1941, *3. Re-equipping of Polish Forces in Russia.*

CAB 79/19 C 518460,War Cabinet, Chiefs of Staff Committee (COS (41) 89th meeting), 19 March 1942, *2. Evacuation of Polish Forces from Russia.*
CAB 79/19 C 518461, War Cabinet, Chiefs of Staff Committee (COS (42) 92nd meeting), 23 March 1942, *1. Evacuation of Polish Forces from Russia.*
CAB 79/19 C 518461, War Cabinet, Chiefs of Staff Committee (COS (42) 94th meeting), 24 March 1942, *7. Evacuation of Polish Forces from Russia.*
CAB 79/20 C 518461, War Cabinet, Chiefs of Staff Committee (COS (42) 101st meeting) 31 March 1942, *5. Evacuation of Polish Forces from Russia.*
CAB 79/20 C 518461, War Cabinet, Chiefs of Staff Committee (COS (42) 109th meeting), 7 April 1942, *7. Evacuation of Polish Forces from Russia.*
CAB 80/36 C 518461, War Cabinet, Chiefs of Staff Committee (COS (42) 237th meeting), 27 April 1942, *Allocation of Polish Forces.*
CAB/66/36/48, image ref. 0001, War Cabinet, W.P. (43) 198, 10 May 1943, *Polish-Soviet Relations – Memorandum by The Secretary of State for Foreign Affairs.*
FO/954/19B, image ref 508, Foreign Office, 24 May 1943, *Notes of meeting between Eden and Sikorski.*
CAB/66/24/50, image ref. 0001, War Cabinet, 25 May 1942, *USSR, Memorandum by the Secretary of State for Foreign Affairs.*
FO/954/19B, image ref. 527, Foreign Office, 6 November 1943, *Telegram from Cairo to Foreign Office concerning proposed reorganization of Polish 2nd Corps.*
WO/201/1395 C 608708, War Office, *General Pownall's Letters to General Anders Apr–Sept 1943.*

Polish Institute and Sikorski Museum Archives (PISM)

C1291, Chronicle of 13th Infantry Battalion.
C292, Chronicle of 3rd Carpathian Rifle Division 3 May 1942 – 10 December 1943.
C474-1a, Chronicle of 6 Lwów Artillery Regiment
KOL4-2, 1942–43. The Lt Col Zygmunt Borkowski (1894–1976) Collection. File 2: Official and private correspondence, reports and notes of Gen. Sikorski's Chef de Cabinet.
A.XI.1/14 Orders of Battle, II Corps.
A.XII.64/1, Military Attaché in Moscow/Kuybyshev
C56-1, Chronicle of No.6 Troop, 10 Inter Allied Commando.

The following archives have also proved most helpful in assisting my research:
Imperial War Museum, London.
The Tank Museum, Bovington.

Contemporary Newspapers

The Palestine Gazette, No. 1302, Thursday 25 November 1943, p. 1081, Official Communique. (Raids on Palestine Settlements searching for Polish deserters)

The Press and Journal, Friday, 24 April 1942, p. 4, 'Polish Army of 60,000 Now in Middle East', by Leonard Mosley.

Veterans' Magazines
Czwartak Pancerny-Biuletyn Koła Żołnierzy Pułku 4 Pancernego 'Skorpion', editions: 71 (May 1989), 72 (May 1990), 74 (May 1992).

Websites
Dębicki, A.W., *Growing up Wasn't Easy*, http://felsztyn.tripod.com/id23.html 28/01/10.

Published Sources
Anders, Lieutenant General Władysław, *An Army in Exile*, The Battery Press, Nashville, 2004.

Armed Forces Staff College (US), *History of Allied Forces HQ December 1943–July 1944, Part 3, Section 1,* USACGSC Library.

Barbarski, Krzysztof, *Polish Armour 1939–45*, Osprey Publishing Ltd, London, 1982.

Barbarski, Krzysztof and Juliusz Englert, *General Anders*, The Polish Institute and Sikorski Museum, Warszawska Drukarnia Akcydensowa, Poland, 1989.

Biegański, Stanisław (Ed.), *Działania 2 Korpusu we Włoszech,* published by the Historical Commission of II Polish Corps, London, 1963.

Blumenson, Martin, *The Patton Papers 1940–1945, Vol. 2,* Houghton Mifflin, 1974.

Butler, Ewan, *Mason-Mac, The Life of Lieutenant-General Sir Noel Mason-MacFarlane,* Macmillan, London, 1972.

Carton de Wiart, Lieutenant General Adrian, *Happy Odyssey*, PAN-Books LTD, London, 1950.

Central Office of Information (prepared by for the War Office), *PAIFORCE, The official history of the Persia and Iraq Command 1941-1946*, HMSO, London, 1948.

Chocianowicz, Colonel W., *Działna 2 Korpusu we Włoszech od dnia 21.XIII 1943 do 6 VI 1944*, unpublished essay.

Cieślewicz, Stanisław, *Dziennik Karpatczyka 1939–1947,* self published through Amazon, Leipzig, 2009.

Churchill, Winston, *The Second World War, Book I, The Gathering Storm, From War to War 1919–1939*, Heron Books & Editorial-Service S.A., Geneva, 1948.

Churchill, Winston, *The Second World War, Book IV, The Hinge of Fate*, Heron Books & Editorial-Service S.A., Geneva, 1948.

Cooper, Jilly, *Animals in War*, Imperial War Museum, London, 1983.

Czwartek Pancerny Biuletyn Koła Pułku 4 Pancernego 'Skorpion' (4 Polish Armoured Regt. Ex-Servicemen's Association Yearly Bulletin, London, No 71 – May 1990, No 72 – May 1990, No 74 – May 1992, Opole, No 78 – May 1996, No 82 – May 2000.

Danchev, A. and D. Todman (Eds), *War Diaries 1939–1945 Field Marshal Lord Alan Brooke*, Phoenix Press, London, 2002.

Eade, Charles (Ed.), *Victory: The Sixth Volume of Winston Churchill's War Speeches*, Cassell & Co., London, 1946.
Eden, Anthony, *The Eden Memoirs, Facing The Dictators,* Cassell, London, 1965.
Eden, Anthony, *The Eden Memoirs, The Reckoning,* Cassell, London, 1965.
Ellis, John, *Cassino: The Hollow Victory, The Battle for Rome January–June 1944*, Guild Publishing, London, 1984.
Gilbert, Martin, *Road to Victory. Winston S. Churchill 1941–1945*, Heinemann, London, 1986.
Halifax, Viscount (Secretary of State for Foreign Affairs), Miscellaneous No.9 (1939) *Documents concerning German-Polish relations and the outbreak of hostilities between Great Britain and Germany on September 3rd, 1939*, His Majesty's Stationery Office, London, 1939.
Hope, Michael, *Polish Deportees in the Soviet Union. Origins of Post-War Settlement in Great Britain,* Veritas Foundation Publication Centre, London, 2000.
Ismay, Hastings, *The Memoirs of General the Lord Ismay*, Heinemann, London, 1960.
Keegan, John, *Churchill's Generals*, Cassell Military Paperbacks, London, 1991.
Kleczkowski, Stefan, *Poland's First 100,000*, Hutchinson & Co (Publishers) Ltd, London, 1942.
Kochanski, Halik, *The Eagle Unbowed, Poland and the Poles in the Second World War*, Penguin Books, London, 2012.
Komornicki, Stanisław, *Wojsko Polskie 1939–1945 Barwa I Broń*, Wydawnictwo Interpress, Warsaw, 1984.
Kot, Stanisław, *Conversations with the Kremlin and Dispatches from Russia*, Oxford University Press, London, 1963.
Ledwoch, Janusz, *Polskie Shermany vol. II*, Wydawnictwo Militaria, Warsaw, 2003.
Ledwoch, Janusz, *Polish Tanks* Wydawnictwo Militaria, Warsaw 2010.
(The) London Committee of Deputies of the British Jews, *Board of Deputies of British Jews Annual Report 1943,* London, 1944.
Łoziński, Marian, *Przechodniu, Powiedz Polsce*...Wydawnictwo Literackie Kraków, 1972.
Macmillan, Harold, *War Diaries, The Mediterranean Years 1943–1945*, Macmillan, London, 1984.
Macyszyn, Colonel Jacek, *Bitwa o Monte Cassino*, Muzeum Wojska Polskiego, Rossagraph (publishers) Warsaw, 2004.
Madeja, Witold, *The Polish 2nd Corps and The Italian Campaign 1943–1945,* Game Publishing Company, Allentown, Pennsylvania, 1984.
Majdalany, Fred, *Cassino, Portrait of a Battle*, The Popular Book Club (by arrangement with the original publisher, Longmans Green & Co. Ltd), London, 1959.
McGilvray, Evan, *A Military Government in Exile, The Polish Government-in-Exile 1939–1945: A study of discontent,* Helion & Company, Solihull, UK, 2010.
Mead, Richard, *Churchill's Lions*, Spellmount, Stroud, 2007.
Molony, Brigadier C. J. C, with Major-General I.S.O. Playfair, Air Vice-Marshal S.E. Toomer, and Captain F. C. Flynn. History of the Second World War, United Kingdom Military series, *The Mediterranean & Middle East, Volume V, Parts I & II,* Naval & Military Press, Uckfield, 2004.

Molony, Brigadier C. J. C, with Major-General I.S.O. Playfair, Air Vice-Marshal S.E. Toomer, and Captain F. C. Flynn. History of the Second World War, United Kingdom Military series, *The Mediterranean & Middle East, Volume VI, Part I,* Naval & Military Press, Uckfield, 2004.
Murgrabia, Jerzy, *Symbole Wojskowe Polskich Sił Zbronjnych Na Zachodzie 1939–1946*, Wydawnictwo Bellona, Warsaw, 1990.
Nagorski, Andrew, *The Greatest Battle, The Fight For Moscow 1941–42*, Aurum Press Ltd, London, 2007.
National Statistics, Ministry of Defence, *UK Armed Forces Monthly Service Personnel Statistics 1 January 2016,* published February 2016.
North, John (Ed.), *The Alexander Memoirs 1940–1945*, Cassell, London, 1962.
Paff, Lucjan (Ed.), *Kresowa Walczy w Italii*, Referat Kultury I Prassy Kreswej Dywizji Piechoty, Italy, 1945.
Pogue, Forrest, *The Supreme Command* United States Army in World War II, The European Theater of Operations, United States Government, Washington DC, 1954.
Prażmowska, Anita, *Britain and Poland 1939–1943, The Betrayed Ally*, Cambridge University Press, 1995.
Puchalski Zbigniew, *Dzieje Polskich Znaków zaszczytnych,* Wydawnictwo Sejmowe, Warsaw, 2000.
Ranfurly, Countess of, *To War With Whitaker*, Mandarin, Reading, 1995.
Sawicki, Z. and Wielechowski, A. *Polskie Siły Zbrojne Na Zachodzie 1939–1947*, Studio Spartan, Gdynia, 2009.
Schwanek, Matthew R. Kazimierz, 'Sosnkowski as Commander-in-Chief: The Government in Exile and Polish Strategy, 1943–1994', *Journal of Military History*, 2006, Vol.70, No. 3, pp. 743–80.
Szkice Perspektywiczne Terenu Walk 2 Korpusu Monte Cassino Maj 1944, 12th Geographic Company, Italy, 1944.
Teslar, Joseph-Andrew, *Poland Remains A Rock*, The Polish Library, Glasgow, 1942.
Wańkowicz, Melchior, *Szkie Spod Monte Cassino*, Omega, Warsaw, 1978.
Wańkowicz, Melchior, *Monte Cassino*, Instytut Wydawniczy Pax, Warsaw, 1989.
Wawer, Zbigniew, *Monte Cassino – Walki 2 Korpusu Polskiego,* Bellona, Warsaw, 2009.
Wilson, Henry Maitland, *Eight Years Overseas,* Hutchinson & Co, London, 1946.
Zaloga, Steven J. *The Polish Army 1939–1945*, Osprey, Oxford 1982.
[Various] *Monte Cassino, Battle of Six Nations*, published by the Dziennika Zolnierzow APW printing house, Bologna, 1946.

Index

Abadan, 69
  see also Anglo-Iranian Oil Company
Acquafondata, 173, 175, 178–79, 184
Adolf Hitler Line, 157–8, 160
  see also Piedimonte san Germano
Adriatic coast, 137, 146, 157, 198, 227
Advanced Dressing Stations, 177
Agnone, 143, 147
AGPA see Artillery Group Polish Artillery
Ahwaz, 65, 69, 94
Albaneta Farm, 155, 161, 163–4,
  fighting for control of, 186, 201, 204–6
Alexander, General Sir Harold, 63–4, 101, 108, 110–3, 116–17, 230
  see also Operation Diadem
Alexandria, 7, 9, 124
Alfedena, 137, 151
Algiers, 110–11, 108, 140
Ali, Rashid, 8–9
Allied Armies Italy, 148
  15 Army Group, 101, 140, 159
Allied Campaign in Italy, 101–2, 107–9, 111, 116
  difficulties encountered, 135, 157, 174, 227
Allied Forces Headquarters (Mediterranean), 141
Allied Forces (Official) Committee, 18–19
Allied Military Government in Italy, 120, 229

Altun kupri, 89–90
American II Corps, 120, 229
American Embassy in Moscow, 25
American Fifth Army, 107, 140, 147, 228
Amioun, 100, 104
Anders, Lieutenant General Władysław, 1–2, 64–5, 123, 133, 228–31
  in Middle East, 66, 86, 88–90, 92–97, 100, 107–10
  in USSR, 11–13, 20, 25–32, 44
  see also Operation Diadem; Piedimonte san Germano; Polish Army in the East, Polish Army in the USSR; separation of II Corps and Base; Stalin, conference with Polish generals; Wilson, General Sir Henry Maitland, meetings with Anders
Anglo-American Supply Mission, 24–5, 27
Anglo-Iranian Oil Company, 21
Anglo-Polish Military Agreement, 6
Anglo-Polish Pact, 5, 7
Anglo-Soviet invasion of Persia, 21, 49, 62
Anglo-Soviet Military Pact, 13, 21
anti-aircraft artillery, 73, 78, 125, 128, 130, 196–7
  in ground-support role and as infantry at Cassino, 171, 188, 194
  see also Army Group Polish Artillery; stretcher-bearers

Anti-Malaria Control Unit, 199
anti-tank artillery, 125, 144, 170, 205, 207
   M10 Wolverine self-propelled anti-tank guns, 185, 195–6, 201, 212
   see also stretcher-bearers
Anzio, 137, 228
Apennine Mountains, 146, 155
Aquino, 160, 212, 216, 219
Archangel, 17, 22, 24, 26–7
Armour Training Centre, 69, 131
Army Reserve Centre, 117, 120
   Officers Reserve, 65
Army Training Centre, 20, 22, 68–9, 129–32
   see also 7th (Reserve) Infantry Division
Artillery Group Polish Artillery, 78, 86, 105, 125
   actions in Italy, 147, 149, 153, 157, 172
   see also anti-aircraft artillery; Heavy Artillery
artillery observation posts, 139, 147, 150, 153, 170
   Cyklop 2, 212
Atina, 160, 170, 184–5, 187
Auchinlek, General Sir Claude, 8, 30, 63
   advocates use of Polish soldiers, 14, 49, 53–6, 58, 69
Aurunci Mountains, 164
Australia, 9, 232
awards and decorations (Polish), 54, 134, 189
   British, 207, 228
   French, 134

Baghdad, 8–9, 64–5, 76, 82
Baillon, Major General, 90
Balkans, 17, 54–5, 91, 97
Bar Bara Camp, 68, 79, 121, 232
Baran, Sergeant Stanisław, 215
Bari Ordnance Depot, 117, 124, 128–9
   transportation to front from, 132, 146, 174, 198
   see also Lines of Communication
Barletta, 140, 198
Bartnowski, Lieutenant, 217
Bartnowski, Major Leon, 17
Basra, 64, 69, 75–6, 104
Battalion Aid Posts, 176–7
Beaverbrook, Lord, 24–7, 44
Beit Jura, 67–8
Beirut–Haifa railway, 68
Belarus, 22, 53
Belmonte, 160, 170, 184–5 187
Beria, Laurenti:
   head of NKVD, 2, 12
Bersheba, 107
Besser, Lieutenant Wiktor, 204
Bevin, Ernest, PM 232
Białecki, Lieutenant Ludomir, 186–7
Białkiewicz, Second Lieutenant, 206
Blitzkrieg, 1, 4
Bobiński, Lieutenant Colonel Władysław, 78, 212, 214–16, 218–22, 225–6
Bobaka, Lieutenant, 169–70, 186, 195
Bohusz-Szyszko, Major General Zygmunt, 17, 19, 26, 32, 60, 74
   Deputy Commander II Corps, 92, 97, 113, 129
Bojano, 146, 179, 199
Bologna, 229
Bolsheviks, 11–12
Bordeaux, 5
Boruta-Spiechowicz, Major General, 19
Brindisi, 124, 129, 198
British V Corps, 138
British X Corps, 157, 160,
British XIII Corps, 163–4, 193
British 2 Special Service Brigade, 138
British 5th Battalion, The Queens Own Royal West Kent Regiment, 214–7
British 18th Division, 44
British 40 Royal Marine Commando, 139
British 50th Division, 44
British 56th Infantry Division, 139

British 56th Reconnaissance Regiment, 138
British 78th Infantry Division, 142, 168, 171, 193, 207, 212
British 169 Infantry Brigade, 139
British Admiralty, 1
British Base Evacuation Staff, 50, 63–4
British Chiefs of Staff, 18, 27, 30–2, 44, 49
  evacuate Polish Army from USSR, 19, 48, 54 61
British Eighth Army, 107, 111–12, 117, 135, 138, 151
  Battle at Cassino, 156–7, 167–8, 181, 183–4, 206–7, 228
  supply of, 142, 146–7, 174–6
  see also Allied Armies Italy, 15 Army Group; North African Campaign
British Engineering Training Centre (Polish Wing), 130
British Foreign Office, 14, 18–19, 28, 58, 61, 71
  dealings with the Polish Army in the East, 91, 94
  see also Eden, Sir Anthony
British Highland Light Infantry, 50
British Irish Brigade, 168
British Tenth Army, 21, 63
British Middle East Command, 8, 14, 21, 30, 54
  meetings with Polish commanders, 53, 58, 72–3, 98, 140
  training of Polish Army, 64, 100, 231
British Military Hospitals, 75, 127, 147, 198
  Commonwealth hospitals, 51, 53, 62
British Military Mission to the Polish Army, 1, 17, 24, 48, 76
British Military Liaison to Polish II Corps, 130, 183
British Ninth Army, 30, 100, 103, 105
  Middle East Mountain Warfare School, 100, 104
British Persia and Iraq Command, 63–4, 72, 75–6, 82, 85–6

British Royal Army Signals Corps, 81
British specialist surgery units, 197
  British Troops in Iraq, 8–9, 21, 30, 49
British War Cabinet, 28, 59
British War Office, 14, 19, 48, 54, 71–2, 74
  deployment of Polish II Corps, 85, 102, 112
Brooke, General Sir Alan, 44, 48–9, 85, 95, 102, 114
  meetings with Polish Generals, 6, 54–5, 71–3, 98–9, 116–7
Butyrki prison, 11
Buzuluk, 20, 39

Cadogan, Sir Alexander, 14
Cairo, 8, 110, 112
  Big Three conference in, 116–17
  see also British Middle East Command, meetings with Polish commanders; Patton, General George S.; Polish Army Units in the Middle East
Canadian Corps, 169, 193, 225
  Canadian 1st Infantry Division, 212
Cassino town and environs, 156, 163
Casualty Clearing Stations, 127, 147, 178–9, 197
Campobasso, 132, 146–7, 179, 227
Carceri, 139
Cardito, 134, 147–50, 152, 169
Capracotta, 138–9, 142, 148, 150–2
Capriati a Volturno, 157, 168, 169
Carovilli, 143, 147
Carpinone, 157
Carton de Wiart, Lieutenant General Sir Adrian, 1–2, 4, 65
Casalina, 218
Casamasima, 198
Casey, Richard, MP 53, 82
Caspian Sea, 21, 25, 49–50, 63, 71
Castel del Giudice, 138, 143
Castel di Sangro, 143, 150

Castel Vincenzo, 142, 144, 147–9
Castiglione, 143
Castrocielo, 214
Caucasus, 14, 17, 19
   Germans threaten, 26–7, 30, 47, 62, 71, 82
   Transcaucasian Front, 21
Cavendish Road, 169
   'car park', 169, 185
Cerro, 143–4
chaplains, 177, 210
Chamberlain, Neville, PM 4
Churchill, Brigadier Tom, 138
Churchill, Sir Winston, PM 2, 4, 16, 229
   difficulties with Poles 89, 96, 98, 114, 142
   support for Polish Army, 5–6, 36, 58–60, 71–3, 81
   see also Anglo-American Supply Mission; Auchinleck, General Sir Claude; Polish Army in the USSR, difficulties encountered, evacuation from; Roosevelt, US President Franklin D.; Soviet–German Front, British troops to fight in USSR; Stalin, conference with Polish generals
civilian refugees, 60
Clark, Lieutenant General Mark, 140, 228
Clark-Kerr, Ambassador Archibald, 59–60
Coetquidon, 4
collective farms, 2, 45,
Colle del Arena, 148, 150
Colle Maiela, 163
Colle Majola, 161, 163, 186
Colle Sant' Angelo, 187, 191, 201–12, 204, 206–7
   significance of the position, 162–3
concentration camp, 65
convalescent home, 127, 132, 179
convoys, by sea to Italy, 123–5

Countess of Ranfurly, 64, 140
Cripps, Sir Stafford, 14, 16
cross-Channel invasion, 22, 55, 101, 107, 157
Czapski, Major Józef, 64, 82–3
   investigates missing Polish Officers, 20–1
Czechoslovakia, 26
   exile Army, 9
Czynski, Lieutenant, 139

De Gaulle, General Charles, 108
Dębicki, Lieutenant, 190
demobilization of Polish II Corps, postwar, 66, 232
Dempsey, Lieutenant General Sir Miles, 138
Detail Issue Depots, 128, 146, 175
doctors, 2, 46, 63, 127, 189
Doliński, Second Lieutenant Władysław, 217
Donetz Basin, 26
D'Onifrio Ridge, 187
Douglas, Air Chief Marshal Sir William Sholto, 112
Drelicharz, Captain Władysław, 204, 207
Duch, Major General Bronisław, 97, 129, 143, 144, 164
Dudek, Dr Jan, 207
duelling, 6
Dzięciołowski, Captain Antoni, 207
Dziewicki, Lieutenant Władysław, 219

East Africa, 65
East Prussia, 1, 133
Eastern Front, 23, 26, 47, 61
   Russian Front, 31, 34
   see also Soviet–German Front
Eden, Sir Anthony:
   negotiations with Soviets and Poles, 7, 13–4, 16, 28, 30, 44
   relations with Polish II Corps, 88, 91, 96–7, 110, 114

Education & Welfare Section, 83, 127, 132–3
   Entertainment Group, 119, 123, 128, 133
   Parade Theatre, 83
Egypt, 7, 9, 59, 63, 69, 98
   convoys to Italy, 124, 125
   see also North African Campaign; Polish Army Units in the Middle East; Polish Women's Auxiliary Service Corps, transport companies; Stalin, conference with Polish generals
Electrical & Mechanical Engineer Corps (Polish), 125, 130, 146
embassies (Polish), 17, 68, 167
   British, 72
   American, 25
England, 2, 24, 55–6, 79, 104, 99
   see also cross-Channel invasion; Stalin, conference with Polish generals
Engineers, 68, 125, 129
   at Cassino, 172–3, 194, 196, 212, 225, 228
   mine clearance, 188–9, 196, 204–5
Entente, 2
Eisenhower, General Dwight, 101–2, 107–9, 111–13
Erlington, Brigadier, 68, 73
Ezman, Captain Stanisław, 215–6, 220

Falluja, 8
Fanslau, Lieutenant Colonel Karol, 205–6
Field Bakeries, 125, 195,
Field Blood Transfusion Units, 125, 147, 178–9
Field Courts Martial, 120, 132
Field Hygiene, 128
Field Map Section, 125, 127
Field Surgery Units, 178–9
Foggia Plain, 146
Fornelli, 149

Forward Maintenance Centre, 174–5, 179
foxholes, 162
Franco-Polish Alliance, 5
French Expeditionary Force in Italy, 147–8, 155, 160, 164, 193, 206
   2nd Moroccan Division, 147
   artillery, 170
   see also Allied Armies Italy, 15th Army Group
Free French Army, 9, 105, 108
   Senegalese, 105
   see also De Gaulle, General Charles
French Army (1939–40), 2, 9
   exiled Polish Army in France, 4–5
French Levant, 5, 7

Galilee, Sea of, 105
Gamberale, 151–2
Garigliano River, 139
Gaza, 99–100, 104
Gedera Hill 69, 68–69
German Afrika Korps see Rommel, General Erwin
German Air Force, 9, 12, 40, 71, 172, 196
   1st Parachute Division holding Monte Cassino, 162, 193, 202, 206
German anti-gun assaults, 215–17, 219–21, 224
German Army units defending Cassino 162
German Tenth Army, 162, 228
German Fourteenth Army, 228
German 14th SS Division, 230–2
German fortifications, 162, 195–6, 198, 202, 204, 206
   Cassino Fortress, 155–6, 159, 228
   at Piedimonte, 210, 212, 218, 220, 225
German Intelligence
   acts of sabotage, 171
   spies in Middle East, 21, 89
German Jäger companies, 138
German prisoners of war, 151–2, 201, 204, 211, 216, 226
   camps, 132

Gibraltar, 58, 95
Gielgud, Colonel, 47
Glinski, Colonel, 196, 205
Grasett, Lieutenant General Sir Arthur, 85, 103
Greece, 9, 33
  exile Army, 105
Group Bob, Task Force *see* Piedimonte san Germano
Guard Battalion, 125
Gustav Line, 109, 157–8, 206, 227–8

Habbaniya, relief of 8
Haller, General Stanisław, 19
Hamadan, 21, 69, 83
Harriman, Avril, 24–5, 27, 31, 37
Heavy Artillery, 79, 86
  field guns, 137, 148, 209, 212
  see also Army Group Polish Artillery
Heidrich, General, 162, 206
Highway 6 175, 193, 207, 209, 214–21, 224–6
  strategic significance, 155, 163
Highway 85 147
Hill 124 221
Hill 444 164
Hill 553 218, 220–2, 224, 226
Hill 710 211
Hill 852 210–11
Hill 893 211–12
Hill 912 211–12
Hill 945 211
Hitler, Adolf, 8, 13, 17, 28, 156
Hoff, Lieutenant Zbigniew, 216
Holmes, Lieutenant General William, 100, 103–5
Hołszczuk, Second Lieutenant, 215
Homs, 15
Hopko, Lieutenant Mieczysław, 195
House of Commons, 17, 142
Hulda, 118
Hulls, Colonel Leslie, 20, 50, 58, 72, 76

Hungary, 4–5
Huntzinger, General, 7

India, 8, 31–2, 65, 230
Indian 4th Infantry Division, 135, 156, 163
Indian 8th Infantry Division, 82, 135
Indian 10th Infantry Division, 135
Indian 21 Infantry Brigade, 214
  see also British 5th Battalion, The Queens Own Royal West Kent Regiment
Inferno Gorge and Track, 171, 173, 175, 178, 185, 197
Intelligence Corps, 9, 172
Iraq Force, 21,
Iraqi government, 8, 91
Iraqi rebellion, 8
Iran, 35, 37, 39, 79
  see also Persia
Ironside, General Edmund, 4
Isernia, 142–3, 146–8
Ismay, Lieutenant General Sir Hastings, 24–6, 31, 44, 81, 98
Italian Combat Group, 147–9
Italian 68 Infantry Regiment, 149
Italian 185th Parachute Battalion, 153
Italian *Bersagalieri* Battalions, 149, 153
Italian Alpine Battalion, 149
Italian *d'Arditi* (commando) Battalion, 149
Italian 11 Light Artillery Regiment, 149
Italian prisoners-of-war, 9
Italian troops in North Africa, 7–8
Iwanowski, Captain Władysław, 185, 187, 195, 207

Jadwisiak, Lieutenant Adolf, 215–16
Japan, 35, 37, 44, 48, 116
Jerusalem, 7, 46, 68, 105, 119, 120
Jesionka Stawiowa, 2
Jews, 39, 46, 61
  desertions of Jewish soldiers, 117

Polish-Jewish communities in Palestine, 94, 99, 118–19, 120

Julius, 68, 100
Junacki see Junior Cadets Schools
Junior Cadets Schools, 120
JWŚW see Polish Army Units in the Middle East

Karaszewicz-Tokarzewski, Lieutenant General, 19, 97, 119
Katyn massacre, 86, 88, 90, 231
Kavzin, 25, 65
Kesselring, Field Marshal, 181, 228
Kazakhstan, 2
Kermanshah, 70
Khanaquin, 70, 74, 79, 82, 86, 89
Kiedacz, Major Zbigniew, 211
Kilo 89 Camp, 100,
Klimecki, Major General Tadeusz, 54–5, 71–4, 89
   as Chief of General Staff, 93, 95, 97
Kochanowski, Second Lieutenant, 204
Koczy, Second Lieutenant Jan, 219
Kondratik, Colonel, 12
Kopański, Major General Stanisław, 54
Kot, Ambassador Stanisław, 25, 32, 35, 42, 46
Kozlov, General, 21
Krasnovodsk, 59, 60, 72
Kermin, 47
Krakow, 177
Kremlin, 37, 60
Khrulov, General, 38, 47
Kuczuk-Pilecki, Captain Alfred, 225
Kukiel, Major General Marian, 54–5
Kuibyshev, 30–2, 39, 60
Kurdish militants, 89
Kurek, Colonel Wincenty, 188, 201
Kyrgyzstan, 62

La Falconara, 148
Lakinski, Colonel, 205

Landing Ship Tanks, 117
Latrun, 105
Lebanon, 5, 9, 30, 94
   mountain warfare training, 100, 104, 135
Leese, Lieutenant General Oliver, 129, 135–6, 140–1, 157
   Monte Cassino, 158, 183, 191, 193, 227–8
   Piedimonte san Germano, 209, 214, 221
Le Mainarde, 148–50, 153
Lenino, Battle of, 114
Lesiak, Warrant Officer Jerzy, 217
Levant–Caspian Front, 63
Libya, 9, 22, 40, 44, 54, 67
Lickindorf, Lieutenant Stanisław, 209–10
Light Artillery Regiments (including horse artillery), 86, 105, 144, 149–50
   at Cassino, 170, 172–3, 190–1, 202, 209–10
   at Piedimonte, 212, 214, 222
Light Transport Companies, 176
Lines of Communication, 64, 89, 140, 146–7, 173, 197
Liri Valley, 155, 157, 163–4, 184
   Eighth Army advances into, 191, 193, 206–7
   see also Piedimonte san Germano
Lubianka prison, 11–12, 17
Lubomirski, Captain Prince Eugeniusz, 167
Lucera, 146
Luftwaffe see German Air Force
Lwów, Polish city, 96, 120

Machowiak, Sergeant, 206
Macmillan, Harold, 110, 116, 157, 167
MacReady, General Sir Gordon, 25, 27
Main Dressing Stations, 177–8
Maisky, Soviet Ambassador Ivan, 13–14, 16
Malaria, 46, 75–6, 85, 93–4, 99–100
   and other diseases, 50–1, 62, 71, 129
   recovery from, 105, 172

see also Anti-malaria Control Unit; Junior Cadet Schools
Marseilles, 5
Mason-MacFarlane, Major General Sir Noel, 17–20, 25, 27, 32, 61
  Governor of Gibraltar, 58, 95
Massa Albaneta, 162–3, 186
Masztak, Lieutenant Stanisław, 216
merchant vessels, 124, 128
  Soviet convoys in Caspian Sea, 50, 62–3, 65
Meretskov, General Kirill, 13
Mersa Matruh, 9, 59
Mignano, 167, 174, 176
Mikołajczyk, Polish Prime Minister Stanisław, 96–7
mines, 139, 150, 162, 205–6, 219, 225
  glass anti-personnel, 198
  clearance, 186, 189, 204
Minsk, 2
Military Hospitals, 68, 75, 78, 83, 93–4, 119
  in Italy, 127–9, 132, 141, 146–7
  during the Battle of Monte Cassino, 179, 188–9, 198–9
  see also Polish Army in the USSR
Military Police
  operations in Italy, 125, 175, 185
  search for deserters in Palestine, 117–18
Military Prison, 94–5, 120, 129, 132
Młotkowski, Second Lieutenant, 215
Molotov, Vyacheslav, 26–7, 30, 45, 58–9, 114
  see also Stalin, conference with Polish generals
Monastery Hill, 163, 170, 193, 201, 207, 228
Monte Cairo, 185, 196, 209, 210, 227
  German positions, 155, 162, 170, 186
Monte Cassino
  Polish losses, 191, 227
  strategic significance, 155–6, 157–8, 193, 228
  see also Operation Diadem

Monte Cassino Abbey, 155, 163, 184, 205
  Polish capture of, 207–8
Monte Castellone, 155, 161–4, 209
Monte Cifalco, 170
Monte Corno, 160
Monte Curval, 143, 147, 151
Monte della Metta, 149, 152
Monte D'Onofrio, 187
Monte Mare, 149, 160
Monte Marrone, 152–3
Monte Pagano, 143–4, 147
  tunnel, 150
Montenero, 143–4, 147–8, 151
Monte Valle Martina, 139
Montgomery, Lieutenant General Sir Bernard, 63, 112
morphine, 177
Moscow, 14, 16–18, 24–5, 31, 44, 110
  Churchill visits, 71–2
  German assault upon, 12, 28, 30, 47
  see also Soviet Government; Stalin, conference with Polish Generals
Mosul, 68, 70, 82, 83
Motor Ambulance Convoys
  31 Polish, 178, 179
  567 American, 147, 175, 178
Mottola, 127–9, 132, 142, 198
mules, 150, 176–7
Mussolini, 8

Naples, 107, 124, 131, 169, 176
Napoleonic Polish Legion, 133–4
Nazareth, 105, 121
Nebelwerfers, 162, 187
newspapers, 82, 86, 132
  Eighth Army News, 141, 153
Newton Abbot, Polish Veterans' Home, 233
New Zealand
  II Army Corps, 68, 111, 137, 158, 175
  2nd Infantry Division, 156
New Zealand abandoned tanks, 169, 195, 196

NKVD, 2, 19, 21, 59, 86
  Blocking Units, 28
  Central Office, 11–12, 17
North African Campaign, 30, 44, 78, 156, 170, 198
  Rommel's Afrika Korps, 8–9, 63
  see also Tobruk
Nowak, Second Lieutenant Władysław, 219
Nowina-Sawicki, Colonel Witold, 201, 209
Nowogrodek Cavalry Brigade, 1
Nóżka, Second Lieutenant Antoni, 217
nurses, 51, 65, 68–9, 178
Nuseirat, 104

oilfields, 26, 47, 82, 85
  Baku, 62
  see also Anglo-Iranian Oil Company
Okulicki, Colonel, 49, 93
Onufrejczyk, Warrant Officer Michail, postwar trial 232
Operation Barbarossa, 13
Operation Countenance, 21
Operation Diadem
  planning, 140–2, 147–8, 156–9, 161–4, 181
  Polish infantry divisions in, 169, 171–6, 183–6, 190–1, 193, 201–8
Operation Exporter, 9
Operation Honker, 183
Operation Overlord see cross-Channel invasion
Operation Typhoon, 28
Operation Virile (training exercise), 100, 104–5
ordnance depots, 119, 125, 128, 176
  ammunition expenditure, 174, 196
orphans, 51, 232
Osmakiewic, Major Franciszek, 218
Ostrowski, Colonel Bolesław, 120

Pahlavi, Shah of Persia, 21
Pahlevi, 25, 49–51, 69, 75

evacuation and reception camps, 53, 61–2, 63, 65
Palagiano, 127, 198
Panzerfausts, 224
Pamir Mountains, 45
Panfilov, General Alexei, 17, 19–20, 22, 35, 37–42, 47
Paris, 4, 167
Passo Corno, 188, 202, 209, 211–12, 214, 221
  German positions on, 155, 184
Paszkiewicz, Major General Gustaw, 57, 97
Patton, General George S., 107, 123
Pay Corps, 132
PEME see Electrical and Mechanical Engineers (Polish)
Pétain, Marshal, 5
penicillin, 198
Persia, 27–8, 31–2, 34, 48–9, 69
  see also Iran; Operation Countenance; Polish-Soviet Military Agreement (1941); Trans-Persian Supply Route
Persia & Iraq Command, 63–4, 75–6, 82, 85–6
  defend against German invasion, 62, 71–2
Persian government, 49, 62
  accepts arms from Germany, 21
  voices concerns over Anders' actions, 94
Pescopennataro, 138, 143, 150, 152
petrol filling centres, 146, 176
Phantom Ridge, 161, 163–4, 188–90, 196, 201–4, 206–7
pharmacists, 198
Piedimonte San Germano, 206, 209, 212
  Group Bob Task Force, 212, 214–16, 218–22, 224–7
  tank turret fortifications, 218–20
Piłat, Colonel Karol,
Pizzone, 144, 149, 151
Płońska, Colonel Antonina, 127
Point 505 201

Point 517 189
Point 569 162, 186, 201, 205–6
Point 575 163, 187, 201–2, 204, 206–7
Point 593 161–3, 187, 201, 204–6
Point 596 186
Poland
  border with USSR, 17, 42, 85, 140, 230
  envisaged post-war reconstruction, 74, 93, 98–9, 111, 121, 133
  post-war election controversy, 231
Polish Air Force, 6, 18, 24, 32, 54–5, 172
  recruitment into from Army, 40, 49, 56, 71, 73, 111–12
Polish I Army Corps (Scotland), 54, 93
  reinforcements for, 42, 56, 71, 98
Polish II Army Corps, 54–6, 64, 93, 96–105, 108–14, 116–17
  establishes in Italy, 123–4, 128–9, 132–4
  post-war fate, 227, 229–33
  see also Operation Diadem; Piedimonte san Germano; Polish Army Units in the Middle East; Sangro River
Polish II Corps Base, 97, 114, 117, 123–4, 127, 129–31
  in Italy, 132–3, 140, 142, 146–7, 173–4
  see also Polish Army in the East, separation of II Corps and Base
Polish II Corps Headquarters, 79, 89, 100, 104, 113
  establishes in Italy, 125, 128, 142, 146
  Monte Cassino, 167, 172, 191
Polish II Corps Headquarters Defence Company, 212, 218, 221, 225
Polish II Corps Sub Area Headquarters, 183
Polish III Army Corps, 54, 56
  see also Polish Army in the USSR
Polish 1 (2, 5) Krechowiecki Armoured Regiment, 69, 104, 169
Polish 2 Armoured (Tank) Brigade, 67, 69, 73, 78–9 85–6, 104

in action, 168–9, 173, 176, 205, 212
moves to Italy, 117, 124
Polish 3rd Carpathian Rifle Division, 56, 67–9, 73
  in Iraq, 76, 78, 82, 90, 97
  in Palestine and Egypt, 100, 102–4, 117, 124
  see also Sangro River, Polish divisions on; Operation Diadem, Polish divisions in; Piedimonte san Germano, Group Bob Task Force
Polish 4th Rifle Division, 56, 67, 73
Polish 4 (1) Skorpion Armoured Regiment, 69, 104, 169, 173
  squadrons at Cassino, 185–6, 189, 195, 196, 201, 204–7
  support attack on Piedimonte san Germano, 218
Polish 5th Kresowa Infantry Division, 20, 22, 30, 39, 42, 45, 47
  in Middle East, 70, 73–4, 76, 78, 85
  moves to Italy, 125, 128
  see also Sangro River, Polish divisions on; Operation Diadem, Polish divisions in; Polish III Army Corps; Piedimonte san Germano, Group Bob Task Force
Polish 6 Children of Lwów Armoured Regiment, 104, 169
  in Corps reserve at Cassino, 205
  see also Piedimonte san Germano, Group Bob Task Force,
Polish 6th (Lwów) Infantry Division, 20, 32, 45
  in Middle East, 69–70, 73, 78–9, 82, 85–6
  see also Polish III Army Corps; Polish 2 Tank Brigade
Polish 6 Troop 10 Inter Allied Commando, 138–41, 143
  at Monte Cassino, 164, 194, 201–2, 204
Polish 7th Reserve (Infantry) Division, 22, 42, 47, 56

in Italy, 117, 129–31, 142
in Middle East, 70, 73, 78–9, 82, 85–6, 93
see also Polish III Army Corps; Army Training Centre
Polish 7 Reserve Reconnaissance Regiment, 131
Polish 7th Reserve Tank Battalion, 131, 169
Polish 8th Infantry Division, 42, 73
Polish 9th Forward Delivery Squadron, 131, 169, 196
Polish 9th Infantry Division, 42, 53, 67
Polish 10th Infantry Division, 42, 67
Polish 12 Podolski Lancers Regiment, 78
  in action, 152, 186, 207, 212, 218–22, 226
Polish 15 Poznan Lancers Regiment, 78, 148–9, 152
  in action, 152, 194, 201, 209, 210–12
Polish Carpathian Lancers Regiment, 69, 78, 125, 128, 148
  in action, 164, 209–11
Polish Army in the East, 74, 76–9, 81–3, 86–8, 95, 98
  personnel to reinforce units in UK, 102, 111–12
  separation of II Corps and Base, 89, 92–4, 97
Polish Army in the East – advanced echelon, 114, 124
Polish Army in the USSR, 12, 14, 17, 19
  difficulties encountered, 22–3, 26, 28, 32, 58
  evacuation from, 46–50, 53–63, 66
  see also Stalin, conference with Polish Generals
Polish Army Units in the Middle East, 119–20
  Territorial Units in the Middle East, 120
Polish Campaign (1939), 1, 2
Polish Consular Delegates, 45–6
Polish Council of Ministers, 91–2, 95
Polish General Staff, 2, 4, 42, 70, 93, 95
Polish Government (1939) 2, 4

Polish Government in Exile, 13–4, 16–7, 19, 31–2, 48
  difficulties with II Corps, 88, 96, 228, 231
  USSR breaks relations with, 86
Polish Home Army, 158, 230
Polish Independent Carpathian Rifle Brigade, 5, 7–9, 14, 54, 56, 67
Polish Military Mission to USSR, 17–9, 47
Polish National Committee, 13–4
Polish Navy, 1, 6, 18, 32, 40, 49, 54, 56
Polish Officers Legion, 7
Polish prisoners of war in USSR, 11, 13–14 60
Polish Resettlement Act 1947, 232
Polish Resettlement Corps, 232–3
Polish Rifle Corps (Middle East), 56
Polish Sappers' Road, 172–3, 185, 205
Polish-Soviet Military Agreement (1941), 13–7, 46
  breakdown of, 61, 66
Polish-Soviet Pact 1941, 16, 70
Polish Women's Auxiliary Service Corps, 23, 65, 69, 120, 130, 177
  field kitchen canteens, 127, 179, 194–5
  transport companies, 81, 119, 127–8, 131–2, 175, 198
Pontecorvo, 212
Portelle, 173, 175, 178
Pownall, Lieutenant General Sir Henry, 85–6, 88–90, 92, 94, 99–100
Pozzilli, 175, 177, 179
Pratta, 157, 169, 176
Przewłocki, Major General Marian, 93
Printing and Publication Section, 121, 131
Public Relations Section, 83, 195
PWSK *see* Polish Women's Auxiliary Service Corps

Qassasin, 123
Qizil Ribat, 65, 70, 74, 79, 82, 89
  wildlife, 75, 83
  see also Military Prison; Wojtek

Quadrant Conference, 101
quartermasters, 81, 93, 146, 167
Quastina, 67–8
Quebec Conference, 98, 101
Queen Alexandra's Royal Army Nursing Service, 51
Queen's Royal Regiment, 139
Quinan, General Sir Edward, 8, 21, 49, 83

Raczkiewicz, Polish President Władysław, 96
railway stations, 146, 151
   railheads, 25, 45, 65, 132, 185–6
Rakowski, Major General Bronisław, 97
Ramat Hakovesh, 118–19
Ranfurly, Countess of, 64, 140
Rapido, River, 155, 158, 191
   Valley, 170, 172, 181
Red Army, 11, 20–2, 24, 45–7, 60, 71
   defence of Moscow, 28, 30–1
   enters Poland (1944), 140
   see also Lenino, Battle of
Red Cross, 68–9, 83, 120, 127
   at Monte Cassino, 178
Reinforcements (Polish II Corps), 66, 93, 97, 100, 109, 111
   from Poles in German Army, 116, 141
   military draft office, 142
   see also Polish 7th Reserve (Infantry) Division
Riardo, 174
Riga, Treaty of, 13
Rionero, 143–4, 147–8
Rochetta, 149
Rokossovsky, General Konstantin, 13
Romania, 1–2, 4–5
Rome, 155–6, 158
   liberation of, 227–8
Romer, Ambassador Tadeusz, 92, 95
Rommel, General Erwin, 8–9, 63
Roosevelt, Franklin D., US President 24, 30, 33
Ross, Lieutenant Colonel A., 50–1, 62

Rostov, 30
Royal Air Force, 4, 8, 44
Royal Army Medical Corps, 178
Royal Army Service Corps, 173, 176
Rudnicki, Colonel Klemens, 196, 201, 209
Rydz-Śmigły, Marshal Edward, 1
Rygor, 9

Salerno, 107
Salvage units, 196
San Angelo river crossing, 138
San Biagio, 148–50, 152
San Pietro, 143, 147, 171
San Pietro Avellana, 139, 143, 151
Sangro River, 137, 138, 144
   Polish infantry divisions on, 112, 129, 135, 139–44, 146–51
San Basilio, 127–9, 131–2
San Michele, 169, 175, 178, 185, 196, 205–7
   supply dump, 173, 197
Santa Scolastica, 214
Santa Teresa Transit Camp, 127–30, 140
Sappers *see* Engineers
Sciullo, 139
Scratch Infantry Battalions, 193–4
Scontrone, 144
Scotland, Polish Army in, 33, 35, 54–7, 68, 138
   see also Polish I Army Corps
Scott, Brigadier T.P.D., 164
Second Front, 21–2, 33
   see also cross-Channel invasion
Selby, Major General, 91, 102
Shaposhnikov, Marshal Boris, 17
Sherman M4A2 tanks, 104, 169, 185, 226
shrapnel wounds, 198, 225
Siberia, 2
Sicily, 107
Siczek, Lieutenant, 196
Signals units, 125, 172, 212
   telephone network, 171
   women volunteers, 127–8

Singapore, 37, 44
Sikorski, General Władysław, 4–7, 9, 105
  Middle East, 67, 70–4, 76, 85–6, 88–97, 100
  USSR, 12–4, 16, 24–5, 31
  see also Polish Army in the USSR; Stalin, conference with Polish Generals
ski patrols, 138–9, 144
Smereczyński, Captain Jozef, 194
Smolensk, 86
Smrokowski, Captain Władysław, 138–9, 194
Snakeshead Ridge, 163, 187
Śniechowski, Second Lieutenant J., 219
Sokołowski, Captain Bronisław, 185
Sosnkowski, General Kazimierz, 4, 13, 16
  as Commander-in-Chief Polish Army, 96–9, 102–4
  negotiates II Corps entry to Italian Campaign, 107–14, 116–17, 119
  see also Operation Diadem, planning
Southampton, 232
Soviet Government, 13, 26–8, 34, 46, 59–61, 86
  postwar dealings with Polish authorities, 229, 23–1
  see also Moscow; Polish-Soviet Military Agreement (1941)
Soviet-German Front, 18, 25–6, 32, 42, 55, 61
  British troops to fight in USSR, 22, 30, 44
  see also Eastern Front ; Lenino, Battle of; Operation Barbarossa; Operation Typhoon; Soviet Government, postwar dealings with Polish authorities
Soviet Levy Commission, 42, 45–6
Soviet Military Mission to Polish Army, 19
Soviet-occupied Poland (1939), 2
Soviet propaganda newspapers, 90
Stalin, 12, 24, 31–2, 54, 71, 101–2, 116

conference with Polish Generals, 32–42
  see also Polish Army in the USSR, evacuation from; Polish-Soviet Military Agreement (1941); Soviet-German Front, British troops to fight in USSR; Soviet Government, postwar dealings with Polish authorities
Strauss, Henry, 1st Baron Conesford, MP 229
stretcher-bearers, 177, 194–5, 197, 202
Stryjewski, Captain Stanisław, 210
Stuart Light Tanks, 176, 196, 216, 226
  used as ambulances, 177
Suez, 7, 76, 123
Sulik, Major General Nikodem, 93, 149–50, 164, 189, 193
Supply & Transport Corps, 81, 84, 128, 130
  in Italy, 146,173–6, 178, 195–6
  see also Lines of Communication; Polish Army Units in the Middle East; Polish Women's Auxiliary Service Corps, transport companies
Świeclicki, Lieutenant Colonel Henryk, 220
Syria, 30, 33, 71, 76, 114, 120
  planned location of II Corps in, 94, 98–9
  training in, 104, 135
  see also Operation Exporter; Polish Independent Rifle Brigade
Szarecki, Lieutenant General Dr Bolesław, 49
Szymanski, Colonel Adam, 95

tank transporters, 168
Taranto, 107, 123–5 127–9, 131–2, 138
  Polish hospitals in, 156–7, 198
Tarkowski, Major Ludomir, 222
Tashkent, 45

Tatra Mountains, 1–2
Tatishchev, 20, 35
Tehran, 42, 50, 69, 72–3, 94
   Allied conferences in, 116–17, 142
   Polish civilians in, 53, 65
Tekliński, Second Lieutenant Henryk, 218–19
Tel-Aviv, 68, 104–5
Terelle, 184, 196
The Great Terror, 13
Tiberias, 105
Tobruk, 9, 33, 35, 69, 164
Totskoye, 20–1, 35, 38
Trans-Jordan, 30, 68
Trans-Persia supply route, 25, 30
Treaty of Riga, 13
Trejdosiewicz, Lieutenant, 189
Trojanowska, Lieutenant Colonel Maria, 132
Tunisia, 9
Turkestan, 39
Turkey, 35, 37, 76
Turkmenistan, 2
Tymieniecki, Second Lieutenant Bohdan, 216–17

Ujecki, Major General Stanisław, 55
Ukraine, 22, 54
United Kingdom Home Forces, 6
Ural Mountains, 20
USSR *see* Soviet entries
Uzbekistan, 39–40, 42, 62, 75

Valentine Mk III tanks, 96
   bridge-laying tanks, 199, 206
Valle Zintone, 139
Vairano, 174–6, 196
Vasilevski, General Alexander, 17
Vastogiraidi, 153
Venafro, 142, 147, 173–5, 188, 196–7
Vichy French Forces, 7, 9

Villa Santa Lucia, 162, 214, 218, 221–2
Vinciaturo, 142
Vistula, River, 1
Volga, River, 20, 30
Volkovyski, Colonel, 20, 38
Volturno, River, 157, 168, 174

Walking Wounded Collection Post, 177
Warsaw, 1
Western Desert Force, 8
West Kents *see* British 5th Battalion, The Queens Own Royal West Kent Regiment
Wiatr, Major General, 93, 97
Wilson, General Sir Henry Maitland, 7, 30, 81–3, 94, 108
   meetings with Anders, 64–5, 72–4, 76, 85, 99, 103–5
   Polish II Corps operational deployment, 112–14, 116, 140, 159
Wind, Major General Jozef, 119
Wiśniowski, Colonel Kazimierz, 78, 113
Wojtek, 83–4, 104, 195
Wolikowski, Major General, 47
Wołoszowski, Captain Stanisław, 139
Wysłouchowa, Lieutenant Colonel Bronisława, 194

Yalta Conference, 229
Yangiyul, 45
YMCA, 83, 120

Zaleski, August, 16
Zalewski, Lieutenant Stefan, 139
Zając, Lieutenant General Józef, 53–4
Zhukov, Red Army General Georgi, 30, 47
Zhukov, NKVD General Georgi, 17, 19–20, 48, 60–1, 72
Zolnierczyk, Second Lieutenant, 196